Innovation and Progress in Artificial Intelligence

Innovation and Progress in Artificial Intelligence

Edited by **Jeremy Rogerson**

New York

Published by Willford Press,
118-35 Queens Blvd., Suite 400,
Forest Hills, NY 11375, USA
www.willfordpress.com

Innovation and Progress in Artificial Intelligence
Edited by Jeremy Rogerson

International Standard Book Number: 978-1-68285-022-0 (Hardback)

Printed in the United States of America.

Contents

Preface

Artificial Intelligence is the field which aims to develop digital computers, softwares, artificial robotics and systems which can mimic and emulate human intellectual processes like the capability to reason, apprehend, analyse and learn from past experiences. It is widely used for designing and programming advanced systems that can perform complex tasks with high proficiency and accuracy. There has been rapid progress in this field and its applications are finding their way across multiple industries. The book aims to shed light on some of the important aspects of A.I. such as knowledge reasoning and knowledge engineering, cognitive stimulation, general and social intelligence, and also the recent researches within this field. For all those who are interested in artificial intelligence, this book can prove to be an essential guide.

Significant researches are present in this book. Intensive efforts have been employed by authors to make this book an outstanding discourse. This book contains the enlightening chapters which have been written on the basis of significant researches done by the experts.

Finally, I would also like to thank all the members involved in this book for being a team and meeting all the deadlines for the submission of their respective works. I would also like to thank my friends and family for being supportive in my efforts.

Editor

A comment on "Robust linear optimization under new distance measure"

Yu Wuyang

Institute of Management Decision and Innovation, Hangzhou Dianzi University, 310018, Zhejiang, P. R. China.
E-mail: yu_wuyang@163.com.

Zhang et al. (2012) proposed a new robust counterpart for linear optimization, and shown the effectiveness of the new model by numerical results of AFIRO and ADLITTLE. In this comment, it is shown that the numerical results in their paper are not true, conversely, the model of Bertimas and Sim (2004) has better optimality than that of Zhang et al. (2012) if the same probability bounds that the i-th constraint violated is maintained.

Key words: Robust optimization, probability bounds, Netlib.

INTRODUCTION

Recently, Zhang et al. (2012) proposed a new robust counterpart to solving linear optimization problems with uncertain data, and claimed to reduce the conservatism of the solution compared to the well-known model of Bertsimas and Sim (2004). This claim was illustrated by numerical results for AFIRO and ADLITTLE, which are test problems of the Netlib (Dongarra et al., 2003), a collection of mathematical software, papers and databases. However, it is pointed out that the comparison given by Zhang et al. (2012) for the performance of the two methods is not valid.

Consider the nominal linear optimization problem as follows:

$$\max c'x$$
$$s.t. Ax \le b \qquad\qquad (1)$$
$$l \le x \le u$$

In Equation 1, assume that data uncertainty only affects the elements in matrix A. Consider a particular row i of the matrix A and let J_i represent the set of coefficients in row i that are subject to uncertainty. Ben-Tal and Nemirovski (2000) modeled each entry $a_{ij}, j \in J_i$ as a symmetric and bounded random variable $\tilde{a}_{ij}, j \in J_i$ that takes values in $[a_{ij} - \hat{a}_{ij}, a_{ij} + \hat{a}_{ij}]$. By defining random

variable $\eta_{ij} = (\tilde{a}_{ij} - a_{ij})/\hat{a}_{ij}$, associated with the uncertain data $\tilde{a}_{ij}$, Bertsimas and Sim (2004) proposed a robust linear optimization model and shown that the probability of i-th constraint is violated at most

$$\Pr(\sum_j a_{ij} x_j^* > b_i) \le \exp(-\frac{\Gamma_i^2}{2|J_i|}) \qquad\qquad (2)$$

Where x^* is assumed to be the optimal solution of the method, and the parameter $\Gamma_i \in [0, |J_i|]$ is introduced to adjust the robustness against the level of conservatism of the solution.

Let $X \subseteq R^n$ be compact set and $x, y \in X$, Wu and Yang (2002) and Zhang and Chen (2004) proposed a distance measure to research AFCM clustering problems as follows:

$$dist(x, y) = \sqrt{1 - \exp(-\beta \| x - y \|^2)} \qquad\qquad (3)$$

Where $\| \cdot \|$ denotes the norm.

For every row i, Zhang et al. (2012) introduced a parameter β_i, the role is to adjust the robustness of the

Table 1. Comparison of different models under different disturbance values (AFIRO, $\Gamma_i = 0.5, \beta_i = \Gamma_i \sqrt{\mu_i^*}$).

$\hat{a}_{23} = \hat{a}_{36}$	Bertsimas and Sim (2004) model		Zhang et al. (2012) model	
	Optimal value	% change	Optimal value	% change
0.2	-448.4359	3.51	-438.6455	5.62
0.4	-432.1186	7.02	-415.8014	10.53
0.6	-415.8014	10.53	-395.6448	14.87
0.8	-399.4841	14.04	-377.7278	18.73
1.0	-383.1669	17.55	-361.6968	22.17
1.2	-366.8496	21.07	-347.2689	25.28
1.4	-350.5323	24.58	-334.2151	28.09
1.6	-334.2151	28.09	-322.3480	30.64
1.8	-317.8978	31.60	-311.5128	32.97
2.0	-301.5806	35.11	-301.5806	35.11

Table 2. Comparison of different models under different adjustment factors (AFIRO, $\hat{a}_{23} = \hat{a}_{36} = 0.6, \beta_i = \Gamma_i \sqrt{\mu_i^*}$).

Γ_i	Bertsimas and Sim (2004) model		Zhang et al. (2012) model	
	Optimal value	% change	Optimal value	% change
0.2	-454.1724	4.21	-433.8362	6.65
0.4	-425.5917	8.43	-407.4438	12.33
0.6	-406.0110	12.64	-384.6502	17.24
0.8	-386.4303	16.85	-364.7665	21.51
1.0	-366.8496	21.07	-347.2689	25.28
1.2	-361.6968	22.17	-331.7521	28.62
1.4	-357.2980	23.12	-317.8978	31.60
1.6	-353.4991	23.94	-305.4525	34.28
1.8	-350.1852	24.65	-48.6359	89.54
2.0	-347.2689	25.28	-48.6359	89.54

proposed method against the level of conservatism of the solution, and used the distance function of Equation 3 to set up a new robust counterpart of linear optimization as follows:

$$\max c'x$$
$$s.t. \sum_j a_{ij}x_j + \beta_i \sum_{j \in J_i} \sqrt{1 - \exp(-\|\tilde{a}_{ij} - a_{ij}\|^2)} y_j \le b_i, \forall i \qquad (4)$$
$$-y_j \le x_j \le y_j, \forall j \in J_i$$
$$l \le x \le u$$
$$y \ge 0$$

This counterpart is the same as the model of Berstimas and Sim (2004), only with a different formation of the first constraint. Zhang et al. (2012) have shown that the probability of the i-th constraint is violated at most

$$\Pr(\sum_j a_{ij}x_j^* > b_i) \le \exp(-\frac{\beta_i^2}{2\mu_i^* |J_i|}) \qquad (5)$$

Where

$$\mu_i^* = \max\{\frac{\hat{a}_{ij}^2}{1 - \exp(-\hat{a}_{ij}^2)}\} .$$

Zhang et al. (2012) claimed to reduce the conservatism of the solution compared to the model of Bertsimas and Sim (2004) by illustrating numerical results for AFIRO and ADLITTLE. In their paper, Tables 1 and 3 show the comparison of different models under different disturbance values when $\Gamma_i = \beta_i = 0.5$, while Tables 2 and 4 show the comparison of different models under different adjustment factors when $\hat{a}_{23} = \hat{a}_{36}$ and $\hat{a}_{161} = \hat{a}_{176} = \hat{a}_{177} = 0.6$, respectively, then they claimed that their model obtained the optimal value under the influence of the uncertain parameters which have a smaller rate of change. Unfortunately, their comparisons are meaningless since they have given these results under the condition that $\Gamma_i = \beta_i$. In fact, it is meaningful to

Table 3. Comparison of different models under different disturbance values (ADLITTLE, $\Gamma_i = 0.5, \beta_i = \Gamma_i \sqrt{\mu_i^*}$).

$\hat{a}_{161} = \hat{a}_{176} = \hat{a}_{177}$	Bertsimas and Sim (2004) model		Zhang et al. (2004) model	
	Optimal value	% change	Optimal value	% change
0.0001	225495.5	0.0002	225495.9	0.0004
0.001	225500.0	0.0022	225504.4	0.0042
0..01	225545.5	0.0224	225588.5	0.0415
0.1	226021.8	0.2336	226366.8	0.3866
0.3	227332.3	0.8148	230050.4	2.0202
0.5	244221.4	8.3046	254412.8	12.8241
0.7	259360.5	15.0183	278566.0	23.5353
0.9	273173.2	21.1438	298384.5	32.3242

Table 4. Comparison of different models under different adjustment factors (ADLITTLE, $\hat{a}_{161} = \hat{a}_{176} = \hat{a}_{177} = 0.6, \beta_i = \Gamma_i \sqrt{\mu_i^*}$).

Γ_i	Bertsimas and Sim (2004) model		Zhang et al. (2004) model	
	Optimal value	% change	Optimal value	% change
0.2	226863.1	0.6067	228149.1	1.1770
0.4	242671.7	7.6173	251849.1	11.6872
0.6	260820.5	15.6658	280747.3	24.5027
0.8	277016.9	22.8484	303567.8	34.6228
1.0	291121.3	29.1032	322595.6	43.0611
1.5	319379.2	41.6347	357570.1	58.5712

compare the optimal values only if the probability bounds of Equations 2 and 5 are the same, that is $\beta_i = \Gamma_i \sqrt{\mu_i^*}$.

Here, the comparisons of the methods of Bertimas and Sim (2004) and Zhang et al. (2012) was given under the condition that $\beta_i = \Gamma_i \sqrt{\mu_i^*}$, any other parameters defined as in Zhang et al. (2012).

Tables 1 and 2 compare the results of AFIRO, while Tables 3 and 4 compare results of ADLITTLE.

Conclusion

All comparisons pointed out that the model of Bertimas and Sim (2004) has better optimality than that of Zhang et al. (2012) if maintaining the same probability bounds that the i-th constraint is violated.

ACKNOWLEDGEMENTS

The author is grateful to the referee for careful reading and useful comments. This work is supported by the Ministry of Education of Humanities and Social Science Project of China (Grant No. 10YJC630360).

REFERENCES

Ben-Tal A, Nemirovski A (2000). Robust solutions of linear programming problems contaminated with uncertain data. Math. Program. 88:411-424.

Bertsimas D, Sim M (2004). The price of Robustness. Oper. Res. 52:35-53.

Dongarra J, Grosse E, Bjorstad P, Bowman M, Gay D, Hopkins T, Moler C (2003). Netlib. Website: http://www.netlib.org.

Wu KL, Yang MS (2002). Alternative c-means clustering algorithms. Pattern Recog. 35:2267-2278.

Zhang DQ, Chen SC (2004). A comment on "Alternative c-means clustering algorithms." Pattern Recog. 37:173-174.

Zhang JK, Liu SY, Ma XJ (2012). Robust linear optimization under new distance measure. IJPS 7:1175-1181.

Digital in-line holography for blood cell

Adnan Salih[1]* and Khawla J. Tahir[2]

[1]College of Science for Women, Baghdad University, Iraq.
[2]College of Science, Karbala University, Iraq.

This paper investigates the application of Fresnel based numerical algorithms for the reconstruction of Gabor in-line holograms. A simple in-line digital holographic system was used to record blood cell. The Fresnel transformation (FS) method was used for reconstruction of the hologram. High contrast blood cell images were used to demonstrate numerical reconstruction process by Matlab. Sine, cosin, and amplitude holograms were reconstructed. This method provides new insights into the dynamics of the red blood cells and will be further used to investigate the effect of physiological and pharmacological effectors on RBCs. The spontaneous cell membrane fluctuations (CMF) of the red blood cell (RBC) was investigated, by calculating both thickness and refraction index of the cell blood.

Key words: Digital holography, blood cell, refractive index.

INTRODUCTION

Holography (Gabor, 1948; Leith and Upatnieks, 1964) is an imaging technique made up of two parts, recording and reconstruction. Digital holography differs from conventional holography in that a digital camera (Charge coupled device/complementary metal oxide semiconductor; CCD/CMOS) is used in place of photographic film or holographic plates. Reconstruction of the hologram is then performed numerically on a computer (Kreis, 2005; Schnars and Jüptner, 2004). The concept of digital holography emerged in the 1960s, as reviewed in Lesem et al. (1968). Numerical reconstruction techniques for optically recorded holograms had been applied. Digital holography greatly simplifies the hardware setup for cinematic holographic recording and reconstruction (Goodman and Lawrence, 1967). Despite these promising prospects, digital holography is inherently limited by the poor resolution of solid-state image sensors. Currently, the pixel size of most scientific CCD sensors is in the range of 6 to 10 μm, compared with the silver-halide holographic films with an equivalent pixel size down to 0.1 μm. Because the digital sensor elements cannot resolve interference fringes finer than the pixel size, the permissible angle between object wave and reference wave is limited to a few degrees (Pereira and Gharib, 2002; Murata and Yasuda, 2000). A digital

hologram is created by the interference between a coherent object and reference beam, which is digitally recorded by CCD camera and processed by computational methods to obtain the holographic images. The digital hologram contains not only amplitude information of the object, but also phase (Myuny et al., 2006). Moreover, the ability of the CCD camera to quantify recorded light gives rise to a number of post processing methods that can for instance be used to calculate optical thickness or refractive index variations of an object provided knowledge of one of the other is available. Digital holography not only offers quantitative information phase but high fidelity and high resolution images (Peng et al., 2001).

This advance was facilitated by the availability of digital cameras with high spatial resolution and high dynamic range. The output of a numerical reconstruction is, in general, a complex two-dimensional representation of the wave front at a single distance from the camera plane, and so we refer to the digital capture combined with numerical reconstruction as an imaging system. The novel microscopic principle originally proposed by Gabor (1948) is the simplest realization of holography and has been coined digital in-line holographic microscopy (DIHM) (Coupland and Bera, 2008). Essentially, all past and present light microscopy of biological systems has been achieved through the lens of the compound microscope, which yields high spatial resolution at the cost of shallow depth of focus and has, in the process,

---

*Corresponding author. E-mail: dradnan_salih@yahoo.com.

condemned biological microscopy to a century of histological study made possible only through microtomy. Digital in-line holography (DIH) has come to represent a new tool for biological applications, supplementing conventional compound light microscopy, its simplicity of the microscope: In-line holography is microscopy without objective lenses. The hardware required is a laser, pinhole, and a CCD camera (Wenbo et al., 2001).

This configuration leads to a new application field, named as digital holographic microscopy (DHM), which takes the advantages of digital holography concerning the numerical manipulation of the complex object wave front in addition with the appealing properties provided by microscopy. In that sense, microscopy expands up the capabilities of digital holography in a similar way than digital holography, and also improves some aspects of microscopy by avoiding the limited depth of focus in high numerical aperture (NA) lenses and the high magnification ratios needed in conventional optical microscope imaging. Thus, DHM is coherent imaging methods allowing instantaneous and quantitative acquisition of both amplitude and the phase information of the objects have diffracted wave front. Imaging of phase distributions with high spatial resolution can be used to determine refractive index variations as well as the thickness of the specimen (Cuche et al., 1999).

The main aim of this study is to use in-line digital holography to record blood cell, investigate the spontaneous cell membrane fluctuations (CMF) of the red blood cell (RBC), and to demonstrate the numerical reconstruction process of holograms in different planes based on the Fresnel transformation (FS). This approach to digital hologram recording and numerical reconstruction not only eliminates wet chemical processing and mechanical scanning but also enables the use of complex amplitude information that is inaccessible in optical reconstruction.

METHODOLOGY

Fresnel transformation method

The FS is the most commonly used method in holographic reconstruction, because of the computational efficiency. The approximation of a spherical Huygens wavelet by a parabolic surface allows the calculation of the diffraction integral using a single Fourier transform. PSF can be simplified by the Fresnel approximation as (Montfort et al., 2006; Charri`ere et al., 2006):

$$S(x,y;z) = -\frac{ik}{2\pi z}\exp[ikz + i\frac{k}{2z}(x^2 + y^2)] \tag{1}$$

Where s(x, y; z) Fresnel diffraction, z is distance and k is the wave number of light $K = 2\pi/\lambda$

And the reconstructed wave field is;

$$E(x,y;z) = -\frac{ik}{2\pi z}\exp[ikz + \frac{ik}{2z}(x^2 + y^2)]$$
$$\times \iint E_0(x_0, y_0)\exp[\frac{ik}{2z}(x_0^2 + y_0^2)]$$
$$\times \exp[-\frac{ik}{2z}(xx_0 + yy_0)]dx_0 dy_0$$
$$= \exp[\frac{ik}{2z}(x^2 + y^2)]\xi[E_0 S] \tag{2}$$

Where $E_0(x_0, y_0)$ is the modified wave field, x_o, y_o of the point object, and the spatial variation governed by a sine function with a quadratic spatial dependence. x, y and $\xi[E_0 S]$ denote the spatial coordinates in the hologram and reconstruction plane, respectively

Fresnel diffraction of a beam during propagation. The resolution $\Delta\alpha$ of the reconstructed images determined directly from the Fresnel diffraction formula will vary as a function of the reconstruction distance z (Gabolde and Trebino, 2006).

$$\Delta\alpha = \frac{\lambda z}{N \Delta x_0} \tag{3}$$

Where N is the number of pixels and Δx_0 is the pixel width of the CCD camera, $\lambda = 532\ nm$ (wave length). As with the Huygens convolution method, there is a minimum z distance requirement set by Equation 4 (Schnars and Jueptner, 1994).

$$z_{min} = \frac{a_x^2}{n_x \lambda} \tag{4}$$

Where $a_x = n_x \Delta x$ is the size of the hologram and n_x, Δx are the number and size of pixels, λ is wave length of light. At a very close distance, the spatial frequency of the hologram is too low and aliasing occurs. Normally, the object is placed just outside this minimum distance. Camera (1024 × 1024 pixels) resolution ($\Delta\alpha$ = 0.225 µm), (NA = 1.4),

Reconstruction in-line digital holography

This represents the reconstruction of sine-hologram, the sine-hologram and the cosine hologram will be expressed in terms of spatial frequencies. Therefore, we have (Lohmann and Rhodes, 1978; Poon, 2006; Poon and Kim, 2006; Yamaguchi and Zhang, 1997)

$$i_c(x,y) = Re\left[\int \mathcal{F}^{-1}\{\mathcal{F}|\Gamma_o|^2 OTF_\Omega\}dz\right]$$
$$= Hsin\ (x, y) \tag{5}$$

$$i_s(x,y) = Im[\int \mathcal{F}^{-1}\{\mathcal{F}\{|\Gamma_o(x,y;z)|^2 OTF_\Omega\}\ dz]$$
$$= Hcos\ (x, y) \tag{6}$$

Where

$$OTF_\Omega(k_x, k_y; z) = \exp\left[-j\frac{z}{2k_o}(k_x^2 + k_y^2)\right]$$
$$= OTF\ (k_x, k_y; z) \tag{7}$$

$Im[.]$ denotes the imaginary part of the quantity within the bracket, Re[.] denotes the real part of the content inside the bracket, OTF_Ω optical transfer function, an amplitude transparency of $\Gamma_o(x, y; z)$

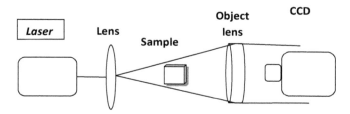

Figure 1. In-line digital holographic setup.

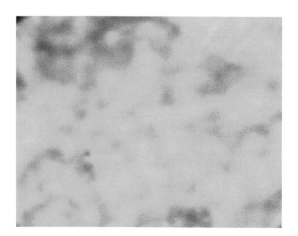

Figure 2. Recorded hologram.

Figure 3. Reconstructed hologram (1024 × 1024) pixels.

located at a distance $z, \mathcal{F}^{-1}$. The spatial impulse response of the optical system shows the sine-hologram and the cosine-hologram. Since the two holograms can be stored digitally, we can also construct a complex digital hologram by using Equation 8.

$$H_{c\pm}(x,y) = H_{cos}(x,y) \pm jH_{sin}(x,y)$$
$$= \int \{|\Gamma_o(x,y;z)|^2 * \frac{k_o}{2\pi z} \exp[\pm j \frac{k_o}{2\pi z}(x^2 + y^2)]\}dz \quad (8)$$

$H_{c\pm}(x,y)$ is called a complex hologram; $H_{cos}(x,y)$ is the

cosine hologram, and $H_{sin}(x,y)$ is the sine hologram; the sine-hologram will be expressed in terms of spatial frequencies. To obtain real image reconstruction formed in front of the hologram, we will use the following equation:

$$H_{any}(x,y) * h(x,y;z_o) \quad (9)$$

Where $H_{any}(x,y)$ represents any holograms, that is, the sine-hologram, the cosine-hologram or the complex hologram.

For digital reconstruction, we will simply convolve the above holograms with the spatial impulse response in order to simulate Fresnel diffraction for a distance of Z_o. To obtain real image, reconstruction is formed in front of the hologram, a planar object at a distance of Z_o away from the x-y scanning mirrors, that is,

$$|\Gamma_o(x,y;z)|^2 = I(x,y)\delta(z - z_o)$$

Where $I(x,y)$ is the planar intensity distribution.

Reconstructed real image is

$$H_{C+}(x,y) = H_{cos}(x,y) + jH_{sin}(x,y) \quad (10)$$

Note that the complex hologram is constructed as

$$H_{C-}(x,y) = H_{cos}(x,y) - jH_{sin}(x,y) \quad (11)$$

Experiments

The experimental setup is shown in Figure 1. The sample (blood smear) illuminated with a green 532 nm Nd:YAG laser. A digital camera (1024 × 1024 pixels) resolution ($\Delta\alpha$ = 0.225 µm), (NA = 1.4), replaces the film. The unscattered part of the illumination wave serves as the reference wave to interfere with the waves scattered by the particles (object). The interference fringes, whose spatial frequency is proportional to the angle formed by the scattering direction and the reference beam direction.

In digital holography, an image sensor records the interference pattern between the light beam scattered by the object under study and a reference beam as shown in Figure 2. This interference pattern is processed in the computer to reconstruct an image of the diffracting object by simulating the reference and using Fresnel propagation.

Then it will have a reconstructed virtual image that is located at a distance of Z_o behind the hologram by computer simulation of digital holography which has been developed (Matlab).

RESULTS AND DISCUSSION

The recording hologram was reconstructed by using Fresnel propagation; the program was designed using Matlab. A reconstructed image for blood cell is shown in Figure 3. The color of the image is shown by Matlab program. To get a clear and magnifying picture, Equations 5 and 6 were solved using Matlab. The results are shown in Figure 4a and b.

Where sigma = $Z_o/2K_o$

We can also construct a complex hologram by using

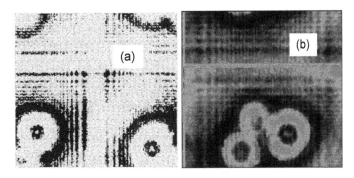

Figure 4. (a) Recorded sine hologram, (b) reconstruction sine hologram.

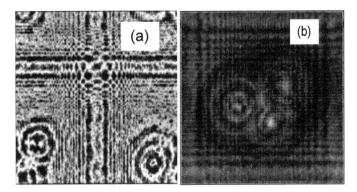

Figure 5. (a) Recorded cosine, (b) reconstruction cosine hologram.

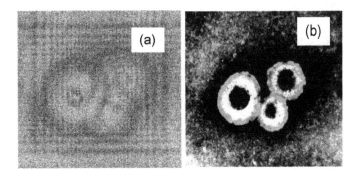

Figure 6. (a) Phase image, (b) amplitude image.

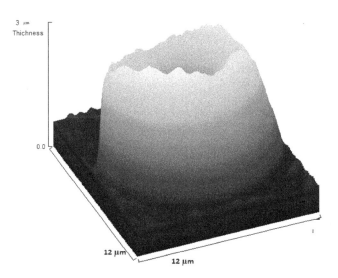

Figure 7. Draw surface of a red blood cell

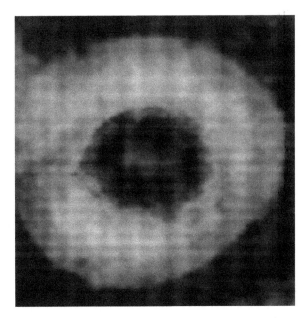

Figure 8. Red blood cell.

Equation 8. For digital reconstruction, we will simply convolve the above holograms with the spatial impulse response in order to Fresnel diffraction for a distance of Z_o. To obtain real image reconstruction formed in front of the hologram where we have used Equation 9 with the spatial frequency response, to obtain the last step (Figure 4b and 5b) which show the reconstruction of the sine-hologram and the cosine-hologram, respectively.

The complex hologram obtained and reconstructed virtual image that is located at a distance of Z_o behind the hologram by solving Equations 10 and 11 images was formed as shown in Figure 6a and b, respectively.

Thickness of the red blood cell was calculated by taking a picture shown in Figure 7, and it was plotted in a three-dimensional Matlab program and cell shape as shown in Figure 8, and the thickness of the cell was 2.2 μm.

From Figure 7, one can be able to know the aid in the diagnosis of malaria disease. The pathogenesis of malaria is largely due to stiffening of the infected RBCs, contemporary understanding ascribe the loss of RBC deformability.

The spontaneous CMF of the RBC has been investigated. DHM as an interferometric technique is able to accurately provide the wave front deformation induced by a transparent specimen. After learning, thickness could account for refraction index by Equation (12) (Curl et al., 2005) as follows:

$$n_{c,i} = \frac{1}{h_i} \int_0^{h_i} n_{c,i}(z)\,dz \qquad (12)$$

Where z is the axial coordinate, h_i is the cellular thickness, $n_{c,i}(z)$ is the function representing the value of the intracellular refractive index along the cellular thickness h_i. The refraction index values ($n_{c,i} = 1.3847 \pm 0.0003$) and the mean refraction index measurements of different erythrocyte regions do not present statistically significant spatial variations. Such a spatially homogeneous intracellular refractive index is consistent with a homogeneous erythrocyte cytoplasm

Conclusion

This paper investigates the application of Fresnel based numerical algorithms for the reconstruction of Gabor in-line holograms. We focus on the two most widely used Fresnel approximation algorithms, the direct method. Both algorithms involve calculating a Fresnel integral, but they accomplish it in fundamentally different ways. The algorithms are performed differently for different physical parameters such as distance, CCD pixel size, and so on. We investigate the constraints for the algorithms when applied to in-line Gabor DHM. We show why the algorithms fail in some instances and how to alter them in order to obtain useful images of the microscopic specimen. We verify the altered algorithms using an optically captured digital hologram. This way was used to get a clear picture of the magnifying, as well as the erythrocyte CMF. This method provides new insights into the dynamics of the RBCs and will be further used to investigate the effect of physiological and pharmacological effectors on RBCs.

REFERENCES

Charri`ere F, Colomb T, Montfort F, Cuche E, Marquet P, Depeursinge C (2006). Shot-noise in flounce on the reconstructed phase image signal to noise ratio in digital holographic microscopy. Appl. Opt. 45(29):7667-7673.

Coupland J, Bera JL (2008). Optical tomography and digital holography. Meas. Sci. Tech. P. 19.

Cuche E, Marquet P, Depeursinge C (1999). Simultaneous amplitude-contrast and quantitative phase contrast microscopy by numerical reconstruction of Fresnel off-axis holograms. App. Opt. 38(34):6994-7001.

Curl CL, Bellair CJ, Harris T, Allman BE, Harris PJ, Stewart AG, Roberts A, Nugent KA, Delbridge LM (2005). Refractive index measurement in viable cells using quantitative phase-amplitude microscopy and confocal microscopy. Cytometry A65(1):88-92.

Gabolde P, Trebino R (2006). Single-shot measurement of the full spatial -temporal field of ultra short pulses with multi-spectral digital holography. Opt. Express 14:11460-11467.

Gabor D (1948). A new microscopic principle. Nature 16:777.

Goodman JW, Lawrence RW (1967). Digital image formation from electronically detected holograms. Appl. Phys. Lett. 11:77.

Kreis T (2005). Handbook of Holographic Interferometry. Wiley-VCH GmbH & Co. KGaAWeinheim.

Leith EN, Upatnieks J (1964). Wavefront Reconstruction with Diffused Illumination and Three-Dimensional Objects. J. Opt. Soc. Am. 54:1295.

Lesem LB, Hirsch PM, JA Jordan (1968). Computer synthesis of holograms for 3-D display. Commun. ACM 11:661.

Lohmann AW, Rhodes WT (1978). Two-pupil synthesis of optical transfer functions. Appl. Opt. 17:1141-1150.

Montfort F, Charri`ere F, Colomb T, Cuche E, Marquet P, Depeursinge C (2006). Purely numerical compensation for microscope objective phase curvature indigital holographic microscopy: Influence of digital phase maskposition. J. Opt. Soc. Am. A23(11):2944-2953.

Murata S, Yasuda SN (2000). Potential of digital holography in particle measurement. Opt. Laser Tech. 32:567-574.

Myuny KK, Lingfeng Y, Christopher JM (2006). Interference techniques in digital holography. J. Opt. A8:518-523.

Peng X, Miao J, Asundi A (2001). Studies of digital microscopic holography with applications to microstructuretesting. Appl. Opt. 40:5046-5051.

Pereira FP, Gharib M (2002). Defocusing digital particle image velocity and the three dimensional characterization of two phase flows. Meas. Sci. Tech. 13:683-694.

Poon TC (2006). Horizontal-parallax-only optical scanning holography, in chapter 10 of Digital Holography and Three-Dimensional Display: Principles and Applications, T.C. Poon ed., Springer, New York, USA.

Poon TC, Kim T (2006). Engineering Optics with MATLAB®. WorldScientific Publishing Co., Singapore.

Schnars U, Jueptner WP (1994). Direct recording of holograms by a CCD target and numerical reconstruction. Appl. Opt. 33:179-181.

Schnars U, Jüptner WPO (2004). Digital Holography, Springer. Ch. 7.

Wenbo Xu, Jericho MH, Meinertzhagen IA, Kreuzer HJ (2001). Digital in-line holographyfor biological applications. PNAS 98:20.

Yamaguchi I, Zhang T (1997). Phase-shifting digital holography. Opt. Lett. 22:1268-1270.

3

Performance evaluation of multi objective differential evolution algorithm (MDEA) strategies

Fred Otieno and Josiah Adeyemo

Durban University of Technology, P. O. Box 1334, Durban, 4000, South Africa.

This study presents the results of comparison of the four strategies of multiobjective differential evolution algorithm (MDEA) namely, MDEA1, MDEA2, MDEA3 and MDEA4 in solving five test problems and an engineering design problem. The test problems are ZDT1, ZDT2, ZDT3, ZDT4 and ZDT6. MDEA is a multiobjective algorithm developed from differential evolution, which is an evolutionary algorithm, to solve multiobjective optimization problems. The strategies were also compared with the results obtained from two other similar algorithms: NSGAII and DEMO. It was found that strategies of MDEA named MDEA1 and MDEA2 with binomial crossover method outperformed other two strategies named MDEA3 and MDEA4 with exponential crossover method in solving ZDT1 and ZDT4 while MDEA3 and MDEA4 outperformed MDEA1 and MDEA2 in solving ZDT2 and ZDT6. All the strategies performed equally in solving the engineering design problem presented. It was concluded that the strategies of MDEA are comparable/better than similar algorithms presented in solving the test problems and the engineering design problem.

Key words: Multiobjective differential evolution algorithm (MDEA), multiobjective, evolutionary algorithm, differential evolution.

INTRODUCTION

Differential evolution (DE) has grown over the years with several extensions to solve multiobjective problems (Abbass and Sarker, 2002; Angira and Babu, 2005; Babu and Jehan, 2003; Chakraborti et al., 2009; Madavan, 2002; Nariman-Zadeh et al., 2009). They are competing well with other multiobjective evolutionary algorithms (MOEAs) and they are producing good results (Angira and Babu, 2005; Ascia et al., 2012; Branke et al., 2009; Fan et al., 2006). However, more strategies of existing MOEAs and development of new ones are necessary to overcome some of the shortcomings and to develop more efficient and faster algorithms. The performance of different MOEAs based on differential evolution and their strategies are yet to be determined. This performance test will aid the modifications necessary to the existing algorithms and development of new ones. Several

MOEAs have been developed over the past decade. They are based on different algorithms (Deb, 1999; Robic and Filipic, 2005; Sarker and Ray, 2009; Wang et al., 2009; Xue et al., 2003; Zitzler and Thiele, 1999). They have been applied to real world problems with success (Konstantinidis et al., 2012; Lee et al., 2008; Marcelloni and Vecchio, 2012). The advantages of MOEA in solving real world optimization problems cannot be overemphasized. They are better than classical methods in solving multiobjective problems. They are faster, easy to use and with few control parameters especially differential evolution. The objectives in design problems are increasing every day and they are usually conflicting with multiple constraints. This growth has necessitated the development of more powerful algorithms to find solutions to them. Researchers in MOEAs are rising up to

Table 1. Formulations of the four different strategies of multi-objective differential evolution algorithm (MDEA).

Strategy	Description	Formulation
MDEA1	DE/rand/1/bin	$v(g,i,j) = x(g,r_3,j) + F * [x(g,r_1,j) - x(g,r_2,j)]$
MDEA2	DE/rand/2/bin	$v(g,i,j) = x(g,r_5,j) + F * [x(g,r_1,j) + x(g,r_2,j) - x(g,r_3,j) - x(g,r_4,j)]$
MDEA3	DE/rand/1/exp	$v(g,i,j) = x(g,r_3,j) + F * [x(g,r_1,j) - x(g,r_2,j)]$
MDEA4	DE/rand/2/exp	$v(g,i,j) = x(g,r_5,j) + F * [x(g,r_1,j) + x(g,r_2,j) - x(g,r_3,j) - x(g,r_4,j)]$

Source: Adeyemo and Otieno (2010).

this challenge with the development of more powerful algorithms. Researchers are not working in isolation. They are developing hybrid algorithms using the advantages of different algorithms to develop a hybrid algorithm better than the algorithms (parents) themselves. This phenomenon is similar to DE algorithms and at large evolutionary algorithms (EAs) where the offspring produced from the parents is usually better than the parents.

While the objective of single objective optimization problem is to come up with a solution to a problem, multiobjective presents many non-dominated solutions. The solutions are non-dominated in the sense that no solution is superior to another one in a set of non-dominated solutions when all the objectives are considered (Deb, 2001). A final solution is thus chosen based on other information available to a user.

Multiobjective differential evolution algorithm (MDEA) has been widely used to solve multiobjective problems with multiple constraints especially crop planning and optimum cropping patter determination (Adeyemo and Otieno, 2010). While MDEA was tested on test problems and engineering design problem, other strategies developed, MDEA2, MDEA3 AND MDEA4 are yet to be tested on test problems to determine their performance using different problems. The objective of this study was to determine the performance of the four different strategies of MDEA using different test problems and an engineering design problem. We wanted to find out the right parameter setting for each of the strategies for their optimum performance. Furthermore, we wanted to find out the best strategy for different types of problems and to find out any improvement needed for their optimum performance.

Strategies of multiobjective differential evolution algorithm (MDEA)

MDEA was proposed by Adeyemo and Otieno (2009). The algorithm is based on the first strategy of differential evolution which is DE/rand/1/bin which denotes that it uses binomial crossover and one vector for perturbation (Storn and Price, 1997). Later they proposed three other strategies and named them MDEA2, MDEA3 and MDEA4 and named the original one MDEA1 (Adeyemo and

Otieno, 2010). MDEA2, MDEA3 and MDEA4 use the description DE/rand/2/bin, DE/rand/1/exp and DE/rand/2/exp as their formulations respectively (as presented in Table 1) from the ten strategies proposed by Storn and Price (1997).

Initially, practical advice by Price and Storn (2008) was followed in choosing crossover constant (CR) and scaling factor (F) but the values were later varied to get the best results from the strategies of the MDEA.

In MDEA, the vectors are randomly generated to create initial solutions to the problem. The generated solutions are allowed to undergo mutation, crossover and selection for the chosen number of generations just like the traditional differential evolution. The evolved solutions in the final generation are checked for domination and the dominated solutions are removed. Usually from previous experiment of this algorithm with crop planning problem and test problems, all the solutions turned out to converge to Pareto fronts (Adeyemo and Otieno, 2009, 2010). The trial solution survives to the next generation if its objective function is better or equal in all the objectives to the target solution. MDEA handles multiple constraints using penalty function proposed by Deb (2001). This algorithm combines the advantages of DEMO (Robic and Filipic, 2005) and the algorithm by Fan et al. (2006). However, MDEA runs faster with more quality Pareto optimal solutions than both algorithms (Adeyemo and Otieno, 2009).

RESULTS

The four strategies of MDEA namely MDEA1, MDEA2, MDEA3 and MDEA4 were tested using five of the six test problems proposed by Zitzler et al. (2000). The description of the test problems are given in Table 2. These are unconstrained test beds. They are labeled ZDT1, ZDT2, ZDT3, ZDT4 and ZDT6. They have two objectives to be minimized. The population size for all the problems was set at 300. The number of parameter, D was 30 in ZDT1, ZDT2 and ZDT3 while D was 10 for ZDT4 and ZDT6 and the maximum generation was 2000 at a step of 500. These steps are named convergence Stages A, B, C and D for 500, 1000, 1500 and 2000 iterations, respectively. The results were recorded at each stage (500 iterations). For ZDT1, CR and F were set at 0.2 and 0.3 respectively. These control parameters were set by trial and error to determine the best for each problem and each strategy. For ZDT1, all the 300 solutions converged to the Pareto optimal front within 500 iterations (Stage A) for MDEA1 and MDEA2. While the

Table 2. Description of test problems used in this study.

Problems	N	Variable bounds	Objective functions	Optimal solutions	Comments
ZDT1	30	[0,1]	$f_1(x) = x_1$ $$f_2(x) = g(x)\left[1 - \sqrt{\left(\frac{x_1}{g(x)}\right)}\right]$$ $$g(x) = 1 + \frac{9}{n-1}\sum_{i=2}^{n} x_i$$	$x \in [0,1]$ $x_i = 0$ $i = 2,\ldots,n$	Convex
ZDT2	30	[0,1]	$f_1(x) = x_1$ $$f_2(x) = g(x)\left[1 - \left[\frac{x_1}{g(x)}\right]^2\right]$$ $$g(x) = 1 + \frac{9}{n-1}\sum_{i=2}^{n} x_i$$	$x \in [0,1]$ $x_i = 0$ $i = 2,\ldots,n$	Nonconvex
ZDT3	30	[0,1]	$f_1(x) = x_1$ $$f_2(x) = g(x)\left[1 - \left[\sqrt{\frac{x_1}{g(x)}}\right] - \frac{x_1}{g(x)}\sin(10\pi x_1)\right]$$ $$g(x) = 1 + \frac{9}{n-1}\sum_{i=2}^{n} x_i$$	$x \in [0,1]$ $x_i = 0$ $i = 2,\ldots,n$	convex, disconnected
ZDT4	10	$x_1 \in [0,1]$ $x_i \in [-5,5] = 2,\ldots n$	$f_1(x) = x_1$ $$f_2(x) = g(x)\left[1 - \sqrt{\left(\frac{x_1}{g(x)}\right)}\right]$$ $$g(x) = 1 + 10(n-1) + \sum_{i=2}^{n}\left(x_i^2 - 10\cos(4\pi x_i)\right)$$	$x \in [0,1]$ $x_i = 0$ $i = 2,\ldots,n$	Nonconvex
ZDT6	10	[0,1]	$$f_1(x) = 1 - e^{-4x_1}\sin^6(6\pi x_1)$$ $$f_2(x) = g(x)\left[1 - \left(\frac{f_1(x)}{g(x)}\right)^2\right]$$ $$g(x) = 1 + \frac{9}{n-1}\sum_{i=2}^{n} x_i$$	$x_1 \in [0,1]$ $x_i = 0$ $i = 2,3,\ldots,n$	Nonconvex, Nonuniformly spaced solutions on Pareto front, Low density of solutions near Pareto front

convergence was maintained after 500 iterations for MDEA1, the solutions started diverging after 500 iterations for MDEA2 (Stage B). MDEA3 could not converge with CR = 0.2 and F = 0.3, therefore, we tried CR = 0.85 and F = 0.5. After 2000 iterations (Stage D), only 154 non-dominated solutions converged to the Pareto front. Divergence was noticed after 2000 iterations (Stage D). It was found that 71, 129, 160 and 154 non-dominated solutions were noticed at convergence stages A, B, C and D respectively. We had to experiment MDEA3 with different values of CR and F of 0.95 and 0.9 respectively to achieve the convergence of all the 300 solutions at convergence Stage D. We noticed a faster convergence of 278, 293, 298 and 300 at convergence Stages A, B, C and D respectively. For MDEA4, when we used CR = 0.2 and F = 0.3, only 87, 123, 194 and 185 solutions converged at convergence Stages A, B, C and D respectively. We could not achieve 100% convergence of non-dominated solutions (300) until we changed our CR and F to 0.95 and 0.9 respectively. It can be concluded that for test problem ZDT1, higher values of CR and F (0.95 and 0.9, respectively) could made the solutions converge to Pareto fronts for MDEA3 and MDEA4 while lower values of CR and F (0.2 and 0.3 respectively) achieved fast convergence for MDEA1 and MDEA2.

Performance measures

The common performance measures for multi-objective algorithms are employed in this study. Two performance metrics are used for adequately evaluating both goals of multi-objective optimization. One performance metric evaluates the progress towards the Pareto-optimal front and the other evaluates the spread of solutions. The descriptions of convergence metric Υ and diversity metric Δ used to evaluate strategies of MDEA are given below. They are:

Convergence metric Υ

This metric measures the distance between the obtained non-dominated front, Q and the set, P* of the Pareto-optimal solutions. It is defined as:

$$\Upsilon = \frac{\sum\limits_{i=1}^{|Q|} d_i}{|Q|} \qquad (1)$$

where Q is the number of non-dominated vectors found by the algorithm being analysed and d_i is the Euclidean distance (in the objective space) between the obtained non dominated front Q and the nearest member in the true Pareto front P.

Diversity metric Δ

This metric measures the extent of spread achieved using the non-dominated solutions. It is defined as:

$$\Delta = \frac{d_f + d_l + \sum\limits_{i=1}^{|Q|-1}\left(d_i - \bar{d}\right)}{d_f + d_l + \left(|Q|-1\right)\bar{d}} \qquad (3)$$

where d_i is the Euclidean distance (measured in the objective space) between consecutive solutions in the obtained non-dominated front Q, and $\bar{d}$ is the average of these distances. The parameter d_f and d_l are the Euclidean distances between the extreme solutions of the Pareto front P* and the boundary solution of the obtained front Q. Also an algorithm having a smaller value of diversity metric Δ is better.

All the 300 solutions converged to Pareto front at convergence Stage A for MDEA1 and MDEA2 for ZDT2 using CR =0.1 and F = 0.3. CR and F were increased to 0.95 and 0.9 respectively as with ZDT1 to achieve convergence of all the 300 solutions at convergence Stage C for MDEA3 and MDEA4. When we increased F to 0.95, all the solutions (300) converged to the Pareto front at convergence Stage B for MDEA4.

For ZDT3, CR = 0.5 and F=0.5 were used for MDEA1 and MDEA2 to achieve a convergence of 297 and 288 solutions respectively at Stage C. Only 280 and 287 solutions converged to the Pareto front at convergence Stages C and D respectively for MDEA3 and MDEA4 (Figure 1). For ZDT4, we experimented with CR = 0.2 and F=0.3 for MDEA1 and MDEA2 and all the 300 solutions converged to Pareto front at convergence Stage A. Only 168 and 164 solutions converged to Pareto front at Stage A using the same parameters for MDEA3 and MDEA4 respectively. The parameters were changed to CR = 0.95 and F = 0.9 for MDEA3 and MDEA4 for all the 300 solutions to converge to Pareto front at convergence Stage A.

We experimented ZDT6 with CR = 0.6 and F = 0.2 for MDEA1 and MDEA2 and all the 300 solutions converged to Pareto front at convergence Stage A. 205 solutions converged at convergence Stage A for MDEA3 and no convergence was noticed for MDEA4 using the same parameters. However, all the 300 solutions converged to Pareto front at Stage A for both MDEA3 and MDEA4 when the parameters were changed to higher values (CR = 0.95 and F = 0.9) Figure 2 and 3.

The four strategies were further tested on an engineering design problem of cantilever design (Deb et al., 2001). The description of this problem is given by Deb et al. (2001). It has two decision variables, two conflicting objectives to be minimized, two constraints and two bound constraints. The population size used for this problem was 100, CR = 0.8 and F = 0.3 were used for MDEA1 and MDEA2 with only 50 solutions converging to Pareto front at convergence Stage A. At higher values of CR = 0.95 and F = 0.9, 50 solutions also converged to Pareto front at Stage A for MDEA3 and MDEA4 (Figure 4).

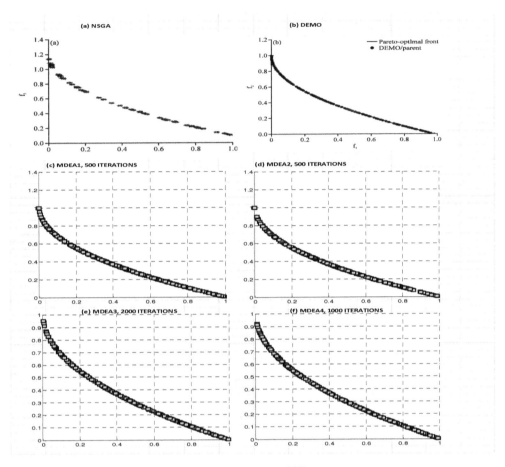

Figure 1. Results of different algorithms on test problem ZDT1.

Performance of the strategies

It was observed that MDEA1 and MDEA2 behave alike and MDEA3 and MDEA4 form another group. For convergence to be achieved, lower values of CR and F were suitable for MDEA1 and MDEA2 while higher values of CR and F (close to 1) favour the convergence of MDEA3 and MDEA4. It can be concluded that MDEA1 and MDEA2 with binomial crossover method perform better with lower values of CR and F and MDEA3 and MDEA4 with exponential crossover method perform better with higher values of CR and F (very close to 1) (Adeyemo and Otieno, 2010; Price and Storn, 2008) (Figure 5).

MDEA1 and MDEA2 converge within convergence Stage A (500 iterations) in all the test problems except ZDT3 which is a difficult optimization problem (Zitzler et al., 2000) and mostly all the solutions converged to the Pareto front except in cantilever problem where only half of them converged. In contrast, convergence to Pareto front only occurred at convergence Stages C and D for MDEA3 and MDEA4 except ZDT4 and ZDT6 and cantilever problem where it occurred at convergence Stage A. Also, not all the solutions converged to

the Pareto front in all the problems using MDEA3 and MDEA4. In ZDT3 which is a difficult optimization, only 280 and 287 solutions converged to the Pareto front for MDEA3 and MDEA4 respectively. Half of the solutions in cantilever problem converged to the Pareto front like MDEA1 and MDEA2. Therefore, it can be concluded that MDEA1 and MDEA2 which use binomial crossover method, have been shown to show superior performance than MDEA3 and MDEA4 in the test problems except in the engineering design problem where they performed equally. This shows that all the strategies of MDEA are capable of solving the engineering problem with reasonable time (within 100 iterations). We also experimented with different values of CR and F for all the strategies when solving the engineering cantilever problem. It was found that all the strategies performed very well with any combination of values of CR and F. It further confirmed that all the strategies of MDEA are capable of solving the engineering design problem presented (Adeyemo and Otieno, 2010).

In Figure 1(a-f), the non-dominated solutions for NSGA, DEMO, MDEA1, MDEA2, MDEA3 and MDEA4 are presented. It is found that the non-dominated solutions for MDEA1 are of more quality than those of the other algorithms as can be deduced from convergence and diversity metrics in Tables 3 and 4. Though the generated Pareto optimal fronts are similar in all the algorithms, those of strategies of MDEA outperformed those of NSGA and DEMO (Tables 3 and 4). Also those of MDEA1 and MDEA2 outperform MDEA3 and MDEA4 on the same ZDT1 problem (Tables 3 and 4). We can conclude that MDEA is better in achieving quality Pareto front than the other algorithms.

Figure 2(a-f) shows the Pareto optimal fronts for test problem ZDT2 for all the algorithms. It was found that MDEA3 and MDEA4 produced Pareto fronts of higher quality than MDEA1 and MDEA2 in terms of diversity and convergence (Tables 3 and 4). MDEA2 produced the worst Pareto front in terms of convergence with solutions scattered on the Pareto front (Table 3). Though MDEA1 and MDEA2 converged faster at convergence Stage A while MDEA3 and MDEA4 converged at convergence Stage C, still their Pareto fronts are worse than MDEA3 and MDEA4 in convergence as can be seen in Table 3. MDEA1, MDEA3 and MDEA4 have superior Pareto fronts than the other algorithms (NSGAII and DEMO) but MDEA2 have an inferior Pareto front in test problem ZDT2 in diversity and convergence as in Tables 3 and 4.

Further observation on MDEA3 is presented in Figure 3. Figure 3a shows the non-dominated solutions' convergence at CR = 0.85 and F = 0.5. It was found that at convergence Stage A, only 219 solutions were non-dominated with scattered solutions on the Pareto front. At convergence Stage B (1000 iterations), only 268 solutions were non-dominated (Figure 3b). We therefore decided to increase CR to 0.95 and F to 0.9. It was found that 293 solutions were non-dominated at convergence Stage A (Figure 3c); 300 solutions at convergence Stage C, respectively (Figures 3d). The quality of the Pareto front in Figure 3d also improved. This shows that MDEA3 can only perform excellently with higher values of CR and F (close to 1) for a problem like ZDT2.

In Figure 4, ZDT3 optimization results are presented for all the algorithms. It was found that only MDEA1 and MDEA4 produced high quality non-dominated solutions interms of convergence and diversity in Tables 3 and 4. MDEA3 produced poorest non-dominated solutions in convergence and diversity as in Tables 3 and 4. It took MDEA4 2500 iterations to produce 287 non-dominated solutions and MDEA1 produced 297 non-dominated solutions in 1500 iterations (convergence Stage C). Though MDEA2 had more non-dominated solutions (288) than MDEA4, the non-dominated solutions of MDEA4 are said to be of better qualities because they spread evenly (that is, more diversity) (Table 4).

ZDT4 solutions are presented in Figure 5. It was observed that MDEA1 and MDEA2 have higher qualities of non-dominated solutions with more diversity than MDEA3 and MDEA4 though all the solutions are comparable/better than the ones by NSGAII and DEMO (Tables 3 and 4). The non-dominated solutions by the

MDEAs were generated at the convergence Stage A (under 300 iterations).

ZDT6 test problem solutions are presented in Figure 6. It was found that all the strategies of MDEA produced 100% non-dominated solutions at the convergence Stage A (within 500 iterations). MDEA3 and MDEA4 have non-dominated solutions with higher diversity (Table 4). The solutions are well spread on the Pareto fronts unlike MDEA1 and MDEA2. All the non-dominated solutions are comparable/better in convergence and diversity than NSGAII and DEMO (Table 4). It was found that MDEA3 and MDEA4 are better than MDEA1 and MDEA2 in diversity and convergence in the test problems ZDT2 and ZDT6 which have similar concave shape Pareto fronts. Also MDEA1 and MDEA2 are better in convergence and diversity in ZDT1 and ZDT4 which have similar convex shape Pareto fronts (Tables 3 and 4). Therefore, the results agree with the findings of (Adeyemo and Otieno, 2010) that MDEA strategies with binomial crossover method (MDEA1 and MDEA2) can perform better than MDEA strategies with exponential crossover method (MDEA 3 and MDEA4) in some problems. Furthermore, we can now establish that MDEA3 and MDEA4 with exponential crossover method are also better in someproblems than MDEA1 and MDEA2 with binomial crossover method. Also, MDEA1 and MDEA4 are better than MDEA2 and MDEA3 in solving similar problems but MDEA1 has faster convergence than MDEA4 while MDEA4 has more diversity of non-dominated solutions than MDEA1 in similar problems.

We therefore proceeded to solving engineering cantilever problem with the algorithms. The results are presented in Figure 7. We set lower values of CR and F (CR = 0.8 and F = 0.3) for MDEA1 and MDEA2 as in the previous test problems. We set higher values of CR and F (CR = 0.95 and F = 0.9; close to 1) for MDEA3 and MDEA4. All the four strategies performed well in solving the problem and producing non-dominated solutions. The solutions further confirm our previous results that MDEA1 and MDEA2 outperform MDEA3 and MDEA4 in finding solutions on convex shaped Pareto fronts. The solutions of all the strategies of MDEA are comparable to the ones by DEMO and NSGAII. It is further confirmed that all the strategies of MDEA are capable of solving the engineering cantilever design problem presented with ease.

Conclusions

Strategies of multiobjective differential evolution algorithm (MDEA) are presented in this study. They were tested on five different test problems with different shapes of Pareto fronts. They were later tested on an engineering design problem. The strategies are based on the crossover methods and number of vectors used for the perturbation. MDEA1 and MDEA2 use binomial crossover method

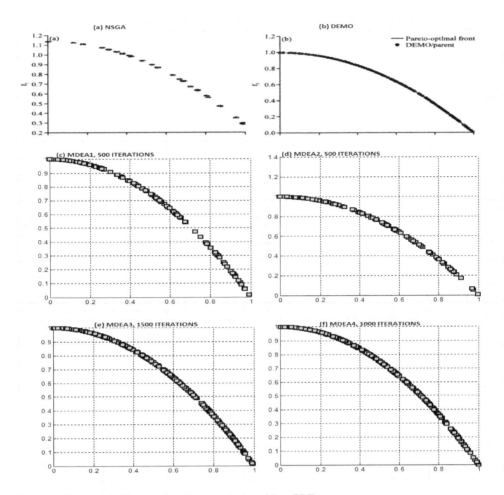

Figure 2. Results of different algorithms on test problem ZDT2.

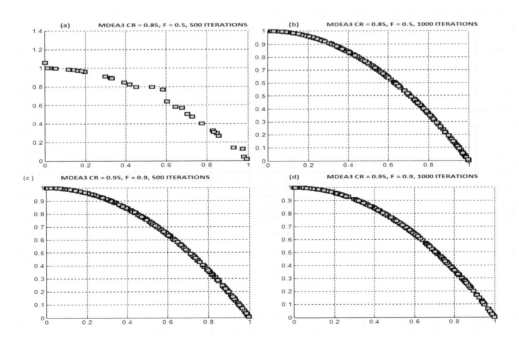

Figure 3. Experiment of the convergence on test problem ZDT2 by MDEA3.

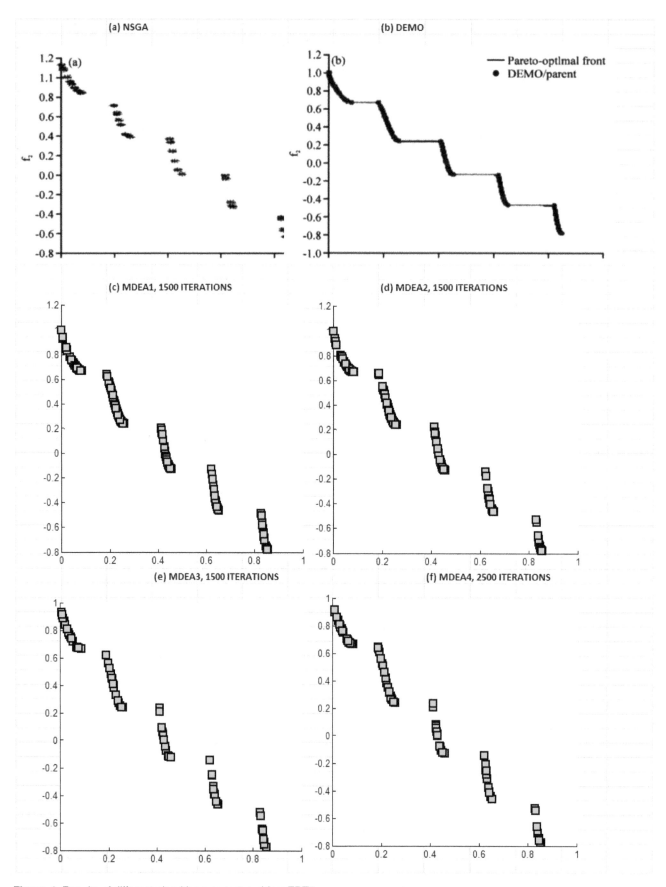

Figure 4. Results of different algorithms on test problem ZDT3.

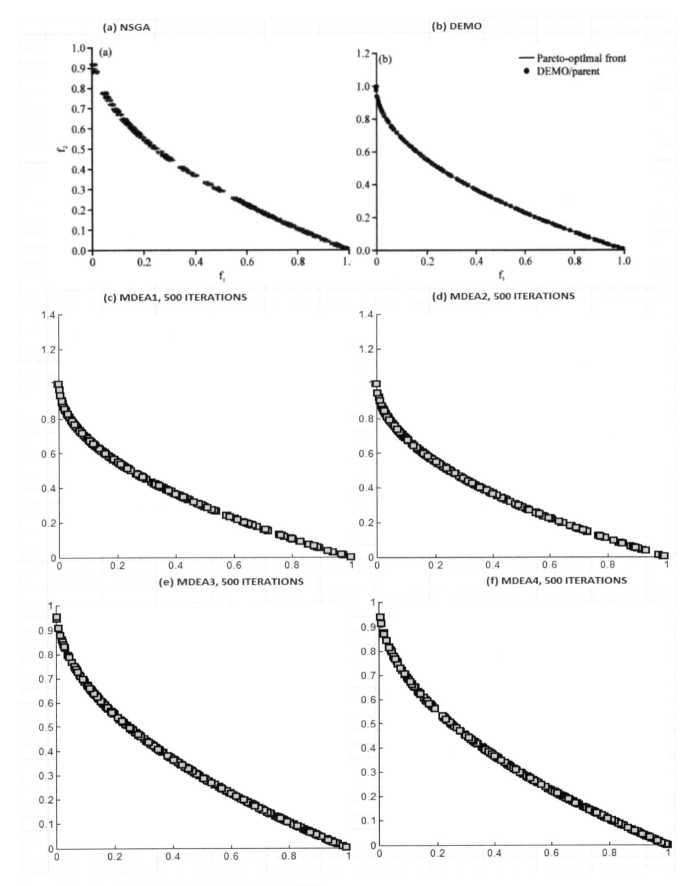

Figure 5. Results of different algorithms on test problem ZDT4.

Table 3. Statistics of the convergence metrics results on all the test problems.

Algorithm	ZDT1	ZDT2	ZDT3	ZDT4	ZDT6
NSGA-II	0.033482±0.004750	0.072391±0.031689	0.114500±0.004940	0.513053±0.118460	0.296564±0.013135
DEMO	0.001113±0.000134	0.000820±0.000042	0.001197±0.000091	0.001016±0.000091	0.000630±0.000021
MDEA1	0.000921±0.000005	0.000640±0.000000	0.001139±0.000024	0.048962±0.536358	0.000436±0.000055
MDEA2	0.000911±0.000010	0.080635±0.000841	0.001200±0.000000	0.041892±0.618792	0.000520±0.000111
MDEA3	0.000103±0.000008	0.000600±0.000016	0.019050±0.005011	0.215873±0.230000	0.000561±0.000212
MDEA4	0.000113±0.000015	0.000605±0.000051	0.001099±0.000028	0.221000±0.025893	0.000542±0.000252

Table 4. Statistics of the diversity metrics results on all the test problems.

Algorithms	ZDT1	ZDT2	ZDT3	ZDT4	ZDT6
NSGA-II	0.390307±0.001876	0.430776±0.004721	0.738540±0.019706	0.702612±0.064648	0.668025±0.009923
DEMO	0.319230±0.031350	0.335178±0.016985	0.324934±0.029648	0.359600±0.026977	0.461174±0.035289
MDEA1	0.283708±0.002938	0.450482±0.004211	0.299354±0.023309	0.406382±0.062308	0.305245±0.019407
MDEA2	0.280015±0.006014	0.460023±0.002102	0.3110000±0.000030	0.412000±0.000055	0.356000±0.001113
MDEA3	0.301500±0.000552	0.310560±0.005101	0.315100±0.000001	0.612000±0.000321	0.111000±0.000555
MDEA4	0.298012±0.000412	0.320050±.0002300	0.201000±0.003000	0.551000±0.000022	0.161000±0.000021

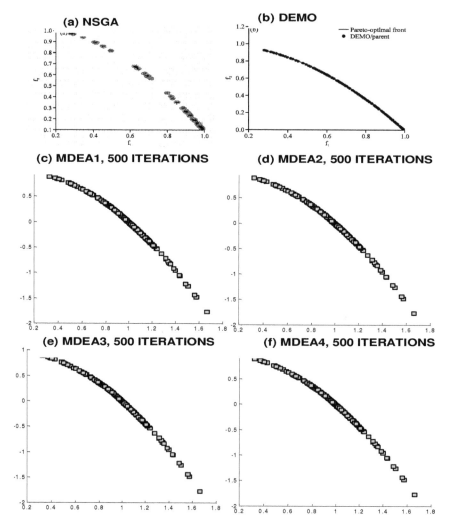

Figure 6. Results of different algorithms on test problem ZDT6.

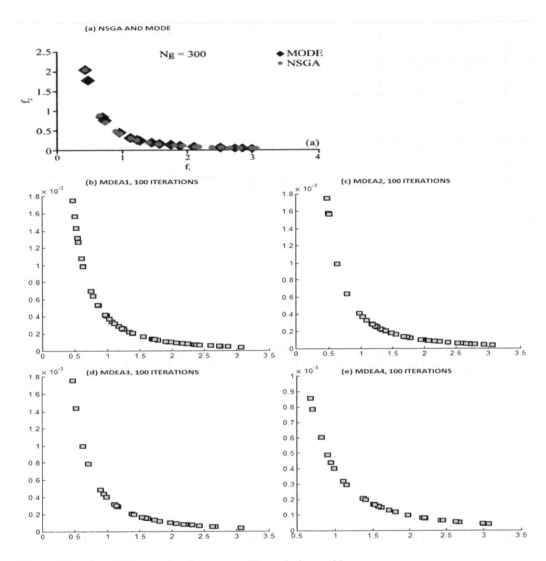

Figure 7. Results of different algorithms on cantilever design problem.

while MDEA3 and MDEA4 use exponential crossover method. MDEA1 is based on DE/rand/1/bin, MDEA2 on DE/rand/2/bin, MDEA3 on DE/rand/1/exp and MDEA4 on DE/rand/2/exp. MDEA2 and MDEA4 use two vectors for their perturbation while MDEA1 and MDEA3 use one vector for their perturbation. All the strategies of MDEA produced non-dominated solutions that converge to the Pareto fronts in the five different test problems. MDEA1 and MDEA2 outperformed MDEA3 and MDEA4 in finding solutions on convex shaped Pareto fronts that is, ZDT1 and ZDT4 while MDEA3 and MDEA4 outperformed MDEA1 and MDEA2 in finding solutions on concave shaped Pareto fronts i.e. ZDT2 and ZDT6. In all, it was found that MDEA1 and MDEA4 are better than MDEA2 and MDEA3 in solving all the test problems. It was however, found that MDEA4 produced non-dominated solutions of better quality and more diversity than MDEA1 though with higher iterations. In the engineering design

problem, all the strategies of MDEA performed excellently with MDEA1 and MDEA2 outperforming MDEA3 and MDEA4. It was concluded that all the strategies of MDEA are comparable/better than the other two algorithms compared (NSGAII and DEMO) in solving the test problems and the engineering cantilever design problem presented. It is suggested that modifications should be made to the strategies of MDEA to make them perform better in terms of diversity especially, MDEA2 and MDEA3.

REFERENCES

Abbass HA, Sarker R (2002). The Pareto differential evolution algorithm. Int. J. Artif. Intell. Tools 11(4):531-552.

Adeyemo J, Otieno F (2010). Differential evolution algorithm for solving multi-objective crop planning model. Agric. Water Manag. 97(6):848-856.

Adeyemo JA, Otieno FAO (2009). Multi-objective differential evolution algorithm (MDEA) for solving engineering problems. J. Appl. Sci. 9(20):3652-3661.

Angira R, Babu BV (2005). Non-dominated sorting differential evolution for multi-objective optimization. 2nd Indian Int. Conf. Artif. Intell. (IICAI-05):1428-1443.

Ascia G, Catania V, Di Nuovo AG, Palesi M, Patti D (2012). Performance evaluation of efficient multi-objective evolutionary algorithms for design space exploration of embedded computer systems. Appl. Soft Comput. 11(1):382-398.

Babu BV, Jehan MM (2003). Differential evolution for multi-objective optimization. Paper presented at the Congress on Evolutionary Computation (CEC-2003), Canberra, Australia. pp. 2696-2703.

Branke J, Scheckenbach B, Stein M, Deb K, Schmeck H (2009). Portfolio optimization with an envelope-based multi-objective evolutionary algorithm. Eur. J. Oper. Res. 199(3):684-693.

Chakraborti N, Sreevathsan R, Jayakanth R, Bhattacharya B (2009). Tailor-made material design: An evolutionary approach using multi-objective genetic algorithms. Comput. Mater. Sci. 45(1):1-7.

Deb K (1999). Multi-Objective Genetic Algorithms: Problem Difficulties and Construction of Test Problems. Evol. Comput. 7(3):205-230.

Deb K (2001). Multi-Objective Optimization using Evolutionary Algorithms. John Wiley & Sons, Chichester, UK. pp. 22-25.

Deb K, Agrawal S, Pratap A, Meyarivan T (2001). A Fast Elistist Non-Dominated Sorting Genetic Algorithm for Multi-Objective Optimization: NSGA-II. Kanpur Genetic Algorithms Laboratory (KanGAL) Indian Inst. Technol. Kanpur. pp. 182-197.

Fan H-Y, Lampinen J, Levy Y (2006). An easy-to-implement differential evolution approach for multi-objective optimizations. Engineering Computations: Int. J. Comput-Aided Eng. Softw. 23(2):124-138.

Konstantinidis A, Yang K, Zhang Q, Zeinalipour-Yazti D (2012). A multi-objective evolutionary algorithm for the deployment and power assignment problem in wireless sensor networks. Comput. Netw. 54(6):960-976.

Lee LH, Chew EP, Teng S, Chen Y (2008). Multi-objective simulation-based evolutionary algorithm for an aircraft spare parts allocation problem. Eur. J. Oper. Res. 189(2):476-491.

Madavan NK (2002). Multi-objective optimization using a Pareto differential evolution approach. Paper presented at the Congress on Evolutionary Computation (CEC '2002). pp. 1145-1150.

Marcelloni F, Vecchio M (2012). Enabling energy-efficient and lossy-aware data compression in wireless sensor networks by multi-objective evolutionary optimization. Inf. Sci. 180(10):1924-1941.

Nariman-Zadeh N, Felezi M, Jamali A, Ganji M (2009). Pareto optimal synthesis of four-bar mechanisms for path generation. Mech. Mach. Theory 44(1):180-191.

Price K, Storn R (2008). Differential evolution homepage (web site of Price and Storn) as at 2008. http:\\www.ICSI.Berkeley.edu/~storn/code.html, vol 2008.

Robic T, Filipic B (2005). DEMO: Differential evolution for multiobjective optimization. Paper presented at the 3rd Int. Conf. on Evolutionary Multi-Criterion Optimization, EMO 2005. pp. 520-533.

Sarker R, Ray T (2009). An improved evolutionary algorithm for solving multi-objective crop planning models. Comput. Electron. Agric. 68(2):191-199.

Storn R, Price K (1997). Differential evolution a simple and efficient heuristic for global optimization over continuous spaces. J. Glob. Optim. 11:341-359.

Wang J-Y, Chang T-P, Chen J-S (2009). An enhanced genetic algorithm for bi-objective pump scheduling in water supply. Expert Syst. Appl. 36(7):10249-10258.

Xue F, Sanderson AC, Graves RJ (2003). Pareto-based multi-objective evolution. Paper presented at the Congress on Evolutionary Computation, Canberra, Australia. 2:862-869.

Zitzler E, Deb K, Thiele L (2000). Comparison of multiobjective evolutionary algorithms: Empirical results. Evol. Comput. 8(2):173-195.

Zitzler E, Thiele L (1999). Multiobjective evolutionary algorithms: A comparative case study and the strength pareto approach. IEEE Trans. Evol. Comput. 3(1999):257-271.

4

Adaptive neuro-fuzzy inference system (ANFIS) islanding detection based on wind turbine simulator

Noradin Ghadimi and Behrooz Sobhani

Department of Electrical Engineering, Ardabil Branch, Islamic Azad University, Ardabil, Iran.

This paper presents a passive islanding detection method based on means of a neuro-fuzzy approach for wind turbines. Several methods based on passive and active detection scheme have been proposed. While passive schemes have a large Non detection zone (NDZ), concern has been raised on active method due to its degrading power quality effect. Reliably detecting this condition is regarded by many as an ongoing challenge as existing methods are not entirely satisfactory. The proposed method is based on voltage measurements and processing of the hybrid intelligent system called the Adaptive neuro-fuzzy inference system (ANFIS) for islanding detection. This new method based on passive methods will help to reduce the NDZ without any perturbation that deteriorates the output power quality opposite active methods. This method detects the islanding conditions with the analysis of these signals. The studies reported in this paper are based on an experimental system (wind turbine simulator). The results showed that, the ANFIS-based algorithm detects islanding situation accurate than other islanding detection algorithms. Moreover, for those regions which are in need of a better visualization, the proposed approach would serve as an efficient aid such that the mains power disconnection can be better distinguished.

Key words: Distributed generation, islanding detection, non detection zone, adaptive neuro fuzzy inference system, fuzzy subtractive clustering.

INTRODUCTION

The increase of distributed resources in the electric utility systems is indicated due to recent and ongoing technological, social, economical and environmental aspects. Distributed generation (DG) units have become more competitive against the conventional centralised system by successfully integrating new generation technologies and power electronics. Hence, it attracts many customers from industrial, commercial, and residential sectors. DGs generally refer to Distributed Energy Resources (DERs), including photovoltaic, fuel cells, micro turbines, small wind turbines, and additional equipment (Jiayi et al., 2008). The total global installed wind capacity at the end of 2010 was 430 TWh annually,

which is 2.5% of the total global demand. Based on the current growth rates, World Wide Energy Association (WWEA) predicts that, in 2015, a global capacity of 600 GW is possible. By the end of the year 2020, at least 1500 GW can be expected to be installed globally (http://www.renewableenergyworld.com/rea/news/article/2011/05/worldwind). However, connecting wind turbines to distribution networks produces some problems, such as islanding.

Islanding when occurred, DG and its local load become electrically isolated from the utility grid (Behrooz et al., 2011). However, the wind turbine produces electrical energy and supplies the local load. Islanding creates many problems in system and causes the existing standards not to permit DGs to be utilized in islanding mode (Smith et al., 2000). Some of these reasons are:

i) Create safety hazard for personals,
ii) Power quality problems for customers load,
iii) Overload condition of wind turbine generator,
iv) Out of phase recloser connection (Vachtsevanous and Kang, 1989; Zeineldin et al., 2006).

Thus, islanding conditions should be detected and interrupted. This application should be done in less than 2 s (Vachtsevanous and Kang, 1989). Originally, the methods of islanding detections are divided to two methods: communication methods and local methods
    Local methods have been classified as active and passive techniques (Smith et al., 2000). Active techniques are based on directly interact with the on-going power system operation, such as impedance measurement (IEEE, 2003), frequency shift, active frequency drift (IEEE, 2003), sandia frequency shift (IEEE, 2003; Karimi et al., 2008) sandia voltage shift (IEEE, 2003; Karimi et al., 2008), phase shift, current injection (Hernandez-Gonzalez and Iravani, 2006), negative sequence current injection method (IEEE, 1999). Passive techniques are based on measurement and information at the local site, such as under/over frequency (IEEE, 2003), under/over voltage (IEEE, 2003), voltage phase jump, voltage unbalanced and total harmonic   distortion (http://www.renewableenergyworld.com/rea/news/article/2011/05/worldwind), rate of change of frequency (Hung et al., 2003), vector surge (Hung et al., 2003; Hopewell et al., 1996), phase displacement monitoring (Hopewell et al., 1996), rate of change of generator power output (IEEE, 2003), comparison of rate of change of frequency (Imece et al., 1989).
    In this paper, a new method based on Discrete Wavelet Transform (DWT) has been proposed for islanding detection of wind turbines. The proposed technique, which is suitable for asynchronous DGs, is explained in Section 3. Section 4 explains the simulation and experimentally test system used to verify the effectiveness of the proposed technique. Section 5 explores the effectiveness of the proposed technique applied on simulation and experimentally test system, Section 6 concludes the paper. The simulation test systems were simulated in MATLAB/ SIMULINK using SimPowerSystemBlockSet. Simulation and experimentally results show that, the proposed islanding detection technique works well in discriminating between switching and islanding conditions.

Adaptive neuro-fuzzy inference system (ANFIS)

Artificial intelligence, including neural network, Fuzzy logic (FL) inference (Gupta and Rao, 1994; Yen et al.,

1995) has been used to solve many nonlinear classification problems. The main advantages of a Fuzzy logic system (FLS) are the capability to express nonlinear input/output relationships by a set of qualitative if-then rules. The main advantage of a neural network (NN), on the other hand, is the inherent learning capability, which enables the networks to adaptively improve its performance. The key properties of neuro-fuzzy network are the accurate learning and adaptive capabilities of the neural networks, together with the generalization and fast learning capabilities of FLS. The ANFIS is a very powerful approach for modeling nonlinear and complex systems with less input and output training data with quicker learning and high precision. ANFIS is an adaptive network which permits the usage of neural network topology together with FL. It not only includes the characteristics of both methods, but also eliminates some disadvantages of their lonely-used case. Basically a Fuzzy inference system (FIS) is composed of five functional blocks (Figure 1).
    Operation of ANFIS looks like feed-forward back propagation network. Consequent parameters are calculated forward while premise parameters are calculated backward. There are two learning methods in neural section of the system: Hybrid learning method and back-propagation learning method. In fuzzy section, only zero or first order Sugeno inference system or Tsukamoto inference system can be used. The ANFIS approach learns the rules and membership functions from data. The objective of ANFIS is to adjust the parameters of a fuzzy system by applying a learning procedure using input-output training data.
    The basic structure of the type of FIS is a model that, maps input characteristics to input membership functions, input membership function to rules, rules to a set of output characteristics, output characteristics to output membership functions, and the output membership function to a single-valued output or a decision associated with the output.
    This section introduces the basics of ANFIS network architecture and its hybrid learning rule. The Sugeno fuzzy model was proposed by Takagi, Sugeno, and Kang in an effort to formalize a systematic approach to generating fuzzy rules from an input-output dataset. A typical fuzzy in a Sugeno fuzzy model has the format:

If x is A and y is B then z = f (x, y)

Where A and B are fuzzy sets in the antecedent; $z = f(x,y)$ is a crisp function in the consequent. Usually f(x, y) is a polynomial in the input variable x and y, but it can be any other functions that can appropriately describe the output of the system within the fuzzy region specified by the antecedent of the rule. When f(x, y) is a first-order polynomial, this first order sugeno fuzzy model is proposed in sugeno (1998). When f is a constant, then, the zero order Sugeno fuzzy model, which is functionally

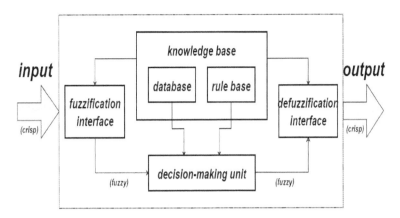

Figure 1. Fuzzy inference system.

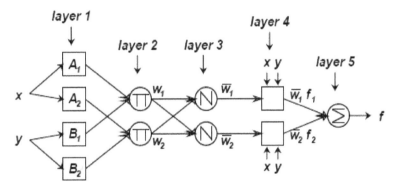

Figure 2. ANFIS architecture.

equivalent to a radial basis function network under certain minor constraints. The architecture of ANFIS with two inputs, one output and two rules is given in Figure 2. In this connected structure, the input and output nodes represent the training values and the predicted values, respectively, and in the hidden layers, there are nodes functioning as membership functions (MFs) and rules. This architecture has the benefit that, it eliminates the disadvantage of a normal feed forward multilayer network, where it is difficult for an observer to understand or modify the network. Here x, y are inputs, F is output, the circles represent fixed node functions and squares represent adaptive node functions.

Consider a first order Sugeno FIS which contains two rules:

Rule 1: If X is Al and Y is B1, then f1 = P1x + q1y+r1
Rule 2: If X is A2 and Y is B 2 then f2 = P2x + q2y+r2

Where, P1, P2, q1, q2, r1, andr2 are linear parameters and A1, A2, B1, and B2 are nonlinear parameter. ANFIS is an implementation of a FL inference system with the architecture of a five-layer feed-forward network. The system architecture consists of five layers, namely, fuzzy layer, product layer, normalized layer, de-fuzzy layer and total output layer. With this way, ANFIS uses the advantages of learning capability of neural networks and inference mechanism similar to human brain provided by FL. The operation of each layer is as follows: Here the output node i in layer l is denoted as O_i^l.

Layer 1 is the fuzzification layer. Every node i in this layer is an adaptive node with node function:

$$O_i^1 = \mu_{A_i}(x), \quad O_{i+2}^1 = \mu_{B_i}(y) \quad i = 1,2$$

(1)

Where, x is the input to i_{th} node, O_i^l is the membership grade of x in the fuzzy set Ai. Generalized bell membership function is popular method for specifying fuzzy sets because of their smoothness and concise notation, and defined as:

$$\mu_{A_i}(x) = \frac{1}{1+\left|\dfrac{x-c_i}{a_i}\right|^{2b_i}}$$

(2)

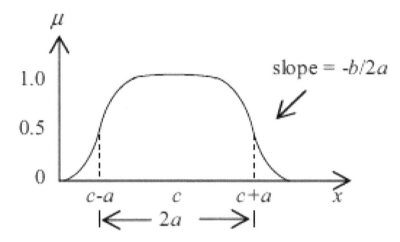

Figure 3. Generalized bell function.

Here $\{a_i, b_i, c_i\}$ is the parameter set of the membership function. The center and width of the membership function is varied by adjusting c_i and a_i. The parameter b_i is used to control the slopes at the crossover points. Figure 3 shows the physical meaning of each parameter in a generalized bell function. The parameters in this layer are called premise parameters. This layer forms the antecedents of the fuzzy rules (*IF* part).

Layer 2 is the rules layer. Every node in this layer is a fixed node and contains one fuzzy rule. The output is the product of all incoming signals and represents the firing strength of each rule:

$$O_i^2 = w_i = \mu_{A_i}(x)\mu_{B_i}(y), \quad i = 1,2 \tag{3}$$

Layer 3 is the normalization layer. Every node in this layer is a fixed node and i_{th} node calculates the ratio of i_{th} rule's firing strength to the sum of all rules' firing strengths. Outputs of this layer are called normalized firing strengths computed as:

$$O_{3,i} = \overline{w_i} = \frac{w_i}{w_1 + w_2} \quad i = 1,2 \tag{4}$$

Layer 4 is the consequent layer. Every node in this layer is an adaptive node and computes the values of rule consequent (then part) as:

$$O_i^4 = \overline{w_i}f_i = \overline{w_i}(p_i x + q_i y + r_i) \tag{5}$$

Here w_i is the output of Layer 3 and the parameters $\{p_i, q_i, r_i\}$ are known as consequent parameters. Layer 5 is the summation layer and it consists of single fixed node which calculates the overall output as the summation of all incoming signals as:

$$O_i^5 = \sum_i \overline{w_i}f_i = \frac{\sum_i w_i f_i}{\sum_i w_i} \tag{6}$$

ROPOSED DETECTION ALGORITHM

In this study, we propose to use a hybrid intelligent system called ANFIS for islanding detection. We combine the ability of a NN to learn with FL to reason in order to form a hybrid intelligent system called ANFIS.

ANFIS training algorithm can be efficiently used to build fuzzy rules from correct input-output numerical data pairs. The main motivations for such an investigation are:

i) The ANFIS is a well known and successful solution
ii) It can be used directly on the data recorded in the learning stage, and so it can be further considered for a real-time implementation
iii) It stands as a classical algorithm, with trustful implementation as the one included in MATLAB.

More specifically, in the forward pass of the hybrid learning algorithm, node outputs go forward until layer 4 and the consequent parameters are identified by the least-squares method. In the backward pass, the error signals propagate backwards and the premise parameters are updated by gradient descent. We don't necessarily have a predetermined model structure based on characteristics of variables in our system. There will be some modeling situations in which we can't just look at the data and discern what the membership functions should look like. Rather than choosing the parameters associated with a given membership function arbitrarily, these parameters could be chosen so as to tailor the membership functions to the input-output data in order to account for these types of variations in the data values.

These techniques provide a method for the fuzzy modeling procedure to learn information about a data set, in order to compute the membership function parameters that best allow the associated FIS to track the given input/output data. Using a given input/output

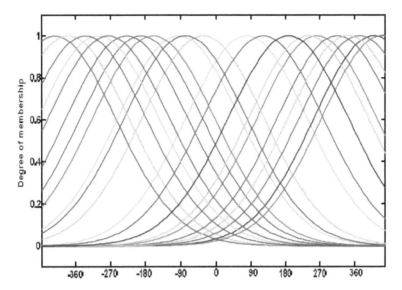

Figure 4. Membership function.

data set, the ANFIS constructs a FIS whose membership function parameters are tuned (adjusted) using either a back propagation algorithm. This allows our fuzzy systems to learn from the data they are modeling.

The proposed approach is based on the passive method of islanding detection considering the data clustering approach. In addition, this method includes building a simplified and robust fuzzy classifier initialized by the subtractive clustering and makes a FIS for islanding detection. As a result of the increasing complexity and dimensionality of classification problems, it becomes necessary to deal with structural issues of the identification of classifier systems. Important aspects are the selection of the relevant features and determination of effective initial partition of the input domain. The purpose of clustering is to identify natural groupings of data to produce a concise representation of a system's behavior. Subtractive clustering is a fast, one-pass algorithm for estimating the number of clusters and the cluster centers in a set of data.

In this paper, an ANFIS models which takes voltage signal as inputs and islanding condition as output. Firstly, voltage data taken from the DG for provide a dataset. The next step, construct a FIS that could best predict the islanding condition or normal condition. ANFIS training can use alternative algorithms to reduce the error of the training. A combination of the gradient descent algorithm and a least squares algorithm is used for an effective search for the optimal parameters. The main benefit of such a hybrid approach is that, it converges much faster, since it reduces the search space dimensions of the back propagation method used in neural networks. ANFIS was trained with the first half epochs and the next half epochs were used for validation. The Root mean squared error (RMSE) from each of the validating epochs was calculated. Averages of RMSE per patient were calculated for all patients to give the average RMSE. Thus before training a FIS, the data set has been divided into training set and test sets. The training set is used to train a fuzzy mode, while the test set is used to determine when training should be terminated to prevent over fitting. After training, for verify the model FIS we calculate, the RMSE of the system generated by the training data that, it is equal to 0.1068. To validate the generalize ability of the model; we apply test data to the FIS that, it is equal 0.018. Figure 4 shows the membership function obtained only from dataset for all conditional of islanding and normal operation without any setting of threshold for islanding

detection parameter. In this paper, we can overcome the problem of setting the detection thresholds for islanding detection.

ANFIS models takes voltage as inputs and islanding condition as output. If the islanding is detected, the output ANFIS is higher than 0.6. Conversely, if the islanding is not detected, the output ANFIS is around 0 or less than 0.5. The result obtained indicates that, ANFIS is effective method for islanding detection.

CASE STUDY

Figure 5 shows a schematic diagram of a wind turbine unit. The DG unit is a wind turbine induction generator, and a capacitor bank is used to improve the power factor. The local load is a three-phase parallel RL before the circuit breaker (CB), in which "r" denotes the series resistance inductance and V_f indicates the voltage drop across the parallel load. The parallel RL is conventionally adopted as the local load for the evaluation of islanding detection methods when the load inductance is tuned to the system frequency. This system, as shown in Figure 5, is connected to a Point of Common Coupling (PCC) with a step-up transformer. To obtain the experimental results, a wind turbine simulator, as shown in Figure 6, was implemented. Figures 7 and 8 showed the implemented simulator system. The implemented system parameters are given in Table 1. The parallel load inductance is considered infinite. Thus, the parallel load is only a resistance, and hence the unit of "L" is "inf". Figure 9 shows the motor saturation curve. In the grid-connected condition, the switches SW1 and SW2 are closed. The islanding condition occurs when SW2 is open.

The voltage and frequency of DG should have admissible values in both grid-connected and islanded modes. In the grid-connected mode, the voltage magnitude and frequency of the local load at the PCC are regulated by the grid.

IMPLEMENTATION RESULTS

In this study, the simulation is conducted in four scenarios to illustrate the effectiveness of the proposed method.

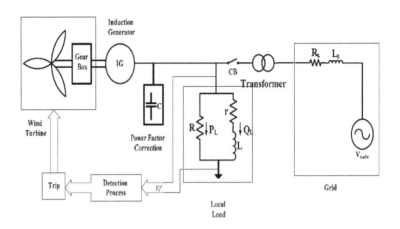

Figure 5. Single line diagram of study system.

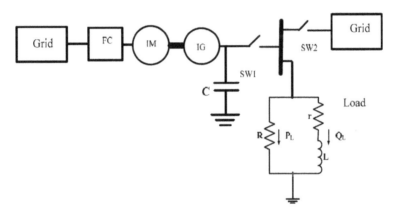

Figure 6. Single line diagram of implementation system in order to islanding condition detection.

Figure 7. Implementation system in order to islanding condition detection.

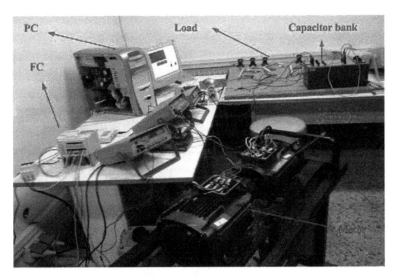

Figure 8. Implementation system in order to islanding condition detection.

Table 1. Parameters of the implemented system.

Parameter		Value
Induction motors	Sn	2 KVA
	Vn	400 V
	F	50 HZ
	PF	0.78 Lag
	Rs, Rr	2.3541 Ω
	Lr, Ls	0.01678 H
	Lm	0.275 H
Local load	R	180 Ω
	L	Inf
Capacitor	C	36.75 μF

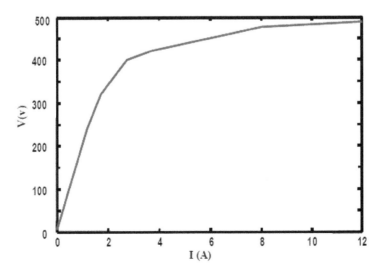

Figure 9. Motor and generator saturation curves.

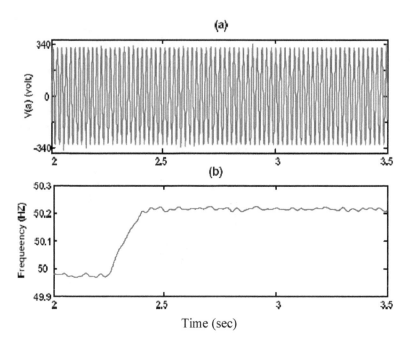

Figure 10. Match power condition: (a) phase voltage, (b) frequency.

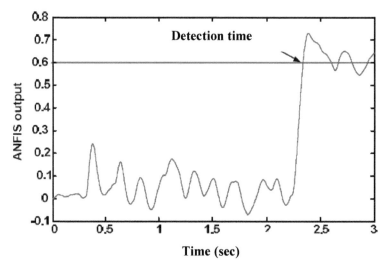

Figure 11. ANFIS output for match power conditional.

Match power condition

In this test, the active and reactive power of local load is 0.8 KW and 0Kvar, respectively. The value of capacitor is 36.0 μF, the distributed generator is assumed to separate from the grid, where the event is assumed to take place at 2.2 s. In Figure 10a and b, the waveforms of phase voltage and frequency of DGs are individually depicted. Immediately following this loss of utility, proposed method relay fails to detect islanding condition. Figure 11 shows the output of proposed method algorithm result. ANFIS

output is rich to above "0.5" value which leads to islanding detection. So the ANFIS based protection algorithm produced the trip signal and sends it to DG.

Mismatch power condition

At first, the amount of capacitor bank is lesser than nominal condition. The active power set to 0.66 KW and reactive power set to 0.1 Kvar, respectively. The distributed generator is assumed to separate from the

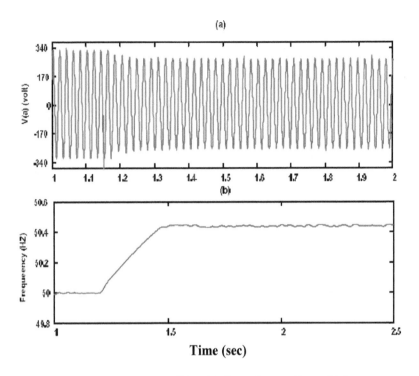

Figure 12. Mismatch power condition: (a) three phase voltage, (b) frequency.

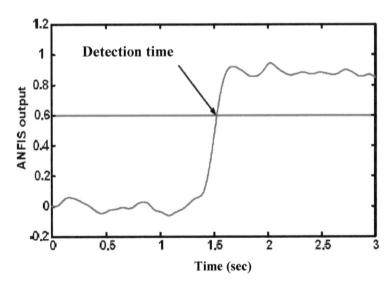

Figure 13. ANFIS output for Mismatch power condition.

grid, where the event is assumed to take place at 1.15 s. In Figure 12a and b, the waveforms of phase voltage and frequency of DGs are individually depicted. Immediately following this loss of utility, frequency is increase and voltage is drop. Figure 13 shows the ANFIS output that is rich to higher than "0.5" value which leads to islanding detection. So the ANFIS based protection algorithm produced the trip signal and sends to DG.

At the next test, the amount of capacitor bank is higher than nominal condition and set to 40 µF. The active power set to 0.66 KW and reactive power set to 0.1 Kvar, respectively. After islanding event at 2.6 s, Figures 14a and b and c shows the waveforms of instantaneous phase voltage, RMS phase voltage and frequency of DGs, respectively. As can be seen, frequency is drop and voltage is increase. Figure 15 shows the ANFIS output that is rich to higher than "0.5" value which leads to islanding detection. So the ANFIS based protection

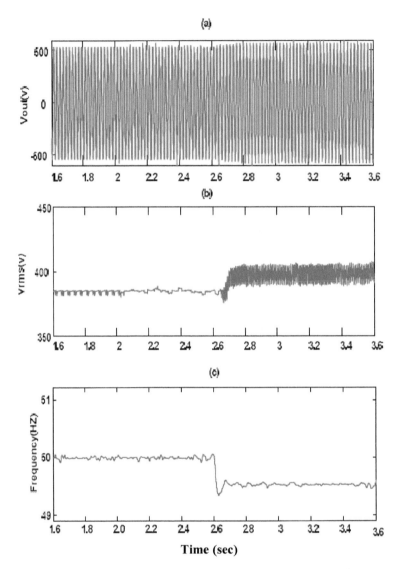

Figure 14. Mismatch power condition: (a) phase voltage, (b) RMS voltage value, (c) frequency.

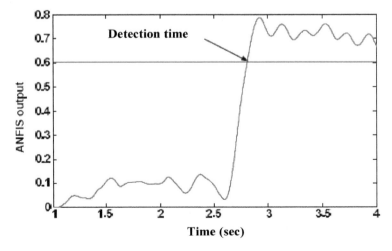

Figure 15. ANFIS output for mismatch power condition (2).

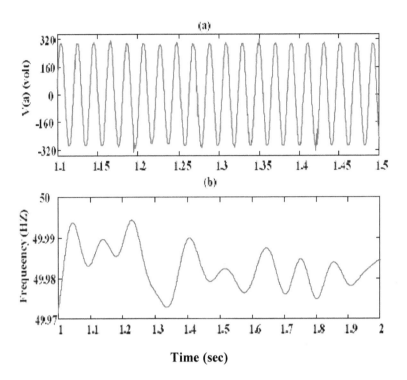

Figure 16. Motor starting condition: (a) three phase voltage, (b) frequency.

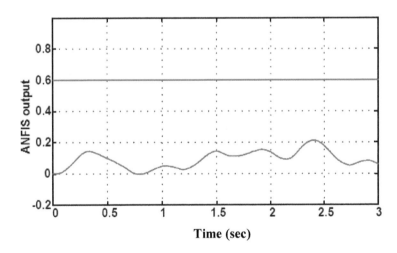

Figure 17. ANFIS output for motor starting.

algorithm produced the trip signal and sends to DG.

Motor starting condition

The starting of induction motors may cause a malfunction of the islanding detection algorithm. To study the reliability of the proposed algorithm, at t = 1.15 min an induction motor with P = 1KW and Q = 1.1 Kvar is starting and connected to the PCC. Figure 16a and b shows the waveforms of phase voltage and frequency of

DGs, respectively. Figure 17 shows the ANFIS results at this condition. The value of neural network output is not reach to threshold value. Therefore, the proposed method does not send a trip signal to DG and works in a reliable mode.

Capacitor bank switching condition

Large capacitor bank switching in distribution power systems initiates disturbances. These disturbances are

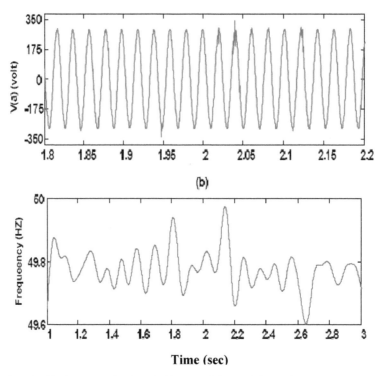

(b)

Figure 18. Capacitor bank switching condition: (a) three phase voltage, (b) frequency.

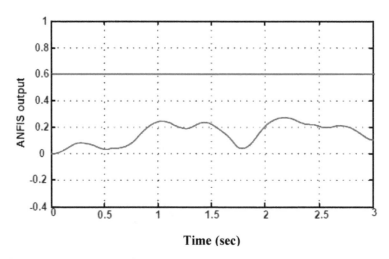

Time (sec)

Figure 19. ANFIS output for motor starting.

propagated in the distribution system and have some effects on the proposed method. To test the proposed algorithm, at t = 2 s, a large 30 μF capacitor bank was switched at the PCC in the non-islanding case. In Figure 18a and b, the waveforms of phase voltage and frequency of DGs are individually depicted. Figure 19 shows the neural network response. The value of neural network output is not reach to threshold value too. Therefore, the system continue to working without any

mistaken trip.

Conclusion

A new technique for islanding detection of DG is proposed based on ANFIS. Following the increased number and enlarged size of distributed generating units installed in a modern power system, the protection against islanding has become extremely challenging nowadays. Islanding detection is also important as islanding operation of distributed system is seen a viable option in the future to improve the reliability and quality of the supply. The islanding situation needed to be prevented with DG due to safety reasons and to maintain quality of power supplied to the customers. By case studies with numerical simulations, the proposed approach was verified with feasibility, flexibility and robustness.

REFERENCES

Behrooz S, Hossein KK, Adel A (2011). A Mixed Active-Passive Algorithm for Islanding Detection of Wind Turbine DG Units. Int. Rev. Elect. Eng. 6(2):992-999.

Gupta MM, Rao DH (1994). Neuro-Control Systems: Theory and Applications. Piscataway, NJ: IEEE press.

Hernandez-Gonzalez G, Iravani R (2006). Current injection for active islanding detection of electronically-interfaced distributed resources. IEEE Trans. Power Deliv. 21(3):1698-705.

Hopewell PD, Jenkins N, Cross AD (1996). Loss-of-mains detection for small generators. IEE Proc – Elect Power Appl. 143(3):225-30.

http://www.renewableenergyworld.com/rea/news/article/2011/05/worldw ind- outlook-down-but-not-out.

Hung GK, Chang CC, Chen CL (2003). Automatic phase-shift method for islanding detection of grid-connected photovoltaic inverters. IEEE Trans. Energy Convers. 18(1):169-173.

IEEE (2003). Standard for Interconnecting Distributed Resources into Electric Power Systems, IEEE Standard 1547TM, June 2003.

Imece AF, Jones RA, Sims TR, Gross CA (1989). An approach for modeling self commutated static power converters for photovoltaic islanding studies. IEEE Trans. Energy Convers. 4(3):397-401.

Jiayi H, Chuanwen J, Rong X (2008). A review on distributed energy resources and micro-grid. Renew. Sust. Energ Rev. 12:2472e83.

Karimi H, Yazdani A, Iravani R (2008). Negative-sequence current injection for fast islanding detection of a distributed resource unit. IEEE Trans. Power Elect. 23(1):298-307.

Smith GA, Onions PA, Infield DG (2000). Predicting islanding operation of grid connected PV inverters. IEEE Proc – Elect. Power Apply. 147(1):1-6.

Vachtsevanous G, Kang H (1989). Simulation studies of islanded behavior of grid connected photovoltaic systems. IEEE Trans. Energy Convers. 4(2):177-83.

Yen J, Langari R, Zadeh LA (1995). Industrial Applications of fuzzyLogic and Intelligent Systems. IEEE Press, New York, NY. P. 190.

Zeineldin HH, El-Saadany EF, Salama MMA (2006). Impact of DG interface control on islanding detection and non-detection zones. IEEE Trans. Power Deliv. 21(3):1515-23.

5

New monitoring method based principal component analysis and fuzzy clustering

Khaled Ouni[1] , Hedi Dhouibi[1], Lotfi Nabli[2] and Hassani Messaoud[2]

[1]The High Institute of Applied Sciences and Technology of Kairouan, Kairouan, Avenue Beit ElHekma, 3100 Kairouan, Tunisia.
[2]The National Engineering School of Monastir, Avenue Ibn ElJazzar, 5019 Monastir, Tunisia.

This work concerns the principal component analysis applied to the supervision of quality parameters of the flour production line. Our contribution lies in the combined use of the principal component analysis technique and the clustering algorithms in the field of production system diagnosis. This approach allows detecting and locating the system defects, based on the drifts of the product quality parameters. A comparative study between the classification performance by clustering algorithms and the principal component analysis has been proposed. Locating parameters in defect is based on the technique of fault direction in partial least square.

Key words: Fuzzy clustering, fault detection, fault location, principal component analysis (PCA).

INTRODUCTION

During the last years, health monitoring of complex manufacturing, which is markedly useful, durable and dependable for the modern industrial drive systems has become very significant in decreasing the unprogrammed downtimes of the appropriate production lines. The accurate and fast isolation of defects can assess the performance process, and the current defect flour processing industry improves the efficiency process and product quality. Early defect detection may help avoid many breakdown and incidents in a flour production line. To use historical data for process monitoring, we have to isolate abnormal process data from a mixture of normal data and abnormal historical data. Accordingly, detecting defects is essential to obtain a high flour quality. The validity of the delivered information is so important to compute an efficient control.

A flour production line is a multi variable complex system. For this kind of system, it is generally not appropriate to use the analytical redundancy methods through an input-output model. In fact, it is often difficult to design a mathematical model which allows obtaining an efficient diagnosis system. To reach this target, we may consider the implicit modeling approaches (Yingwei and Yang, 2012), based on the data driving techniques such as the Principal component analysis (PCA). These methods are well adapted to emphasize the relationships between the plant variables, without the explicit expression of the system model (Kresta et al., 1991).

In the literature associated with the field of diagnosing defects in the industrial systems, we find many statistical techniques designed to make use of the historical data and relations between the variables. Among these techniques, we can mention the use of the correlation matrix in the data sample, using the PCA to capture the most important directions in the correlation amongst the variables.

These statistical techniques are pre-calculated, based on a reference data sample; and as soon as the new data become available, the statistical approach can be quickly calculated on the parameters. These statistical methods have also been spread out for the monitoring of flexible processes of a complex manufacturing production. During the treatment of the process containing a great number of variables, the PCA can be used to reduce them, by grouping them into new sub-spaces of a reduced dimension. In determining the structure and classifying data, the fuzzy clustering techniques offer an important insight, while producing the affiliation functions for each group or cluster. A considerable number of fuzzy clustering algorithms have been developed with widely known methods like the Fuzzy C-Means (FCM), the Gustafson Kessel (GK) and Gath-Geva (GG) algorithms (Pal et al., 2005; Oliveira and Pedrycz, 2007).

This literature evaluation indicates an increasing tendency concerning the contribution of the statistical method like the PCA with the artificial intelligence method, as well as neural networks and the fuzzy logic. Bouhouche et al. (2007) proposed a combined use of the PCA and SOM algorithms. In this combined method, new detection indexes, based on metric distances, were used; all these indexes were used in the diagnosis phase. The SOM algorithm showed a bad classification compared to the PCA and the PCA-SOM. Ahvenlampi et al. (2005) proposed in these works, an approach of diagnosis of a digester system. In this study, measurements and some statistical variables are combined with fuzzy logic to produce key factors for the diagnosis. The combination between the PCA and the fuzzy logic has shown interesting results for the detection of defects and the diagnosis.

Also, many works have combined the PCA with the clustering techniques for the detection of defects and the classification of regions. Sebzalli and Wang (2001) presented in this work, an industrial study that uses the PCA and clustering algorithms to identify the operational spaces. This is a case study applying the PCA and the Fuzzy C-Means technique to the data of a refinery liquid. Ahvenlampi and Kortela (2005) presented an application on a quality parameter called kappa. It is a quality measurement in the kitchen processes. The clustering technique and the defect diagnosis system are used to control the quality variables. Peter et al. (2005) proposed in their work, a combined approach between the PCA and the k-means clustering algorithm. The defects are detected by the PCA and the classifier, in the form of regions with and without defects, using the k-means clustering. This approach is efficient in detecting and isolating defects in a process of industrial films. Ouni et al. (2011) presented a combined approach between the non linear PCA and the partial least square (PLS) for the monitoring in the tobacco manufacturing industry. The SPE statistic and the PLS-2 are applied to the defect detection and the region classification, respectively.

This work puts forward a combined approach of detecting and locating parameters of quality, in defect based on real data in a flour production line.

In this paper, we present a new analysis of flour quality variables using the statistical methods and fuzzy clustering techniques. The PCA is used to find the correlations between the quality parameters. The PCA and its statistical indexes SPE and T^2 guarantee the detection of defects in all the data space. Contribution calculations can facilitate the isolation of defects, but these contributions do not always provide variable results. Improving the isolation of parameters in defect can be realized by the method combining the PCA and the Fisher Discriminant Analysis (Peter et al., 2005). Likewise, our combined approach based on the PCA and fuzzy clustering technique aims at separating between the normal and abnormal data in the form of regions in a 2D space. The directions of these regions are used as a new approach of contribution calculations in PLS.

In this paper, we suggest to extend this approach by using a PCA proposed in Ouni et al. (2011) and Chaouch et al. (2011). Also, we present an improvement of the operating region definition by studying the dynamic of the squared predictor error and the statistic T^2. These regions are visualized in a 2D space, using the clustering algorithms. Therefore, we suggest the technique of PLS defect direction between the regions two to two. The weights of its directions are used in isolating the defected quality parameters.

This paper is organized as follows: The lines coming afterwards are firstly devoted to the situation of our contribution. After a brief description of the PCA technique, our contribution is highlighted at the level of the different modules of functional decomposition of the proposed diagnosis system. The last part of this work is devoted for an industrial application on a flour production line, and to a comparative study between the classification performance by FCM, GK, GG clustering and the PCA.

Principal component analysis (PCA)

The PCA is a multidimensional statistical method, which allows us to synthesize a set of data, while identifying the existing redundancy in them (Jollife, 1986). If at the origin of its development, it has been known to be attractive, while showing how to graphically represent the data groups, we should highlight the correlations between observations and variables. It is actually with the recent developments that a method of quantitative appreciation has known an informative content of the observations, which allows us to comprehend many problems such as searching a model structure, identifying model parameters, detecting aberrant values, detecting changes of the functioning flow rates, and diagnosing the systems functioning (Harket et al., 2006).

The PCA principle

We consider a vector of centered measurements

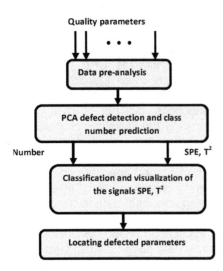

Figure 1. Detecting and locating defected quality parameters.

(nil average), $x = [x_1, x_2, ..., x_m]^T \in \Re^m$, and $\Sigma \in \Re^{m \times m}$ is a symmetrical covariance matrix which represents the estimated variance of the data matrix $X \in \Re^{N \times m}$, where X, is a matrix of N observations at m variables. The transformation matrix $P \in \Re^{m \times m}$ is called the loading matrix of the covariance or correlation matrix of the original data samples. T is called the score matrix or the principal component matrix, which is the projection of original data in the sub-space of principal components.

$$T_{N \times m} = X_{N \times m} P_{m \times m} \tag{1}$$

$P = [p_1, p_2, ..., p_m]$ is a set of vectors, orthonormal in $\Re^{m \times m}$. A PCA model is often established from the collected data in the form of information that can be measured on sensors or indicators of quality.
In fact, the data matrix X is decomposed into the two following parts:

$$X = \hat{X} + E \tag{2}$$

Where $\hat{X}$, the estimated part of X and E presents the variations caused by modeling errors. The two components are orthogonal, one to the other, because they are in the complementary sub-spaces of $\Re^{N \times m}$.

$$\hat{X} E^T = 0 \tag{3}$$

Determining the structure of PCA model

In the structure of the PCA model, we first choose an adequate number of principal components to represent the process optimally (Valle et al., 1999). Dunia and Qin

(1998) proposed to choose the number of principal components based on best reconstruction of the process variables. An important characteristic of this approach shows that the index has a minimum, corresponding to the best reconstruction. The variance of reconstruction error for the ith sensor is:

$$v_i = \frac{\tilde{\xi}_i^T \Sigma \tilde{\xi}_i^T}{\left(\tilde{\xi}_i^T \tilde{\xi}_i^T \right)^2}, \ i = 1, ... m \tag{4}$$

Where $\tilde{\xi}_i = \left(I - \hat{C} \right) \xi_i$ and $\tilde{\xi}_i^T \tilde{\xi}_i = (1 - c_{ii})$. The VRE is defined to represent all the sensors:

$$VRE = \sum_{i=1}^{m} \frac{v_i}{\text{var}(x_i)} \tag{5}$$

Where $\text{var}(x_i) = \xi_i^T \Sigma \xi_i$ signifies the variance of the ith element of the observation vector. $VRE(\ell)$ can be calculated recursively, using only the values and loadings of the covariance matrix Σ, until $\ell \leq m$; until the method of the variance of the reconstruction error chooses the number of principal components that gives a minimum VRE.
Once the number of components ℓ is determined, the PCA model is then identified, and the data matrix $X \in \Re^{N \times m}$ can be approximated from the first principal components.

$$\hat{X} = \sum_{i=1}^{\ell} T_i p_i^T = \sum_{i=1}^{\ell} X p_i p_i^T \tag{6}$$

Knowing that $\sum_{i=1}^{\ell} p_i p_i^T = \hat{P} \hat{P}^T$ and that we will note it as $\hat{C}$, the estimation of X is formulated as follows:

$$\hat{X} = X \hat{C} \tag{7}$$

Proposed monitoring approach

In Figure 1, we show the steps of our monitoring approach on the measurements of quality parameters in a factory of flour manufacturing. These measurements contain at the same time, the normal measurements and illogical others, which show the non quality of the product. These abnormal or defected data can always lead to controlling the production quality, which not only causes a great energy loss in the form of wastes, but also affects the quality of flour. To manufacture flour, it can influence the ordinary quality of flour and dough.

Our proposed monitoring approach is composed of four steps: The pre-analysis, the detection of defects and the prediction of the number of classes, the classification and visualization of classes and the location of defected parameters.

The pre-analysis

During this phase, the measurements of quality parameters of flour are treated in a way to be significant and valid. This pre-analysis phase consists in centering and reducing the data.

The detection of defects and the prediction of the number of classes

After formulating the PCA model, the defect detection is realized by the statistics SPE (Square Prediction Error), T^2 Hotelling and the combined statistic φ. According to the evolution of detection statistics, their signals are divided up into classes with and without defects.

Classification and visualization of classes

According to the evolution of its detection statistics, we distinguish regions without defects and others with defects that go beyond classification of these regions and the visualization of these classes in a 2D space. The classification and visualization phase is introduced, using the clustering algorithms. A comparative study of classification is proposed using the FCM, GK and GG algorithms and the PCA. In our application, the classification is applied on the detection statistics SPE and T^2.

The location of defected parameters

The location of defected quality parameters is realized by the principle of defect direction in PLS between classes.

In our application we have used the steps of the algorithm for the offline monitoring while respecting the following instructions:

1. Get the data that represent the process at its state of normal functioning.
2. Center and reduce the data.
3. Get the PCA model, by determining the number of principal components.
4. Determine the control limits for the statistics SPE, T^2 and φ.
5. Classify the normal and abnormal regions using the fuzzy clustering tools.
6. Use the defect directions two by two in PLS to isolate variables in defect.

7. Use the contributions of weight and their directions to isolate the parameters in defects.

Pre-analysis

Beforehand, an essential pre-treatment consists in centering and reducing the variables to obtain an independent result of the units used for each variable.

Detection of defects

The detection of defects using the PCA models is normally accomplished based on the statistics SPE, T^2 and φ. The SPE statistic, known as the Q statistic measures the projection of an x vector in the residual space.

$$SPE(k) = e^T(k)e(k) = \sum_{i=1}^{N}(x_i(k) - \hat{x}_i(k))^2 \qquad (8)$$

Where $e = (I - P_\ell P_\ell^T)x$ is the residue of the x vector which represents the distance squared at each observation, perpendicular to the sub-space of principal components, and measures the residues that cannot be represented by the PCA model. The process is considered wrong at the instant k if;

$$SPE(k) < \delta_\alpha^2 \qquad (9)$$

Where δ_α is the trust threshold of the SPE. The approximation of the detection limit for the SPE statistic with an α covariance level is then represented by:

$$\delta_\alpha = \theta_1 \left[\frac{1 - \theta_2 h_0(1 - h_0)}{\theta_1^2} + z_\alpha \frac{(2\theta_2 h_0^2)^{\frac{1}{2}}}{\theta_1} \right]^{\frac{1}{h_0}} \qquad (10)$$

Where $\theta_1 = \sum_{i=1}^{m}\lambda_i, \theta_2 = \sum_{i=1}^{m}\lambda_i^2, \theta_3 = \sum_{i=1}^{m}\lambda_i^3, h_0 = 1 - \frac{2\theta_1\theta_3}{3\theta_2^2}$

The statistic T^2, which measures the variation of the score vector in the space of principal components, is expressed by:

$$T^2 = t^T A^{-1} t = x^T P A^{-1} P^T x = x^T D x \qquad (11)$$

Where A, is a diagonal matrix containing the principal components used in the PCA model, and $D = P A^{-1} P^T$ is a semi positive matrix. The detection limit is obtained, using the distribution of Fisher (Vermasvuori, 2008) and will depend on the freedom degrees available for the estimation of Σ.

Case 1: Known covariance matrix

This statistics is used as a big-sized sample whose distribution follows the rule of chi-square centered with ℓ degrees of freedom. A limit threshold in a α trust interval is expressed by $\chi^2_{\alpha,n}$.

Case 2: Unknown covariance matrix

When the covariance matrix Σ is unknown, it should be estimated using the T^2 statistics given by:

$$T^2 = (x-\mu)S^{-1}(x-\mu)^T \tag{12}$$

Where S is the estimation of the covariance matrix Σ. The exact detection limits are given at the α trust level:

$$HCL = \frac{m(N^2-1)}{N(N-P)}F_{1-\alpha}(m, N-m)$$
$$LCL = \frac{m(N^2-1)}{N(N-P)}F_{\alpha}(m, N-m) \tag{13}$$

Where HCL, high detection limit at the trust level $(1-\alpha)$, and LCL, low detection limit at the trust level α.

The statistics SPE and T^2 are complementary one to the other and can measure the variation in the whole measurement space. The combined statistic proposed by Yue and Qin (2001) introduces the two metrics SPE and T^2 together. This combined index is defined as an addition of the statistic SPE and T^2, balanced against their threshold limit.

$$\varphi = \frac{SPE(x)}{\delta^2} + \frac{T^2}{\tau^2} = x^T \Phi x \tag{14}$$

Where $\Phi = \frac{I - PP^T}{\delta^2} + \frac{PA^{-1}P^T}{\chi^2_\alpha(\ell)}$. The detection threshold limit for the combined index is given in the following equation:

$$\varphi \geq g\chi^2_\alpha(\ell) = \zeta^2 \tag{15}$$

Classification and visualization with clustering algorithms

In today's flour production industry, the massive quantity of data is easily available; whereas, visualizing highly-dimension data is difficult. However, the radial plots (Nottingham et al., 2001) and parallel coordinates (Albazzaz et al., 2005) methods are usually applicable to small sets of data; because of this limitation, these methods cannot be applied to the visualization of flour quality parameters due to the big number of samples and variables. Generally, if the highly-dimension data cannot be represented in a space of 2 or 3 dimensions, the use of clustering algorithms provides a general frame for visualizing and exploring big sets of multi-varied data.

The clustering is a technique of a non supervised study; its objective is to group the points of similar data. A clustering algorithm assigns a great number of data points to a smaller number of groups such as the data points in the same group sharing the same properties, whereas in the different groups, they are dissimilar. The clustering technique has many applications, including the image segmentation, the knowledge extraction, the form recognition and the classification (Liang et al., 2005; Hung et al., 2006; Luukka, 2009).

Fuzzy C-means classification (FCM)

The FCM calculates the distance measured between two vectors, where each component is a trajectory instead of a real number. Thus, this FCM algorithm is rather flexible than being able to eliminate the classes and their combination. The FCM is a classification technique, which introduces the fuzzy set notion in the presentation of classes. In the traditional FCM algorithm, an object is assigned only to one group (Rezaee et al., 1998; Dulyakran and Ransanseri, 2001). This is valid before that the groups are split or separated. But if the groups are nearing one another or are overlapping, then, an object can belong to more than one group. In this case, the FCM technique is the best to be used. Particularly, the version proposed by Bezdek is the best applied one. It is based on minimizing the following objective function (Bezdek, 1981; Höpper et al., 1999; Pedrycs, 1997).

$$J_m = \sum_{i=1}^{N}\sum_{j=1}^{C}(u_{ij})^m d^2 \|x_i - c_j\|^2, 1 \leq m \leq \infty \tag{16}$$

Where m, is a real number higher than 1; μ_{ij} is the membership degree of x_i in the j cluster; x_i is the ith data of measurements; c_j is the cluster center, and $\|*\|$ is the norm between a measured datum and the center.

The fuzzy division is affected by an iterative optimization of the J_m function, by updating the μ_{ij} membership and the cluster center c_j:

$$u_{ij} = \cfrac{1}{\displaystyle\sum_{k=1}^{C} \left(\cfrac{\|x_i - c_j\|}{\|x_i - c_k\|} \right)^{\frac{1}{m-1}}} \tag{17}$$

Where $c_j = \cfrac{\displaystyle\sum_{i=1}^{N} u_{ij}^m x_i}{\displaystyle\sum_{i=1}^{N} u_{ij}^m}$. The k iterations stop when

$$\max_{ij} \left| u_{ij}^{k+1} - u_{ij}^k \right| < \varepsilon$$

Where ε is a benchmark between 0 and 1.

Fuzzy C-means model steps

1. Randomly select the j number of the center (c_j).
2. Determine the fuzzy membership μ_{ij} starting from equation 17.
3. Compute the fuzzy center c_j.
4. Repeat steps 2 and 3 until the minimum of J_m is achieved.

The gustafson-kessel algorithm

The Gustafson-Kessel algorithm is an extension of the FCM. This technique uses an adaptive distance norm which detects the clusters of different geometric forms in a data set (Graves and Pedrycz, 2007; Krishnapuram and Kim, 1999). Each cluster has its own norm expressed as follows:

$$D_{ikA}^2 = (x_k - v_i)^T A_i (x_k - v_i), \ 1 \le i \le c, \ 1 \le k \le N \tag{18}$$

The objective function of the GK algorithm is the following:

$$J(X;U,V,A) = \sum_{i=1}^{c} \sum_{k=1}^{N} (\mu_{ik})^m D_{ikA_i}^2 \tag{19}$$

The Gath-Geva algorithm

The Gath-Geva algorithm is also known as the mixed gaussian decomposition. It is an algorithm similar to the FCM, where the Gaussian distance is used instead of the Euclidean distance. The clusters do not have any definite form and can have various sizes. The Gaussian distance is expressed as follows:

$$d_{ie} = \frac{1}{P_i} \sqrt{\det(A_i)} \exp(\frac{1}{2}(x_e - v_i)^T A^{-1} (x_e - v_i)) \tag{20}$$

The different steps of the Gath-Geva are detailed in many works (Gath et al., 1989; Park et al., 2004).

Locating defects

We apply fault direction in the PLS to normal data and to each class of defect data to find a defect direction, which optimally moves each defect of data apart from normal data. We use weights in defect directions to generate contribution plots for defect diagnosis. The PLS-DA is a PLS-based model, where the general model form can be as follows:

$$X b = y \tag{21}$$

Where y is a column vector of observations of a dependent variable and $X \in \Re^{N \times m}$ is a matrix which results from N observations of the m variables. The column vector b contains the m regression coefficients. To solve this equation, we have suggested (Vance, 1996):

$$X^T X b = X^T y \tag{22}$$

We have the vector y whose components take the classes $c_1 \ldots c_p$. In our study, the vector y consists of p classes.

$$y = \left[c_1 \ldots c_1, c_2 \ldots c_2, c_3 \ldots c_3, \ldots, c_p \ldots c_p \right]^T \tag{23}$$

So at the first step, to bring to fruition the algorithm of less partial squares, the standardization of the vector y consists in having a nil average $\alpha_1 c_1 + \alpha_2 c_2 + \ldots + \alpha_p c_p = 0$ where, α_p is the number of occurrence of c_p. y is an n-dimensional vector whose components take on the two considered classes c_1 and c_2, which are the class of normal data and each class of defect data, respectively. Then, to satisfy the normalization of the first step of the PLS algorithm, we should rescale y to have a zero mean $\alpha_1 c_1 + \alpha_2 c_2 = 0$, where α_i is the number of occurrence of c_i. We arbitrarily choose $c_1 = 1$, which implies $c_2 = -\cfrac{\alpha_1}{\alpha_2}$. Accordingly, the right hand side of the equation (21) is reduced to:

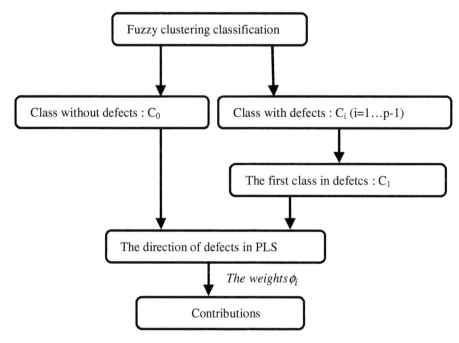

Figure 2. Locating defects for p classes.

$$X^T y = \sum_{j=1}^{n_1} a_{kj} - \frac{\alpha_1}{\alpha_2} \sum_{j=n_1+1}^{n} a_{kj} \qquad (24)$$

Where a_{kj} is an element of X and $1 \le k \le m$. This can be written as follows:

$$X^T y = \alpha_1 (\mu_1 - \mu_2) \qquad (25)$$

Where μ_1 is the m-dimensional mean whose corresponding variable has a c_1 class. As a result, $X^T y$ is in the same direction as the line connecting the means of the two classes of y. Then, the final solution vector b obtained by the PLS is given by:

$$X^T X b = \alpha_1 (\mu_1 - \mu_2) \qquad (26)$$

$$b \square \Sigma^{-1} (\mu_1 - \mu_2) \qquad (27)$$

Where the covariance matrix is $\Sigma = \frac{1}{n} X^T X$.

Therefore, we have a PLS direction, where $\phi_1 = (\mu_1 - \mu_2)$, which is the needed one. So, we define this ϕ_i direction as the defect direction for class c_i. This weight in ϕ_i is used to generate the contribution plot for the defected class.

$$\phi_i = \left[\phi_1, \phi_2, ..., \phi_j, ..., \phi_m \right] \qquad (28)$$

For the fault direction, the jth element ϕ_j is the contribution from the jth variable. For p classes, we determine two to two the class fault direction. All the abnormal data are used by the PLS model to determine the directions of defects (Figure 2). The weights of these defect directions are calculated within the regions of normal and abnormal data two by two.

Application

Process description

Grinding wheat into flour or semolina is done in a progressive industrial mill. Wheat flour is worked out from wheat grains; we partially eliminate the bran and the germ and we crush the rest into enough fine powder. In Figure 3 we present the different steps of a line of grinding wheat into standard flour.

Water level (H): The flour water level is an important parameter that must be between 10 and 16% in such a way that we can properly preserve the flour. The moisture meter measurement ensures a rapid determination of the level of water. The moisture meters are used on the sites of reception. The measurement of an electric characteristic of the grains, which are variable in function of their moisture state, is linked after calibration to the water level of the grains.

Ash content (C): The ash rate is an official means used

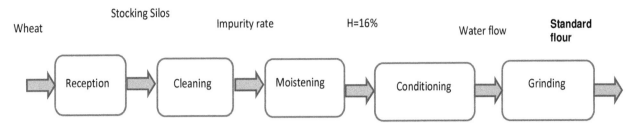

Figure 3. Line of grinding wheat.

Table 1. Signification of quality parameters of the chopin alveograph.

Symbols	Signification
P	It is called pressure, and it measures the tenacity and firmness of the dough and its resistance to deformation
G	The rising tallies with the air quantity instilled into the dough, till its bursting.
L	It is the width of the graphic design, and it shows the curve extensibility and indicates the dough elasticity and the processing extension
W	This value measures the necessary work to deform the dough roll till bursting; we use also the term "baking power" of the flour
$P/L = r$	It is the link that shows the balance and unsteadiness between the dough's tenacity and extensibility
Ie	Rate of elasticity: $Ie\ (\%) = (P_{200}/P)*100$

for characterizing the flour purity. The ash determination makes it easy to know the global mineral material content of wheat and its derivatives.

Protein content (Pr): Having a good idea about the content of protein, combined with that of wheat variety, provides significant information about the technological flour capacity. We have picked out relatively high protein contents, which vary between 11.45 and 17%. The determination of protein content by infrared spectrometry is also a known method.

In addition, we distinguish six other indicators of flour quality by a method of indirect measurement using a device called the alveograph of CHOPIN, with which we measure the dough's resistance and elasticity. That is why we will make the dough to fall down completely. These different measurements permit us to get the flour baking power. The principle measurement is based on raising a dough sample subjected to air pressure. The formed bubble volume is determined in relation to the extensibility of the dough. The bubble pressure evolution in function of time is measured and carried forward in the form of a curve called alveogram. In Table 1, we present the signification of quality parameters of the CHOPIN alveograph.

Pre-analysis

We set out the historical measurements of nine variables, representing the quality parameters of flour. The data base is used in our application form of historical measurements of quality parameters in a flour manufacturing line. The measurement (528 × 9) is the data test composed of 528 observations of 9 flour quality parameters. First, we should start by creating normalized data. In Figure 4, we present the reduced centered variables.

Among the principle components, we should not keep only the one carrying significant data, allowing us to explain the different variables, to estimate those which are not original. Then, we determine the structure of the PCA model; that is, we determine the number of components to keep or to retain in the PCA model.

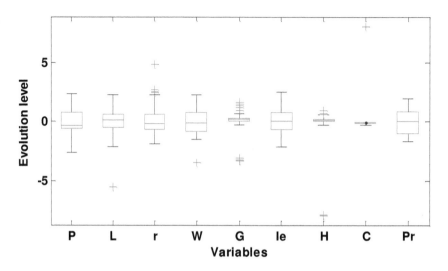

Figure 4. Evolution of reduced centered variables.

Table 2. Variance of reconstruction error with m = 8 and $\min_{\ell} \sum_{i=1}^{m} \rho_i(\ell) = 3$

i	ℓ							
	1	2	3	4	5	6	7	8
1	0.25	0.98	0.56	0.79	0.91	0.54	0.96	0.95
2	0.18	0.83	0.38	0.40	0.82	0.54	0.23	0.24
3	0.17	0.11	0.06	0.12	0.75	0.47	0.14	0.13
4	0.66	0.06	0.11	0.05	0.06	0.01	0.01	0.11
5	0.92	0.04	0.04	0.05	0.05	0.01	0.01	0.05
6	0.54	0.02	0.02	0.02	0.02	0.01	0.01	0.01
7	0.97	0.01	0.01	0.01	0.01	0.01	0.01	0.01
$\sum_{i=1}^{m} v_i(\ell)$	3.69	2.05	1.18	1.44	2.62	1.59	1.37	1.5

Determining the number of principal components

To determine the number of principal components, we use the method of the method of the variance of reconstruction error. The number of components which minimizes $VRE(\ell)$ is $\ell = 3$. We have three principle components in the PCA model (Table 2).

Once the component number ℓ is determined, the PCA model is then identified. In Figures 5 and 6, we present the measurement development of the variables P and L, as well as their estimation determined by the PCA model

Detection of defects and prediction of classes

In Figures 7, 8 and 9, we present the evolution of the statistics SPE, T^2 and φ. Thus, we notice that the derivatives are only detected by the statistics SPE and

T^2. The detection by the statistic φ is not effective, so this statistic will not be used in the classification phase. From the development from the statistics SPE and T^2, we distinguish 5 regions, where B and D are two regions in defect and A, C and E make up three regions without defects.

Classification and visualization of regions

We present, in this section, the classification and visualization of quality parameters of flour by the clustering algorithms. The distances determined by the FCM, GK and GG algorithms are projected into a 2D space.

The validity indexes of clusters used in our application are the partition coefficient PC and the partition entropy

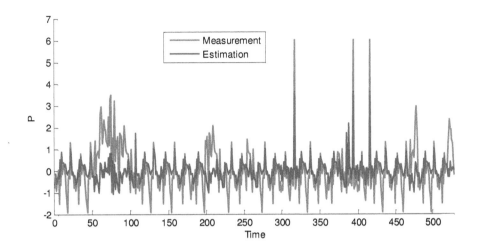

Figure 5. Measurements and estimation of pressure P.

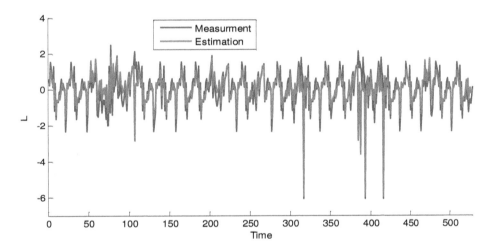

Figure 6. Measurements and estimation of width L.

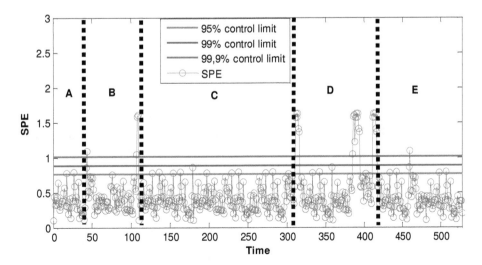

Figure 7. The evolution of the statistic SPE.

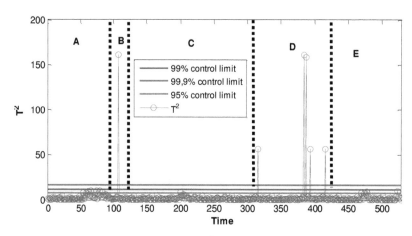

Figure 8. The evolution of the statistic T².

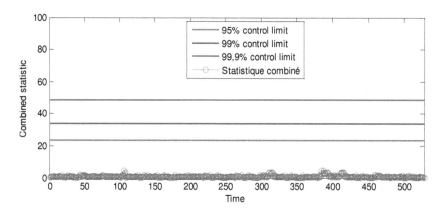

Figure 9. The evolution of the statistic φ .

Table 3. Validation Parameters of the FCM, GK and GG clustering.

	PC	EC	PI	SI	XB
FCM	0.6851	0. 4137	0.2568	0.0004	3.1271
GK	0.7820	0. 5811	0.1990	0.0007	6.2296
GG	0.9228	NaN	NaN	NaN	NaN

EC. They are sensitive to noise and to the variation of the exponent m. The optimal cluster number is pointed out by the minimum *PC* value. The *EC* index measures the cluster fuzziness, which is similar to a division coefficient. The optimal cluster number is pointed out by the maximum *EC* value.

The other indexes *PI* and *XB* are proposed, respectively by Fukayama, Sugeno and Xie-Beni (Xie et al., 1991; Fukuyama et al., 1989). *PI* is sensitive to high and low values of m, and *XB* gives good responses onto a great choice for $c = 2,\ldots,10$ and $1 < m \leq 7$. The *XB* index measures how many clusters are compact; and *PI* is

a further term that measures how many clusters are separated. The distance-based separation index *SI* is the most used function that reduces the total distance in the cluster variation to the minimum. To determine these validation parameters of these algorithms, we have used the Fuzzy Clustering toolbox (Balasko et al., 2005).

Classification of SPE and T² signals

The classification is applied to both SPE and T² signals, using the clustering algorithms. In our application of the FCM, GK and GG algorithms, we have fixed the number of clusters $c = 5$ and $1 \leq m \leq 7$. The validation parameters of the FCM, GK and GG clustering algorithms are gathered in the Table 3.

During the application of clustering algorithms, both FCM and GK algorithms ensure the classification, whereas the GG algorithm diverges.

When applying the FCM algorithm, the *PC* index is minimum and the *EC* index is maximum, compared with the GK algorithm. So, the cluster optimum number is

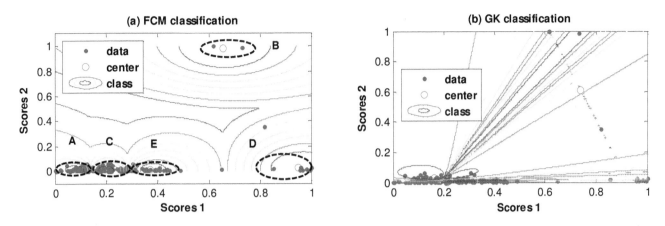

Figure 10. FCM and Gk clustering of the data m = 2 and c = 5, and the recalculated membership contours.

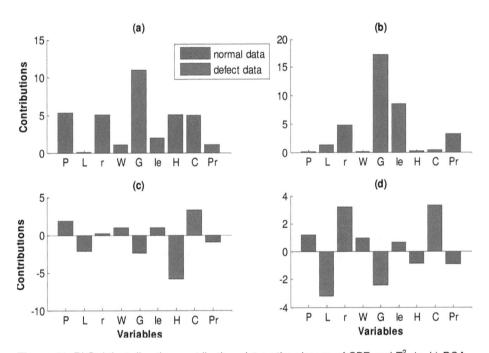

Figure 11. PLS defect direction contribution plot on the classes of SPE and T^2, (a, b) PCA contribution plot.

indicated by the minimum *PC* value and the maximum *EC* value. In our application, for the FCM and GK algorithm, we have a minimum *PI* coefficient that indicates a better division of clusters. So, the *SI* separation index guarantees a minimum separation distance between clusters. The XB index indicates how many clusters are compact; we have almost 3 groups, showing the three regions without defects. On the other hand, for the GK algorithm, we have almost 6 compact groups, which show that the classification by the GK algorithm does not ensure a separation between the regions with and without defects.

In the Figure 10, the blue dots are the measurements, the 'o's in red indicate the center of the cluster or class.

The contour-map circles points out the limits of each cluster. The contour-map of Figure 10a of the FCM classification presents three compact classes, which are the classes with defects and two other separated classes. The classification Figure 10b by the GK algorithm shows an unclear classification; we cannot distinguish between the classes.

Based on expertise, we notice that the two classes D and B are the two regions in defect. The groups A, C and E are more compact clusters than the two other groups D and B, which make up the A, C and E regions without defects.

The classification of the detection signals SPE and T^2, using the clustering algorithms, is efficient for the

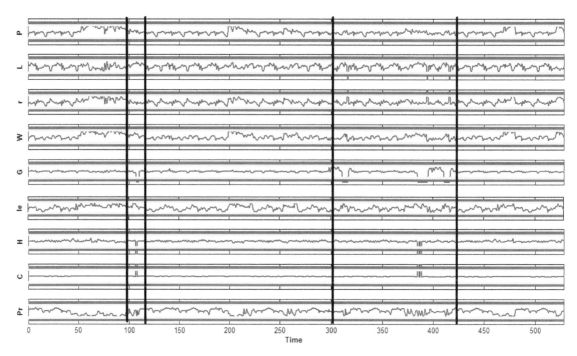

Figure 12. Simulated measurements of flour quality parameters.

separation between the data with and without defects.

RESULTS AND DISCUSSION

After classifying the process data in classes with and without defects, we put forward in Figure 11 the contribution plot based on directing PLS defects and PCA for all the used measurement. Figure 11c and d show the contribution plot of the defects B and D. The PCA based contribution plot draw in Figure 11a and b.

Defect B

In Figure 11c, the PLS defect direction contribution of variables has shown that parameter H (water level: moisture) and C (ash content) have the highest contribution, compared with other variables. The development of variables in Figure 12 shows that the parameters G (inflating), H and C are the cause of this B defect. However, the contribution calculation is based on the classical PCA in Figure 11a; only the variable G is identified, but other C and H parameters are not identified.

Defect D

In Figure 11d, the PLS defect direction contribution of variables has shown that the variable L (elasticity), r (ratio

of tenacity and stretchability of the dough) G and C have the highest contribution, compared with other variables. Thus, these parameters are considered in defect.

The PCA-based contribution calculation, in Figure 11b, shows the variables G and Ie (elasticity rate) which have the highest contribution. Therefore, these two parameters are considered in defect. The development of parameters in Figure 12 shows that the variables L, r, G, H and C are the cause of the defect D. Then, the location of defects by the PLS defect direction technique is much more efficient than the PCA contribution calculation. So, the location of parameters in defect on the SPE and T^2 signals is validated, and the location results are efficient on the detection signals SPE and T^2.

The results of this analysis show that combining the PCA and the fuzzy clustering techniques is useful in extracting the abnormal data out of the set of flour quality parameters starting from these multidimensional, and in simplifying the data interpretation to detect and isolate defects. A comparative study of our monitoring approach and the isolation by PCA contribution calculations is well presented (Figure 11). Extracting abnormal regions, thanks to the combination of the PCA and the fuzzy clustering technique, has proved its contribution in isolating defects in PLS.

Our approach of isolating abnormal data from the set of historical measurements is efficient in relation to the isolation by linear PCA contribution. The isolation is based on the classification of regions by fuzzy clustering, and the PLS defect direction has a positive impact in determining parameters in defect.

Conclusion

In this study, the PCA defect detection and the clustering technique, for the monitoring of quality parameters, are applied and validated to the process of producing flour. The proposed monitoring approach implemented in our process is based on combining the PCA and the clustering algorithms.

In our application, we suggest data-processing to extract the detection signals SPE and T^2, in order to make a classification depending on their development. Then, we suggest a comparative study between the classification by the clustering algorithms FCM, GG and GK, and the classification by the PCA. The development of the results of locating defected parameters, using the classification on the SPE and T^2 signals, is validated. The location technique of defect direction in PLS has shown its performance, compared with the location, using the PCA for determining defected parameters.

The method has been assessed with historical measurements of flour quality and with the possibility of carrying out this combined approach of monitoring in an online automatization system.

REFERENCES

Albazzaz H, Wang XZ, Marhoon F (2005). Multidimensional visualization for process historical data analysis: a comparative study with multivariate statistical process control. J. Proc. Cont. 15:285-294.

Ahvenlampi T, Tervaskanto M, Kortela U (2005). Diagnosis System for Continuous Cooking Process. 16th IFAC World Congress. 16:1-6.

Ahvenlampi T, Kortela U (2005). Clustering Algorithms in Process Monitoring and: Control Application to Continuous Digesters, Informatica. 29:101-109.

Bezdek JC (1981). Pattern recognition with fuzzy objective function algorithms. Plenum, New York.

Bouhouche S, Lahreche M, Moussaoui A, Bast J (2007). Quality Monitoring Using Principal Component Analysis and Fuzzy Logic Application in Continuous Casting Process. Am. J. A Sci. 4(9):637-644.

Balasko B, Abonyi J, Feil B (2005). Fuzzy Clustering and Data Analysis: Matlab Toolbox. pp. 75-79.

Chaouch H, Ouni K, Nabli L (2011). ECG signal monitoring using linear PCA. Int. J. Comput. Appl. 33(8):48-54.

Dulyakran P, Ransanseri Y (2001). Fuzzy c-means clustering using spatial information with application to remote sensing. 22nd Asian Conference on Remote Sensing. http://www.actapress.com/Abstract.aspx?paperId=31118.

Dunia R, Qin SJ (1998). A subspace approach to multidimensional fault identification and reconstruction. AIChE J. 44(13):1813-1831.

Fukuyama Y, Sugeno M (1989). A new method of choosing the number of clusters for the fuzzy c-means method. Proc. Fifth Fuzzy Syst. Symp. pp. 247-250.

Gath I, Geva AB (1989). Unsupervised optimal fuzzy clustering. IEEE Transactions on Pattern Analysis and Machine Intelligence. 11(7):773-781.

Graves D, Pedrycz W (2007). Fuzzy C-Means, Gustafson-Kessel FCM, and Kernel-Based FCM: A Comparative Study. Adv. Soft Comput. 41:140-149.

Harket MF, Mourot G, Ragot J (2006). An improved PCA scheme for sensor FDI: Application to an air quality monitoring network. J. Proc. Control 16(6):625-634.

Hung WL, Yang MS, Chen DH (2006). Parameter selection for suppressed fuzzy c-means with an application to MRI segmentation. Pattern Recogn. Lett. 27(5):424-438.

Höpper F, Klawonn F, Kruse R, Renklu T (1999). Fuzzy cluster analysis for classification data analysis and image recognition. John Wiley and Son. pp. 35-37.

Jollife I (1986). Principal Component Analysis. Springer Verlag.

Krishnapuram R, Kim J (1999). A note on the Gustafson-Kessel and adaptive fuzzy clustering algorithms. IEEE Trans. Fuzzy Syst. 7(4):453-546.

Kresta JF, MacGregor JF, Marlin TE (1991). Multivariate statistical monitoring of process operating performance. Can. J. Chem. Eng. 69(1):35-47.

Liang GS, Chou TY, Han TC (2005). Cluster analysis based on fuzzy equivalence relation. Eur. J. Oper. Res. 166(1):160-171.

Luukka P (2009). PCA for fuzzy data and similarity classifier in building recognition system for post-operative patient data. Expert Syst. Appl. 36(2):1222-1228.

Nottingham QJ, Cook DF, Zobel CW (2001). Visualization of multivariate data with radial plots using SAS. Comput. Ind. Eng. 41:17-35.

Ouni K, Nabli L, Messaoud H (2011). A Monitoring Method Based on Fuzzy Detection and PCA Diagnosis. Int. J. Intell. Control Syst. 16(1):19-27.

Ouni K, Dhouibi H, Nabli L, Hassani M, Simeu-Abazi Z (2011). Monitoring Approach Using Nonlinear Principal Component Analysis, CCCA. 1:1-6.

Oliveira JV, Pedrycz W (2007). Advances in Fuzzy Clustering and its Applications. John Wiley and Sons. DOI:10.1002/9780470061190.

Pal NR, Pal K, Keller JM, Bezdek JC (2005). A Possibilistic C-Means Clustering algorithm. IEEE Trans. Fuzzy Syst. 13(4):517-530.

Peter Q, He S, Qin J, Wang J (2005). A New Fault Diagnosis Method Using Fault Directions in Fisher Discriminant Analysis. AIChE J. 51(2):555-571.

Park HS, Yoo SH, Cho SB (2004). A Fuzzy Clustering Algorithm for Analysis of Gene Expression Profiles. Trends Artif. Intell. 3157:967-968.

Pedrycs W (1997). Fuzzy clustering with partial supervision. IEEE Transactions on Systems, Man and cybernetics, Part B. Cybernetics. 27(5):787-795.

Rezaee MR, Lelieveldt BPF, Reiber JHC (1998). A new cluster validity index for the fuzzy c-mean. Pattern Recogn. Lett. 19(3-4):237-246.

Sebzalli YM, Wang XZ (2001). Knowledge discovery from process operational data using PCA and fuzzy clustering. Eng. Appl. Artif. Intell. 14:607-616.

Vance F (1996). Partial Least Squares, Conjugate Gradient And The Fisher Discriminant. Los Alamos National Laboratory, Los Alamos New Mexico. 3958:1-17.

Valle S, Li W, Qin SJ (1999). Selection of the number of principal components: The variance of the reconstruction error criterion with a comparison to other methods. Am. Chem. Soc. 38(11):4389-4401.

Vermasvuori M (2008). Methodology for utilising prior knowledge in constructing data-based process monitoring systems with an application to a dearomatisation process. Ph. D, Helsinki University of Technology.

Xie L, Beni G (1991), A validity measure for fuzzy clustering, IEEE Transaction. Pattern Anal. Mach. Intell. 13(8):841-847.

Yue H, Qin SJ (2001). Reconstruction-based fault identification using a combined index. Ind. Engin. Chem. Res. 40(20):4403-4414.

Yingwei Z, Yang Z (2012). Process monitoring, fault diagnosis and quality prediction methods based on the multivariate statistical techniques. IETE J. Res. 27(5):406-420.

6

A method of dual-process sample selection for feature selection on gene expression data

Quanjin Liu[1,2], Zhimin Zhao[1] , Ying-xin Li[3] and Xiaolei Yu[4]

[1]College of Science, Nanjing University of Aeronautics and Astronautics, Nanjing 210016, China.
[2]School of Physics and Electronic Engineering, Anqing Normal College, Anqing 246011, China.
[3]Institute of Machine Vision and Machine Intelligence, Beijing Jingwei Textile Machinery New Technology Co., Ltd., Beijing 100176, China.
[4]Jiangsu Institute of Standardization, Nanjing 210029, China.

A method of dual-process sample selection based on support vector machine (SVM) is proposed to select informative features in this paper. Samples in a training set are used to train a SVM model, and the samples excluding support vector samples are chosen to select critical features in the procedure of recursive feature elimination (RFE). The effect of the dual-process sample selection method on feature selection is evaluated using the classification and the clustering performance of the selected features. The proposed dual-process sample selection method is applied to five gene expression datasets, and the experimental results show that the method is useful to improve the performance of the feature selection method based on fuzzy interactive self-organizing data algorithm (ISODATA). This indicates the method is reliable and effective for selecting informative genes from gene expression data.

Key words: Feature selection, support vector machine, fuzzy interactive self-organizing data algorithm (ISODATA), dual-process sample selection.

INTRODUCTION

Feature selection method removes irrelevant features and selects a small portion of features with strong classification ability from the original dataset (Theodoridis and Koutroumba, 1999). Depending on the classification models used, feature selection method can be classified into the "filter" and the "wrapper" method. The former method takes the characteristics of the dataset itself into account and utilizes the divisibility index of samples to select informative features (Duda et al., 2001; Uncua and Türkşenb, 2007). In contrast, the latter method conducts the feature selection based on some classification models. The integration of those two methods is the major focus of the research on the feature selection from high-dimensional datasets (Guyon and Elisseeff, 2003;

Jensen and Shen, 2009).

For cancer classification and diagnosis, many literatures studied how to select informative genes from microarray dataset, which has thousands of genes and only dozens of samples. On one hand, filter method was used to filtered the "irrelevant" genes and select critical genes (Golub et al., 1999; Lan and Vucetic, 2011). On the other hand, wrapper methods were applied to informative genes selection. For instance, Guyon et al. (2000) proposed the feature selection method (SVM-RFE) based on SVM to select critical genes in the process of recursive feature elimination. Tang et al. (2008) designed a recursive fuzzy granular support vector machine to select informative genes for cancer diagnosis. In addition, ensemble method was applied to wrapper method based on the difference between gene subsets (Abeel et al., 2010). Meanwhile, unsupervised learning algorithm was also used to analyze microarray dataset and select discriminant genes (Alon et al., 1999). Liu et al. (2012) proposed the feature selection method based on fuzzy Interactive Self-Organizing Data Algorithm (RFE-ISODATA) and selected informative genes from 5 cancer microarray datasets.

Sample selection method is to select the key sample to build the classification decision function. SVM only uses the information of the support vector samples (SVs) for the classification decision, thus it can work with a high speed. However, for the dataset with the uneven number of heterogeneous samples, it is inappropriate to use SVs to carry out classification (Akbani et al., 2004). Tang et al. (2009) later improved the SVM classification performance by re-sampling techniques. Lyhyaoui et al. (1999) conducted and improved the clustering for various samples, by selecting two samples with the closest distance from each cluster to establish the classifier.

This paper proposes a dual-process Sample Selection Support Vector Machine (SS-SVM) method for selecting informative genes form microarray dataset. We demonstrate the impact of SS-SVM on the feature selection method RFE-ISODATA, based on five cancer microarray datasets. According to the proportion of 3:1:1, the original dataset is randomly divided into the training set, validation set and independent test set. RFE-ISODATA is conducted on the samples selected by SS-SVM and all samples from the training set respectively. Experimental results show that SS-SVM method can effectively improve the classification and clustering capabilities of the informative genes selected by RFE-ISODATA.

The rest of this paper is organized as follows. Subsequently, the feature selection method of RFE-ISODATA is described, after which the dual-process sample selection method (SS-SVM) is proposed. This is followed by a presentation of the results of the feature selection experiments based on SS-SVM and an evaluation of the performance of the feature selection methods. Finally, this paper is concluded.

FEATURE SELECTION BASED ON FUZZY INTERACTIVE SELF-ORGANIZING DATA ALGORITHM

Fuzzy ISODATA is a kind of clustering algorithm with simple structure and high running speed (Bezdek, 1976; Marcelloni, 2003). The sample $X_i = \{x_{i1}, ..., x_{ij}, ..., x_{im}\}$ in training set belongs to s clusters and the kth cluster center is represented as $V_k = \{v_{k1}, ..., v_{kj}, ..., v_{km}\}$. Membership u_{ki} of sample X_i which belongs to the kth cluster is defined as (Bezdek, 1981; Marcelloni, 2003):

$$u_{ki} = \frac{1}{\sum_{t=1}^{s} \left(\frac{\|X_i - V_k\|}{\|X_i - V_t\|} \right)^{\frac{1}{r-1}}} \tag{1}$$

Membership u_{ik} regards the distance between the sample X_i and the cluster center V_k as the important indicator. Membership implies the relationship between features of sample and class of sample, so the features determine the membership value of sample to a certain class. The sensitivity formula of the jth feature of samples to the membership (Liu et al., 2012) is defined as

$$S(j) = \sum_{k=1}^{s} |S(k, j)| = \sum_{k=1}^{s} \left| \sum_{i=1}^{n} \sum_{p=1}^{n} \frac{\partial u_{ki}}{\partial x_{pj}} \right| \tag{2}$$

$S(k, j)$ represents the sensitivity of the jth feature to membership and reflects the contribution of the jth feature to the kth cluster. $S(j)$ can be regarded as the importance index of the feature in fuzzy ISODATA Clustering.

RFE-ISODATA method selects features based on the sensitivity index in the process of recursive feature elimination. In the process of feature sensitivity analysis, the "cluster" formed by the fuzzy ISODATA based on sample similarity reveals the underlying structure of the data. The discriminant function established by the features with high sensitivity has the high recognition ability.

As we know, the longer distance between sample and the center of other categories and the shorter distance between sample and the center of its own class will make the higher membership value of the samples. If the samples on the border of different classes are removed, spacing between different types of samples can be increased relatively and the remaining samples would have high membership value to their own classes in new round of fuzzy ISODATA clustering and the features with high sensitivity would carry more class information.

DUAL-PROCESS SAMPLE SELECTION BASED ON SVM (SS-SVM)

The support vector machine algorithm is a kind of machine learning algorithm developed by Vapnik based on the structural risk minimization principle and the statistical learning theory, which can obtain good generalization ability in the case of limited samples (Vapnic, 1998).

Let $X_i \in R^m$ be a sample of the training set X and $y_i \in \{+1, -1\}$ be a class label of X_i, that is, each sample X_i corresponds to a class indicator y_i. Linear discriminant function is given by $g(x) = \alpha \cdot x + b$ and the hyperplane $g(x) = \alpha \cdot x + b = 0$ can classify the training samples. Thus the margin, which is defined as the distance between the pair of parallel hyperplanes described by $\alpha \cdot x + b = \pm 1$, is determined by α which characterizes the direction of the hyperplane. To search for the maximum possible margin, quadratic programming problem is defined as below:

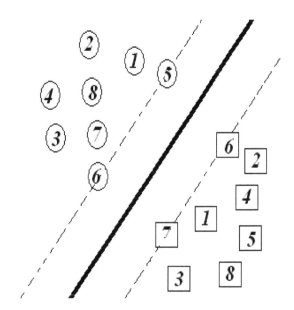

Figure 1. Distribution of two types of samples.

Minimize: $\Phi(\omega) = \dfrac{1}{2}\|\omega\|^2$

Subject to: $\quad y_i(\omega^T \cdot X_i + b) \geq 1, i = 1,2,...,n \qquad (3)$

Based on the method of Lagrange multipliers, the optimal SVM classification discriminant function is obtained as follows:

$$f(x) = \text{sgn}\left\{ \sum_{i=1}^{sv} \lambda_i^* y_i (X_i \cdot x) + b^* \right\} \qquad (4)$$

The sample X_i with nonzero Lagrange multiplier λ_i^*, which lies on both hyperplanes, is called support vector sample (SV) (Vapnic, 1996). sv is the number of SVs. The SVs on the hyperplanes are only a small part in the training set, and are used as samples to define classification border.

As shown in Figure 1, 16 samples $(X_i, y_i), i = 1,...16, X_i \in R^2$ belong to the positive and negative categories, respectively marked by the circular and square icons. The thick line in the middle refers to the optimal classification line and the dotted lines on both sides are 'support lines' of positive class and negative class. Six samples of the eight positive ones are at the upper left corner, the other two samples on the support line are the positive SVs. Six samples of the eight negative ones are at the lower right corner, the other two samples on the negative support line are the negative SVs.

Figure 1 indicates that if the SVs are removed, the spacing between the heterogeneous samples can be increased and cohesion of within-class samples can be enhanced relatively. Due to the fact that SVs only account for a small part of the training set, the removal of SVs will not affect the original information structure of dataset. In other words, if the samples excluding SVs are selected, not only the original class information of dataset can be retained, but also the spacing between different classes can be expanded, coupled with the shortening of inner-class distance. The dispersion between classes and compactness within-class are just

the key factors to determine the class separability of feature in feature selection (Theodoridis and Koutroumbas, 1999). In view of this, this paper proposes a dual-process sample selection method (SS-SVM), which trains SVM on training set and selects samples other than SVs, for improving the performance of feature selection method.

EXPERIMENTAL RESULTS

The SS-SVM method is applied to feature selection method RFE-ISODATA and the impact of SS-SVM on RFE-ISODATA is studied via experiments. The flowchart of feature selection based on SS-SVM is shown in Figure 2. The SS-SVM method is added to recursive feature selection process: all samples in training set are used to train SVM, the samples selected by SS-SVM are used for feature selection. Based on these samples, features are sorted by RFE-ISODATA to generate candidate feature subsets.

To evaluate the class information of the candidate feature subsets reliably, classification and clustering tests are respectively done on the candidate feature subsets. The SVM and K nearest neighbor (KNN) classifiers trained by training set are used to identify the type of samples of the validation set for investigating the classification capability of the candidate feature subsets. Meanwhile, hierarchical clustering experiments are carried out on the validation set to check the clustering performance of the candidate feature subsets. The AUC(Area Under the receiver operating characteristic Curve) (Li et al., 2012; Provost and Fawcett, 1997) value and the correct rate of classification and clustering experiments on the validation set are used to build the objective function $Object(F)$ of the candidate feature subset F in the RFE process:

$$Object(F) = (AUC_{SVM}(F) + AUC_{KNN}(F) + AUC_{Cluster}(F) + right_{SVM}(F) + right_{KNN}(F) + right_{Cluster}(F))/6$$

$$(5)$$

where AUC represents the AUC value of classification or clustering test, and $right$ stands for the right rate of classification or clustering test. The candidate feature subset with the highest value of the objective function is the optimal feature subset with the strongest classification and clustering performance in the validation test.

The classification and clustering performance of the optimal feature subset is further verified on the independent test set. The higher the AUC value and the right rate are, the stronger the classification and clustering ability of the optimal feature subset will be. SVs in SS-SVM algorithm will change along with the different features during the process of RFE. Despite of the shrinking range of feature selection, the scope of the sample selection remains all the samples of the training

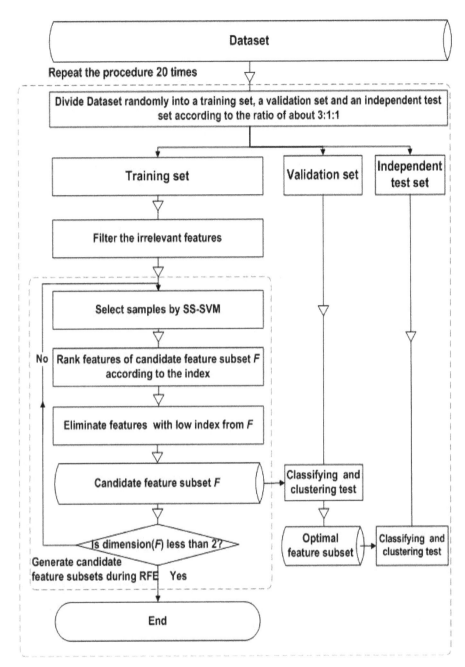

Figure 2. The illustration of the process of feature selection based on SS-SVM.

set. Fixed scope of sample selection ensures the stability of the classification information of the selected features.

Microarray datasets

To verify objectively the effect of SS-SVM method on RFE-ISODATA, feature selection experiments are carried out on the 5 gene expression datasets (Alon et al., 1999; Goloub et al., 1999; Shipp et al., 2002; Singh et al., 2002; Zhan et al., 2002). As shown in Table 1, the number of

genes in the datasets is greater than the number of samples, and different types of samples are unevenly distributed. In Table 1, the first column lists names of the datasets, the second column indicates the initial number of genes, and the third columns lists the number of samples of two different types. The samples of datasets are randomly assigned into the training set, validation set and independent test set by the proportion of 3:1:1 in the experiments.

On one hand, informative gene selection experiments based on RFE-ISODATA are carried out on the samples

Table 1. The datasets used for feature selection experiments.

Dataset	Features	Samples(+/-)	Training set/Validation set /Independent test set	Search scope of features
Colon	2000	62(40/22)	38/12/12	500
Acute Leukemia	7129	72(47/25)	44/14/14	100
Multiple myeloma	7129	105(74/31)	63/21/21	100
DLBCL	7129	77(58/19)	47/15/15	1000
Prostate	12600	102(52/50)	62/20/20	1000

selected by SS-SVM from the training set (RFE-ISODATA without SVs); on the other hand, informative gene selection experiments based on RFE-ISODATA are carried out on all samples of the same training set (RFE-ISODATA). To prevent the impact of uneven distribution of the samples on the feature selection, datasets are divided into three parts twenty times randomly. Consequently, both of feature selection methods are carried out on the three parts of the dataset each time. The statistical results of the feature selection experiments are used to evaluate the effect of SS-SVM on RFE-ISODATA.

Experimental configuration

The experiments are conducted with MATLAB on a PC with 2.2 GHz Intel Core 2 CPU and 2.0 GB.

The number of features in the datasets is greater than that of samples, with only part of features related to sample class. As a result, the irrelevant genes should be filtered before feature selection in order to reduce the search scope and the complexity of calculation. Bhattacharyya distance (Duda et al., 2001; Theodoridis and Koutroumba, 1999) between the heterogeneous samples in the training set is considered as criteria to filter the irrelevant genes. The number of filtered genes is determined through the filtering and classification tests on the five datasets. Table 1 lists the search scope for the next feature selection process.

For fuzzy ISODATA algorithm we set r = 2, s = 2, and ε = 0.0001. We set the kernel function of SVM as linear function and set 5 neighbors for the KNN algorithm. For the hierarchical clustering algorithm, we set the Euclidean distance as distance between pair-wised samples and construct the hierarchical cluster tree based on average distance.

Validation tests

Figure 3 shows the performance of classification and clustering in terms of objective function of 2 feature selection methods (RFE-ISODATA without SVs and RFE-ISODATA). The x-axis presents the number of the genes

of the candidate feature subsets and the y-axis indicates the average value of the objective function in the validation tests during the 20 rounds of experiments.

The curve of objective function reflects the classification and clustering capabilities of candidate feature subsets in validation tests. The curves of "RFE-ISODATA without SVs" are higher than that of RFE-ISODATA, which indicates that the classification and clustering performance of the candidate feature subsets selected by the former is superior to the latter.

The curves of objective function indicate that SS-SVM method can improve the proportion of class information of the candidate feature subsets and is conductive for RFE-ISODATA.

Independent tests

The candidate feature subset with the highest objective function value is selected as the optimal feature subset. Genes in the optimal feature subset are considered as informative genes for cancer classification and diagnosis. To illustrate the effect of SS-SVM on feature selection methods, RFE-ISODATA is compared with "RFE-ISODATA without SVs" in terms of AUC value and right rate of classification and clustering in the independent tests.

Figure 4 illustrates the performance of the optimal feature subsets selected by the 2 feature selection methods from the 5 cancer microarray datasets respectively. The results indicate the mean and standard deviation of AUC value and right rate in the independent tests during the 20 rounds of feature selection experiments.

From Figure 4, we find the AUC value of classification and clustering tests of the optimal feature subsets selected by "RFE-ISODATA without SVs" is higher than that selected by RFE-ISODATA. Right rate of classification and clustering tests of the optimal feature subsets selected by "RFE-ISODATA without SVs" is higher than that selected by RFE-ISODATA, except the SVM classification performance on the Prostate dataset. Comparison of the independent test result in Table 2 indicates that the classification and clustering performance of the informative genes selected by "RFE-

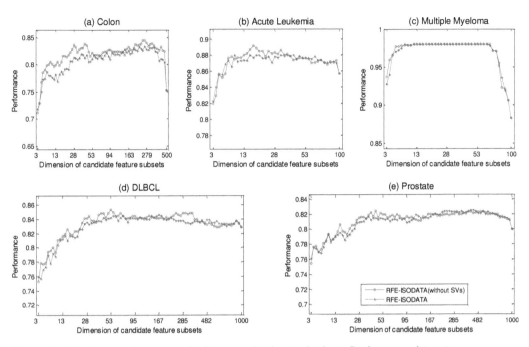

Figure 3. Objective function curve of 2 feature selection methods on 5 microarray datasets.

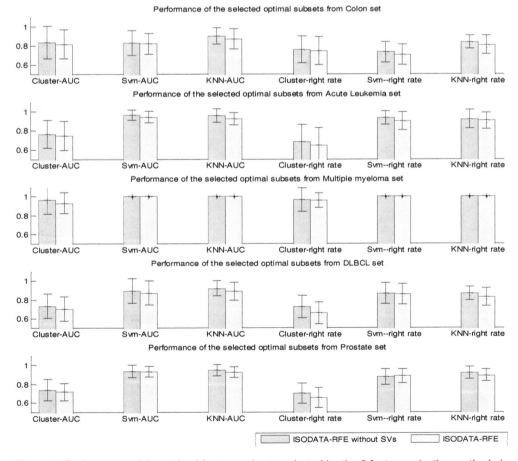

Figure 4. Performance of the optimal feature subsets selected by the 2 feature selection methods in the independent tests.

Table 2. Performance of the selected optimal feature subsets in the independent tests.

Microarray dataset	Feature selection method	Dimension	AUC			Right rate		
			SVM	KNN	Hierarchical clustering	SVM	KNN	Hierarchical clustering
Colon	RFE-ISODATA without SVs	18.35	0.839±0.133	0.903±0.088	0.837±0.172	0.733±0.085	0.838±0.069	0.758±0.145
	RFE-ISODATA	18.35	0.821±0.109	0.871±0.106	0.816±0.155	0.704±0.106	0.808±0.098	0.746±0.149
Acute Leukemia	RFE-ISODATA without SVs	8.95	0.966±0.052	0.962±0.070	0.762±0.148	0.946±0.061	0.932±0.047	0.725±0.160
	RFE-ISODATA	9.00	0.943±0.062	0.941±0.067	0.726±0.156	0.914±0.082	0.921±0.065	0.711±0.157
Multiple Myeloma	RFE-ISODATA without SVs	4.75	1.000±0.000	1.000±0.000	0.967±0.151	1.000±0.000	1.000±0.000	0.967±0.078
	RFE-ISODATA	4.00	1.000±0.000	1.000±0.000	0.932±0.111	1.000±0.000	1.000±0.000	0.960±0.053
DLBCL	RFE-ISODATA without SVs	20	0.895±0.131	0.903±0.080	0.733±0.130	0.863±0.111	0.863±0.073	0.723±0.119
	RFE-ISODATA	19.55	0.875±0.128	0.888±0.094	0.703±0.128	0.860±0.110	0.823±0.098	0.657±0.119
Prostate	RFE-ISODATA without SVs	21.8	0.936±0.064	0.949±0.061	0.738±0.112	0.873±0.082	0.918±0.067	0.703±0.107
	RFE-ISODATA	17.05	0.932±0.058	0.926±0.056	0.717±0.093	0.883±0.076	0.890±0.062	0.653±0.110

ISODATA without SVs" is superior to that selected by RFE-ISODATA. It shows that the class information carried by the informative genes selected by "RFE-ISODATA without SVs" is much more than that selected by RFE-ISODATA. This indicates that SS-SVM method can effectively improve the performance of RFE-ISODATA on the 5 microarray datasets.

Integrating the results of 20 rounds of feature selection experiments by the 2 feature selection methods on the 5 cancer microarray datasets, it verifies that the removal of SVs can expand the distance between heterogeneous classes, shrink the sample dispersion within-cluster in fuzzy ISODATA clustering, increase the sensitivity of feature to sample membership and enhance the classification performance of the selected informative genes.

Results of the experiments show SS-SVM can improve the recognition ability and clustering performance of the selected informative genes by RFE-ISODATA. It means the application of SS-SVM on feature selection is useful to cancer diagnosis and findings of subtype of cancer.

Conclusions

This paper proposes a new method of dual-process sample selection based on SVM (SS-SVM) and studies the impact of SS-SVM on feature selection method RFE-ISODATA. In this paper, we show that SS-SVM is able to relatively contract the dispersion within class and extend the distance between the classes by removing SVs, and thus improve the clustering quality of fuzzy ISODATA and the feature selection performance of RFE-ISODATA.

Informative gene selection experiments based on 5 microarray datasets show that SS-SVM method can effectively improve the performance of RFE-ISODATA algorithms. SS-SVM combined with RFE-ISODATA achieved high clustering performance on the independent test sets, implying this combined method has the potential to identify cancer subtypes. Thus, SS-SVM could have its application potential in cancer diagnosis and drug response.

As the 5 cancer microarray datasets contain only dozens of samples, we will take further feature selection tests based on SS-SVM on the datasets with more samples.

This paper develops the sample selection method (SS-SVM) which helps feature selection method to identify the key genes with abundant class information from the gene expression datasets. Experimental results prove that SS- SVM plays an important role in improving the performance of feature selection method based on clustering model. In the future, we will study the impact of SS-SVM on the feature selection methods based on the classification model.

ACKNOWLEDGEMENTS

This work is supported by the National Natural Science Foundation of China (NO.10172043, NO.61173068), the Specialized Research Fund for the Doctoral Program of Higher Education of China (NO.200932181100024), International Science and Technology Cooperation Grant (NO.BZ2010060), Key Program of the Jiangsu Municipal Bureau of Quality and Technical Supervision (NO. KJ122714) and the Natural Science key Foundation of the Department of Education of Anhui Province of China (NO.KJ2010A226).

REFERENCES

Abeel T, Helleputte T, Van de Peer Y, Dupont P, Saeys Y (2010). Robust biomaker identification for cancer diagnosis with ensemble feature selection methods. Bioinformatics 26:392-298.

Akbani R, Kwek S, Japkowicz N (2004). Applying support vector machines to imbalanced datasets. In: J.-F. Boulicaut et al. (Eds.): ECML 2004, LNAI 3201 pp. 39-50.

Alon U, Barkai N, Notterman DA, Gish K, Ybarra S, Mack D, Levine AJ (1999). Broad patterns of gene expression revealed by clustering analysis of tumor and normal colon tissues probed by oligonucleotide arrays. PNAS USA 96:6745-6750.

Bezdek JC (1976). Physical interpretation of fuzzy ISODATA. EEE SMC, SMC-6 pp. 387-390.

Bezdek JC (1981).Pattern Recognition with Fuzzy Objective Function Algorithms, Plenum Press, New York.

Duda RO, Hart PE, Stork DG (2001). Pattern Classification. 2nd ed, John Wiley & Sons.

Goloub TR, Slonim DK, Tamayo P, Huard C, Gaasenbeek M, Mesirov JP, Coller H, Loh ML, Downing JR, Caligiuri MA, BloomÞeld CD, Lander ES (1999). Molecular classification of cancer: Class discovery and class prediction by gene expression monitoring. Sciences 286:531-537.

Guyon I, Elisseeff A (2003). An Introduction to Variable and Feature Selection, J. Mach. Learn. Res. 3:1157-1182.

Guyon I, Weston J, Barnhill S, Vapnik V (2000). Gene selection for cancer classification using support vector machines. Mach. Learn. 46(13):389-242.

Jensen R, Shen Q (2009). Feature Sejhiojlection for Aiding Glass Forensic evidence analysis, Intel. Data Anal. 13(5):703-723.

Lan L, Vucetic S (2011). Improving accuracy of microarray classification by a simple multi-task feature selection filter. Int. J. Data Min. Bioinforma. 5(2):189-208.

Li Y-X, Ji S, Kumar S, Ye J, Zhou, Z-H (2012). Drosophila gene expression pattern annotation through multi-instance multi-label learning. ACM/IEEE Trans. Comput. Biol. Bioinforma. 9(1):98-112.

Liu QJ, Zhao ZM, Li Y-X, Li YY (2012). Feature Selection Based on Sensitivity Analysis of Fuzzy ISODATA. Neurocomputing 85:29-37.

Lyhyaoui A, Martínez M, Mora I, Vázquez M, SanchoJ, R Figueiras-Vidal A (1999). Sample selection via clustering to construct support vector-like classifiers. IEEE Trans. Neural Netw. 10(6):1474-1481.

Marcelloni F (2003). Feature selection based on a modified fuzzy C-means algorithm with supervision. Inform. Sci. 151:201-226.

Provost F, Fawcett T (1997). Analysis and visualization of classifier performance: comparison under imprecise class and cost distributions. In: Proc. Third Int. Conf. on Knowledge Discovery and Data Mining. AAAI Press, Menlo Park, CA, pp. 43-48.

Shipp MA, Ross KN, Tamayo P, Weng AP, Kutok JL, Aguiar R CT, Gaasenbeek M, Angelo M, Reich M, Pinkus GS, Ray TS, Koval MA, Last KW, Norton A, Lister A, Mesirov J, Neuberg DS, Lander ES, Aster JC, Golub TR (2002). Diffuse large B-cell lymphoma outcome prediction by gene-expression profiling and supervised machine learning. Nat. Med. 8(1):68-74.

Singh D, Febbo PG, Ross K, Jackson DG, Manola J, Ladd C, Tamayo P, Renshaw AA, D'Amico AV, Richie JP, Lander ES, Loda M, Kantoff PW, Golub TR, Sellers WR (2002). Gene expression correlates of clinical prostate cancer behavior. Cancer Cell 1(2):203-209.

Tang YC, Zhang YQ, Clhawla NV, Krasser S (2009). SVMs modeling for highly imbalanced classification, IEEE Trans. Syst., Man, Cybern. - Part B Cybern. 39:281-288.

Tang YC, Zhang YQ, Huang Z, Hu XH, Zhao YC (2008). Recursive fuzzy granulation for gene subsets extraction cancer classification, IEEE Trans. Inform. Technol. Biomed. 12(6):723-730.

Theodoridis S, Koutroumbas K (1999). Pattern Recognition, Academic Press, New York.

Uncua Ö, Türkşenb IB (2007). A novel feature selection approach: Combining feature wrappers and filters. Inf. Sci. 177(2):449-466.

Vapnic VN (1998). Statistical Learning Theory. John Wiley and Sons, New York.

Vapnic VN (1996). The Nature of Statistical Learning Theory. Springer, New York.

Zhan F, Hardin J, Kordsmeier B, Bumm K, Zheng MZ, Tian E, Sanderson R, Yang Y, Wilson C, Zangari M, Anaissie E, Morris C, Muwalla F, Rhee FV, Fassas A, Crowley J, Tricot G, Barlogie B, John Shaughnessy JJ (2002). Global gene expression profiling of multiple myeloma, monoclonal gammopathy of undetermined significance, and normal bone marrow plasma cells. Blood 99:1745-1757.

7

On enhanced control charting for process monitoring

Saddam Akber Abbasi[1] and Muhammad Riaz[2]

[1]Department of Statistics, the University of Auckland, Auckland, New Zealand.
[2]Mathematics and Statistics Department, King Fahd University of Petroleum and Minerals, Dhahran, Saudi Arabia.

The information on auxiliary characteristics helps significantly in increasing the efficiency of control charts for detecting shifts in process parameters. In this study we proposed Shewhart type control charts, namely the A_r chart, the D_r chart and the K_r chart, which utilizes information on two auxiliary characteristics (X and Z) for improved monitoring of process location parameter with respect to a single quality characteristic of interest (Y). Assuming trivariate normality of (Y, X, Z), a general control chart structure is developed in the form of the three sigma and the probability limits. The performance of the proposed charts is compared with the usual Shewhart $\overline{Y}$ chart, the M_r chart of Riaz (2008a), the control limits of Zhang (1984) and Wade and Woodall (1993). It has been observed that the proposed charts perform superior, in terms of discriminatory power, as compared to the above mentioned counterparts, depending upon the correlation structure among the auxiliary characteristics and the quality characteristic of interest. The said superiority zone of the correlation structures, favoring the proposed charts, needs to be identified very carefully to apply it in a given situation.

Key words: Auxiliary characteristics mean control charts, location parameter, normality, power curves, quality characteristics.

INTRODUCTION

A process is generally described by its characteristics and out of these some are of main concern and others are of a supplementary nature. The characteristics of main concern are termed as quality characteristics of interest while the other characteristics are termed as auxiliary characteristics. The auxiliary characteristics need to be identified very carefully along with the characteristics of interest. An auxiliary characteristic may be an early measurement in a process, crude but simple to obtain measurement, a property that would be monitored etc. The quality characteristic of interest may be any current variable of major interest which needs to be monitored for example, weight of a machine component, diameter of a shaft, spinning speed of wheel etc.

It is a common practice to take benefit out of the information available on auxiliary variable(s), along with the main study variable(s) of interest, in order to improve the efficiency in statistical terms. There is a variety of literature available in this regard for example, Kiregyera (1984), Mukerjee et al. (1987), Singh (2001), Singh et al. (2004), Kadilar and Cingi (2005), Joarder (2009), (2011) and Omar and Joarder (2011). This idea of using information on some additional characteristic(s) (for example, auxiliary characteristic(s)) which are associated with the main quality characteristic of interest has also been used in quality control literature. Particularly in control charting methodology, it has been used in the form of cause-selecting and regression-adjusted control charts (for example, Mandel (1969); Zhang (1984); Hawkins (1991, 1993); Wade and Woodall (1993); Shu et al. (2005) and auxiliary information based control charts (for example, Riaz (2008a, b); Riaz and Does (2009)) for the sake of an improved process monitoring with respect to the quality characteristic of interest.

Riaz (2008a) proposed a location control chart, namely the M_r chart, in which he used the information of single auxiliary characteristic on regression pattern. Riaz (2008b) and Riaz and Does (2009) gave proposals for variability control charts based on a single auxiliary characteristic in which they used the auxiliary information on regression and ratio patterns respectively. There may be many real situations when more than one auxiliary characteristics are available to be used e.g. to monitor the inner diameter of a shaft its outer diameter and weight may be the two possible auxiliary characteristics. For the sake of simplicity we assume that there are two auxiliary characteristics available along with the quality characteristics of interest.

The rest of this article is organized as follows: The design structure of the proposed charts, performance evaluation measures and a comparison of the proposed charts with the usual Shewhart $\overline{Y}$ chart and the M_r chart of Riaz (2008a), the steps for using the proposed chart with help of simulated examples and finally, the paper ends with conclusions.

THE PROPOSED CHARTS

Suppose that the quality characteristic of interest is denoted by Y and the two auxiliary characteristics by X and Z. We write these three variables of this study in the form of a triplet as

$$(Y, X, Z) \quad . \quad \text{Let} \quad (Y, X, Z) \square N_3(\underline{\mu}, \Sigma) \quad \text{where}$$

$$\underline{\mu} = \begin{pmatrix} \mu_y \\ \mu_x \\ \mu_z \end{pmatrix} \text{ and } \Sigma = \begin{bmatrix} \sigma_{yy} & \sigma_{yx} & \sigma_{yz} \\ \sigma_{xy} & \sigma_{xx} & \sigma_{xz} \\ \sigma_{zy} & \sigma_{zx} & \sigma_{zz} \end{bmatrix}.$$

Here N_3 represents the trivariate normal distribution, μ_y, μ_x and μ_z represent the means of Y, X and Z, respectively; σ_{yy}, σ_{xx} and σ_{zz} represent the variances of Y, X and Z, respectively; σ_{yx}, σ_{yz} and σ_{xz} represent the co-variances between Y, X; Y, Z and X, Z; respectively.

Now the objective is to monitor the variations in Y by exploiting the information on X and Z. We consider here the case when the auxiliary characteristics X and Z remain stable over time. Also we assume that the spread parameters of Y is in-control so the only

parameter we are concerned with is the location parameter of Y, that is, μ_y. In a broader sense we can consider any process without cascade property (cf. Hawkins (1993)) where each variable may undergo a distributional change without affecting the other variables of the process.

To monitor the behaviour of Y, in terms of μ_y, taking into account the information on X and Z we need an estimator for μ_y which capitalizes the information on X and Z as well along with the information of Y. Let $(y_k, x_k, z_k) \text{ where } k = 1, 2, \ldots n$ be a trivariate random sample of size n drawn from (Y, X, Z). We considered three estimators of process location which uses the information of auxiliary characteristics X and Z, given as:

The regression type estimator given in Kadilar and Cingi (2005), defined as:

$$A_r = \overline{y} + b_{yx}(\mu_x - \overline{x}) + b_{yz}(\mu_z - \overline{z}) \tag{1}$$

The ratio type estimator proposed by Abu-Dayyeh et al. (2003), defined as:

$$D_r = \overline{y} \left(\frac{\mu_x}{\overline{x}} \right)^{\alpha_1} \left(\frac{\mu_z}{\overline{z}} \right)^{\alpha_2} \tag{2}$$

The ratio type estimator proposed by Kadilar and Cingi (2003), defined as:

$$K_r = \overline{y} \left(\frac{\mu_x}{\overline{x}} \right)^{\beta_1} \left(\frac{\mu_z}{\overline{z}} \right)^{\beta_2} + b_{yx}(\mu_x - \overline{x}) + b_{yz}(\mu_z - \overline{z}) \tag{3}$$

where $\overline{y}$, $\overline{x}$ and $\overline{z}$ are the sample means of Y, X and Z respectively. The quantities b_{yx} and b_{yz} are defined as:

$$b_{yx} = s_{yx} / s_{xx} \quad \text{and} \quad b_{yz} = s_{yz} / s_{zz}$$

where s_{xx} and s_{zz} are the sample variances of X and Z, respectively, s_{yx} and s_{yz} are the sample co-variances between Y, X and Y, Z, respectively. We used the optimal choices of $\alpha_1, \alpha_2, \beta_1$ and β_2 as reported in Abu-Dayyehh et al. (2003) and Kadilar and Cingi (2005), respectively, that is:

$$\alpha_1 = \frac{c_y b_{yx.z}}{c_x}, \alpha_2 = \frac{c_y b_{yz.x}}{c_z}, \beta_1 = \frac{s_y}{r_1 s_x} \rho_1^* \text{ and } \beta_2 = \frac{s_y}{r_2 s_z} \rho_2^*$$

Where

$$c_y = \frac{s_y}{\bar{y}}, \quad c_x = \frac{s_x}{\bar{x}}, \quad c_z = \frac{s_z}{\bar{z}}, \quad b_{yx.z} = \frac{\rho_{yx} - \rho_{yz}\rho_{xz}}{1-\rho_{xz}^2}, \quad b_{yz.x} = \frac{\rho_{yz} - \rho_{yx}\rho_{xz}}{1-\rho_{xz}^2}$$

$$\rho_1^* = \frac{\rho_{xz}(\rho_{yx}\rho_{xz} - \rho_{yz})}{1-\rho_{xz}^2} \quad \text{and} \quad \rho_2^* = \frac{\rho_{xz}(\rho_{yz}\rho_{xz} - \rho_{yx})}{1-\rho_{xz}^2}$$

The population means of the two auxiliary characteristics that is, μ_x and μ_z are assumed to be known in Equation 1 to 3. We will refer to the charts based on A_r, D_r and K_r estimators as the A_r chart, the D_r chart and the K_r chart, respectively.

Some distributional results

A general control chart structure that can be used with any of the three estimators will develop here.

First we define a pivotal quantity G, which is based on the sample statistic, say T, given as:

$$G = \sqrt{n}(T_r - \mu_y)/\sigma_y \qquad (4)$$

Here T represents any of the sample statistic given in Equation 1 to 3, that is, A_r, D_r or K_r. The distributional behaviour of G entirely depends on the four quantities namely n, ρ_{yx}, ρ_{yz} and ρ_{xz}. Here ρ_{yx}, ρ_{yz} and ρ_{xz} represent the correlations between Y, X; Y, Z and X, Z; respectively, where $\rho_{ij} = \sigma_{ij}/\sqrt{\sigma_{ii}\sigma_{jj}}$. Now we let the following:

$$\left. \begin{array}{l} \mu_G = g_2, \\ \sigma_G = g_3 \text{ and} \\ \alpha^{th} \text{ quantile of } G = G_\alpha \end{array} \right\}, \qquad (5)$$

where μ_G, σ_G and G_α are the mean, standard deviation and αth quartile of the distribution of G. The asymptotic results for coefficients g_2 and g_3 considering different choices of T are provided in the Appendix.

The results given in Appendix can be used satisfactorily for larger values of n or ρ_{ij} ($i = y, x, z = j$ where $i \neq j$).

For other choices of n and ρ_{ij}s, we need the true results for g_2, g_3 and G_α which may be obtained either analytically or through Monte Carlo simulations. To avoid

the analytical complications of dealing with the distributional properties of G in the form of g_2, g_3 and G_α, we have written a code in R language to obtain the simulation results for these quantities. For some representative values of n and ρ_{ij}s the simulation results of g_2 and g_3 are given in Table 1 while the lower and upper quartiles of G at $\alpha = 0.01, 0.005$ and 0.0027 are given in Tables 2 to 4, respectively for the A_r chart. The standard errors for the simulated results (reported in Tables 1 to 4) are less than 1%, which is acceptable in control chart studies (Schaffer and Kim, 2007). These simulation results are based on 1000 repetitions of 10,000 Monte Carlo simulations. Similar results can be easily obtained for D_r and K_r charts.

Control chart design

Based on the results given above, we are now in a position to define the design structure of a general control chart namely the T_r Chart. From the expressions given in (4) and (5) above, we have the following:

$$\left. \begin{array}{ll} \mu_G = g_2 & \Rightarrow \mu_{T_r} = \mu_y + g_2\sigma_y/\sqrt{n} \\ \sigma_G = g_3 & \Rightarrow \sigma_{T_r} = g_3\sigma_y/\sqrt{n} \\ G_\alpha = \alpha^{th} \text{ quantile of } G & \Rightarrow T_{r_\alpha} = \mu_y + G_\alpha\sigma_y/\sqrt{n} \end{array} \right\} \qquad (6)$$

where μ_{A_r}, σ_{A_r} and T_{r_α} are the mean, standard deviation and αth quartile of the distribution of T_r, respectively. Based on these results for μ_{T_r}, σ_{T_r} and T_{r_α}, we can define the control limits of the T_r charts, using the three sigma limit and the probability limit approaches, as:

Three Sigma Limits

$$CL = \mu_{T_r}, \quad LCL = \mu_{T_r} - 3\sigma_{T_r} \text{ and } UCL = \mu_{T_r} + 3\sigma_{T_r} \qquad (7)$$

where CL, LCL and UCL refer to the Central Line, Lower Control Limit and Upper Control Limit on the T_r chart and the results for μ_{T_r} and σ_{T_r} are given in (6).

Probability Limits

$$ML = T_{r_{0.50}}, \quad LPL = T_{r_{\alpha/2}} \text{ and } UPL = T_{r_{(1-\alpha/2)}} \qquad (8)$$

Table 1. Control chart coefficients g_2 and g_3 for the proposed A_r chart.

n	ρ_{xz}	ρ_{yx}	ρ_{yz}							
			0.2	0.5	0.6	0.7	0.2	0.5	0.6	0.7
			g_2				g_3			
5	0.1	0.2	0.02528	0.01118	0.00286	-0.02103	1.37879	1.25962	1.19871	1.11642
		0.5	0.02124	0.00101	0.00559	0.01226	1.25305	1.12344	1.09129	1.00844
		0.7	-0.00531	0.01388	-0.00072	0.00301	1.10444	0.98864	0.88997	0.7833
	0.4	0.2	0.00062	-0.00609	0.0072	0.01235	1.38015	1.33266	1.22746	1.1622
		0.5	-0.02645	-0.00976	-0.002	-0.00839	1.32587	1.22778	1.18168	1.10548
		0.7	-0.00705	0.00271	-0.0174	0.01366	1.15595	1.10066	1.06812	0.99845
	0.6	0.2	-0.00197	0.00907	0.01026	0.00406	1.46208	1.33059	1.27938	1.18668
		0.5	-0.00711	-0.02869	-0.00815	-0.00565	1.35712	1.33152	1.25687	1.16798
		0.7	-0.01363	-0.0016	-0.01275	0.00543	1.14878	1.19654	1.14881	1.10673
10	0.1	0.2	-0.00563	-0.00288	-0.00945	0.00688	1.08122	0.98617	0.92521	0.84061
		0.5	-0.00461	0.01465	0.00944	-0.00743	0.98483	0.8928	0.81227	0.71503
		0.7	-0.00273	0.00824	-2e-04	0.00255	0.83997	0.72319	0.63659	0.51959
	0.4	0.2	0.02833	0.01165	0.01507	-0.01221	1.11388	1.02812	0.96857	0.90049
		0.5	0.0087	-0.0062	0.00074	-0.01407	1.03116	0.98071	0.92882	0.86788
		0.7	0.00306	0.00767	0.00337	-0.00634	0.8959	0.87357	0.81322	0.75689
	0.6	0.2	-0.02319	-0.01109	0.00263	0.02549	1.15461	1.0691	1.02283	0.92831
		0.5	0.01838	0.01306	-0.01017	-0.00651	1.06936	1.04593	1.00541	0.95394
		0.7	0.00656	0.01254	0.00046	0.01008	0.93079	0.94729	0.92794	0.89932
15	0.1	0.2	0.001	-0.00371	-0.00448	-0.00194	1.04659	0.93876	0.85827	0.78882
		0.5	0.01472	-0.00889	-0.00796	0.01011	0.93186	0.82375	0.76034	0.66147
		0.7	-0.00161	-0.0061	0.01524	-0.00027	0.79915	0.67325	0.58489	0.45589
	0.4	0.2	-0.01385	0.00744	-0.00434	0.01175	1.06876	0.96603	0.92541	0.85329
		0.5	-0.0112	0.0072	0.00733	0.00566	0.96556	0.91324	0.88048	0.80839
		0.7	-0.00789	-0.00359	0.02181	-0.01146	0.84572	0.81578	0.7686	0.71474
	0.6	0.2	0.00597	0.00838	-0.00581	0.01725	1.08526	0.99464	0.94147	0.88688
		0.5	-0.00031	0.01003	-0.00629	0.01038	1.00483	0.97996	0.95624	0.89657
		0.7	0.00443	0.00981	0.01118	-0.00304	0.87396	0.91137	0.88681	0.84288

where ML, LPL and UPL refer to the Median Line, Lower Probability Limit and Upper Probability Limit on the T_r chart and the results for T_{r_α}s are given in (6). Here α is a pre-specified false alarm rate which is equally divided on both the tails to define the probability limits.

In probability limits approach it is preferable to replace the CL by ML as we did in (8). The control limits given in (7) and (8) are the specified parameters versions of the three sigma and probability limits structures of the T_r chart. In case of unspecified parameters the estimated versions may used by replacing μ_y and σ_y by their estimators $\hat{\mu}_y$ and $\hat{\sigma}_y$, where $\hat{\sigma}_y$ may be obtained from some spread control chart e.g. the R chart and $\hat{\mu}_y = \overline{T}_r$

based on an initial set of say m samples from the process in a stable situation. The choices of T as A_r, D_r and K_r will be referred as the proposed A_r chart, D_r chart and K_r chart, respectively.

PERFORMANCE EVALUATION AND COMPARISONS

To evaluate the performance of a control chart discriminatory power is a very popular measure. We evaluate here the performance of our proposed control charts using the same performance measure. Let the in control value of μ_y be denoted by μ_y^0 and the shifted value by μ_y^1. We define here μ_y^1 in terms of μ_y^0 and

Table 2. Quantile points of the distribution of G when $\alpha = 0.01$ for the proposed A_r chart.

			ρ_{yz}							
			0.2	0.5	0.6	0.7	0.2	0.5	0.6	0.7
n	ρ_{xz}	ρ_{yx}	Lower quantile points				Upper quantile points			
5	0.1	0.2	-3.97102	-3.78103	-3.6426	-3.65317	4.14905	3.73057	3.8889	3.43684
		0.5	-3.62557	-3.27497	-3.16787	-2.92716	3.78079	3.31657	3.38637	3.01347
		0.7	-3.44537	-3.12252	-2.82657	-2.58031	3.37663	3.07759	2.69982	2.61299
	0.4	0.2	-4.11569	-4.19893	-3.73861	-3.59456	4.30716	4.07241	3.77613	3.56266
		0.5	-4.41764	-3.683	-3.54701	-3.39483	3.71978	3.78464	3.80811	3.46128
		0.7	-3.60466	-3.36004	-3.34861	-2.9802	3.65047	3.5377	3.35836	3.04366
	0.6	0.2	-4.50682	-4.23655	-3.98565	-3.68707	4.41788	3.85878	3.88798	3.76618
		0.5	-4.23524	-4.55563	-3.95808	-3.67121	3.94551	3.86092	3.88779	3.40115
		0.7	-3.61571	-3.88482	-3.75627	-3.44119	3.34483	3.52922	3.48809	3.41596
10	0.1	0.2	-2.86258	-2.59285	-2.46205	-2.24404	2.82898	2.68028	2.42749	2.30314
		0.5	-2.64839	-2.3952	-2.22006	-1.98339	2.67217	2.39217	2.23577	1.94372
		0.7	-2.25481	-2.03972	-1.80749	-1.58932	2.15949	2.01814	1.77604	1.52854
	0.4	0.2	-2.96395	-2.83776	-2.54074	-2.4675	3.06357	2.85225	2.72894	2.49768
		0.5	-2.83123	-2.7103	-2.51405	-2.51962	2.72242	2.70332	2.5911	2.36777
		0.7	-2.47889	-2.46715	-2.23234	-2.20898	2.3918	2.45258	2.30924	2.17702
	0.6	0.2	-3.14441	-2.84443	-2.87916	-2.55466	3.09088	2.95342	2.7877	2.66518
		0.5	-2.9006	-2.81961	-2.71347	-2.78393	2.88504	2.96454	2.7522	2.55112
		0.7	-2.54317	-2.57074	-2.64255	-2.57708	2.65917	2.711	2.67683	2.61477
15	0.1	0.2	-2.72483	-2.36326	-2.27587	-2.0561	2.70286	2.53425	2.19781	2.01474
		0.5	-2.36822	-2.19739	-1.99993	-1.75113	2.43056	2.18883	2.00273	1.75705
		0.7	-2.06945	-1.82418	-1.59031	-1.29214	2.15204	1.78648	1.60332	1.33872
	0.4	0.2	-2.82178	-2.58514	-2.53264	-2.22029	2.78592	2.54471	2.42061	2.33632
		0.5	-2.46588	-2.28677	-2.30213	-2.20105	2.48775	2.38369	2.40907	2.17542
		0.7	-2.24404	-2.23402	-1.9964	-1.97943	2.26355	2.15898	2.0529	1.89697
	0.6	0.2	-2.7444	-2.60271	-2.45856	-2.31174	2.86499	2.56944	2.43297	2.47822
		0.5	-2.64485	-2.53601	-2.70039	-2.52149	2.66358	2.54752	2.57133	2.51461
		0.7	-2.40357	-2.45853	-2.31856	-2.38694	2.33469	2.44131	2.47169	2.38482

$\delta\sigma_y$ as:

$$\mu_y^1 = \mu_y^0 + \delta\sigma_y \tag{9}$$

Now the ability of the three sigma and the probability limits based design structures of the proposed charts is given by the following power expressions:

$$Power_{TChart} = Pr((T_r < LCL \text{ or } T_r > UCL) / \mu_y^1 = \mu_y^0 + \delta\sigma_y) \tag{10}$$
$(\text{for three sigma limits})$

$$Power_{TChart} = Pr((T_r < LPL \text{ or } T_r > UPL) / \mu_y^1 = \mu_y^0 + \delta\sigma_y) \tag{11}$$
$(\text{for probability limits})$

These power expressions for the proposed A_r chart may be evaluated using the distributional results given above. It is a common practice to evaluate such expressions by varying the values of δ and we do the same here in this article. By varying the values of δ from 0.0 to 3.0, we have evaluated the power expressions for different n by fixing the false rate at α level. It is to be mentioned that for power evaluation, the shifts are taken in μ_y in terms of σ_y units. The resulting powers/power curves are provided in the following sub-sections along with the comparison with other charts. We expect that the proposed control charts should detect any shift in the parameter of interest with a high probability, keeping the false alarm rate at fixed low level. We compare the

Table 3. Quantile points of the distribution of G when $\alpha = 0.005$ for the proposed A_r chart.

			ρ_{yz}							
			0.2	0.5	0.6	0.7	0.2	0.5	0.6	0.7
n	ρ_{xz}	ρ_{yx}		Lower quartile points				Upper quartile points		
5	0.1	0.2	-4.54539	-4.33528	-3.97429	-3.97104	4.74617	4.56065	4.17105	4.07236
		0.5	-4.47279	-4.31902	-4.18939	-3.77039	4.80639	3.96592	3.64165	3.71793
		0.7	-3.99686	-3.69871	-3.27888	-3.15671	4.04841	3.72148	3.69719	3.13192
	0.4	0.2	-5.2083	-4.82689	-4.35783	-4.14606	5.23378	4.41552	4.34827	4.09887
		0.5	-4.94663	-4.46005	-4.30744	-4.25492	4.75222	4.42103	4.13466	3.88508
		0.7	-4.17621	-3.93938	-3.87112	-3.97246	3.89642	3.93888	3.71839	3.65786
	0.6	0.2	-5.38393	-4.99306	-4.47041	-4.14798	5.42804	4.92632	4.58492	4.3932
		0.5	-4.81035	-4.49234	-5.05762	-4.555	4.66916	4.44825	4.45817	4.33252
		0.7	-4.31651	-4.25503	-4.01866	-4.20301	4.46666	4.15392	4.31538	4.16839
10	0.1	0.2	-3.15883	-2.94136	-2.71138	-2.5647	3.30012	2.89895	2.67749	2.70204
		0.5	-2.91722	-2.67483	-2.58528	-2.07595	2.80245	2.55839	2.48538	2.34822
		0.7	-2.59091	-2.22275	-1.98301	-1.86076	2.64974	2.22036	2.08953	1.71718
	0.4	0.2	-3.29782	-2.96312	-2.86768	-2.75342	3.22129	2.8768	2.91972	2.81218
		0.5	-3.09865	-3.09822	-2.8358	-2.79805	3.09848	3.01829	2.89781	2.71626
		0.7	-2.7672	-2.69623	-2.62449	-2.39855	2.66776	2.70528	2.67277	2.40624
	0.6	0.2	-3.48474	-3.14002	-2.9252	-2.94404	3.58448	3.12041	3.09335	2.92391
		0.5	-3.18597	-3.34953	-3.35038	-2.84796	3.42229	3.31241	2.99185	2.96006
		0.7	-2.81364	-2.92902	-2.91798	-2.77572	3.08454	3.055	2.91007	2.8502
15	0.1	0.2	-2.85949	-2.75897	-2.51351	-2.15714	3.04247	2.68486	2.51987	2.34164
		0.5	-2.77216	-2.46103	-2.1907	-1.90911	2.64823	2.22662	2.21324	1.87076
		0.7	-2.31086	-1.87003	-1.75189	-1.51016	2.39498	2.04127	1.70571	1.51232
	0.4	0.2	-3.09685	-2.83138	-2.49248	-2.53114	3.14351	2.94631	2.59407	2.51537
		0.5	-2.71765	-2.62582	-2.54215	-2.52317	2.66559	2.70403	2.57528	2.39982
		0.7	-2.37308	-2.45781	-2.36547	-2.33688	2.51149	2.49198	2.44836	2.23488
	0.6	0.2	-3.19168	-3.01762	-2.8691	-2.55438	3.23773	2.99301	2.87793	2.66199
		0.5	-2.94557	-3.18495	-2.72081	-2.79505	3.04275	3.07343	2.89973	2.75213
		0.7	-2.67956	-2.8704	-2.69916	-2.6941	2.69604	2.72166	2.69453	2.61663

performance of the proposed A_r, D_r and K_r charts, in terms of discriminatory power, with the existing counterparts serving the same purpose. These exiting counterparts are the M_r chart of Riaz (2008a) and the usual Shewhart $\bar{Y}$ chart. An indirect comparison with the control limits of Zhang (1984) and Wade and Woodall (1993) is also provided.

Comparison of proposed A_r, D_r and K_r charts with M_r and $\bar{Y}$ charts. We have evaluated the power expression (11) of the proposed A_r, D_r and K_r charts for $n = 15$, $\alpha = 0.01$ and $\delta = 0.0 - 0.3$ for different representative combinations of ρ_{yx}, ρ_{yz} and ρ_{xz}. These powers are plotted against δ and the resulting power curves are shown in the Figures 1 to 9 whereas Figure 10 presents power curves for a specific case when $n = 25$, to investigate the effect on sample size on the performance of the proposed chart. We have varied the values of ρ_{yx} and ρ_{xz} between Figures 1 to 10 and within each figure we have taken different choices of ρ_{yz}. The similar power curves for the M_r chart of Riaz (2008a) and the usual Shewhart $\bar{Y}$ chart are also provided in Figures 1 to 10.

The symbols used in Figures 1 to 10 are defined as:

$\bar{Y}$ refers to the power curve of the usual $\bar{Y}$ chart; $M_{r_{0.5}}$ refers to the power curve of the M_r chart when $\rho_{yx} = 0.5$;

Table 4. Quantile points of the distribution of G when $\alpha = 0.0027$ for the proposed A_r chart.

n	ρ_{xz}	ρ_{yx}	ρ_{yz} 0.2	0.5	0.6	0.7	0.2	0.5	0.6	0.7
			Lower quartile points				Upper quartile points			
5	0.1	0.2	-5.39974	-5.00368	-5.43807	-4.58529	5.01409	5.1413	5.01839	5.07115
		0.5	-4.52258	-5.14223	-5.18399	-4.04945	4.89941	4.66119	4.86417	4.38703
		0.7	-4.90532	-4.25886	-4.17131	-3.94228	4.7847	3.87925	4.36303	4.01529
	0.4	0.2	-5.50985	-5.12604	-4.94594	-4.99818	5.24367	5.46468	4.72265	4.79616
		0.5	-5.34707	-5.2568	-5.02791	-4.46698	5.13957	4.94856	4.7503	4.52779
		0.7	-5.14314	-4.12201	-4.77943	-4.28963	4.97546	4.12672	4.25718	4.49008
	0.6	0.2	-5.52532	-5.81717	-6.24932	-5.17663	7.13212	5.40913	5.56254	5.39732
		0.5	-6.33033	-5.10441	-4.90417	-5.89414	5.52745	5.18017	5.71029	5.04137
		0.7	-5.65621	-5.24406	-4.69353	-5.63756	5.52347	5.35344	5.33113	5.1099
10	0.1	0.2	-3.27143	-3.22835	-3.01715	-2.63105	3.22923	3.13473	3.13884	2.78724
		0.5	-3.05905	-2.8379	-2.69147	-2.37552	3.09342	2.98674	2.7367	2.38318
		0.7	-2.56669	-2.35595	-2.17836	-2.04356	2.85726	2.40829	2.21894	2.09169
	0.4	0.2	-3.58836	-3.79965	-3.46405	-3.03036	3.62924	3.27544	3.25358	3.03745
		0.5	-3.32176	-3.47487	-2.9817	-3.1034	3.23131	3.2391	3.28229	2.88333
		0.7	-3.03735	-2.76057	-2.95401	-2.63614	3.11502	3.12867	2.70669	2.59237
	0.6	0.2	-3.67768	-3.61903	-3.42601	-3.4583	3.93277	3.83308	3.446	3.25822
		0.5	-3.68748	-3.52476	-3.64232	-3.23163	3.3837	3.40624	3.4675	3.44901
		0.7	-3.06349	-3.36299	-3.16347	-3.55088	3.14006	3.3475	3.27739	3.26034
15	0.1	0.2	-3.0439	-2.90463	-2.71473	-2.37663	3.12921	2.96994	2.66318	2.40894
		0.5	-2.98606	-2.55459	-2.40091	-2.23551	2.95396	2.55838	2.31413	2.09056
		0.7	-2.58221	-2.10444	-1.76171	-1.54547	2.53261	2.06038	1.87562	1.68233
	0.4	0.2	-3.41324	-3.14535	-2.78668	-2.70091	3.23811	3.00637	2.80955	2.79875
		0.5	-3.053	-3.02028	-2.72883	-2.6213	3.25452	2.98602	2.58218	2.54357
		0.7	-2.73916	-2.66978	-2.4749	-2.5905	2.73159	2.57113	2.53498	2.42894
	0.6	0.2	-3.54761	-3.02662	-3.16646	-2.99985	3.39046	3.18865	3.32626	2.83037
		0.5	-3.10087	-3.02705	-3.01128	-2.90399	3.34941	3.10859	3.08018	2.92046
		0.7	-2.87782	-2.84046	-2.96856	-2.81365	2.6707	3.05733	2.96639	2.76807

$A_{r_{0.5}}$ refers to the power curve of the A_r chart when $\rho_{yz} = 0.5$; $D_{r_{0.5}}$ refers to the power curve of the D_r chart when $\rho_{yz} = 0.5$; $K_{r_{0.5}}$ refers to the power curve of the K_r chart when $\rho_{yz} = 0.5$;

Similarly the other symbols are defined.

The power curve analysis advocates the following for the proposed charts:

The D_r chart is performing better than all the other competing charts followed by the K_r chart. A_r chart although less efficient then D_r and K_r charts, performs better then M_r and $\overline{Y}$ charts. For a fixed value of ρ_{xz}, power of the proposed A_r, D_r and K_r charts increases with an increase in ρ_{yx} and ρ_{yz} (Figures 1 to 3). Power of the proposed charts decreases with an increase in ρ_{xz} and vice versa (Figures 1 and 4).

The proposed charts performs better than both the $\overline{Y}$ and M_r charts for low and moderate values of ρ_{xz} irrespective of the values of ρ_{yx} and ρ_{yz} (that is, for low, moderate and high values of ρ_{yx} and ρ_{yz}, the proposed

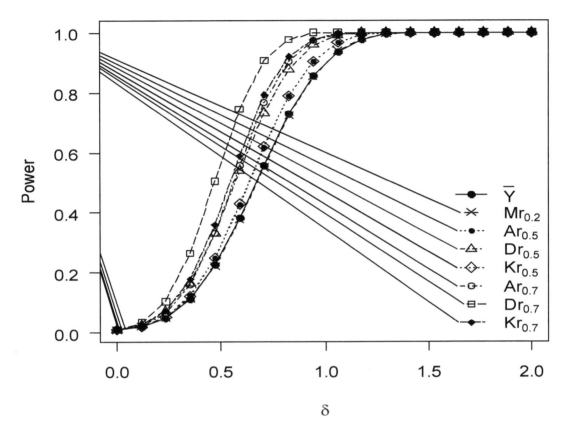

Figure 1. Power curves of $\bar{Y}, M_r, A_r, D_r$ and K_r charts for $\rho_{xz} = 0.1, \rho_{yx} = 0.2$ and $\rho_{yz} = 0.5$ and 0.7.

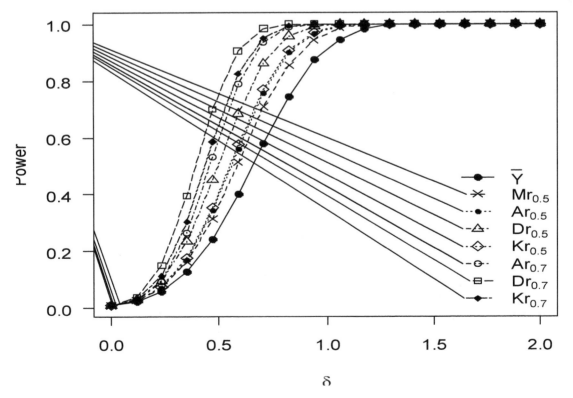

Figure 2. Power curves of $\bar{Y}, M_r, A_r, D_r$ and K_r charts for $\rho_{xz} = 0.1, \rho_{yx} = 0.5$ and $\rho_{yz} = 0.5$ and 0.7.

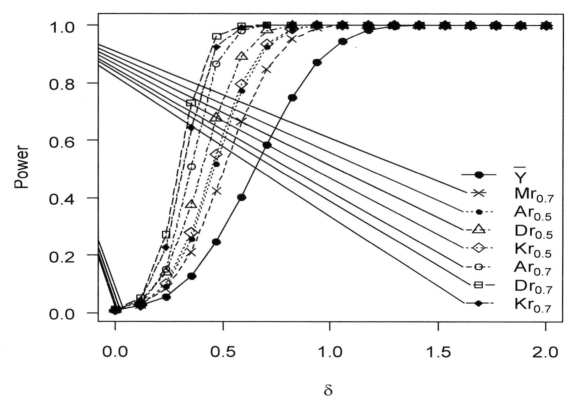

Figure 3. Power curves of $\bar{Y}, M_r, A_r, D_r$ and K_r charts for $\rho_{xz} = 0.1, \rho_{yx} = 0.7$ and $\rho_{yz} = 0.5$ and 0.7.

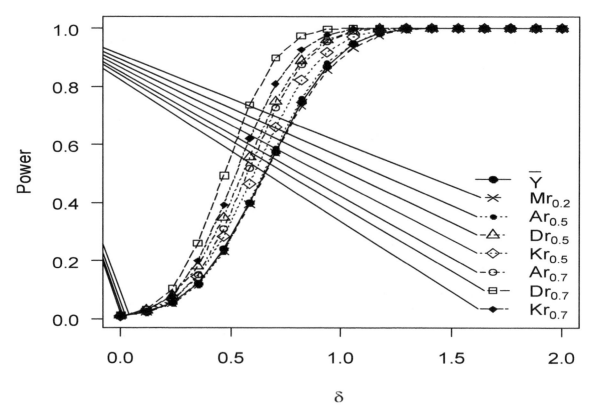

Figure 4. Power curves of $\bar{Y}, M_r, A_r, D_r$ and K_r charts for $\rho_{xz} = 0.4, \rho_{yx} = 0.2$ and $\rho_{yz} = 0.5$ and 0.7.

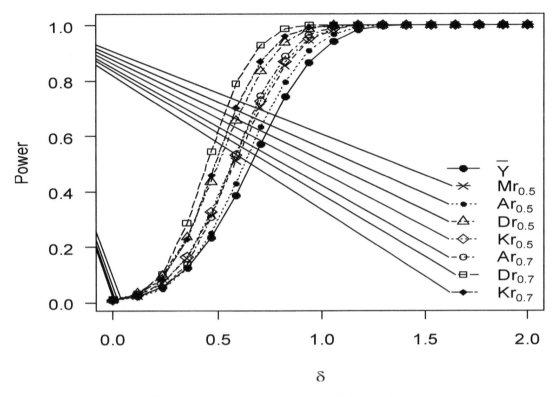

Figure 5. Power curves of $\bar{Y}, M_r, A_r, D_r$ and K_r charts for $\rho_{xz} = 0.4, \rho_{yx} = 0.5$ and $\rho_{yz} = 0.5$ and 0.7

provided ρ_{xz} is not high (Figures 1 to 6)). The M_r chart unconditionally performs better than the $\bar{Y}$ chart (Figures 1 to 10).

In brief, the proposed charts has shown better performance for the case when the auxiliary variables (X and Z) are not much correlated with each other but strongly/moderately correlated with main variable (Y). To be specific, the correlation between X and Z (that is, ρ_{xz}) should not exceed 0.50 while the correlations of X and Z with Y (that is, ρ_{yx} and ρ_{yz}) should be at least 0.30 in order to have a superior performance from the proposed charts. An important point to be noted is that these constraints on ρ_{xz}, ρ_{yx} and ρ_{yz} keeps relaxing with an increase in the value of n. This can be examined by looking at Figures 5 and 10. One can easily see the gaps among the curves in Figures 10 are more than those of in Figures 5. It means that the conditions on the correlation structures ρ_{xz}, ρ_{yx} and ρ_{yz} have been relaxed with the increase in sample size n.

A_r Chart vs. Zhang (1984); Wade and Woodall (1993) Zhang (1984) proposed an improvement over the separate use of the usual Shewhart's $\bar{Y}$ charts. Later Wade and Woodall (1993) gave an improvement over

Zhang (1984) by proposing their prediction limits. Riaz (2008a) proved superiority of the M_r chart over the control limits of Zhang (1984); Wade and Woodall (1993). We have shown from above that the charts proposed in this study perform better than the M_r chart. Hence we can indirectly draw the conclusion that the proposed A_r, D_r and K_r charts will perform better than the control limits of Zhang (1984); Wade and Woodall (1993).

ILLUSTRATIVE EXAMPLES

In this section we will illustrate the application procedure for one of the three proposed charts that is, the A_r chart. Let us consider the data in which we have two auxiliary characteristics (X and Z) and one quality characteristic of interest (Y). Suppose we have samples of size $n = 10$ available on 30 time points and the sample on each time point comes from one of the following two mechanisms:

Example 1: In all the 30 samples as a whole, 90% of the observations come from $N_3 \left(\begin{pmatrix} 0.0 \\ 0.0 \\ 0.0 \end{pmatrix}, \begin{bmatrix} 1.0 & 0.5 & 0.6 \\ 0.5 & 1.0 & 0.1 \\ 0.6 & 0.1 & 1.0 \end{bmatrix} \right)$ and

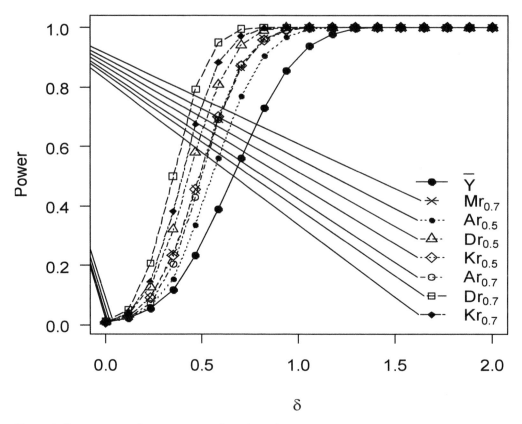

Figure 6. Power curves of $\bar{Y}, M_r, A_r, D_r$ and K_r charts for $\rho_{xz} = 0.4, \rho_{yx} = 0.7$ and $\rho_{yz} = 0.5$ and 0.7.

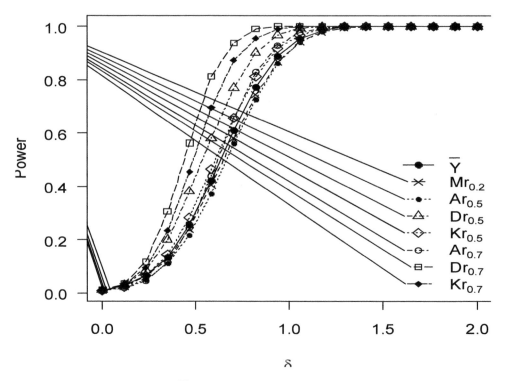

Figure 7. Power curves of $\bar{Y}, M_r, A_r, D_r$ and K_r charts for $\rho_{xz} = 0.6, \rho_{yx} = 0.2$ and $\rho_{yz} = 0.5$ and 0.7.

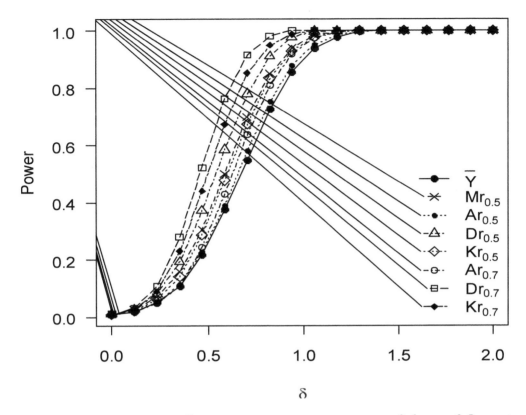

Figure 8. Power curves of $\bar{Y}, M_r, A_r, D_r$ and K_r charts for $\rho_{xz} = 0.6, \rho_{yx} = 0.5$ and $\rho_{yz} = 0.5$ and 0.7

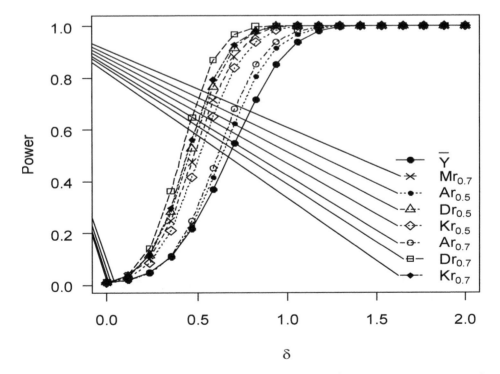

Figure 9. Power curves of $\bar{Y}, M_r, A_r, D_r$ and K_r charts for $\rho_{xz} = 0.6, \rho_{yx} = 0.7$ and $\rho_{yz} = 0.5$ and 0.7.

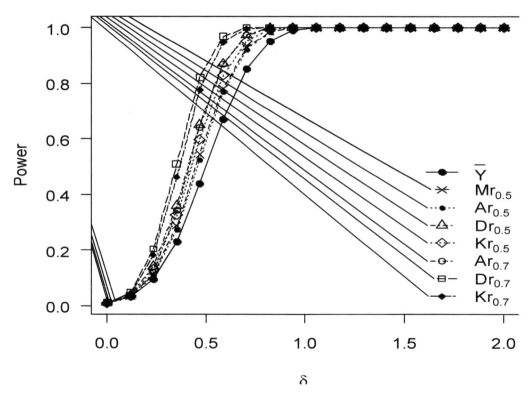

Figure 10. Power curves of $\bar{Y}, M_r, A_r, D_r$ and K_r charts for $\rho_{xz} = 0.4, \rho_{yx} = 0.5$ and $\rho_{yz} = 0.5$ and 0.7 when $n = 25$.

rest of the 10% come from $N_3 \left(\begin{pmatrix} 1.0 \\ 0.0 \\ 0.0 \end{pmatrix}, \begin{bmatrix} 1.0 & 0.5 & 0.6 \\ 0.5 & 1.0 & 0.1 \\ 0.6 & 0.1 & 1.0 \end{bmatrix} \right)$.

Example 2: First 20 samples are from $N_3 \left(\begin{pmatrix} 0.0 \\ 0.0 \\ 0.0 \end{pmatrix}, \begin{bmatrix} 1.0 & 0.5 & 0.6 \\ 0.5 & 1.0 & 0.1 \\ 0.6 & 0.1 & 1.0 \end{bmatrix} \right)$ and the last 10 samples are

from $N_3 \left(\begin{pmatrix} 1.0 \\ 0.0 \\ 0.0 \end{pmatrix}, \begin{bmatrix} 1.0 & 0.5 & 0.6 \\ 0.5 & 1.0 & 0.1 \\ 0.6 & 0.1 & 1.0 \end{bmatrix} \right)$. We have simulated the

datasets for the above mentioned two mechanisms of examples 1 and 2 so that we can have datasets with the known characteristics. The resulting datasets are used to calculate the required quantities for the proposed chart. The sample statistic A_r as defined in (1) and R_y (the sample range) are calculated for both the examples and are provided in the following Table 5.

The control limits for the proposed A_r chart are calculated using $\alpha = 0.01$ for the two examples under discussion. The two sets of limits are given as:

(For example 1)

$LCL = \bar{A}_r + G_{0.005}\hat{\sigma}_y/\sqrt{n} = -0.535$

$CL = \bar{A}_r = 0.121$

$UCL = \bar{A}_r + G_{0.995}\hat{\sigma}_y/\sqrt{n} = 0.781$

where $\hat{\sigma}_y = \bar{R}_y/d_2 = 2.874/3.078 = 0.934$, $G_{0.005} = -2.220$, $G_{0.995} = 2.236$,

$\rho_{xz} = 0.1, \rho_{yx} = 0.5, \rho_{yz} = 0.6, n = 10, \alpha = 0.01$

(For example 2)

$LCL = \bar{A}_r + G_{0.005}\hat{\sigma}_y/\sqrt{n} = -0.728$

$CL = \bar{A}_r = -0.061$

$UCL = \bar{A}_r + G_{0.995}\hat{\sigma}_y/\sqrt{n} = 0.611$

where $\hat{\sigma}_y = \bar{R}_y/d_2 = 2.925/3.078 = 0.9502$, $G_{0.005} = -2.220$, $G_{0.995} = 2.236$,

$\rho_{xz} = 0.1, \rho_{yx} = 0.5, \rho_{yz} = 0.6, n = 10, \alpha = 0.01$

Now values of the statistic A_r given in Table 5 are plotted against their respective control limits given above. The resulting control chart displays of the A_r chart are presented in Figures 11 and 12 for Examples 1 and 2 respectively.

According to our decision rule for the proposed A_r chart, we received out-of-control signals at time points

Table 5. Sample statistics A_r and R_y fro the simulated data sets.

Sample Number	Example 1		Example 2	
	A_r	R_y	A_r	R_y
1	-0.1953	3.4072	-0.2522	2.3536
2	0.9956	3.4576	-0.5479	3.7193
3	0.3632	3.3511	-0.0228	3.1412
4	0.3848	2.4604	0.3154	5.0663
5	0.0504	3.2620	-0.3051	2.4668
6	-0.2662	1.8949	-0.0692	2.6307
7	-0.3812	1.7086	0.2455	3.8516
8	1.4919	2.2800	0.1176	1.4283
9	-0.2341	2.2169	0.0573	2.9638
10	0.1919	3.9100	-0.2906	2.8699
11	-0.2110	2.3610	-0.0198	3.2805
12	0.0577	2.9506	-0.0261	2.6952
13	-0.1008	2.3926	0.0244	2.1876
14	-0.4243	2.4553	-0.4366	2.8410
15	-0.0554	2.8706	-0.1345	2.8980
16	0.1396	2.7692	0.1654	1.9662
17	-0.1152	2.3398	-0.0683	1.9612
18	0.6356	2.9082	0.2092	3.6413
19	0.1922	3.4963	0.1461	3.5290
20	-0.0131	2.1525	-0.3310	3.0069
21	0.1314	2.2191	1.0648	2.4157
22	0.1363	2.5550	0.7475	3.1311
23	1.0418	3.4011	0.7258	2.7343
24	-0.0354	2.9528	0.6691	2.3613
25	-0.2625	2.3061	0.7959	3.3186
26	-0.1491	2.9588	0.9752	5.4543
27	0.1727	2.3281	0.9220	2.6533
28	0.2465	4.1356	1.0267	2.7691
29	-0.5724	3.9148	1.0901	3.8828
30	0.4033	4.8015	0.9544	2.9581

#2, 8, 23 and 29 as can be seen in Figure 11. Similarly the out-of-control signals are received at time point's #21 to 30 as can be seen in Figure 12 (which is infact a permanent shift in the location parameter μ_y).

Conclusions

In this study we proposed three Shewhart type control charts, namely the A_r chart, the D_r chart and the K_r chart. These charts exploit the information of two auxiliary characteristics for the sake of an improved monitoring of the location parameter of the quality characteristic of interest. The design structure of the proposed charts has been developed in the form of the three sigma and the probability limits based on trivariate normality

assumption. Comparison of the proposals has been made with the existing counterparts including the usual $\overline{Y}$ chart and the proposals of Zhang (1984); Wade and Woodall (1993); Riaz (2008a). The comparisons revealed that the D_r chart is best among all the charts investigated in this study. All the new proposals outperformed the said existing counterparts in terms of discriminatory power. This superiority of the proposed chart demands the auxiliary characteristics to be highly/moderately correlated with the main quality characteristic of interest but not having high correlations with each other.

The proposals of this article are of Shewhart type, focusing on an improved monitoring of the location parameter. However EWMA and CUSUM type structures can also be devised by using these location estimators,

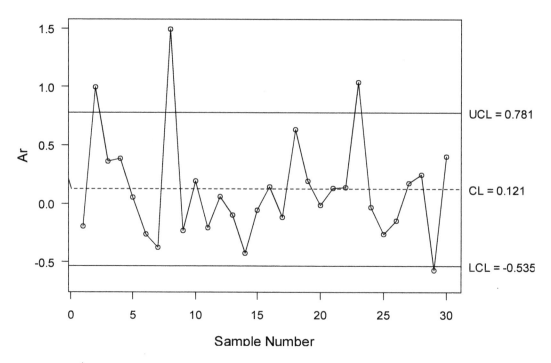

Figure 11. A_r chart for Example 1.

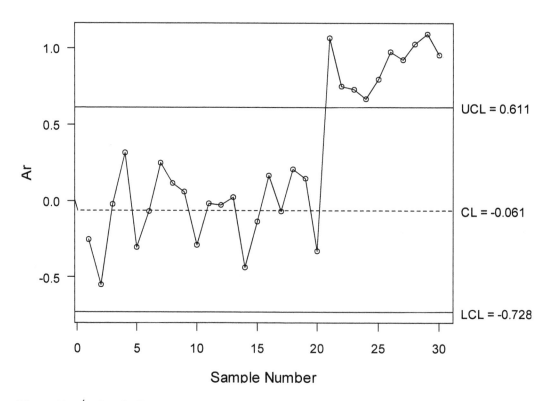

Figure 12. A_r chart for Example 2.

for efficient detection of small deviations from the parameter value or alternatively some extra sensitizing rules can also be carefully planned to be used with its control structure.

REFERENCES

Abu-Dayyeh WA, Ahmed MS, Ahmed RA, Muttlak HA (2003). Some estimators of a finite population mean using auxiliary information. Appl. Math. Comput. 139:287-298.

Hawkins DM (1991). Multivariate quality control based on regression-adjusted variables. Technometrics 33:61-75.

Hawkins DM (1993). Regression adjustment for variables in multivariate quality control. J. Qual. Technol. 25(3):170-182.

Joarder AH (2009). Moments of the product and ratio of two correlated chi-square random variables. Stat. Pap. 50(3):581-592.

Joarder AH (2011). Robustness of correlation coefficient and variance ratio under elliptical distributions. Tech. Rep., No. 422 - Department of Mathematics and Statistics, King Fahd University of Petroleum and Minerals - Saudi Arabia.

Kadilar C, Cingi H (2005). A new estimator using two auxiliary variables. Appl. Math. Comput. 162(2):901-908.

Kiregyera B (1984). Regression type estimators using two auxiliary variables and the model of double sampling form finite populations. Metrika 31:215-226.

Mandel BJ (1969). The regression control chart. J. Qual. Technol. 1:1-9.

Mukerjee R, Rao TJ, Vijayan K (1987). Regression type estimator using multiple auxiliary information. Aust. J. Stat. 29:244-254.

Omar MH, Joarder AH (2011). Some moment characteristics of the ratio of correlated sample variances. Technical Report No. 4223 - Department of Mathematics and Statistics, King Fahd University of Petroleum and Minerals - Saudi Arabia.

Riaz M (2008a). Monitoring process mean level using auxiliary information. Stat. Neerlandica 62(4):458-481.

Riaz M (2008b). Monitoring process variability using auxiliary information. Comput. Stat. 23(2):253-276.

Riaz M, Does RJMM (2009). A process variability control chart. Comput. Stat. 24(2): 345-368.

Schaffer JR, Kim MJ (2007). Number of replications required in control chart Monte Carlo simulation studies, Communications in Statistics: Simulation and Computation. 36(5):1075-1087.

Shu L, Tsung F, Tsui KL (2005). Effects of estimation errors on cause-selecting charts. IIE Trans. 37:559-567.

Singh GN (2001). On the use of transformed auxiliary variable in the estimation of population mean in two phase sampling. Stat. Transit. 5:405-416.

Singh HP, Upadhyaya LN, Chandra P (2004). A general family of estimators for estimating population mean using two auxiliary variables in two phase sampling. Stat. Transit. 6:1055-1077.

Wade M, Woodall WH (1993). A review and analysis of cause-selecting control charts. J. Qual. Technol. 25:161-169.

Zhang GX (1984). A new type of control charts and a theory of diagnosis with control charts. World Quality Congress Transactions. Am. Soc. Qual. Control, Lond. 25:175-185.

APPENDIX

Here we will present asymptotic results of g_2 and g_3 for different choices of T

1. When $T = A_r$

From Kadilar and Cingi (2005), we have:

$$g_2 \approx 0$$
$$g_3 = \sqrt{1 - \rho_{yx}^2 - \rho_{yz}^2 + 2\rho_{yx}\rho_{yz}\rho_{xz}}$$

2. When $T = D_r$

From Abu-Dayyeh et al. (2003), we have:

$$g_2 = \frac{1}{2\sqrt{n}}\left[\frac{\sigma_x}{\mu_x}b_{yx.z} + \frac{\sigma_z}{\mu_z}b_{yz.x} - \frac{\sigma_y}{\mu_y}b_{y.xz}\right]$$

$$g_3 = \sqrt{(1 - \rho_{y.xz}^2) - \frac{1}{4n}\left(\frac{\sigma_x}{\mu_x}b_{yx.z} + \frac{\sigma_z}{\mu_z}b_{yz.x} - \frac{\sigma_y}{\mu_y}b_{y.xz}\right)^2}$$

3. When $T = K_r$

From Kadilar and Cingi (2005), we have:

$$g_2 = \frac{\sqrt{n}}{\sigma_y}E\left\{\left(-\alpha_1\frac{\mu_y}{\mu_x} - b_1\right)(\bar{x} - \mu_x) + \left(-\alpha_2\frac{\mu_y}{\mu_z} - b_2\right)(\bar{z} - \mu_z) + (\bar{y} - \mu_y)\right\}$$

$$g_3 = \sqrt{\begin{array}{l} 1 + (\rho_1^* + \rho_{yx})^2 + (\rho_2^* + \rho_{yz})^2 + 2(\rho_1^* + \rho_{yx})(\rho_2^* + \rho_{yz})\rho_{xz} - 2(\rho_1^* + \rho_{yx})\rho_{yx} - 2(\rho_2^* + \rho_{yz})\rho_{yz} - \\ \left(\frac{n}{\sigma_y}\right)^2\left(E\left\{\left(-\alpha_1\frac{\mu_y}{\mu_x} - b_1\right)(\bar{x} - \mu_x) + \left(-\alpha_2\frac{\mu_y}{\mu_z} - b_2\right)(\bar{z} - \mu_z) + (\bar{y} - \mu_y)\right\}\right)^2 \end{array}}$$

8

Multi-core large-scale image-based modeling

Kun Li, Chao Song, Jingyu Yang and Jianmin Jiang

Tianjin University, Tianjin 300072, China.

Large-scale image-based modeling is a challenging and important research topic, which has wide applications in various areas. Existed serial methods consume a significant amount of time for large problems. With the emergence of multi-core computers, it is possible to speed up the method using central processing unit (CPU) parallelism. In this paper, we present the design and implementation of multi-core large-scale image-based modeling that exploits hardware parallelism to efficiently solve the large-scale 3-D scene reconstruction problem. We explore the use of multi-core CPU to achieve high speedups for the whole problem. The speedup ratio can be close to the number of cores. Experimental results show that our method achieves the acceleration of the whole algorithm and also ensures the accuracy of the 3-D reconstruction.

Key words: Large-scale image-based modeling, multi-core, central processing unit (CPU) parallelism, 3-D reconstruction, speedup ratio.

INTRODUCTION

Image-based modeling is a classic and hot issue in computer vision and image processing, and its goal is to create 3-D models from a collection of 2-D image measurements. Some methods (Lavoie et al., 2004; Wang et al., 2012) achieve the 3-D reconstruction with the help of structured light, but it is difficult for them to recover the textures of the scene. Another category of methods (Rander et al., 1997; Liu et al., 2011) depend on multi-camera arrays to obtain high quality 3-D models, but the costs of building multi-camera systems are very high. Recently, there has been a renewed interest in large-scale image-based modeling systems, especially those of which use the images captured by uncalibrated cameras, or collected from the Internet (Agarwal et al., 2010; Snavely et al., 2006). The problem for this kind of methods is usually large-scale: with hundreds of or thousands of input images. Many methods adopt serial processing mode, which needs several days to reconstruct a 3-D model from several hundreds of images. With the rapid development of parallel computation resources, Agarwal et al. (2009) achieve distributed computation running on a cluster of computers, and significantly shorten the running time. Since the hard disk space is local and not shared, they need to consider the problem of data distribution and communication. The emergence of multi-core computers motivates Wu et al. (2011) to propose a multi-core bundle adjustment algorithm (a key component of the problem) and achieve a 10x to 30x boost in speed over existing systems.

In this paper, we present a multi-core implementation for the whole framework of large-scale image-based modeling, which significantly improves the computational efficiency without loss of reconstruction quality. We use central processing unit (CPU) parallelism to achieve high speedups over existing serial systems. The speedup ratio can be close to the number of cores.

THE PROPOSED METHOD

Pipeline of the large-scale image-based modeling

As show in Figure 1, the large-scale image-based modeling

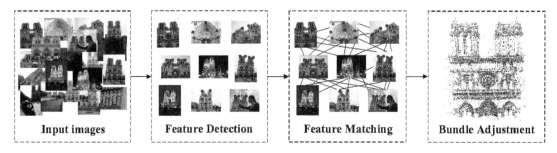

Figure 1. The pipeline of classic large-scale image-based modeling.

method mainly contains three steps: feature detection, feature matching, and bundle adjustment. The input images are captured with uncalibrated cameras or collected from the Internet, and the number of images is usually large. In the first step, existed methods process the images one by one: extracting the EXIF tags, recording the focal length, and generating a shell script which processes the operations of converting file formats, detecting the features with scale-invariant feature transform (SIFT), and compressing the features in a serial manner. The second step uses the Approximate Nearest Neighbor (ANN) library (Arya et al., 1998) to match SIFT features, which costs about half of the whole processing time. Given a set of measured image feature locations and correspondences, the goal of the final step is to find 3-D point positions and camera parameters that minimize the reprojection error. The optimization problem is usually formulated as a non-linear least squares problem and solved by the Levenberg-Marquardt (LM) algorithm (Nocedal and Wright, 2006).

Multi-core parallelized scheme

In this section, we present our multi-core parallelized scheme for the three steps of the large-scale image-based modeling.

Feature detection

Although shell programming does not support multi-thread, there is still a way to parallelize the work by creating children processes in a multi-core environment. We first divide the input images into M lists that are saved in M files, where M is the number of available cores. Then, we generate a script of extracting the EXIF tags and recording the focal length for each list, and create a child process to complete the corresponding operation. The same is used for generating the shell script for feature detection.

Feature matching

We use message passing interface (MPI), instead of multi-thread, to parallelize this step in distributed environment. MPI does not share variables in the global scope but maintains independent code and data for each process. These processes communicate with each other by the respective data buffer. Therefore, the features generated in the first step are not shared by these processes, which must be read more than once. Fortunately, we find that reading these data does not cost too much time and the time of reading keys for all these processes is the same as reading these keys once. We adopt master-slave mode to achieve process collaboration. The main process is responsible for dividing tasks and then also participates in the calculation. Denote $f(i)$ as the

matching number for the image i. The amount of computation for the process j that is assigned the task of matching the images from m to n is:

$$F(j) = \sum_{i=m}^{n} f(i). \qquad (1)$$

Hence, the main process divides the tasks so that the computation of each process is roughly equal, and then sends the image indexes to the corresponding process. Finally, the main process maintains the last task for its own computation.

Bundle adjustment

In this step, we use the computation interface provided by the PBA method (Wu et al., 2011). The reconstruction accuracy of the PBA method is less than that of the original serial method (Snavely et al., 2006), which will affect the initialization and further the final reconstruction. Therefore, for some important initialization, we use the original bundle adjustment method (Snavely et al., 2006), and then adopt the PBA method to speed up.

RESULTS

We evaluate the performances of the proposed method on three datasets: *Rilievo* (93 pictures) captured with a Samsung digital camera, *NotreDame1* (103 pictures) and *NotreDame2* (204 pictures) provided by Noah Snavely (Snavely et al., 2006). All the experiments are individually performed on two workstations: one with three-core CPUs clocked at 3.2 GHz and 4 GB RAM running a 32-bit Ubuntu operating system, and the other with eight-core CPUs clocked at 0.8 GHz and 16 GB RAM running a 64-bit OpenSUSE operating system (Figure 2).

Table 1 gives the quantitative evaluation of the proposed method for the three datasets, compared with a serial method (Snavely et al., 2006). The speedup ratio is $S = t_s / t_p$, which is the ratio of serial time t_s over parallel time t_p. This is an intuitive evaluation of how much is accelerated. The efficiency is $E = S / n$, where n is the number of threads or processes. The cost is $C = t_p \times n = t_s / E$. The degree of contribution of the

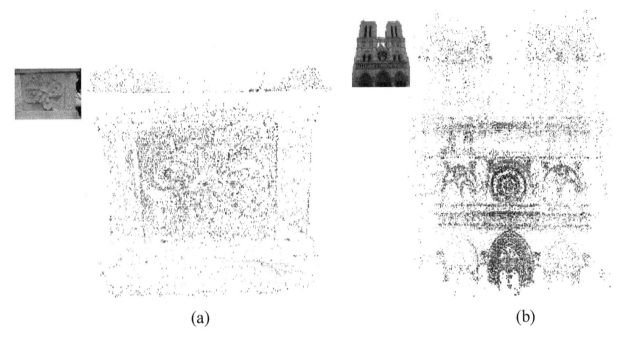

Figure 2. 3-D point clouds of (a) *Rilievo* and (b) *NotreDame1* reconstructed by our method.

Table 1. Quantitative evaluation of the proposed method for three datasets.

Dataset	Step	Serial time	Parallel time	Cores	Speedup ratio	Efficiency (%)	Cost	Proportion (%)	Degree of contribution
R	FD	5m22s	1m56s	3	2.78	92.53	5m48s	17.09	1.12
	FM	9m44s	3m27s	3	2.82	94.04	10m21s	31.00	1.25
	BA	16m18s	1m58s	3	8.29	276.27	5m54s	51.91	1.84
	All	31m18s	7m7s	3	4.33	131.24	23m51s		
N1	FD	40m20s	9m1s	5	4.58	91.68	45m5s	26.68	1.26
	FM	1h21m47s	21m27s	5	3.81	76.25	1h47m15s	54.10	1.66
	BA	29m3s	6m28s	5	4.49	89.85	32m20s	19.22	1.18
	All	2h40m43s	35m33s	5	4.52	90.42	2h57m45s		
N2	FD	1h23m2s	19m17s	5	4.31	86.12	1h36m25s	14.93	1.13
	FM	6h32m44s	1h32m4s	5	4.27	85.32	7h40m20s	70.92	2.19
	BA	1h20m22s	52m5s	5	1.54	30.86	4h50m25s	14.45	1.05
	All	8h36m31s	2h41m28s	5	3.20	63.98	13h27m20s		

R, Rilievo; N1, NotreDame1; N2, NotreDame2; FD, feature detection; FM, feature matching; BA, bundle adjustment.

step i is $Q_i = \frac{1}{1+q_i(1/s_i-1)}$, where q_i is the proportion of the computation of the step i in the whole system, and s_i is the speedup ratio of the step i. The more the degree of contribution is, the larger the played acceleration role is.

As shown in Table 1, for feature detection step, the speedup ratio is close to the number of cores due to the small computation of serial component, which complies with Amdahl's law. The same is used for feature matching step. For *Rilievo* dataset in the bundle adjustment step, the speedup ratio is larger than the number of cores, and the execution efficiency is even equal to 276.27%. This is because our approach is not simply the parallelization of the original program, but replacing its part with other parallelized process, which does not meet the condition of Amdahl's law. The total execution time of each dataset is less than the sum of phased execution times, since the separate implementation of each step requires some additional overhead such as process creation. It can be seen that the proportion of the feature matching step increases with the expansion of the scale of the problem. The high degree of parallelism in the feature matching step has an important role to improve the execution efficiency of the whole system. Figure 1 gives the 3-D point clouds of *Rilievo* and *NotreDame1* reconstructed by our method. The left-top corner of each subfigure shows one of the input images. It can be observed that our method maintains high quality of reconstruction when speeding up the algorithm.

Conclusion

In this paper, we present multi-core solutions to the problem of large-scale image-based modeling that run on currently available CPUs. These systems deliver a significant boost in speed over existing serial systems while maintaining the high quality of 3-D reconstruction. In the future, we would like to further improve the parallelism of various steps, especially for bundle adjustment, and at the same time ensure the high accuracy of 3-D reconstruction.

ACKNOWLEDGEMENTS

This work is supported by the NSF of China (61072062), Ph.D. Programs Foundation of Ministry of Education of China (20120032120040), the Tianjin Research Program of Application Foundation and Advanced Technology (12JCYBJC10300, 13JCQNJC03900), and the Research Academy of China Space Technology.

REFERENCES

Agarwal S, Snavely N, Simon I, Seitz S, Szeliski R (2009). Building Rome in a day. In: Proceeding of Int. Conf. Computer Vision, pp. 72–79.

Agarwal S, Snavely N, Seitz S, Szeliski R (2010). Bundle adjustment in the large. In: Proceeding of Eur. Conf. Computer Vision, pp. 29–42.

Arya S, Mount DM, Netanyahu NS, Silverman R, Wu AY (1998). An optimal algorithm for approximate nearest neighbor searching fixed dimensions. J. ACM. 45(6):891–923.

Lavoie P, Ionescu D, Petriu EM (2004). 3-D object model recovery from 2-D images using structured light. IEEE Trans. Instrumentation and Measurement. 53(2):437–443.

Liu Y, Stoll C, Gall G, Seidel HP, Theobalt C (2011). Markerless Motion Capture of Interacting Characters Using Multi-view Image Segmentation. In: Proceeding of IEEE Int'l Conf. Computer Vision and Pattern Recognition.

Nocedal J, Wright SJ (2006). Numerical Optimization. (2ed.). Springer.

Rander P, Narayanan PJ, Kanade T (1997). Virtualized reality: constructing time-varying virtual worlds from real world events. In: Proceeding of IEEE Conf. Visualization, Phoenix, Arizona, United States, pp. 277–284.

Snavely N, Seitz S, Szeliski R (2006). Photo tourism: exploring photo collections in 3D. ACM Transactions on Graphics (TOG). 25(3):835–846.

Wang J, Zhang C, Zhu W, Zhang Z, Xiong Z, Chou PA (2012). 3D scene reconstruction by multiple structured-light based commodity depth cameras: In: Proceeding of Int. Conf. Acoustics, Speech, and Signal Processing, Kyoto, Japan.

Wu C, Agarwal S, Curless B, Seitz S (2011). Multicore bundle adjustment. In: Proceeding of IEEE Conf. Computer Vision and Pattern Recognition, pp. 3057–3064.

9

Iris localization through Hough clustering

Lili Pan and Mei Xie

University of Electronic Science and Technology of China, 2006 Xiyuan Avenue, Gaoxin West Zone, 611731, Chengdu, China.

Occlusion, reflections and iris shape deformations are the obstacles that stand in the way of a complete solution to iris localization problem. How to reject outliers caused by occlusion and reflections as much as possible before ellipse or spline fitting is a key challenge. For this reason, we proposed a Hough clustering method, which utilizes the shape configuration of iris edge points and their local appearance characteristics to distinguish iris from non-iris edge points. The experimental results show an improved localization performance of the proposed algorithm on CASIA2.0 and 3.0 databases.

Key words: Hough clustering, local edge point experts.

INTRODUCTION

Iris recognition is one of the most reliable biometric identifier and is the preferred mode for biometric recognition (Daugman, 1993). As an emerging subfield in biometric recognition, iris recognition has enjoyed much attention in recent years (Daugman, 1993; Du et al., 2010; He et al., 2009; Wildes, 1997), and substantial progress has been made since the initial works by Du et al. (2009). Nonetheless, many aspects of iris recognition remain only partially solved.

One crucial, yet elusive, component of iris recognition is the iris localization problem. As with other biometric recognition problems, registration is a key to accurate iris recognition since it allows "apples-to-apples" comparisons. Imprecision in iris localization is the principal cause of miss-match errors (He et al., 2009).

The difficulty of iris localization stems from the complexities of real-world images, such as, the presence of eyelid/eyelash occlusion, specular reflections and out-of-axis gazing. The difficulty of the problem is compounded by the typical expectation of real-time processing speeds, which limits the range of solutions that can be employed.

Most existing methods to iris localization effect a compromise between the goals of robustness and efficiency. A common theme amongst these methods is the use of a simplifying assumption about iris geometry coupled with an exhaustive search procedure. An example includes the early work of Daugman (1993), where the integro-differential operator was proposed for robust iris localization. Another case is that of Wildes (1997), where the use of Hough voting was proposed for iris localization. The drawbacks of these methods are: (1) a strict circular shape hypothesis cannot account for person specific iris characteristics as well as perspective deformations; (2) an exhaustive search over a 3D parameter space is computationally expensive. Remedies for these drawbacks have been proposed in recent works (Du et al., 2009; Zuo and Schmid, 2010; Proença, 2010). These methods typically precede two stages. First, the iris region is detected by some learning based method (that is, adaboost, neural network, etc.). This significantly reduces the number of candidates for iris edge points. Second, an ellipse or smoothing spline is applied to fit these edge points. Although, this two stage scheme typically incurs low computational cost, it depends on the accurate delineation between iris and non-iris edge points in the first stage. As such, in this work, we propose an approach that more accurately detects relevant edge points and their physiological assignment (that is, iris inner and outer edges).

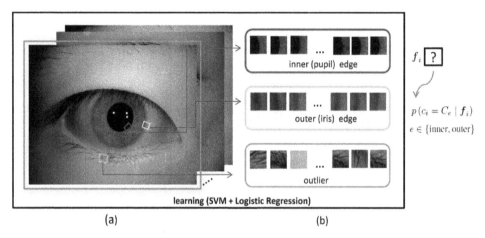

Figure 1. Local edge point experts.

PROPOSED METHODS

Here, we will first describe how to detect image edge points using multi-scale theory. Next, we introduce the local edge point experts' model for estimating the confidence of one edge point belonging to iris edge only according to its local patch appearance. Also, we explain Hough clustering for iris edge point selecting from all edge points. Finally, we present smooth spline fitting as our curve fitting method.

Edge point detection

We firstly detect image edge points based on multi-scale theory (Lindeberg, 1998). Based on multi-scale theory, detecting edges at a coarse scale can exclude noise and high frequency image texture as much as possible, while localizing edges at a finer scale has high localization precision. Therefore, we first detect edge points at a detection scale (coarse scale) to avoid the influence of eyelash and noise, and then localize the edge points detected at a coarse scale to a finer scale. In this paper, the multi-scale edge detection method based on local directional derivatives (Lindeberg, 1998) was adopted to obtain a set of edge points $(x_1; y_1)^T$; $(x_2; y_2)^T \dots (x_N; y_N)^T$ along with their gradient directions $\{\hat{A}_1; \hat{A}_2; \dots \hat{A}_N\}$. In addition, the gradient direction of every edge point was calculated at a coarse image scale to avoid the disturbing of noise and iris texture.

Local edge point experts

Local discriminative model is an efficient way to measure the similarity between the testing local feature and the learned features; however, it is seldom used in iris localization. In this work, we employ it to estimate the likelihood of an edge point belonging to iris inner or outer edge only according to its local patch feature matching. Let $\{f_1; f_2; \dots f_N\}$ denotes the local patch features of edge points. They are extracted from iris image, in which the specular reflections have been removed. The local image patch feature $f_i \in R^M$ of the i-th edge point refers to the vector concatenation of image intensity values within a $P \times P$ region around this position $x_i = (x_i; y_i)^T$. The dimension M is equal to $P \times P$. Given local image patch feature of every edge point, its local expert (the likelihood of f_i being iris inner or outer edge

according to local patch feature matching) can be calculated by employing a support vector machines (SVM) classifier. Similar local experts have been used to creat effect in deformable face fitting (Saragih et al., 2009). In this work, it was used to approximate the probability of an edge point belonging to iris inner or outer edge through local patch feature matching. The local edge point experts of the i-th edge point (located at x_i) is defined as below:

$$p(c_i = C_e \mid f_i) = \text{sig}(w_e^T f_i + b_e); \qquad (1)$$

Where c_i is a discrete random variable denoting whether the local patch feature f_i has pupillary or limbic edge feature (hypothesis $C_e \in \{inner; outer\}$), $\text{sig}(\phi)$ denotes the sigmoid function. $w_e \in R^M$ and $b_e \in R$ are the weight vector and bias of SVM respectively. Figure 1 illustrates the details of local edge point experts model.

For the off-line training, we first manually label the pupillary edge points, limbic edge points and outliers. When training w_{inner} and w_{inner}, positive patch examples are obtained by extracting local patches centered at pupillary edge points, while negative patch examples are obtained by sampling patches centered at other remaining edge points. For the training of w_{outer} and b_{outer} was similar. To reduce the intra-class variations, every patch was normalized with respect to its dominant gradient direction.

Hough clustering

We cannot determine whether an edge point is iris inner or outer edge accurately from the local image patch feature only. However, combing the global spatial configuration of edge points, we can distinguish iris from non-iris edge points accurately. As we know, the shape of iris edge is circle-like, so we can first detect the center location and scale of iris inner or outer edge, and then, discriminate iris and non-iris edge points according to its local patch appearance coupled with their spatial distribution relative to the detected center location and scale. This method is called Hough clustering.

The center and scale detection for iris inner or outer edge can proceed through maximizing the following Hough score (Leibe et al., 2008; Maji and Malik, 2009) formulated under a probabilistic framework that is robust against small iris shape deformations and noise. This formulation also enables the optimal parameter search in a continuous parameter space by using mean-shift algorithm. The Hough score is obtained by marginalizing over all the edge points:

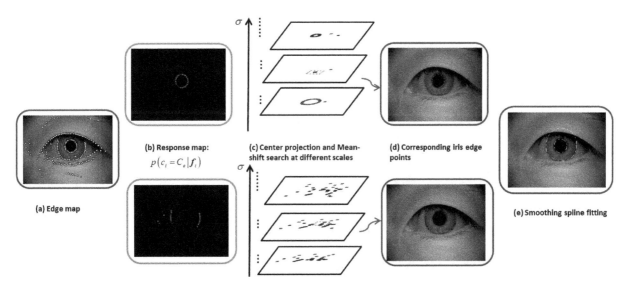

Figure 2. Illustration about selecting corresponding iris inner and outer edge points from non-iris edge points using Hough clustering: (a) the edge map of iris image, (b) the local edge point experts for iris inner or outer edge, (c) the center projection for all the edge points which have high probability of being iris inner and outer edge points through local appearance feature matching, and the Hough clustering results after mean-shift mode-finding, (d) the corresponding iris inner and outer edge points, (e) the smoothing spline fitting results.

$$S(O; C_e; \mu_e) = \sum_{i=1}^{N} p(o_i = O; c_i = C_e; \mu_e; l_i) \tag{2}$$
$$= \sum_{i=1}^{N} p(o_i = O; c_i = C_e; \mu_e \mid l_i) \, p(l_i) ;$$

Where $p(o_i = O; c_i = C_e; \mu_e; l_i)$ represents the probability of an edge point being iris inner or outer edge whose center location and scale can be described by $\mu_e = (x_{ce}; y_{ce}; \frac{3}{4})$. We denote this probability by $\frac{1}{4}_e$. The triple $l_i = (x_i; \acute{A}_i; f_i)$ denote the observed local features of the i-th edge point, where x_i is its 2D location in image domain, $\acute{A}_i$ is its gradient direction and f_i is its local patch feature. The discrete random variable o_i denotes whether the i-th edge point is on a circle-like shape edge (O) or not. c_i is another discrete random variable denoting whether the i-th edge point have iris inner edge or outer edge appearance feature. Assuming a uniform prior over all edge point observations:

$$\frac{1}{4}_e / \; p(o_i = O; c_i = C_e; \mu_e \mid l_i)$$
$$= p(\mu_e \mid o_i = O; x_i; \acute{A}_i) \, p(o_i = O \mid x_i; \acute{A}_i) \, p(c_i = C_e \mid f_i) \tag{3}$$

Where Equation 3 utilizes the independence of o_i and c_i, and that of x_i, $\acute{A}_i$ and f_i is assumed. In Equation 3, the first term is the probabilistic Hough vote for a circular like shape edge's center position and scale. The second term is the probability of an edge point (located at x_i with gradient direction $\acute{A}_i$) being a circular like shape. The last term represents the likelihood of this edge point being iris inner or outer edge through local image patch feature matching. Assuming that the probability $p(o_i = O \mid x_i; \acute{A}_i)$ satisfies uniform distribution.

$$S(O; C_e; \mu_e) / \sum_{i=1}^{N} p(\mu_e \mid o_i = O; x_i; \acute{A}_i) \, p(c_i = C_e \mid f_i) \tag{4}$$

All that Equation 4 says is that, the Hough score is proportional to the sum of all the probabilistic votes about possible center position and scale of iris inner or outer edge and every vote is weighted by the likelihood of that edge point having iris inner or outer edge appearance feature. This likelihood is denoted by $p(c_i = C_e \mid f_i)$ which we get previously. Maximizing the Hough Score $S(O; C_e; \mu_e)$ is equal to maximizing the right hand side of Equation 4. To reduce computational complexity, we leverage the gradient direction of every edge point to formulate every probabilistic vote. If knowing the scale of iris inner or outer edge is $\frac{3}{4}$, based on the fact that the gradient direction of an edge point of iris points towards its center, we can infer that the center position of iris inner or outer edge may be distributed around the below point $x_{ci}^0 (\frac{3}{4}) = (x_{ci}^0 (\frac{3}{4}); y_{ci}^0 (\frac{3}{4}))^T 2 R^2$:

$$x_{ci}^0 (\frac{3}{4}) = x_i \mid \frac{3}{4} \cos \acute{A}_i$$
$$y_{ci}^0 (\frac{3}{4}) = y_i \mid \frac{3}{4} \sin \acute{A}_i \tag{5}$$

Where x_i is the location of the i-th edge point and $\acute{A}_i$ is its gradient direction. In Figure 2b, the red points and blue points are edge points which have high confidence of being iris inner or outer edge through local appearance feature matching, and the center projection for these edge points at different scale $\frac{3}{4}$ are shown in Figure 2c. The probabilistic vote about possible parameter of iris inner or outer edge in Equation 4 is approximated by a kernel density estimate (Comaniciu and Meer, 2002) as follows:

$$S(O; C_e; \mu_e) / \frac{1}{V_b (\frac{3}{4})} \sum_{i=1}^{N} K \left(\frac{x_c \mid x_{ci}^0 (\frac{3}{4})}{b(\frac{3}{4})} \right) w_i \tag{6}$$

Where weight (w_i) is equal to the local edge point expert $p(c_i = C_e \mid f_i)$. Using a kernel density estimate to approximate the vote for every possible parameter $p(\mu_e \mid o_i = O; x_i; \acute{A}_i)$ is to

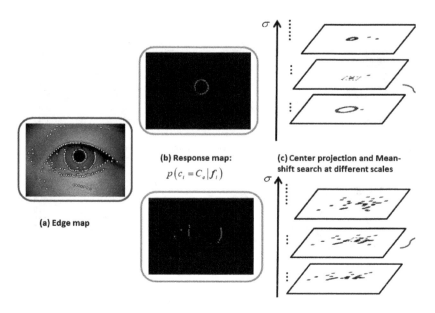

(a) Edge map

(b) Response map: $p\left(c_i = C_a | f_i\right)$

(c) Center projection and Mean-shift search at different scales

Figure 3. Some iris localization example.

tolerate a degree of iris shape deformations, because iris inner or outer edge is not a strict circle due to person specific iris characteristics as well as perspective deformations. This effectively smoothes the underlying distribution, where the degree of tolerance to shape deformation is effected through the kernel bandwidth. For each scale $\frac{3}{4}$, we find the mode of the kernel density estimation (KDE) using the mean-shift algorithm (Comaniciu and Meer, 2002). The optimal center position (X_{ce}^{π}) and scale ($\frac{3}{4}\frac{\pi}{4}$) of iris inner or outer edge are obtained by comparing the maximum of Equation 6 over all possible scales. Because the exhaustive search is only over scale (that is, one dimensional exhaustive search), the computational speed is very fast. The correspondence set of iris inner and outer edge points (Figure 2d) can be determined by selecting points that satisfy $p(\mu_e^{\pi} j \, o_i = O; x_i; Á_i) > ¿_1$ and $p(c_i = C_e j \, f_i) > ¿_2 (¿_1$ and $¿_2$ are two thresholds). That means we select the edge points which have high confidence of being iris inner or outer edge through local appearance feature matching and also distribute under the circle-like shape configuration.

Smoothing spline fitting

After selecting the corresponding set of iris inner and outer edge from all image edge points, the cubic smoothing spline (He et al., 2009) is employed to fit iris inner or outer edge points on polar coordinate system. This is shown in Figure 2e.

EXPERIMENT

This experiment was carried out to evaluate the performance of the proposed method on the problem of iris localization on three different databases: (1) the CASIA version 2.0, (2) the CASIA version 3.0(Lamp) (CASIA, 2008), and (3) the real-world database founded by us in natural environment. The CASIA version 2.0

database contains 1200 images with resolution of 640 × 480 from 60 live human test subjects (20 different images for each subject) with two separate visits (40 days apart). The CASIA Version 3.0 (Lamp) contains 411 human test subjects' 16213 images (640 × 480 pixel resolution). The real-world database contains 3300 iris images (640 × 480 pixel resolution) of 126 persons and the image acquisition device is OKI's IRISPASS-h. This database includes a number of low quality images, including those with eyelid/eyelash occlusion, glasses reflections and out of axis gazing.

The first experiment was designed to test the performance of our method when using different local image features. In this work, we propose two types of local image features namely: raw pixel intensity and intensity gradient. Raw pixel intensity is defined as a vector constructed by the intensity value of the very pixel, and the intensity gradient is defined as a vector that is composed by the intensity gradient of every pixel. By adopting different feature types, we can get different equal error rates (EER) from our method. To calculate the EER, we use our proposed method in the localization part and Daugman's method in normalization and matching parts. The result listed in Table 1.

On these datasets, we also compared four types of iris localization methods: (1) the integro-differential operator proposed by Daugman (1993), (2) the traditional Hough transform proposed by Wildes (1997), (3) pulling and pushing method proposed by He (2009), and (4) the edge point subset selection combined with Smoothing spline fitting (EPSS+SSF) proposed in §2 (Figure 3). To give a fair comparison, we adopted different methods in the iris localization part and the same feature extraction and matching methods proposed by Daugman (1993) to

Table 1. The EER comparison of our method using different local image features on CASIA-V3.0, CASIAV2.0 and our real database.

Data	Raw pixel intensity (%)	Intensity gradient (%)
CASIA-V2.0	0.89	4.52
CASIA-V3.0	3.91	5.26
real-world	2.47	5.10

Table 2. The EER comparison of CASIA-V3.0, CASIAV2.0 and our real database.

Data	Daugman (%)	Wildes (%)	He (%)	EPSS+SSF (%)
CASIA-V3.0	8.97	7.78	4.67	3.91
CASIA-V2.0	3.38	4.51	1.20	0.89
real-world	6.95	7.05	3.89	2.47

compare the different localization algorithms' performance. The tested results of the three databases are shown in Table 2. All algorithms were implemented in Matlab on a 3.98 GHz duo CPU (1.99 G per core) and 2 GB of memory. The average running time for the 4 algorithms on CASIA- V3.0 database are: 10.20, 14.44, 1.99s and 3.31 s respectively. From the accuracy and efficiency comparison, the proposed algorithm was the most accurate localization algorithm though it is slightly slower than that proposed by He (2009).The proposed method's performance is obviously better than that of Daugman's and Wildes' as our method takes into account the shape deformations caused by person specific iris characteristics as well as perspective deformations while Daugman's and wildes' do not. The strict circular shape hypothesis of iris edge in Daugman's and Wildes' method cannot account for any shape deformations leading the non-ideal performance. Moreover, our method's performance was also a little better than He's because our method can determine whether an edge point belongs to iris edge accurately according to its location, intensity gradient direction and local image feature. But He's method discriminate iris and non-iris edge points only according to its spatial distribution relative to the detected iris region and this strategy is not as effective as our proposed method.

Conclusion

In this paper, we present a novel method for iris detection and localization using a weighted kernel voting framework. It improves the performance of iris localization by selecting the right corresponding iris edge point for fitting. A mean-shift search strategy was used to guarantee that the method can tolerate some shape deformations. The validity of the proposed algorithm was verified by testing it on three different iris databases.

REFERENCES

CASIA (2008). CASIA Iris Image Database Version 2.0 and Version 3.0, http://www.cbsr.ia.ac.cn/iris-database.html.

Comaniciu D, Meer P (2002). Mean shift: a robust approach toward feature space analysis. IEEE Trans. Pattern Anal. Machine Intell. 24(5):603-619.

Daugman JG (1993). High confidence visual recognition of persons by a test of statistical independence.IEEE Trans. Pattern Anal. Machine Intell. 15(11):1148-1161.

Du Y, Arslanturk E, Zhou A (2010). Video-based noncooperativeiris image segmentation. IEEE Trans. System, Man, and Cybernetics, Part B. Cybernetics 5(9):1-11.

He Z, Tan T,Sun Z (2009). Toward accurate and fast iris segmentation for iris biometrics.IEEE Trans. Pattern Anal. Machine Intell.. 31(9):1670-1684.

Leibe B, Leonardis A, Schiele B (2008). Robust object detection with interleaved categorization and segmentation, Int. J. Comput. Vision, 77:259-289.

Lindeberg T (1998). Scale-space theory in computer vision, pp.153-157.

Maji S, Malik J (2009). Object detection using a maxmarginhoughtransform, Proc. IEEE Int'l Conf. Computer Vision and Pattern Recognition pp.1038-1045.

Proença H (2010). Iris recognition: on the segmentation of degraded images acquired in the visible wavelength.IEEE Trans. Pattern Anal. Machine Intell. 32(8):1502-1516.

Saragih MJ, Lucey S, Cohn J (2009). Face alignment through subspace constrained mean-shifts.Proc. IEEE Int'l Conf. Computer Vision and Pattern Recognition, pp. 1034-1041.

Wildes RP (1997). Iris recognition: An emerging biometric technology.Proceedings of the IEEE. 85(9):1348-1363.

Zuo J, Schmid NA (2010). Robust iris segmentation algorithm for non-ideal iris image.IEEE Trans. on System, Man, and Cybernetics-Part B 40(3):703-718.

10

Feature subset selection using association rule mining and JRip classifier

Waseem Shahzad, Salman Asad and Muhammad Asif Khan

National University of Computer and Emerging Sciences Department of Computer Science, Sector H-11/4, Islamabad, Pakistan.

Feature selection is an important task in many fields such as statistics and machine learning. It aims at preprocessing step that include removal of irrelevant and redundant features and the retention of useful features. Selecting the relevant features increases the accuracy and decreases the computational cost. Feature selection also helps to understand the relevant data, addressing the complexity of dimensionality. In this paper, we have proposed a technique that uses JRip classifier and association rule mining to select the most relevant features from a data set. JRip extracts the rules from a data set and then association rules mining technique is applied to rank the features. Twenty datasets are tested ranging from binary class problem to multi-class problem. Extensive experimentation is carried out and the proposed technique is evaluated against the performance of various familiar classifiers. Experimental results demonstrate that while employing less number of features the proposed method achieves higher classification accuracy as well as generates less number of rules.

Key words: Feature subset selection, association rules mining, JRip, J48, Ridor, PART.

INTRODUCTION

The speedy growth of data on daily basis have resulted the size of databases to Terabytes, where a lot of useful information is invisible. Discovering such hidden information is called data mining. Data mining can also be defined as a process that is used to analyze data to find the hidden patterns and relationships among data. It helps in making correct prediction. Techniques used in data mining are the combination of multiple fields like databases, machine learning, computational intelligence, statistics, pattern recognition and neural networks (Edelstein, 1999).

Data mining is used in businesses where large transactions are involved. For example, it can detect the characteristics of customer who buy products from store, which help to find what trends are being followed. It can also help in fraud detection if customer's transaction behavior is abnormal. Such predictions are based on

historical data. Data mining techniques can be classified as supervised and unsupervised. Supervised technique takes training set to build a model and learn it. After a predictive model is built, test data is produced to find out the accuracy of the predictive model. In contrast, an unsupervised method has no target class. The unsupervised technique searches for patterns and similarity among the variables on the basis of which they are grouped. Clustering is one of the most common unsupervised data mining techniques.

Classification is one of the important techniques of supervised data mining. Its objective is to build a model by using the training set that can predict the class labels of test set. Applications of classification are fraud detection, weather prediction, customer behavior, risk management (Han and Kamber, 2006). Building classification model, starts with training set or training data. The next step is to find the relationships and hidden patterns in that training data. Different classification algorithm uses different techniques to find the relationships and hidden patterns in training data (Liu et al., 2002; Martens et al., 2007; Parpinelli et al., 2002). These relationships and hidden patterns are then used to build a model. The model can then be used to predict the target value of unknown cases.

The existence of strong and hidden relationship in large databases is the major concern of most of the researchers today. Data mining resolve this issue by providing a technique called association rule mining (ARM). The rules created by association rule mining is in the form on IF – THEN statement. IF part is called the antecedent part of the rule while THEN part is called the consequent of the rule. Support and confidence are the two important factors, associated with the ARM. Collection of important information is also carried out with the help of a feature selection mechanism by choosing a subset of features also known as feature extraction, feature reduction, variable selection or attributes selection. The technique selects the set of most significant features that improve performance and increase the accuracy. Feature selection algorithms can be classified into two categories – feature ranking and feature subset selection. In feature ranking, features are ranked by a metric; while the latter one searches for the optimal subset of features from possible subsets (Wei and Billings, 2007; Yahang and Honavar, 1997; Zhou et al., 2007).

In this paper, for feature selection, we proposed a feature subset selection technique that uses JRipper classifier with association rules mining to select most valuable features of a dataset. First, we build rules using JRipper classifier, then assign ranks to features by using these rules based on support and confidence. Extensive experimentation on various datasets has been performed using the proposed approach and the results greatly showed the worth of proposed technique over other techniques.

RELATED WORK

Feature selection is an important stage of preprocessing. In literature it has been proven that feature selection is an effective mechanism in reducing the dimension to improve the computational efficiency (Kanan et al., 2007; Raymer et al., 2000). Feature subset selection technique can be classified into three categories – filtered based techniques, wrappers, and embedded technique. Filtered approach first searches the data and then use a filtered approach. In wrapper based methods any classification algorithm is used that can go through all data and find a set of relevant features. Wrappers based methods have high computation cost. Embedded technique is embedded in the model and it selects features by making a model.

Approaches used for feature subset selection have number of drawbacks. To avoid such drawbacks many hybrid approaches have been introduced like (Shahzad and Baig, 2010). Yang et al. (2005) concluded that there is no any specific criteria which can be used to pick any filtered algorithm. They introduced a hybrid algorithm by merging different filtered based algorithms and produced better results. The methodology lacks some helpful classification facts and information. It did not explain what difficulties would occur when each gene is treated distinctly. Wang et al. (2005) enhanced the classification process by merging hierarchical clustering, different filters and uniform gene selection classification method. A special filter algorithm is used in their approach for gene ranking and clustered hierarchically the top 50 to 100 genes. Hassan et al. (2009) and Su et al. (2007) suggested the multiple classifier concept for efficient system and better results. A GA-based classifier prototype proposed by Zhang et al. (2009) namely "Genetic Ensemble" uses GA in finding nonlinear association from genes and also in assessing gene sets by groups.

Classification is termed as grouping of similar objects. A number of classification algorithms exist such as decision trees, k-nearest neighbor classifiers, neural networks and support vector machines. Among many classification applications, few are fraud detection, weather prediction, customer behavior, risk management (Baesens et al., 2003; Han and Kamber, 2006). A Naïve Bayes classifier is a simple classifier based on probability (Friedman et al., 1997). It uses a formula of Bayes theorem to calculate probability by counting the frequency of values in the historical order.

Decision tree is a well known classification algorithm which uses conditional probability formula. Decision tree generate rules that can be understand and read easily by human. Decision trees can work for both binary and multi-class classification problems and can also contain categorical and numeric information (Edelstein, 1999). Decision tree finds strong relationships between the values of the data. When a set of values is found having strong relationship than others then that set is grouped and it becomes a branch. The algorithm is recursive and repeats to create more branches. After constructing a rule, instances covered by that rule are removed, so that the remaining dataset is considered for other rules to be constructed.

Ripper is also a well-known algorithm for supervised data classification. Its rule set is easy to understand and usually better than decision tree learners (Cohen, 1995). In ripper classifiers training data is randomly distributed into growing set and pruning set. Each rule keeps on growing until no information gain is possible further.

PROPOSED TECHNIQUE

The proposed technique uses JRipper algorithm with ARM to select

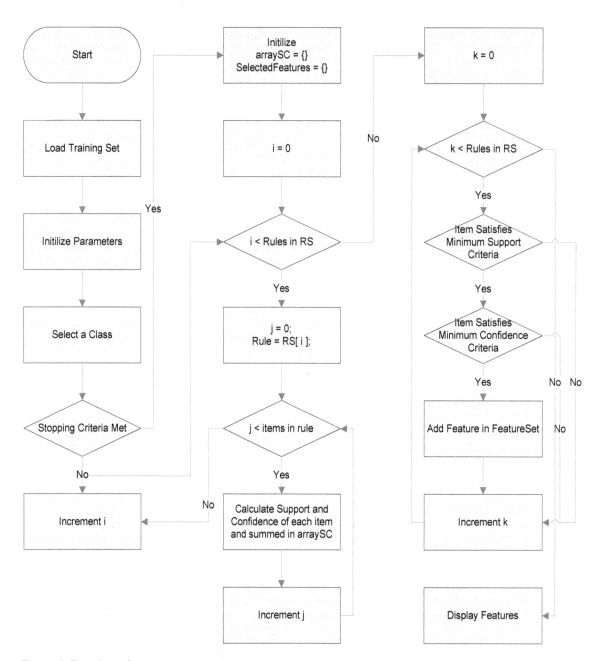

Figure 1. Flowchart of proposed approach.

features of a dataset. Ripper is one of the supervised classification approach where training data is distributed randomly into two sets-growing set and the pruning set. Each rule keeps on growing until no information gain is possible further. After this process, the rule is then passed through a pruning step where unnecessary terms are eliminated in order to maximize the following function given in Equation (1).

$$\frac{p + (N - n)}{P + N} \tag{1}$$

Where p is the number of positive examples covered by rule, N is the number of negative examples in prune set, n is the number of negative examples covered by rule, and P is the number of positive examples in Prune Set. Figure 1 shows the proposed flowchart of the proposed approach followed by the algorithm.

JRip algorithm

JRip is an optimized version of IREP (Cohen, 1995). It was introduced by William W. Cohen. With the repeated incremental pruning JRip produce error reduction.

Initialization

Initialize RS = {}, and from each class from the less frequent one to the most frequent one.

Building stage

Repeat the grow phase and prune phase until there are no positive examples or error rate >= 50%.

(i) Grow phase: Keep on greedily adding terms to the rule until the rule is perfect (100% accurate)

(ii) Prune phase: Each rule is incrementally pruned. Now any finishing sequences can get pruned. The pruning value can be measured using the formula 2p / (p + n) − 1 (Figure 1).

```
Algorithm: An algorithm for the proposed approach
load (TrainingSet);          /*rule set will be initialized as empty*/
Initialize RS = {};
minSupport, minConfidence;          /*this will be set by user*/
for each (class in TrainingSet)
    begin
        while (!positive_examples () && error_rate >= 50)
            begin
                Rule = buildRule();
                Rule = pruneRule();
                addRule(RS, Rule);
            end
    end
        optimizationRules();
        deleteRules(); /*After this stage we have the rules created by
the JRip in ruleset*/
        arraySC[][] = {}; /*stores the support and confidence of each
item*/
        SelectedFeatureList = {}; /*stores the array of selected
features*/
for (int i=0; i<RS.count(); i++)
    begin
        Rule = RS[i];
        for (int j=0; j<rule.count(); j++)
            begin
                Item = rule[j];
                Item_index = findItemIndex(Item);
                Item_support = findItemSupport(Item);
                Item_confidence = findItemConfidence(Item);
                arraySC[Item_index][0] = Item_support;
                arraySC[Item_index][1] = Item_confidence;
                arraySC[Item_index][2]++;  /*Tell the frequency of
item*/
            end
    end
for (int i=0; i<arraySC.rowCount(); i++)
    begin
        if (arraySC[i][0]/arraySC[i][2]>minSupport)
            begin
                if (arraySC[i][1]/arraySC[i][2]>minConfidence)
                    begin
                        SelectedFeatureList.Add(i);
                    end
            end
    end
```

Optimization stage

In this optimization stage of JRip algorithm first initial rule set is identified and is known as {Ri}. Now create two variants by using procedures of grow phase from each rule Ri using random data and prune these variants. Empty rule must be applied for generating

one of the variants and second variant is generated by adding antecedents to the original rule. In this way, the pruning metric used is (TP+TN) / (P+N). Now, for each variant and the original rule, smallest possible DL is calculated. Final representative from the set R is taken on the basis of minimum DL. If there are residual positives after observing {Ri} rules, some more rules are identified using building stage again on the basis of residual positives.

Delete stage

All the rules that increase the DL get deleted, the left set is then added in the resultant set. This resultant set will be denoted as RS.

Association rule mining

Association rule mining (ARM) is one of the important technique of data mining. It is used to find the hidden and interesting patterns in the data. It only works on categorical data.

Rule structure

The rule generated using association rule mining has two parts. First part is called ANTECEDENT or IF part and the second part is the CONSEQUENT or THEN part. Antecedent part contains terms. For example:

$$IF\ term_1\ and\ term_2 \ldots term_n \tag{2}$$

The consequent part contains only the class label. Therefore, the complete rule will look like:

$$IF\ term_1\ and\ term_2 \ldots term_n\ THEN\ class \tag{3}$$

Each term consists of attribute name and value. The structure of a term is given below:

$$AttributeName = AttributeValue \tag{4}$$

For example the term "Outlook = Sunny" has an *Attribute name* "Outlook" and *Attribute value* "Sunny".

Market basket analysis

Market basket analysis is a common example of association rule mining. It is a modeling technique based upon the theory that if an item from a certain group is bought then it is more or less possible that another group of item is bought. The set of items customer buys is referred as the item set. The market basket analysis finds interesting relationships between items. This is done using association rule mining.

Factors of association rule mining

There are two very important factors of association rule mining. These factors are:

(i) Support: Support is used to tell how frequently a rule occurs in the dataset. It's actually the number of instances covered by the rule against total number of transactions/records. The formula for

Table 1. Ranking of features arranged on the basis of support and confidence.

Features with support and confidence			Features arranged on the basis of confidence			Features arranged on the basis of support		
Feature index	Confidence	Support	Feature index	Confidence	Support	Feature index	Confidence	Support
1	0.9	0.02	1	0.9	0.02	10	0.9	0.11
2	0.8	0.05	10	0.9	0.11	1	0.9	0.02
3	0.8	0.05	12	0.9	0.006	12	0.9	0.006
4	0.7	0.08	2	0.8	0.05	2	0.8	0.05
5	0.5	0.02	3	0.8	0.05	3	0.8	0.05
6	0.7	0.02	4	0.7	0.08	4	0.7	0.08
7	0.6	0.005	6	0.7	0.02	9	0.7	0.04
8	0.2	0.001	9	0.7	0.04	11	0.7	0.04
9	0.7	0.04	11	0.7	0.04	6	0.7	0.02
10	0.9	0.11	7	0.6	0.005	7	0.6	0.005
11	0.7	0.04	5	0.5	0.02	15	0.5	0.05
12	0.9	0.006	15	0.5	0.05	5	0.5	0.02
13	0.1	0.02	8	0.2	0.001	14	0.2	0.004
14	0.2	0.004	14	0.2	0.004	8	0.2	0.001
15	0.5	0.05	13	0.1	0.02	13	0.1	0.02

support of a rule X => Y is:

$$Support(X => Y) = P(X \cup Y) \qquad (5)$$

Suppose a database with 10,000 transactions. Out of those 10,000 transactions 1000 include both items 1 and item 2 and 500 of these include item C. Therefore the support of the rule "If items 1 and 2 then item C" is 500/10000=0.05=5%.

(ii) Confidence

The formula for confidence of a rule X => Y is:

$$Confidence(X => Y) = P(Y|X) \qquad (6)$$

Suppose a database with 10,000 transactions. Out of those 10,000 transactions 1000 include both item 1 and item 2 and 500 of these include item C. Therefore the confidence of the rule "If item 1 and item 2 then item C" is 500/1000=0.5=50%.

Feature selection

Feature selection an important technique of data mining. The main task of feature selection is to exclude or remove extra features from the dataset. Feature selection not only removes irrelevant features to reduce computational cost but also increases the accuracy. Feature selection is a very useful technique and has many advantages. The main advantage of feature selection is that as features are removed so learning process will be faster. Secondly, problem will get simpler as irrelevant and redundant features are removed. There is another advantage that accuracy of model will be increased. Feature selection therefore provides us information about the importance of features and this helps us to understand the data.

Feature weightage

After rules are built by JRip they are stored in the rule set. Each rule

has antecedent and consequent part. Each antecedent part has at least one term and each term has an attribute in it. The support and confidence of each rule is summed and assigned to that attribute. Now each attribute has its support sum, its confidence sum and the number of times it appears in the rule list. The equation for assigning support to each feature is given below:

$$FS_i = \frac{\left(\sum_{j=0}^{k} x.Support_j\right)}{\left(\sum_{j=0}^{k} x\right)} \qquad (7)$$

Where FS_i is the support of ith feature, $Support_j$ is the support of jth rule, k is the total number of rules and x will be 1 if the rule contains the ith feature else it will be 0. The equation for assigning the confidence to each feature is given below:

$$FC_i = \frac{\left(\sum_{j=0}^{k} x.Confidence_j\right)}{\left(\sum_{j=0}^{k} x\right)} \qquad (8)$$

Where FC_i is the confidence of ith feature, $Confidence_j$ is the confidence of jth rule, k is the total number of rules and x will be 1 if the rule contains the ith feature else it will be 0.

Ranking of features

All features are sorted on the basis of support and confidence values. First the features are sorted with respect to confidence. After this the feature are again sorted on the basis of confidence. But this will only affect those features whose confidence value is same. For example, suppose we have 15 features in a dataset along with their support and confidence as given in Table 1. There are some features with the same confidence value and same support value.

It is important to note that features with same confidence are now grouped, but still their support value is not sorted. As a second step these values are sorted on the basis of their support. Hence, the

Table 2. Features and there ranking.

Feature index	Confidence	Support	Rank
10	0.9	0.11	1
1	0.9	0.02	2
12	0.9	0.006	3
2	0.8	0.05	4
3	0.8	0.05	5
4	0.7	0.08	6
9	0.7	0.04	7
11	0.7	0.04	8
6	0.7	0.02	9
7	0.6	0.005	10
15	0.5	0.05	11
5	0.5	0.02	12
14	0.2	0.004	13
8	0.2	0.001	14
13	0.1	0.02	15

Table 3. Selected features.

Feature index	Confidence	Support	Rank
10	0.9	0.11	1
1	0.9	0.02	2
2	0.8	0.05	3
3	0.8	0.05	4
4	0.7	0.08	5
9	0.7	0.04	6
11	0.7	0.04	7
6	0.7	0.02	8
15	0.5	0.05	9
5	0.5	0.02	10

features are arranged on the basis of both support and confidence as shown in Table 1.

Feature ranking

In feature ranking a metric (rank no.) is assigned to each feature based on their sorted position (as in Table 1). Feature ranking for all features is shown in Table 2.

Selection of features

Features that meet the minimum threshold are selected and the features that do not meet the minimum threshold criteria are removed. The parameters used are Support = 0.01 and Confidence = 0.5. The selected features using the above parameters are shown in Table 3.

RESULTS

Experimentation results are discussed here. The algorithm is tested on 20 different datasets. The datasets are taken from machine learning repository. Detail of all datasets used is given in Table 4.

Dataset are first discredited and also missing values are removed from it before performing experimentation. The comparisons are done using four different classifiers named JRip (Cohen, 1995), J48 (Quinlan, 1993), PART (Frank and Witten, 1998) and Ridor (Gaines and Compton, 1995). Table 5 also shows the features selected by proposed technique. In most cases the 60 to 70% features are removed and in some cases even 93% features are removed. But it is important that important features not get removed else there will be a fall in accuracy level. Therefore, removing a certain number of

Table 4. Datasets used in experimentation.

S/N	Dataset	Attributes	Instances	Classes	Selected features
1	Audiology	69	226	24	12
2	Autos	25	205	6	13
3	Breast Cancer	9	286	2	4
4	Colic	22	368	2	5
5	Credit –A	15	690	2	1
6	Credit –G	20	1000	2	7
7	Diabetes	8	768	2	3
8	Glass	9	214	6	7
9	Heart –C	13	303	2	6
10	Heart Statlog	13	270	2	7
11	Hepatitis	19	155	2	7
12	Ionosphere	34	351	2	11
13	Iris	4	150	3	2
14	Labor	16	57	2	3
15	Primary Tumor	17	399	21	10
16	Segment	19	2310	7	12
17	Sonar	60	208	2	16
18	Splice	60	3190	3	11
19	Vehicle	18	846	4	14
20	Waveform	40	5000	3	20

Table 5. Comparison between accuracies using different classifiers.

S/N	Dataset	JRip		PART		J48		Ridor	
		Accuracy before feature selection (%)	Accuracy after feature subset (%)	Accuracy before feature selection (%)	Accuracy after feature subset (%)	Accuracy before feature selection (%)	Accuracy after feature subset (%)	Accuracy before feature selection (%)	Accuracy after feature subset (%)
1	Audiology	70.79	73.45	79.64	76.10	78.31	77.43	74.33	76.10
2	Autos	65.36	66.34	69.75	69.26	75.12	78.53	64.39	63.90
3	Breast Cancer	70.27	74.47	69.58	74.12	75.52	75.87	72.02	74.82
4	Colic	86.41	87.50	81.52	84.51	85.05	85.59	82.60	86.14
5	Credit –A	85.21	85.50	84.92	85.50	85.79	85.50	85.36	85.50

Table 5. Contd.

6	Credit Germany	69.60	71.30	72.20	73.10	71.30	72.90	71.10	71.20
7	Diabetes	74.21	75.00	69.53	72.39	74.21	72.65	73.43	74.60
8	Glass	58.41	59.34	60.74	63.08	59.81	61.68	57.00	56.07
9	Heart –C	81.18	83.82	78.87	82.50	77.88	80.85	77.55	80.52
10	Heart Statlog	78.14	82.96	77.40	82.59	77.03	81.85	72.59	81.85
11	Hepatitis	80.64	84.51	81.95	82.58	81.29	81.29	79.35	80.64
12	Ionosphere	86.89	88.88	88.03	88.88	86.32	90.59	86.03	87.74
13	Iris	92.00	91.33	90.00	91.33	90.66	92.00	88.00	92.00
14	Labor	78.94	91.22	85.96	87.71	82.45	94.73	85.96	84.21
15	Primary Tumor	38.93	39.82	38.64	39.23	40.11	36.87	35.39	34.51
16	Segment	91.38	91.68	91.94	92.52	91.94	92.12	91.42	91.25
17	Sonar	73.55	75.96	75.00	77.88	67.78	69.71	69.23	69.71
18	Splice	94.13	95.17	92.50	92.79	94.35	94.51	92.10	94.01
19	Vehicle	59.21	60.16	65.36	65.60	65.48	65.13	64.18	61.34
20	Waveform	75.46	76.72	75.88	76.70	75.16	77.12	72.16	72.24

features will not be a good approach, as we can analyze that in some cases only a few features are removed and in those cases removing more features will cause fall in accuracy.

Figure 2 clearly analyzes the number of features selected. The figure shows the comparison between the original features and the extracted features. The blue bars show the features of original dataset while red bars show the number of features selected by the proposed approach. It can be clearly seen that in most cases 60 to 65% features are removed and in some cases like audiology, colic, credit–A, labor, sonar and splice 85 to 93% features are removed.

Comparison using different classifiers

Using JRip classifier, rules are generated for extracting features. First the accuracy of dataset is calculated with all features and then it is compared with the accuracy achieved by the selected features. The best performance is shown in boldface as given in Table 8. The accuracies of original dataset and the selected feature is calculated using the same classifier that is, JRipper. Even if the accuracy is not much increase but the computational cost has decreased. For example in Credit-A the accuracy is not much increased but the computational cost is very much decreased. The algorithm only picks 1 feature out of 15 features and ignores rest 14 features. 93% of the features are removed in this case and the problem is also very much simpler now. As features are removed so this helps user to understand the dataset more easily. Therefore even if the accuracy is not much increased we can say that two things can be achieved that is, the computational cost is decreased and the other is problem gets simpler and more understandable.

If we analyze it closely then we can easily see that result of Labor dataset is coming very good. Only 3 features out of 16 features are selected which means 81% of the features are removed. But not only features are removed also its accuracy is much better now. There is a 12.28% increase in accuracy now.

With PART classifier (Frank and Witten, 1998), same procedure is followed that is, first the accuracy of dataset with all is computed and then compute accuracy of dataset with the features selected by proposed technique. Table 5 shows the comparison of accuracies of original features and selected features by the proposed technique.

The accuracy of original dataset and the selected feature is calculated using the same classifier that is, PART. In comparison with JRip some of the results are given more good results in selected features. For example on Colic dataset accuracy increased is 1.04% on JRip but in PART

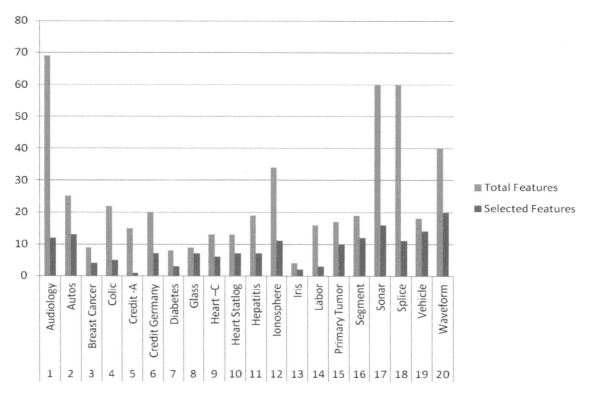

Figure 2. Comparison of feature reduction (total features: left bar, selected feature: right bar).

its 3%. Similarly Heart-C is also providing good results. The results in which accuracies are increased are highlighted in the table. Accuracies on almost all dataset have increased this shows that the features selected are good and it not only gives good result in JRip but also using PART its is giving good results. This shows the robustness of proposed technique.

In J48 classifier, first the accuracy of dataset with full features is calculated and then computes the accuracy of dataset with selected features. Table 5 shows the comparison of accuracies of original features and selected features by the proposed technique. The accuracy of original dataset and the selected feature is calculated using the same classifier that is, J48. The results in which accuracies are increased are highlighted in the table. It seems that the features selected are working fine. As most of the results are giving increases in accuracies. But like JRip and PART, J48 is not giving much good results but still its results are good.

Using Ridor classifier, first the accuracy of dataset with full features is calculated and then accuracy of the dataset with selected features. Table 5 shows the comparison of accuracies of original features and selected features by the proposed technique. The accuracy of original dataset and the selected feature is calculated using the same classifier that is, Ridor. The results in which accuracies are increased are highlighted as bold. After analyzing the results obtained by Ridor,

reflects that features selected by the approach are good. Even if the accuracy is not increase in some cases but in those cases computational cost is decreased and not only computational cost is decreased but also the problem becomes more simple to understand and analyze.

Comparison of proposed approach with CFS using different classifiers

Correlation based feature subset selection (CFS) is a well-known technique that uses correlation based heuristic for feature selection (Hall and Smith, 1999). This algorithm is simple and fast. The algorithm maintains the correlation matrix of target class and another matrix in which every feature's correlation is maintained with every other feature. Using best first search it searches for the appropriate features. Best first is only used because it was giving better results than others were but in some cases hill climbing approach was giving better results.

Table 6 shows the selected features using the correlation based feature subset selection. The indices of selected features using proposed technique are also given. In Table 7, number of selected features of proposed technique and CFS is compared. In the third column number of selected features using CFS is shown and last column contains the number of selected features

Table 6. Comparison of number of features selected using CFS and proposed approach.

S/N	Dataset	CFS	Proposed approach
1	Audiology	15	12
2	Autos	7	13
3	Breast Cancer	5	4
4	Colic	5	5
5	Credit -A	4	1
6	Credit Germany	4	7
7	Diabetes	4	3
8	Glass	6	7
9	Heart –C	8	6
10	Heart Statlog	9	7
11	Hepatitis	9	7
12	Ionosphere	5	11
13	Iris	2	2
14	Labor	7	3
15	Primary Tumor	12	10
16	Segment	9	12
17	Sonar	12	16
18	Splice	22	11
19	Vehicle	8	14
20	Waveform	15	20

using the proposed algorithm. In most cases, the proposed algorithm selects fewer features than CFS. While in some cases it selects more, however, in such cases the accuracy of the proposed approach is far much better than CFS.

Table 7 shows the accuracy of selected features by CFS and proposed technique that clearly demonstrate that the proposed approach is better than CFS in terms of accuracy. The important point to note that despite in cases where more features are selected by the proposed approach, their accuracy still beats CFS. This means the proposed feature selection technique is much better than CFS. For example CFS selects seven features in Autos and the proposed approach selects thirteen features, but the accuracy is better than CFS. Same is the case with Credit Germany, Sonar, Vehicle and Waveform datasets. Only in case of Credit A the accuracy is 0.15% less than achieved by CFS, but in that case just 1 feature is selected and CFS have selected 4 features which reflects that both results seems to be almost equal.

Ionosphere is the only case in which our results are not good. We have selected more features than CFS and our accuracy is also not better than CFS. So Ionosphere is the only case in which CFS is better than the proposed technique. It makes clear that our results are better than CFS. The above results also reveal that there is much difference between accuracies. One of the examples is the big difference between the accuracies in dataset "vehicle". Other than that in most of the cases, the proposed outperforms the CFS. Moreover, Table 7 also shows that the proposed approach produced better results in most of the cases. In three cases - Autos, Vehicle and Labor, the proposed technique has achieved much more accuracies than the CFS. As another example, the proposed approach produced much better results on the datasets heart statlog, vehicle and heart-c as compared to the results produced by the CFS.

Conclusion

Feature selection is an important technique of data mining to exclude or remove insignificant features from the dataset. In other words, it is to choose a subset of significant features for building a learning model. Feature selection not only removes insignificant features to reduce computational cost but it also increases the accuracy. Removal of the most irrelevant and redundant features from the dataset are the main goal of feature selection. Feature selection is very useful technique and has many advantages. The main advantage of feature selection is that as features are removed learning process becomes faster. Secondly, problem will get simpler with the removal of irrelevant and redundant features. Another advantage is that accuracy of the model will increase. Feature selection, therefore, helps researchers to acquire better understanding about their data by telling them which one are the important

Table 7. Accuracies comparison between CFS and proposed approach using different classifiers.

S/N	Dataset	JRip		PART		J48		Ridor	
		Accuracy after feature selection using CFS (%)	Accuracy after feature selection using proposed approach (%)	Accuracy after feature selection using CFS (%)	Accuracy after feature selection using proposed approach (%)	Accuracy after feature selection using CFS (%)	Accuracy after feature selection using proposed approach (%)	Accuracy after feature selection using CFS (%)	Accuracy after feature selection using proposed approach (%)
1	Audiology	73.45	73.45	73.00	76.10	76.10	77.43	73.45	76.10
2	Autos	65.36	66.34	68.78	69.26	67.80	78.53	59.51	63.90
3	Breast Cancer	73.42	74.47	71.32	74.12	73.07	75.87	73.77	74.82
4	Colic	86.41	87.50	84.23	84.51	85.59	85.59	85.05	86.14
5	Credit –A	85.65	85.50	84.34	85.50	86.08	85.50	85.65	85.50
6	Credit Germany	70.70	71.30	72.00	73.10	72.10	72.90	71.00	71.20
7	Diabetes	74.08	75.00	75.26	72.39	75.13	72.65	74.73	74.60
8	Glass	59.81	59.34	60.28	63.08	62.14	61.68	60.28	56.07
9	Heart –C	79.20	83.82	80.52	82.50	79.53	80.85	78.21	80.52
10	Heart Statlog	79.25	82.96	81.48	82.59	79.62	81.85	74.44	81.85
11	Hepatitis	82.58	84.51	81.93	82.58	81.93	81.29	77.41	80.64
12	Ionosphere	89.45	88.88	90.02	88.88	88.31	90.59	87.17	87.74
13	Iris	91.33	91.33	91.33	91.33	92.00	92.00	92.00	92.00
14	Labor	80.70	91.22	82.45	87.71	78.94	94.73	82.45	84.21
15	Primary Tumor	38.93	39.82	41.00	39.23	40.11	36.87	35.39	34.51
16	Segment	88.83	91.68	89.43	92.52	90.34	92.12	89.09	91.25
17	Sonar	72.59	75.96	73.07	77.88	72.59	69.71	71.15	69.71
18	Splice	94.95	95.17	93.38	92.79	94.48	94.51	92.47	94.01
19	Vehicle	48.10	60.16	47.04	65.60	47.39	65.13	43.14	61.34
20	Waveform	76.56	76.72	77.16	76.70	77.26	77.12	73.50	72.24

features and how they are related with each other. The proposed technique used for feature selection is very simple to understand and implement, and also produces better results. JRipper is used because it uses good features only to build concise rules. Furthermore, association rule mining is used to filter the features picked up by the JRipper classifier. The two main factors support and confidence are

used. Experimentation results shows that features selected are of significant impact. Accuracy of selected features is measured using JRip, J48, PART and Ridor to validate that these features are giving at least same or much better results. In some cases, accuracy achieved is not much better while using Ridor, PART and J48. On the other hand, the computational cost is less, causing the solution to be simpler and with a

negligible difference in accuracy. In future, a hybrid approach using ensemble classifiers will be experimented. To decrease the curse of dimensionality and will make data more understandable, change in threshold such as the support and confidence will also be investigated thoroughly to analyze the impact of number of features selected that significantly improve accuracy.

REFERENCES

Baesens B, Gestel TV, Viaene S, Stepanova M, Suykens J, Vanthienen J (2003). Benchmarking state-of-the-art classification algorithms for credit scoring. J. Oper. Res. Soc. 54(6):627-635.

Cohen WW (1995). Fast effective rule induction. In: Proceedings of the 12th International Conference on Machine Learning. pp. 115-123.

Edelstein HA (1999). Introduction to data mining and knowledge discovery. 3rd edn. Two Crows Corporation.

Frank E, Witten IH (1998). Generating Accurate rule sets without global optimization. In: Proceedings of 15th International Conference on Machine Learning. pp. 144-151.

Friedman N, Geiger D, Goldszmidt M (1997). Bayesian network classifiers. J. Mach. Learn. Res. 29:131-163.

Gaines BR, Compton P (1995). Induction of Ripple-Down rules applied to modeling large databases. J. Intell. Inf. Syst. 5(3):211-228.

Hall MA, Smith LA (1999). Feature Selection for Machine Learning: Comparing a Correlation-based Filter Approach to the Wrapper. Comput. Inf. Sci. AAAI Press pp. 235:239.

Han J, Kamber M (2006). Data mining: concepts and techniques, 2nd edn. Morgan Kaufmann Publishers.

Hassan MR, Hossain MM, Bailey J, Macintyre G, Ho JW, Ramamohanarao K (2009). A voting approach to identify a small number of highly predictive genes using multiple classifiers. BMC Bioinformatics. 10(Suppl 1):S19.

Kanan HR, Faez K, Taheri SM (2007). Feature selection using ant colony optimization (ACO): a new method and comparative study in the application of face recognition system. In: Proceedings of the 7th industrial conference on Advances in data. pp. 63-76.

Liu B, Abbass HA, McKay B (2002). Density-based heuristic for rule discovery with ant-miner. In: Proceedings of 6th Australia-Japan Joint Workshop on Intelligent Evolutionary Systems, Canberra, Australia. pp. 180-184.

Martens D, De Backer M, Haesen R, Vanthienen J, Snoeck M, Baesens B (2007). Classification with ant colony optimization. IEEE Trans. Evol. Comput. 11(5):651-665.

Parpinelli RS, Lopes HS, Freitas AA (2002). Data mining with an ant colony optimization algorithm. IEEE Trans. Evol. Comput. 6(4):321-332.

Quinlan JR (1993). C4.5: programs for machine learning. Morgan Kaufmann Publishers, San Mateo, CA. USA.

Raymer ML, Punch WF, Goodman ED, Kuhn LA, Jain AK (2000). Dimensionality reduction using genetic algorithms. IEEE Trans. Evol. Comput. 4(2):164-171.

Shahzad W, Baig AR (2010). A hybrid associative classification algorithm using ant colony optimization. IJICIC 7(12):6815-6826.

Su Z, Hong H, Perkins R, Shao X, Cai W, Tong W (2007). Consensus analysis of multiple classifiers using non-repetitive variables: Diagnostic application to microarray gene expression data. Comput. Biol. Chem. 31(1):48-56.

Wang Y, Makedon FS, Ford JC, Pearlman J (2005). HykGene: A hybrid approach for selecting marker genes for phenotype lassification using microarray gene expression data. Bioinformatics 21(8):1530-1537.

Wei HL, Billings SA (2007). Feature subset selection and ranking for data dimensionality reduction. IEEE Trans. Pattern Anal. Mach. Intell. 29(1):162-166.

Yahang J, Honavar V (1997). Feature subset selection using a genetic algorithm. Pattern Recogn. 13(2):380.

Yang YH, Xiao Y, Segal MR (2005). Identifying differentially expressed genes from microarray experiments via statistic synthesis. Bioinformatics 21(7):1084-1093.

Zhang Z, Yang P, Wu X, Zhang C (2009). An agent-based hybrid system for microarray data analysis. IEEE Intell. Syst. 24(5):53-63.

Zhou H, Wu J, Wang Y (2007). Wrapper approach for feature subset selection using genetic algorithm. In: Proceedings of International Symposium on Intelligent signal Processing and Communication Systems. pp. 188-191.

11

Comparison of the performance of analog and digital hadronic sampling calorimeters

Y. Elmahroug[1]*, B. Tellili[1,2] and S. Chedly[3]

[1]Unité de Recherche de Physique Nucléaire et des Hautes Energies, Faculté des Sciences de Tunis, 2092 Tunis, Tunisie.
[2]Université de Tunis El Manar, Institut Supérieur des Technologies Médicales de Tunis, 1006 Tunis, Tunisie.
[3]Université de Carthage, École Polytechnique de Tunisie, B.P. 743 - 2078 La Marsa, Tunisie.

By using the tungsten as passive element and the Glass Resistive Plate Chambers (GRPCs) as active element, the gaseous hadronic calorimeter is studied as a possible detector for the future International Linear Collider (ILC). The results of the numerical study, using the GEANT4 simulation package, of the performance of this calorimeter when it is exposed to a negative pion beam in an energy range from 5 GeV to 100 GeV are presented in this paper. Operating characteristics of this prototype, such as signal linearity, energy resolution and reconstructed energy have been simulated and examined. Moreover, a comparison between the Digital Hadron Calorimeter (DHCAL) and the Analog Hadron Calorimeter (AHCAL) is made.

Key words: Calorimetry, resistive plate chambers, international linear collider (ILC), GEANT4.

INTRODUCTION

Among the most important objectives of future particle physics experiments at the international linear collider (ILC) [ILC reference design report (RDR); ILC Homepage http://www.linearcollider.org/cms/.] are searching for one or more Higgs particles and the study of their characteristics. Many interesting physics processes will be provided by the electron-positron collisions at the center-of-mass energies between 500 GeV and 1 TeV in ILC such as W, Z and H heavy bosons processes. These processes will be characterized by multi-jet. A very good energy resolution ($30\%/\sqrt{E}$) is required to the reconstruction of heavy bosons (W, Z, H) in hadronic final states (Doroba, 2004; Thomson, 2009).

The most efficient method to achieve this resolution is particle flow algorithm (PFA). This method allows to separate, respectively the deposited energies from photons and due to hadrons and the energies deposited from the charged hadrons and due to neutral hadrons in a jet. The optimal application of this technique requires

highly granular hadronic calorimeter in order to separate the shower (Thomson, 2009). Accordingly, the study of a calorimeter performance is an essential step.

In this context, several kinds of Hadron Calorimeters (HCALs) are under construction and testing (Ammosov, 2002; Ammosov et al., 2004; Andreev et al., 2005, 2006). Among the best HCALs are those which use Resistive Plate Chambers (RPCs) as active elements. This is due to their several advantages compared to other detection technologies, such as their strength and their very good performances in terms of temporal and spatial resolutions (Repond, 2007; Drake et al., 2007; Bilki et al., 2008, 2009). Glass RPCs were chosen instead of bakelite RPCs due to their long-term stability, they do not need oil surface treatment with linseed oil, their fabricate is simple with low production cost and their homogeneity (Calcaterra et al., 2004; Candela et al., 2004; Akindinov et al., 2004; Ammosov et al., 2007; Drake et al., 2007; Va'vra, 2003; Ambrosio et al., 2003; Fonte, 2002).

In this paper, a study based on GEANT4 simulation is conducted to investigate the performance of a HCAL using tungsten as an absorber material and RPCs as active elements. The objective of this study is to simulate the energy resolution, the linearity and the reconstructed

---

*Corresponding author. E-mail: youssef_phy@hotmail.fr.

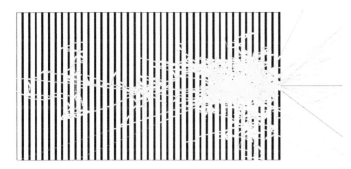

Figure 1. The calorimeter geometry for the simplified in GEANT4 with a 10 GeV pion event. White layers represents the absorber, and the black layers are the sensitive material.

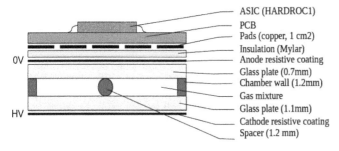

Figure 2. Schematic view of a glass RPC (Ammosov et al., 2007; Bedjidian et al., 2010).

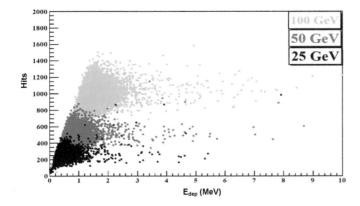

Figure 3. Correlation between the deposited energy and the hits number for 25, 50 and 100 GeV pions energies.

energy of single pions and make a comparison between digital and analog methods.

METHODOLOGY

In this study, the HCAL has been simulated with a Monte Carlo program based on the GEANT4 (Geometry ANd Tracking) version 9.2.4 (Agostinelli et al., 2003; The GEANT4 web page: http://cern.ch/geant4).

This program is inspired from the examples of GEANT4 (novice\exempleN03 and \ovice \exempleN07, extended \persistency: P01 and extended\electromagnetic\TestEm3 and advanced \lAr calorimeter) and uses the ILC Physics. There is a list to simulate the interactions of particles with matter (ILC Physics List Homepage). For analysis of the simulated data by GEANT4, we developed programs based on software Root (ROOT, version 5.30.01. CERN, 2011).

The calorimeter used in this study consisted of 40 layers; each layer is composed of an absorber and a sensitive material. The dimensions of calorimeters are $100 \times 100 \times 104.16$ cm^3 and they are in such away that 95% of hadronic shower cascades energy is deposited in the calorimeter for 100 GeV pion (Adloff et al., 2009; Leroy and Rancoita, 2000). The structure of calorimeter is shown in Figure 1. Each active layer is segmented into 1×1 cm readout cells (pads) and a total of 400000 channels in 40 layers. The absorber is a layer of 2 cm of tungsten and the sensitive detector is a RPCs having a thickness of 6.04 mm, these chambers consisted of two parallel glass plates spaced of 1.2 mm, with a thickness of 0.7 mm on the anode side and 1.1 mm on the cathode one. Between these two plates, we insert a gas mixture composed of R134A (93%), isobutane (5.0%) and a sulfur-hexafluoride (2%) (Camarri et al., 1998), and on the outer faces of the glass we put a graphite film with a thickness of 0.05 mm for the anode side and 0.06 for the cathodes one. Above graphite, we put a mylar layer with 0.05 mm thickness on the anode side and 0.18 mm on the cathode one. Finally, a printed circuit board (PCB) (G10) with 2.7 mm of thickness represents the readout electronics (1.5 mm) and the real PCB (1.2) is deposited on the anode of mylar. The structure of RPC is shown in Figure 2; for more details about the RPC structure see (Ammosov et al., 2007; Bedjidian et al., 2010).

We generated 10000 events of pion in the perpendicular direction of the calorimeter with energies from 5 to 100 GeV with a step equal to 5 GeV. The first 5000 events are used to measure the deposited energy, estimate the number of hits and the rest is for assessing the reconstructed energy.

ENERGY RESOLUTION AND LINEARITY

Deposited energy in analog and digital mode

The first step for analysis of the data simulated by GEANT4 is to measure the total deposited energy by a primary pion in the active medium (the RPCS). This was done by summing the deposited energy in all cells hit (hits or pads) which have an energy greater than the 0.1 minimal ionizing particle (MIP). This concerns the analog mode. For the digital mode, instead of using the deposited energy, we counted the total number of hits which has a deposited energy higher than 0.1 MIP. In fact, the number of hits is proportional to the total deposited energy. This proportional relationship is shown in Figure 3.

The second step for data simulation is plotting and fitting the distributions of the measured energy and number of hits. From the fit parameters, we determined the linearity and the resolution. The distribution of the deposited energy and the distribution of the hits number are shown respectively in Figures 4 and 5. We found that the deposited energy by primary pions follows a Landau distribution with right-hand tail due to the Landau fluctuation, but in the digital mode this fluctuation disappears, and the distribution follows a Gaussian distribution.

Linearity

As indicated previously, the fit parameters of deposited energy distributions and the hits number was used to estimate the linearity of the calorimeter response and the primary pions energy. Indeed,

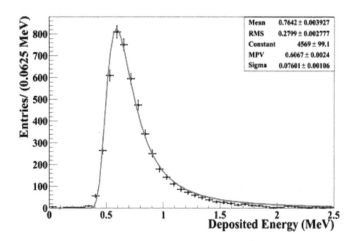

Figure 4. Distributions of deposited energy for 50 GeV pions.

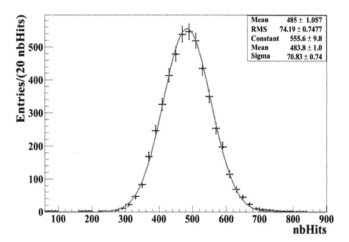

Figure 5. Distributions of hits number for 50 GeV pions.

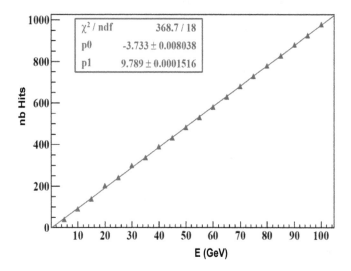

Figure 6. Linearity between the hits number and the primary pions energy for digital readout.

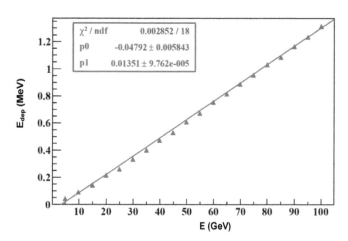

Figure 7. Linearity between the deposited energy and the primary pions energy for analog readout.

for each energy of primary pions, the average value of the Gaussian and Landau distributions was taken, then these values were plotted and fitted by a polynomial function of first degree ($p = p_0 + p_1.x$). The linearity between the calorimeter response and the primary pions energy for digital and analog modes are shown, respectively in Figures 6 and 7. It was observed that the deposited energy and the hits number are proportional to the incident energy. By taking into account the fit parameters, the deposited energy and the hits number are as follows:

$$E_{dep}(MeV) = (0.01351 \pm 0.00009762)E(GeV) - (0.04792 \pm 0.005843)E(GeV) \quad (1)$$

$$N_{hit} = (9.789 \pm 0.0001516)E(GeV) - (3.733 \pm 0.008038)E(GeV) \quad (2)$$

Resolution of the deposited energy and the hits number

The same method used to estimate linearity was used to determine the energy resolution. The fit parameters of the deposited energy distribution or hits number were used. Since the resolution is defined as the ratio between the width at half height and the mean value, it was determined and then we plotted as a function of the primary pion energy. The fitting was done by the following resolution function:

$$\frac{\sigma}{E} = \frac{S}{\sqrt{E}} + \frac{N}{E} + C \quad (3)$$

With S the term of stochastic, C is a constant and N the electronic noise term is not taken into account because there is no electronic noise in Monte Carlo simulations. The energy resolution for digital and analog modes is presented in Figure 8. The fits values ($p_0 = C$ and $p_1 = S$) are shown in Table 1.

At low energies, the energy resolution in the digital mode is better than in the analog mode, this can be explained by the fact that in an analog calorimeter, the deposited energy by a pion in RPCs presents a large tail due to Landau fluctuations. These fluctuations increase the energy resolution for the analog readout compared to the digital case, because these effects are suppressed in the digital mode (Magill, 2003). However, for high energies, the degradation of the resolution in digital mode was observed which is caused by saturation effects of hits number. Indeed, at high incident energy, the shower particle density will be very high, and this increases the

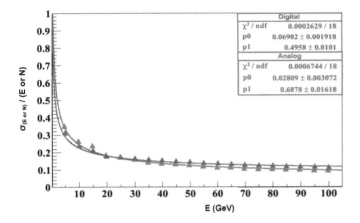

Figure 8. Comparison between the energy resolution of the digital readout and that of the analog (p_0 = C and p_1 = S).

Table 1. Parameters of energy resolution.

Mode	Stochastic (%)	Constant (%)
Digital	49.58 ± 1.01	6.90 ± 0.1918
Analog	68.78 ± 1.618	2.81 ± 0.3072

probability that a cell will be crossed by several secondary particles, but these particles will be counted as one hit (Wigmans, 2000).

RECONSTRUCTED ENERGY

Distribution of reconstructed energy

As previously discussed, the linear relationship between the calorimeter response and the incident pion energy can be translated by Equations 1 and 2. Using these two equations and replacing E by E_{rec}, the reconstructed energy can be written as follows:

$$E_{rec}(GeV)= \begin{cases} (74.01924 \pm 0.53484) \times E_{dep} + (3.547002 \pm 0.458124) & \text{Analog} \\ (0.102155 \pm 1.58 \times 10^{-6}) \times N + (0.381346 \pm 8.2715 \times 10^{-4}) & \text{Digital} \end{cases} \quad (4)$$

From these two equations, we determined the reconstructed energy of each primary pion. As noted previously, the reconstructed energy was calculated using events from 5000 to 10000 and to test and validate our simulation program. Figures 9 and 10 represent the reconstructed energy distributions using the deposited energy and the hits number for primary pions with energies of 50 GeV for two different event groups. The first group is composed by the first 5000 events and the second is constituted by the events from 5000 to 10000. It is clear that the distributions are similar for the two groups of events (parameters of the two distributions are very close). So, our program is valid and for the following work we will use only the second group of events.

It was also noted that the reconstructed energy distribution using the deposited energy has the same shape as that of the deposited energy distribution and also the reconstructed energy distribution using the hits number has the same shape as that of the hits number distribution.

Response and linearity

The linearity between reconstructed energy and primary pions energy is obtained by plotting the mean values of the reconstructed energy distribution according to the incident energy. These points are fitted by a polynomial of degree one. The linearity curves for digital and analog modes are shown respectively in Figures 11 and 12. From the fit parameters, it was deduced that the reconstructed energy can be written in the following form:

$$E_{rec}(GeV)= \begin{cases} (1.0009793 \pm 0.0004368)E(GeV) + (0.0052804 \pm 0.0000992) & \text{Analog} \\ (1.0036925 \pm 0.0011798)E(GeV) + (0.0016034 \pm 0.0000711) & \text{Digital} \end{cases}$$

$$(5)$$

The calorimeter response can also be described by another variable called the nonlinearity which is defined by $\dfrac{E_{rec} - E}{E}$, and presented in Figures 13 and 14 for two readouts. The maximum value of nonlinearity is about 1% for the analog mode and 3% for the digital mode. The linearity degradation in the digital mode is due to the saturation phenomenon. As earlier explained, at high incident energies, the number of counted hits is saturated; for this it does not follow the augmentation of incident energy (Wigmans, 2000).

Resolution of reconstructed energy

To determine the energy resolution $\dfrac{\sigma_{E_{rec}}}{E_{rec}}$, the same procedure which was used to calculate and plot theresolutions $\dfrac{\sigma_N}{N}$ and $\dfrac{\sigma_{E_{dep}}}{E_{dep}}$ was applied. The resolution for digital and analog modes is presented in Figure 15. As well as the deposited energy resolution $\dfrac{\sigma_{E_{dep}}}{E_{dep}}$ and the hits number $\dfrac{\sigma_N}{N}$ at low energies, the digital mode provides a better resolution $\dfrac{\sigma_{E_{rec}}}{E_{rec}}$. This is due to Landau fluctuations of the reconstructed energy in the analog case. At high energies, in the analog mode, the resolution is better than in the digital case because of the effects of hits number saturation (Wigmans, 2000; Magill, 2003). This resolution can be written as follows:

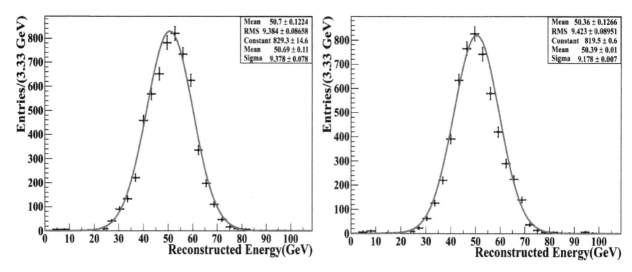

Figure 9. Distributions of reconstructed energy for 50 GeV pions for digital readout. (a) for the first 5000 events and (b) for the events from 5000 to 10000.

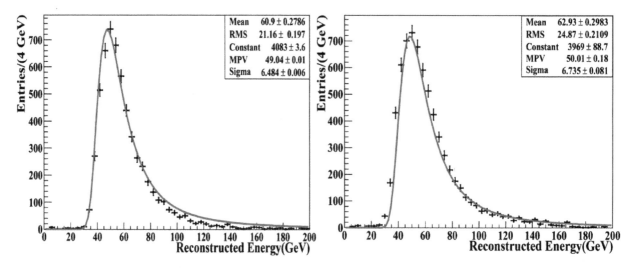

Figure 10. Distributions of reconstructed energy for 50 GeV pions for analog readout. (a) for the first 5000 events and (b) for the events from 5000 to 10000.

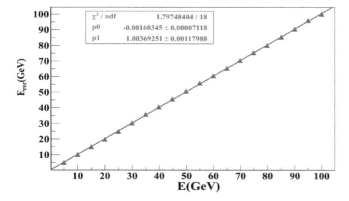

Figure 11. Linearity between the reconstructed energy and the primary pions energy for digital readout.

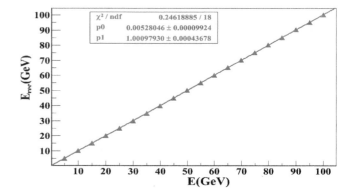

Figure 12. Linearity between the reconstructed energy and the primary pions energy for analog readout.

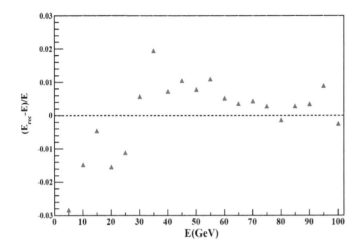

Figure 13. Full scale nonlinearity for digital readout.

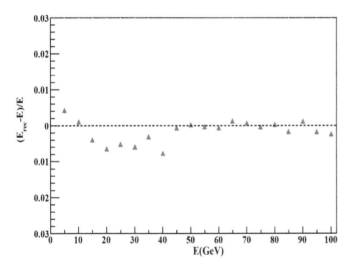

Figure 14. Full scale nonlinearity for analog readout.

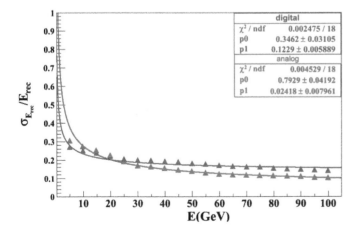

Figure 15. Comparison between the energy resolution of the digital readout and that of the analog, using reconstructed energy ($p_0 = S$ and $p_1 = C$).

$$\frac{\sigma_{E_{rec}}}{E_{rec}} = \begin{cases} \dfrac{(79.29 \pm 4.192)\%}{\sqrt{E(GeV)}} + (2.412 \pm 0.7961)\% \quad \text{Analog} \\[2mm] \dfrac{(34.62 \pm 3.105)\%}{\sqrt{E GeV}} + (12.29 \pm 0.5889)\% \quad \text{Digital} \end{cases} \quad (6)$$

Conclusion

The simulation study of the HCAL characteristics which uses tungsten as an absorber and RPCs as an active medium shows that at low energies, the energy resolution is better for the digital mode than for the analog mode, and the opposite for high energies. However, the calorimeter linearity response is better for the analog mode than for the digital mode. The analog resolution is dominated only by Landau fluctuations, but in the digital mode the resolution and linearity are degraded by the saturation effect which can be suppressed by applying two or three thresholds.

These results are valid for 0.1 MIP thresholds. The effect of thresholds on the calorimeter response, the choice and the optimization thresholds for digital HCAL and the performance study for semi-digital HCAL will be the subjects of the future work. Already, we started studying on the thresholds choice and the results will be published later.

This numerical work can be reproduced for other configurations, for example we can change the type of absorber (iron, lead or steel) and the type of active medium (MICROMEGAS or GEM).

REFERENCES

Adloff C Blaha J, Blaising J, Chefdeville M, Espargilière A, Karyotakis Y (2009). Monte Carlo study of the physics performance of a digital hadronic calorimeter. JINST. 4:P11009.

Agostinelli S, Allison J, Amako K (2003). Geant4 Collaboration. Nucl. Instrum. Methods Phys. Res. A 506:250-303.

Akindinov AV, Alici A, Anselmo A (2004). Study of gas mixtures and ageing of the multigap resistive plate chamber used for the Alice TOF. Nucl. Instrum. Methods Phys. Res. A 533: 93-97.

Ambrosio M, Candela A, Deo MDe, D'Incecco M, Gamba D, Giuliano A, Gustavino C, Lindozzi M, Morganti S, Redaelli N, Tonazzo A, Trapani P, Trinchero GC (2003). Aging measurements on glass RPCs. IEEE Trans. Nucl. Sci. 50(4):820-824.

Ammosov V (2002). TESLA digital hadron calorimeter (requirements, status and plans for R&D). Nucl. Instrum. Methods Phys. Res. A 494:355-361.

Ammosov V, Gapienko V, Ivanilov A, Sefkow F, Semak A, Sviridov Yu, Usenko E, Zaets V (2004). Small pad RPCs as detector for high granularity digital hadron calorimetry. Nucl. Instrum. Methods Phys. Res. A 533:130-138.

Ammosov V, Gapienko V, Ivanilov A, Semak A, Sviridov Yu, Zaets V (2007). Study of RPCs with 1x1 cm² read-out pads operated in the saturated avalanche mode. IHEP. P. 22.

Andreev V, Balagura V, Bobchenko B, Buzhan P (2005). A high-granularity scintillator calorimeter readout with silicon photomultipliers. Nucl. Instrum. Methods Phys. Res. A 540:368-380.

Andreev V, Cvach J, Danilov M, Devitsin E (2006). A high-granularity plastic scintillator tile hadronic calorimeter with APD readout for a linear collider detector. Nucl. Instrum. Methods Phys. Res. A. 564:144-154.

Bedjidian M, Belkadhi K, Boudry V, Combaret C (2010). Performance of Glass Resistive Plate Chambers for a high-granularity semi-digital calorimeter. JINST 6:P02001.

Bilki B, Butler J, Cundiff T, Drake G (2008). Calibration of a digital hadron calorimeter with muons. JINST 3:P05001.

Bilki B, Butler J, May E, Mavromanolakis G, Norbeck E, Repond J, Underwood D, Xia L, Zhang Q (2009). Measurement of the rate capability of Resistive Plate Chambers. JINST. 4: P06003.

Calcaterra A, Sangro R de, Gamba D, Mannocchi G (2004). Test of large area glass RPCs at the DAΦNE Test Beam Facility (BTF). Nucl. Instrum. Methods Phys. Res. A 533:154-158.

Camarri P, Cardarelli R, Ciaccio ADi, Santonico R (1998). Streamer suppression with SF6 in RPCs operated in avalanche mode. Nucl. Instrum. Methods Phys. Res. A. 414:317-324.

Candela A, Deo MDe, Giovanni ADi, Marco NDi, D'Incecco M, Gustavino C, Redaelli N, Tonazzo A, Trinchero GC (2004). Ageing and recovering of glass RPC. Nucl. Instrum. Methods Phys. Res. A 533:116-120.

Doroba K (2004). Precision test of electroweak interactions-what we have learned from LEP and SLC. Acta Phys. Pol. B 35:1173-1189.

Drake G, Repond J, Underwood S, Xia L (2007). Resistive Plate Chambers for hadron calorimetry: Tests with analog readout. Nucl. Instrum. Methods Phys. Res. A 578:88-97.

Fonte P (2002). Applications and new developments in resistive plate chambers IEEE Trans. Nucl. Sci. 49(3):881-887.

ILC Reference Design Report (RDR), ILC Collaboration, ILC-REPORT-2007-001. ILC Homepage: http://www.linearcollider.org/cms/.

Leroy C, Rancoita PG (2000). Physics of cascading shower generation and propagation in matter: Principles of high-energy, ultrahigh-energy and compensating calorimetry. Rep. Prog. Phys. 63:505-606.

Magill S (2003). Comparison of simulated analog versus digital energy measurement in a finely-segmented hadron calorimeter P. 009.

Repond J (2007). Calorimetry at the International Linear Collider. Nucl. Instrum. Methods Phys. Res. A 572:211-214.

ROOT, an object-oriented data analysis framework, version 5.30.01. CERN, 2011. Available:http://root.cern.ch.

The Geant4 web page: http://cern.ch/geant4.

Thomson MA (2009). Particle Flow Calorimetry and the PandoraPFA Algorithm. Nucl. Instrum. Methods Phys. Res. A 611:25-40.

Va'vra J (2003). Summary of session 6: Aging effects in RPC detectors. Nucl. Instrum. Methods Phys. Res. A 515:354-357.

Wigmans R (2000). Calorimetry, Energy Measurement in Pariticle Physics. New York, Oxford University Press.

12

Simulation analysis of the effect graded Zn(O,S) on the performance of the ultra thin copper indium gallium diselenide (CIGS) solar cells

Chihi Adel, Boujmil Mohamed Fethi and Bessais Brahim

Laboratoire Photovoltaïque, Centre des Recherches et des Technologies de l'Energie Technopole BorjCedria
B.P No. 95 2050 - Hammam Lif - Tunisie.

This paper indicated a numerical modeling of ultra thin copper indium gallium diselenide (CIGS) solar cells. An optimum value of the thickness of the structure has been calculated and it is shown that by optimizing the thickness of the cell, efficiency has been increased and cost of production can been reduced. Numerical optimizations have been done by adjusting parameters such as thickness of the layers and the gap. It shows that by optimization of the considered structure, open circuit voltage (V_{co}) increases and an improvement of conversion efficiency has been observed in comparison to the conventional CIGS system.

Key words: Graded pseudo copper indium gallium diselenide (CIGS)-Zn(O,S), solar cells, efficiency enhancement, solar capacitance simulator (SCAPS).

INTRODUCTION

Copper indium gallium diselenide ($CuIn_{1-x}Ga_xSe_2$ or CIGSe) solar cells is a multilayer thin film technology which has been increasingly developed in the last decade; thanks to its relatively low cost combined with high efficiencies. CIGSe is a direct band gap semiconductor with a chalcopyrite structure, a p-type doping and band gap varying continuously with the gallium content x from about 1 eV for pure Cis to about 1.7 eV for CuGaSe. Presently, the highest conversion efficiency never reported in thin film technology, with a record value of 20.3% was recently reported by Zentrum für Sonnenenergie- und Wasserstoff-Forschung Baden-Württemberg (Centre for Solar Energy and Hydrogen

Research) (ZSW) (Jackson et al., 2011). Over the past decade, the CIGSe field experienced an increasing industrial development with the commercialization of high efficiency modules (Powalla et al., 2006). It is now considered as one of the most promising alternative technology to silicon-based solar cells. The p-CIGSe layer can be grown by several vacuum and non vacuum methods, such as co-evaporation (Repins et al., 2008; Thornton, 1984), sputtering (Thornton, 1984; Nakada et al., 1995), ectrodeposition (Lincot et al., 2004) or nano-particles based techniques ()Vijay et al., 2003).

A numerical device model for the electronic and optical processes allows researchers for a good understanding

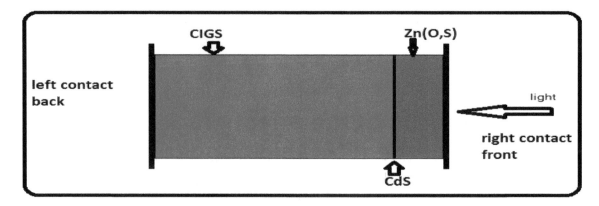

Figure 1. Schematic structure of CIGS based thin film solar cells.

and also, efficient optimization of thin film solar cells. There were several numerical studies for investigation of thin film solar cells that reports to investigate most important parameters of cells such as grain boundary, defects density and thickness which contribute in performance of thin film solar cell.

Several numerical software have been developed by research groups to predict the thin film solar cell performance of the cell, a typical CIGS solar cell structure which composed of three layers, namely a transparent conductive oxide (TCO) contact which composed of n-doped graded Zn(O,S), n-doped CdS buffer layer, and p-doped $CuIn_{1-x}Ga_xSe_2$ layer.

In this paper, in order to investigate the effects of cell composed layers thickness on the performance of the cell, a typical CIGS structure which composed of five layers grille/graded Zn(O,S) / CdS / graded CIGSe / Metalas is shown in Figure 1.

The aim of this article is to illustrate the effects of band gap grading in $Cu(In,Ga)Se_2$ absorber or CIGSe and in Zn(O,S) the purpose is to demonstrate that solar capacitance simulator (SCAPS) can handle such complicated structure.

NUMERICAL SIMULATION METHODOLOGY

In this study, numerical modeling of CIGS thin films solar cell has been carried out by SCAPS-1D, version 3.2.01 computer software to investigate the effects on absorber band gap grading on the overall CIGS solar cell device performance. SCAPS is a one-dimensional solar cell simulation program developed at the department of Electronics and Information Systems (ELIS) of the University of Gent.

Several researchers have contributed to its development (Burgelman et al., 2000; Decock et al., 2011). This version have several features such as almost all parameters can be graded (that is, dependent on the local composition or on the depth in the cell) : E.g, χ, ε, NC, NV, v_{thn}, v_{thp}, μ_n, μ_p, N_A, N_D, all traps (defects)N_t. Poisson equation used for semiconductor device:

$$\frac{\partial}{\partial x}\left(\varepsilon_r \varepsilon_0 \frac{\partial}{\partial x}\Psi(x)\right) = q\left(p(x) - n(x) + N_D - N_A + \rho_{def}\right) \quad (1)$$

Where Ψ is electrostatic potential, q is charge of electron, ε_r and ε_0 are the relative and the vacuum permittivity, respectively, p and n are hole and electrons concentrations, N_D is charge impurities of donor and N_A is acceptor type, ρ_{def} is the defect distribution . The continuity equations for electrons and holes are:

$$-\frac{\partial}{\partial x}J_n(x) + G(x) - R(x) = \frac{\partial n}{\partial t} \quad (2)$$

$$-\frac{d}{dx}J_p(x) + G(x) - R(x) = \frac{\partial p}{\partial t} \quad (3)$$

Where

$$j_n = -\frac{\mu n}{q} n \frac{\partial E_{Fn}}{\partial x} \quad (4)$$

$$j_p = \frac{\mu p}{q} p \frac{\partial E_{Fp}}{\partial x} \quad (5)$$

Where J_n and J_p are electron and hole current densities, E_{Fn} and E_{Fp} are Quasi-Fermi level for electrons and holes, G(x) and R(x) are charge generation and recombination rates. The system of equations described that Equations 1, 2 and 3 are solved numerically, using a Gummel iteration scheme with Newton Raphson substeps (Niemegeers et al., 1998; Selberherr, 1984).

SCAPS calculates solution of the basic semiconductor equations in one-dimensional and in steady state conditions.

Recombination in deep bulk levels and their occupation is described by the Shockley Read Hall (SRH) formalism. The current transport mechanism of our model can be explained in general terms by considering the effect of light on the band diagram.

Since the calculations require the input of device parameters, the surface recombination velocities of both electrons and holes were set at 10^7 cm/s. The solar AM 1.5 radiation was adopted as the illuminating source with power density of 100 mW/cm^2. The light refection of the front and back contacts was set at 0.1 and 1, respectively. The light absorption coefficient for CIGS layer was taken from absorption file. The other simulating parameters are given in Table 1.

RESULTS AND DISCUSSION

This paper indicates a study to optimize the CIGS based solar cell by considering the effects of layer thickness on

Table 1. Summary of the input parameters of the SCAPS demonstration model. The contacts are ohmic ('flat band').

Parameter	Graded p-CIGS	CdS	Graded n- Zn(O,S)
ε_r	13.6	10	9
χ (eV)	4.5	4.2	4.45
Eg(eV)	1.04 - 1.68	2.4	3.6
μ_n(cm^2/Vs)	100	100	100
μ_p (cm^2 /Vs)	100	25	25
N_c (cm^{-3})	2.2×10^{18}	2.2×10^{18}	2.2×10^{18}
N_v(cm^{-3})	1.8×10^{18}	1.8×10^{19}	1.8×10^{19}
N_A(cm^{-3})	2×10^{18}	1	10^{17}
N_D(cm^{-3})	1	10^{16}	1
Ve (cm /s)	10^7	10^7	10^7
V_h(cm /s)	10^7	10^7	10^7

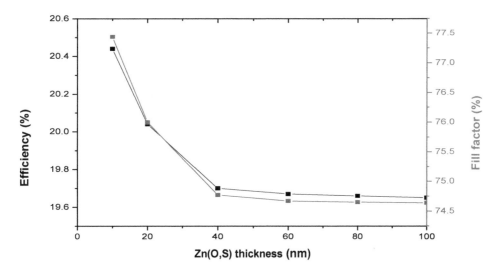

Figure 2. Variation efficiency and FF as a function of graded Zn(O,S) thickness.

the performance of the cell and the graded structure of Zn(O,S). In this respect, the structure of CIGS based thin film solar cell is shown in Figure 1. Figure 2 shows variation of TCO thickness Zn(O,S) versus fill factor (FF) and efficiency. It is shown that by decreasing the thickness of graded n-Zn(O,S), cell efficiency increases. It is due to this fact that n-Zn(O,S) is not fully transparent for light and this layer absorbs and reflects the sunlight. As it is shown in Figure 2 by increasing the Zn(O,S) thickness, light absorption increases and leads to lower efficiency. By decreasing the Zn(O,S) layer from 100 nm to 10 nm, cell efficiency increases from about 19.60 to 20.44; also FF curve has the same increasing rate as it shown in η. Calculation shows that variation of the Zn (O,S) thickness has no effect on the current density.

Figure 3 shows the variation of short circuit current (J_{sc}) and open circuit voltage (v_{oc}) interms of the graded p-CIGS. It is shown that by increasing the thickness from

2 nm to 3 µm, J_{sc} increases and after about 1 µm is constant. Also, Figure 3 demonstrates that by increasing the thickness from 2 nm to 3 µm, V_{oc} decreases exponentially.

Figure 4 shows the variation of η efficiency and FF versus CIGS thickness. It is shown that by increasing the thickness from 10 nm to 0.5 µm, efficiency increases from 18.30 to 20.04; efficiency increases about 10% and after 0.5 µm falls down. From the simulation, results were found that the optimized value of the graded p-CIGS is 0.5 µm which leads to a thinner and cheaper solar cell. Simulation results shows optimized value of CIGS and graded n-Zn(O,S) thickness is 0.5 µm and 10 nm, respectively. By choosing the optimized value J_{sc}, V_{oc} and η are 41.85 mA/cm^2, 0.63 V and 20.44%, respectively. From Figure 5, it is clear that in optimized structure V_{oc} increased, J_{sc} decreases a little but cell efficiency increases from 18.35 to 20.04.

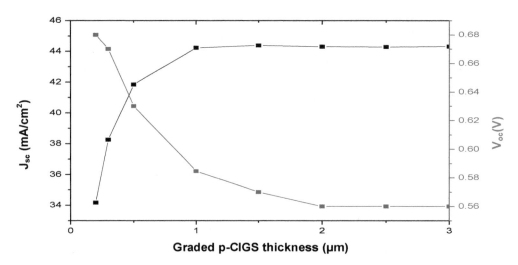

Figure 3. Variation of J_{sc} and V_{oc} as a function of graded CIGS thickness.

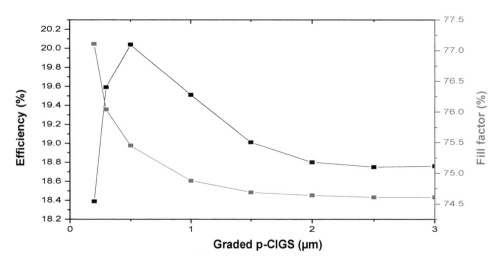

Figure 4. Variations of efficiency and FF as a function of graded CIGS thickness.

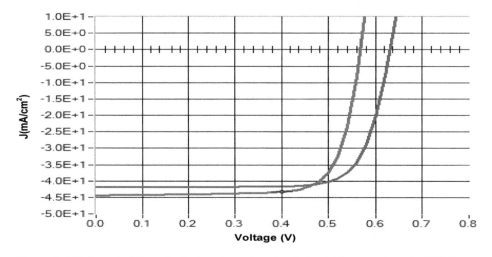

Figure 5. J-V characteristics of typical (red curve) and optimized (blue curve) graded CIGS.

Conclusion

This paper indicated a numerical investigation of graded CIGS based solar cells. Numerical optimizations have been done by adjusting parameters such as the combination of band gap, as well as the specific structure of the cell. From the simulation result, it was found that by optimization of the considered structure, optimized value of CIGS and TCO thickness is 0.6 um and 10 nm and an improvement of conversion efficiency has been observed in comparison to the conventional CIGS which cell efficiency increases from 18.04 to 20.04%.

Conflict of Interests

The author(s) have not declared any conflict of interests

ACKNOWLEDGMENT

The authors gratefully acknowledge Dr. Marc Burgelman, University of Gent, for providing the SCAPS simulation software.

REFERENCES

Jackson P (2011). New world record efficiency for Cu(In,Ga)Se2 thin film solar cells beyond 20%. Progress in Photovoltaics: Res. Appl. 19:894–897. http://dx.doi.org/10.1002/pip.1078

Powalla M (2006). Large-area CIGS modules: Pilot line production and new developments. Solar Ener. Mater. Solar Cells 90:3158–3164. http://dx.doi.org/10.1016/j.solmat.2006.06.052

Repins I, Contreras MA, Egaas B, DeHart C, Scharf J, Perkins CL, To B, Noufi R (2008). 19•9% efficient ZnO/CdS/CuInGaSe2solar cell with 81•2% fill factor. Progress in Photovoltaics: Res. Appl. 16:235–239. http://dx.doi.org/10.1002/pip.822

Thornton JA (1984). Reactive sputtered copper indium diselenide films for photovoltaic applications. J. Vac. Sci. Technol. A: Vacuum, Surfac. Films. 2:307.

Nakada T, Migita K, Niki S. AkioKunioka (1995). Microstructural characterization for sputter-deposited CuInSe films and photovoltaic devices. Japanese J. Appl. Phys. 34:4715–4721. http://dx.doi.org/10.1143/JJAP.34.4715

Lincot D (2004). Chalcopyrite thin film solar cells by electrodeposition. Solar Energy 77:725–737. http://dx.doi.org/10.1016/j.solener.2004.05.024

Vijay K (2003). Ashish Bansal, Phucan Le, Omar Asensio.Non-vacuum processing of CuIn1-xGaxSe2 solar cells on rigid and flexible substrates using nanoparticle precursor inks. Thin Solid Films 431-432:53–57. http://dx.doi.org/10.1016/S0040-6090(03)00253-0

Burgelman M, Nollet P, Degrave S (2000). Modelling polycrystalline semiconductor solar cells, Thin Solid Films, 361:527-532. http://dx.doi.org/10.1016/S0040-6090(99)00825-1

Decock K, Khelifi S, Burgelman M (2011). Modelling multivalent defects in thin film solar cells, Thin Solid Films, 519:7481-7484. http://dx.doi.org/10.1016/j.tsf.2010.12.039

Niemegeers A Gillis S, Burgelman MA (1998). User program for realistic simulation of polyrystallineheterojunction solar cells: SCAPS-1D, Proceedings of the 2nd World Conference on Photovoltaic Energy Conversion, Wien, pp. 672-675.

Selberherr S (1984). Analysis and simulation of semiconductor devices. Springer Verlag Wien-New York, http://dx.doi.org/10.1007/978-3-7091-8752-4

13

Simulation of circular jet outfalls using artificial neural network

Seyed Habib Musavi-Jahromi and Javad Ahadiyan

Faculty of Water Sciences Engineering, Shahid Chamran University (SCU), Ahwaz, Iran.

In the present article, outfall of the circular jet in the stagnant ambient fluid has been investigated. First, dimensional analysis for eleven involved parameters in the process, results in four dimensionless numbers including; relative length of jet trajectory, x/dp; jet convergence angel, θ_c; geometry number of jet, Di/dp and Densimetric Froude Number, Fr_d. Furthermore, using an experimental setup in the hydraulic laboratory of Shahid Chamran University (SCU), a large amount of data was gathered from several runs of physical model. Gathered data include coordinates of trajectory (x, z) and other involved variables. Then Qnet2000 as an artificial neural network (ANN) software was selected for simulation of the jet outfalls. In this regard, 192 runs of Qnet2000 were performed for training and testing processes. Then, in the application step, ANN model was used for predicting two values of z as upper and inferior limits of the jet trajectory. Findings showed that the model could simulate upper and inferior limits of trajectory very successfully.

Key words: Submerged Jet, outfalls, physical modeling, artificial neural network.

INTRODUCTION

The present article undertakes an artificial intelligence approach for predicting hydraulic properties of circular buoyant jets in the static ambient flow. In many cases, due to high concentrations of pollutants, or critical toxicity or even very high temperature wastewaters from nuclear reactors, inevitably dilution of wastewater to reach the limit concentration should be done in shortest time. One way to make quick dilution is using submerged jets in rivers or seas that can relatively in short period dilute large amounts of pollution due to its mixture of high turbulence conditions, and the destructive effects will rapidly reduce (Fischer et al., 1979). Jet behaviors are very important in the environmental field and real ambient flow. Environmental regulations and water quality objectives are mostly set in terms of pollutant concentrations in receiving waters. It is important to be able to predict the concentration distribution in the vicinity (the near field) of a discharge for a given discharge design and location, waste load, and environmental

conditions. This is required for defining mixing zones and minimizing the impact of discharges on sensitive receivers (e.g. nearby beaches for amenities, wetland reserve, or fisheries). The proper design of a submarine outfall can have a profound effect on the water quality actually observed near the discharge (Lee and Chu, 2003).

Turner (1967) and Kunze (1987) have investigated the salt fingering derived from a downward salinity flux. Maxworthy (1983) and Turner (1998) have shown that a two-dimensional surface intrusion, with a low Reynolds Number (R), will actually terminate its surface progression at the same distance and plunge downward. Cuthberston et al. (2008) studied particle deposition process for the case of a round, turbulent, particle-laden, buoyant jet, discharging horizontally into homogeneous receiving fluid that is initially either quiescent or co-flowing. Ahadiyan and Musavi-Jahromi (2008) have investigated variation of efflux momentum in shallow receiving water, using FLOW-3D, and have shown that the momentum flux decreases in the longitudinal distance of jet position, which is agreed with Turner (1967), Kunze (1987), Maxworthy (1983), Turner (1998) and Cuthberston et al. (2008). Vertical round buoyant jets in a cross flow have been investigated by Ben et al. (2004) and Papanicolau and List (1988).

In the present article, outfall of the circular jet in the stagnant ambient fluid is going to be investigated using an experimental set up and artificial neural network, which has not been considered in the literature yet.

Fundamentals

Buoyant jet is a kind of a free turbulence flow (Albertson et al., 1950; Rajaratnam, 1976). French (1986), illustrated hydraulic characteristics of buoyant surface jets and associated phenomena. In this kind of flow, the velocity of the turbulence is proportional to the product of the mixing length and the mean velocity gradient.

If the Reynolds number for fluid efflux, from a submerged boundary outlet is not too low, the mean velocity, v, at any point should depend only on the coordinates x, y and z on the efflux velocity v_0 and on a linear dimension, L_0. Thus, dimensionless relationships between these parameters are:

$$\frac{v}{v_0} = f_1\left(\frac{x}{L_0}, \frac{y}{x}, \frac{z}{x}\right) \tag{1}$$

Equation 1 is considered to involve the magnitude of v and the components of which may be related through the differential continuity equation. The flux of flow, Q, past successive normal sections, may be written as the integral of the differential flux v_x*dA over any normal section. Since the entrainment, Q will vary with the longitudinal distance x from the efflux section, its ratio to the efflux rate Q_0 is as follows:

$$\frac{Q}{Q_0} = \frac{\int_0^\infty v_x dA}{v_0 A_0} = f_2\left(\frac{x}{L_0}\right) \tag{2}$$

In which A_0 is the cross sectional area of the outlet. Similarly, since the momentum flux M may be written as the integral of the volume flux v_x*dA, the longitudinal component of momentum per unit volume ρv_x, ρ being the fluid density, the ratio of M for any section to M_0 for the efflux section should be:

$$\frac{M}{M_0} = \frac{\int_0^\infty (v_x)^2 dA}{(v_0)^2 A_0} = f_3\left(\frac{x}{L_0}\right) \tag{3}$$

The hydrostatic force against jet flow causes the deceleration of the jet and the acceleration of the surrounding fluid is the tangential shear within the mixing region; because this process is wholly internal, it follows at once that the momentum flux must be a constant for all normal sections of a given flow pattern:

$$\frac{M}{M_0} = \frac{\int_0^\infty (v_x)^2 dA}{(v_0)^2 A_0} = 1 \tag{4}$$

If, moreover, viscous action is presumed to have no influence on the mixing process, the diffusion characteristics, and hence the characteristics of the mean flow should be dynamically similar under every condition. In this research, predicting the hydraulic parameters and geometry of the trajectory in the buoyant round jets, including the upper and lower limits and length as shown in Figure 1, are investigated using physical modeling and ANN and artificial neural network.

Learning approach is appealing for artificial intelligence, since it is based on the principle of learning from training and experience. ANNs are well suited for learning, where connection weights are adjusted to improve the performance of a network. An ANN is a network of neurons, connected with directed arcs, each with a numerical weight, specifying the strength of the connection. These weights indicate the influence of previous neuron on the next neuron where positive weights represent reinforcement and negative weights represent inhibition (Gallant, 1993). Generally, the initial connection weights are random.

MATERIALS AND METHODS

Dimensional analysis

According to jet governing parameters, to achieve non-dimensional equation, dimensional analysis has been performed. The variables involved in the jet hydraulic are as follows:

$$f(\rho_a, \mu_j, u_0, d_p, D_i, x, \rho_j, g, Z_u, Z_2, \theta_c) = 0 \tag{5}$$

Where ρ_a, is ambient density; μ_j, is viscosity of jet injection; u_0, is efflux velocity; d_p, is port diameter; D_i, inlet diameter; x, length from jet location; ρ_j, jet injection density; g, acceleration due to gravity; Z_u, height of trajectory upper limit; Z_2, height of trajectory inferior limit and θ_c, is convergence angle of jet nozzle. Finally, using dimensional analysis, the non-dimensional parameters were derived as follow:

$$f\left(\frac{\rho_j.U_0.d_p}{\mu_j}, \frac{U_0}{\sqrt{(\frac{\Delta\rho}{\rho_a}.g.d_p)}}, \frac{Z_u}{d_p}, \frac{Z_2}{d_p}, \frac{x}{d_p}\frac{D_i}{d_p}, \theta_c\right) = 0 \tag{6}$$

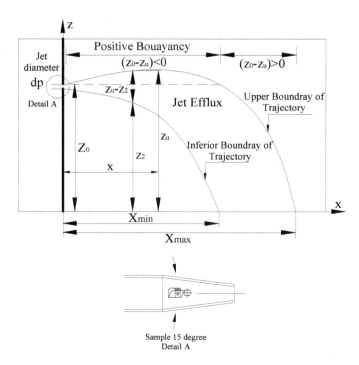

Figure 1. Schematic representation of the jet outfall and its nozzle details.

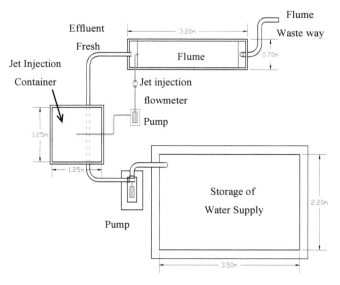

Figure 2. Schematic of the experimental setup.

Where in equation (6) the first parameter, is Reynolds number of jet efflux, the second parameter is Densimetric Froude Number [dimensional analysis gives geometric and hydraulic characteristics of the jet flow in the static ambient fluid as function of Densimetric Froude Number (Adrian and Stephan, 2004; Pantokratoras, 2003)], the third, fourth and fifth parameters denote coordinate of trajectory, the sixth parameter is the geometric number of jet and the last parameter is the convergence angle. In this research, trajectories geometry of round jet, which they had measured with artificial neural network, was predicted. The variables include various

discharges, concentration, and diameter.

The data were gathered, using a constructed physical model, with 3.2 m length, 0.7 m width and 0.95 m height, in the hydraulic laboratory, Shahid Chamran University, Ahwaz, (SCU), Iran (2007 to 2008). The schematic representation of flume and its equipments are shown in Figure 2. This figure represents supply of fresh water from concrete storage tank, using a pump with 20 L/s and 15 m of head. The means of supply pump, experimental flume from fresh water is to be filled. Jet injection through salt density current, is also transferred into experimental flume. Measurements include both

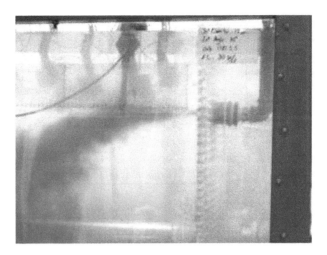

Figure 3. observed trajectory in the stagnant ambient flow in the hydraulic laboratory.

Table 1. Designed experimental scenarios of the research program.

Concentration (g/L)	Diameter (mm)	Discharge L/s	Convergence angle (°)
15			15
30	5	4 cases different	30
50	8	efflux velocity	45
200	15		60
			90

length and height of trajectory under different jet injection concentrations and constant temperature of jet injection. Figure 3 shows the real trajectory in the stagnant ambient flow, developed in the hydraulic laboratory.

As observed in the Figure 3, there are two boundaries for trajectory; one as upper limit of trajectory, and another one as inferior limit. The data gathered include results of experiments which had been performed in three diameters, including 5, 8 and 15 mm of round jet and 4 discharges. In the entire experimental data, thermal condition between jet injection and ambient fluid was constant. In performed experiments, the fluid density was measured, using a hydrometer 151H standardized carried out with ASTM E100 (2003) method, respectively. As shown in Table 1, several scenarios are considered to be investigated.

Artificial neural network

Trained ANNs can be used for prediction of outputs of new unknown patterns (Adineh et al., 2008). The advantages of using of ANNs are; high computation rate, learning ability through pattern presentation, prediction of unknown pattern, and flexibility affronts the noisy patterns (Hagan and Menhaj, 1994). In this research, feed forward networks are used. In addition, Levenberg-Marquardt (LM) regulation learning algorithms was utilized. The network types include:

Feed-forward back-propagation (FFBP)

This network consists of one input layer, one or several hidden layers and one output layer. Usually, back propagation (BP)

learning algorithm is used to train this network (which finally result in learning). In the case of BP algorithm, first, the output layer weights are updated. For each neuron of the output layer, a desired value exists. By this value and the learning rules, weight coefficient is updated. For some problems, the BP algorithm presents suitable results, while it ends to improper results for the others. In some cases, the learning process is upset because of trapping in local minimum. This is because of the answer lying at the smooth part of the threshold function. Figure 4 shows the training process of BP algorithm for the updating weights and biases. During the training of this network, calculations were performed from input of network toward the output, and then the values of errors were propagated to prior layers. Calculations were done layer-to-layer and the output of each layer was the input of next layer.

Cascade-forward back-propagation (CFBP)

This network like FFBP network uses the BP algorithm for updating weights, but the main symptom of this network is that each layer's neurons are related to all the previous layer neurons. Two training algorithms are used for updating the network weights. These algorithms are LM and Bayesian regulation BP algorithms.

For the LM algorithm, gradient-based training algorithms, such as BP, are the most commonly used by researchers. They are not efficient because the gradient vanishes at the solution. Hessian-based algorithms allow the network to learn features of a complicated mapping more suitably. The training process converges quickly as the solution is approached, because the Hessian does not vanish at the solution.

To benefit from the advantages of Hessian-based training, LM algorithm is used. The LM algorithm is a Hessian-based algorithm

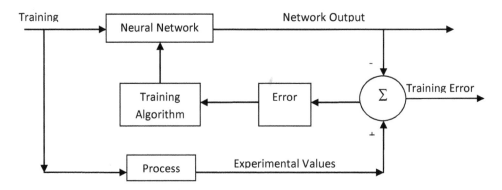

Figure 4. Training process of the back propagation networks.

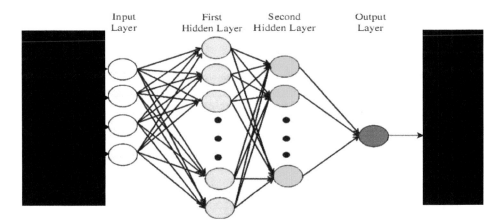

Figure 5. Applied ANN's topology.

for non-linear least squares optimization. The steps involved in training a neural network in batch mode, using LM algorithm, are as follows (Girosi et al., 1995):

1. Introduce all inputs to the network and computing the corresponding network outputs and errors;
2. Computation of the Jacobian matrix J;
3. Solution of LM weight updates equation as follows:

$$x_{k+1} = x_k - \left[J^T J + \mu I \right]^{-1} J^T e \qquad (7)$$

where, x_k is calculated weight in prior step; x, is weight value in new step; μ, is training parameter; $J^T_{k+1} J$, is Hessian matrix; I is the identity matrix; and $J^T e$, is the gradient (where e is the network error vector).
4. Error computation using x + Δx. If this new error is smaller than that computed in step 1, then reduce the training parameter *i ´* by μ⁻ and μ⁺; let x = x + Δx, μ⁻ and μ⁺ are predefined values set by the user.

In the Bayesian regularization (BR) algorithm, training process of BP, with BR algorithm, is initialized with random distribution of initial weights and biases. After presenting input patterns to networks, updating initial weight begins to obtain final distribution using algorithm. This procedure has a good approximation for training step, and can improve generalization performance. In this algorithm, instead of the sum of squared error (SSE) on the training set, a cost function, which is the SSE plus a penalty term, is automatically adjusted (Kozma et al., 1996).

Structural learning with forgetting is the main technique used for regularization (Kozma et al., 1996; Pirmoradian et al., 2009). It has good approximation with arbitrary accuracy for training, and it can improve generalization performance. The BR algorithm foundations are:

1. The performance function used for optimization is as follows:

$$J = SSE + \lambda \sum w^2 \qquad (8)$$

Where λ, is penalty factor within the range [0, 1] and $\sum w^2$ is the sum of square weights (SSW);
2. Network architecture includes selection of hidden layer and threshold function;
3. The prior distribution is setup with Gaussian distribution. Sensitivity analysis is performed in order to decrease the chance of being trapped in a local minimum and to find stable results.
Applying four inputs in all experiments, the output was derived from different situation. The following conditions are considered; networks with four neurons in input layer (relative length of jet trajectory, X/dp, which X is length of positive buoyancy and dp is port diameter; jet convergence angel θc; geometry number of jet Di/dp; Densimetric Froude Number Frd; and one neuron in output layer (relative height of jet trajectory Z/dp) were designed. Figure 5 shows the considered neural network topology, input, and output parameters.

Table 2. Maximum and minimum of parameters before and after normalization.

	x/dp	Θ_c	Di/dp	Fr$_d$	z/dp
Before normalization					
Min	0	15	2.54	7.28	0
Max	414	90	5.08	123.41	130
After normalization					
Min	0	0	0	0	0
Max	1	1	1	1	1

Qnet2000© software is used for this research. The Qnet2000© provides a complete set of functions and a graphical user interface for the design, implementation, visualization, and simulation of neural networks. It supports the most commonly used supervised and unsupervised network architectures and a comprehensive set of training and learning functions (Demuth et al., 2007).

For obtaining the desired answer, FFBP networks was utilized. Training process by this network is repetitive, when the error between desired value and predicted value is minimum and the training process moves towards stability. The increasing method was used for selection layers and neurons for evaluation of various topologies. By this method, when the network traps into the local minimum, new neurons are added to network gradually. This method has the more practical potential for detecting the optimum size of network. The advantages of this method is that network complexity increases gradually by increase in neurons. The optimum size of network is always obtained by adjustments. Monitoring and evaluating local minimum is done during the training process (Kozma et al., 1996). Various threshold functions were used to obtain the optimized status (Kasabov, 1998).

$$Y_j = \frac{1}{1 + \exp(-X_j)} \quad (LOGSIG) \tag{9}$$

$$Y_J = \frac{2}{(1 + \exp(-2X_j)) - 1} \quad (TANSIG) \tag{10}$$

Xj, is sum of weighted inputs for each neuron in the jth layer and can be computed using

$$X_j = \sum_{i=1}^{m} W_{ij} * Y_i + b_j. \tag{11}$$

Where m, is number of output layer neurons; W_{ij}, is the weight between i^{th} and j^{th} layers; Y_i, is the ith neuron output; and b, is the bias of the jth neuron for FFBP network. Experimental values for up and down boundaries are 1709 and 1514 patterns, respectively. About 80% of all data are random for training of network with suitable topology and training algorithms. Data for training step entered to the network, and the network is adjusted according to its error. The remaining data were used for test. Testing data have no effect on training, and provide an independent measure of network performance, during and after the training.

The performance of the neural network model was evaluated, using the root mean square error (RMSE) and coefficient of determination (R^2), between predicted and measur ed values of geometric and hydraulic properties. When the RMSE value is

minimum, and R^2 is ≥ 0.8, a model can be judged as very good. The RMSE can be calculated by the below-mentioned equation, where T denotes the number of data patterns; S, is network output of kth pattern and T_k, is target output of kth pattern (observed data).

$$RMSE = \sqrt{\frac{1}{T} \sum_{K=1}^{T} (S_k - T_k)^2} \tag{12}$$

In addition, the coefficient of determination is

$$R^2 = 1 - \frac{\sum_{k=1}^{T} [S_k - T_k]}{\sum_{k=1}^{T} [S_k - T_m]} \tag{13}$$

with $T_m = \frac{\sum_{k=1}^{T} S_k}{T}$

Another criterion is the mean absolute error, which is calculated from the following equation:

$$MAE = \frac{1}{T} \sum_{k=1}^{T} |S_k - T_k| \tag{14}$$

For increasing the accuracy and processing velocity of network, the input and output data were normalized and de-normalized, before and after the actual application in the network. Input data were normalized at a boundary of [0, 1] using:

$$X_n = \frac{X_i - X_{min}}{X_{max} - X_{min}} \tag{15}$$

Where X_n, is normalized value; X_i, is real value; X_{min}, is minimum real value and; X_{max}, is maximum real value. The maximum and minimum of parameters are shown in Table 2. Qnet2000© is capable of normalizing input and output data automatically.

RESULTS

Jet trajectory has two boundaries, upper and inferior. Using original experimental setup in the hydraulic laboratory of Shahid Chamran University (SCU), Iran, several upper and inferior limits were observed. Longitudinal 2D measured trajectory profiles are shown in Figure 6 for 1.55 m/s jet flow velocity. The coordinate of limit boundary of trajectory are x and z. Due to symmetry towards lateral direction, no y was measured. As shown in Figure 6, the length of the trajectory, upper and lower limits are increased when θ_c is increased. As shown in Figure 6a, however, the length of the lower limit of the trajectory for θ_c = 15° is 1080 mm, it is 1400 mm (30% increase) for θ_c = 90° (Figure 6d). Almost the same

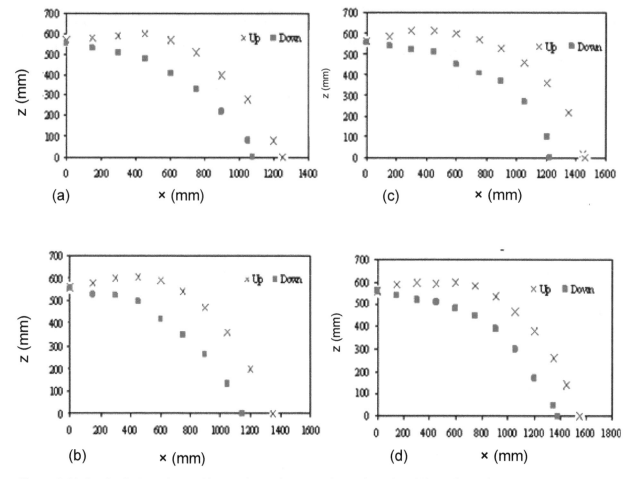

Figure 6. Limits of trajectory observed in experimental tests (a) θ_C = 15°; (b) θ_C = 30°; (c) θ_C = 60° and; (d) θ_C = 90°.

results are shown for the upper limit of the trajectory. For instance, Figure 6a shows this length equal to 1250 mm for θ_c = 15° and in Figure 6d, for θ_c = 90°, it is almost 1575 mm. This phenomenon is due to increasing of efflux momentum, which is reasonable. The momentum force is the major cause of jet power, which drive the jet flow forward. As a result, observation show that the convergence angle of jet nozzle significantly affects length trajectory. Table 3 presents the sample results corresponding to the change of upper limit coordinates.

In Table 3, Z_0 is the highest elevation of the jet diameter, which is constant in all experiments, and c variable is concentration of jet fluid, which plays role in the Densimetric Froude Number. In addition, increase of efflux velocity and Densimetric Froude Number lengthen the trajectory significantly. Table 4 demonstrate the changing of upper limit of trajectory to efflux velocity of jet flow.

DISCUSSION

Generally, on the base of experimental results which a

sample of these results were presented in Table 3, the comparison has shown increasing almost 25 to 30% of the development of trajectory, which has been due to changing of contraction angle from 15 to 90°. Also, as shown in the Table 4, increasing of efflux velocity up to 4 times is the cause of 10 times decreasing of $(Z_0 - Z_u) / x_u$. x_u is the x-coordinate of upper limit of trajectory. The main reason for the length of trajectory and contraction angle correlation is the increase of jet momentum flux, due to increase of contraction angle. The momentum flux is the main cause flow force, which is increased due to increases of contraction angle.

In this research, 96 types of neural networks, with different strategies (various threshold functions and various numbers of nods for hidden layers) for upper limit, and 96 types of neural networks with different strategies for inferior limit, were created. To achieve the goal, FFBP neural network was used. Two strategies were utilized for investigation of different threshold function effects on network optimization that include a one hidden layer and two hidden layers. Both strategies were used for FFBP network, with the learning algorithms of BP. The best results of the used network and algorithm

Table 3. Statistics of contraction angle effects on the upper limit coordinates.

dp = 8 mm, c =30 g/L, Q_0 = 0.026 L/s					
A = 15°		A = 45°		A = 90°	
(x/dp)u	(Z0-Zu)/xu	(x/dp)u	(Z0-Zu)/xu	(x/dp)u	(Z0-Zu)/xu
0.00	0.00	0.00	0.00	0.00	0.00
18.75	-0.04	18.75	-0.01	18.75	-0.05
37.50	0.09	37.50	0.28	37.50	0.06
56.25	0.30	56.25	0.54	56.25	0.28
75.00	0.67	75.00	0.91	75.00	0.49
80.00	0.88	76.25	0.92	93.75	0.70

dp = 8mm, c = 30 g/L, Q_0 = 0.053 L/s					
A = 15°		A = 45°		A = 90°	
(x/dp)u	(Z0-Zu)/xu	(x/dp)u	(Z0-Zu)/xu	(x/dp)u	(Z0-Zu)/xu
0.00	0.00	0.00	0.00	0.00	0.00
18.75	-0.11	18.75	-0.11	18.75	-0.11
37.50	-0.09	37.50	-0.09	37.50	-0.09
56.25	-0.01	56.25	0.01	56.25	-0.06
75.00	0.14	75.00	0.04	75.00	0.01
93.75	0.26	93.75	0.17	93.75	0.09
112.50	0.47	112.50	0.28	112.50	0.22
121.25	0.58	131.25	0.42	131.25	0.30
		141.25	0.50	150.00	0.47

for upper and inferior limits are shown in Tables 5 and 6.

As shown in Table 5, the best results of FFBP network in the first strategy for upper limit are related to 4-7-1 topology that produces RMSE = 0.0415, R^2 = 0.9774 and MAE = 0.005, with train data. For test data, results were RMSE = 0.0452, R^2 = 0.9725 and MAE = 0.0052. Furthermore, in this stage, application of Sigmoid-Sigmoid has a best result, because it produced lower RMSE and MAE values and higher R^2 value.

As presented in Table 6, the best results of FFBP network in the first strategy for inferior limit are related to 4-7-1 topology that produce RMSE = 0.0444, R^2 = 0.9766 and MAE = 0.0045, with train data. For test data result were RMSE = 0.0497, R^2 = 0.9714 and MAE = 0.0051. Furthermore, in this stage, application of Tangent Hyperbolic- Sigmoid has a best result, because it produced less RMSE and MAE values and more R^2 value.

The best results of FFBP network in the second strategy for up boundary are related to 4-7-7-1 topology that produce RMSE = 0.0401, R^2 = 0.9785 and MAE = 0.0045, with train data. For test data, results were RMSE = 0.0435, R^2 = 0.9745 and MAE = 0.0048. Furthermore, in this stage, application of Sigmoid- Sigmoid has a best result, because it produced less RMSE and MAE values and more R^2 value.

The best results of FFBP network in the first strategy for down boundary are related to 4-7-7-1 topology that produce RMSE = 0.0382, R^2 = 0.9827 and MAE = 0.0037, with train data. For test data,

results were RMSE = 0.0454, R^2 = 0.9762 and MAE = 0.0044. Furthermore, in this stage, application of Sigmoid- Sigmoid has a best result, because it produced less RMSE and MAE values and more R^2 value.

Figures 7 and 8 shows the relative length of jet's up and down boundaries versus pattern sequence of topology 4-7-7-1 for train and test data. The best R^2 for upper and inferior limits are shown in Figures 9 and 10, which belong to FFBP network, LM algorithm, and Sigmoid-Sigmoid-Sigmoid threshold functions, with topology 4-7-7-1 for both (up and down). In Figure 9 and 10, predicted values of the jet trajectory were obtained from this network, compared to experimental results (real values). Sensitivity analysis of selected topologies resulted in the weight of each parameter in output value. This process is done by Qnet2000© for upper and inferior limits separately. For upper boundary input values: relative length of jet trajectory, X/dp; jet convergence angel, θ_c; geometry number of jet, Di/dp and; Densimetric Froude Number, Fr_d, have 38.07, 4.13, 30.6 and 27.2% effect on the output (relative height of jet trajectory Z/dp), respectively. For inferior limit input values; X/dp, θ_c, Di/dp and Fr_d, have 33.98, 4.5, 34.76 and 26.76% effect on the output (Z/dp), respectively.

Conclusion

In the present article, jet outfalls in the static ambient fluid have been physically simulated in the Hydraulic

Table 4. Statistics of efflux velocity of the jet flow effects on the upper limit coordinates.

Angle = 15°, dp = 5 mm, C = 15 g/L							
Fr = 34.91; U_0 = 0.5 m/s		Fr = 57.36; U_0 = 1.0 m/s		Fr = 89.78; U_0 = 1.5 m/s		Fr = 119.71; U_0 = 2.0 m/s	
$(x/dp)u$	$(Z_0-Zu)/xu$	$(x/dp)u$	$(Z_0-Zu)/xu$	$(x/dp)u$	$(Z_0-Zu)/xu$	$(x/dp)u$	$(Z_0-Zu)/xu$
0.00	0.00	0	0	0	0	0	0
30.00	-0.18	30	-0.083	30	-0.183	30	-0.117
60.00	-0.06	60	-0.025	60	-0.125	60	-0.092
90.00	0.11	90	0.006	90	-0.083	90	-0.083
120.00	0.39	120	0.138	120	-0.0459	120	-0.071
140.00	0.80	150	0.217	150	0.01	150	-0.063
		180	0.325	180	0.081	180	-0.042
		210	0.45	210	0.14	210	-0.036
		214	0.526	240	0.194	240	0.018
				270	0.283	270	0.076
				290	0.388	290	0.133
						320	0.214
						340	0.331

Angle = 15° dp = 5 mm C = 50 g/L							
Fr = 16.68; U_0 = 0.5 m/s		Fr = 33.36; U_0 = 1.0 m/s		Fr = 47.47; U_0 = 1.5 m/s		Fr = 61.59; U_0 = 2.0 m/s	
$(x/dp)u$	$(Z_0-Zu)/xu$	$(x/dp)u$	$(Z_0-Zu)/xu$	$(x/dp)u$	$(Z_0-Zu)/xu$	$(x/dp)u$	$(Z_0-Zu)/xu$
0.00	0.00	0	0	0	0	0	0
30.00	-0.11	30	-0.116	30	-0.09	30	-0.05
60.00	0.18	60	0.008	60	-0.072	60	-0.092
90.00	0.78	90	0.161	90	-0.0056	90	-0.028
98.00	1.15	120	0.388	120	0.138	120	0.088
		148	0.760	150	0.256	150	0.163
				180	0.458	180	0.303
				200	0.562	210	0.489
						214	0.526

Table 5. Strategies for different neurons and hidden layers for several topologies in the training and test steps, upper limit.

No. of hidden layer	No. of hidden layers node	Upper boundary threshold function		Assessment criteria					
				R^2		RMSE		MAE	
		Hidden layers	Output layers	Train	Test	Train	Test	Train	Test
1	3	Tangent hyperbolic	Secant hyperbolic	0.9671	0.9655	0.0496	0.0511	0.0064	0.0067
1	5	Sigmoid	Sigmoid	0.9722	0.9692	0.0457	0.0483	0.0056	0.0061
1	7	Sigmoid	Sigmoid	0.9774	0.9725	0.0415	0.0452	0.005	0.0052
2	3, 3	Tangent hyperbolic	Sigmoid	0.969	0.9689	0.048	0.0481	0.006	0.0059
2	5, 5	Tangent hyperbolic	Sigmoid	0.9773	0.9718	0.0412	0.0461	0.0047	0.0052
2	7, 7	Sigmoid	Sigmoid	0.9785	0.9745	0.0401	0.0435	0.0045	0.0048

Laboratory of Shahid Chamran University, Iran. A large amount of data has been collected from 192 runs of physical models. Then, gathered observation data has been used for mathematical simulation using Artificial

Table 6. Strategies for different neurons and hidden layers for several topologies in the training and test steps, inferior limit.

No. of hidden layer	No. of hidden layers node	Upper boundary threshold function		Assessment criteria					
				R²		RMSE		MAE	
		Hidden layers	Output layers	Train	Test	Train	Test	Train	Test
1	3	Sigmoid	Secant hyperbolic	0.9681	0.965	0.0518	0.0551	0.0056	0.0061
1	5	Tangent hyperbolic	Sigmoid	0.9748	0.971	0.0468	0.0501	0.0047	0.0052
1	7	Tangent hyperbolic	Sigmoid	0.9766	0.9714	0.0444	0.0497	0.0045	0.0051
2	3. 3	Sigmoid	Secant hyperbolic	0.9649	0.971	0.046	0.05	0.0046	0.0051
2	5.5	Sigmoid	Sigmoid	0.978	0.9742	0.043	0.0472	0.0042	0.0046
2	7.7	Sigmoid	Sigmoid	0.9727	0.9762	0.0382	0.0454	0.0037	0.0044

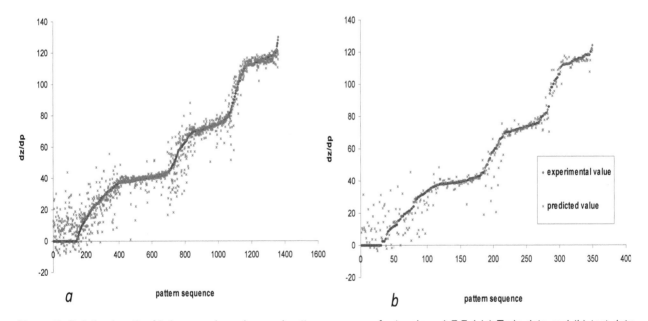

Figure 7. Relative length of jet's upper boundary and pattern sequence for topology 4-7-7-1,(a) Train data and (b) test data (the x axis denotes row number of arranged data from low high values of z/dp).

Neural Networks (ANN). Observed data showed that increase in contraction angle of jet is the main caused for increasing the length of upper and lower limits of the jet trajectory.

Among the ANNs networks, including FFBP network, BP algorithm, and Sigmoid-Sigmoid-Sigmoid threshold functions, with seven neurons for the first hidden layer, and seven neurons for the second hidden layer, were employed in the simulation process. Utilizing more than two hidden layers and seven nodes in hidden layers, in most of topologies, caused fluctuations and lack of stability, and sometimes divergence of neural networks. Neural network training parameters, such as learning rate and momentum factor, based on software recommendations and trial and error, found 0.01 and 0.8, respectively that causes minimal error and stability of training process. Sensitivity analysis of influence of the input parameters on output parameters showed that x/dp and Di/dp had the highest influence on z/dp.

Finally, however, several known and unknown

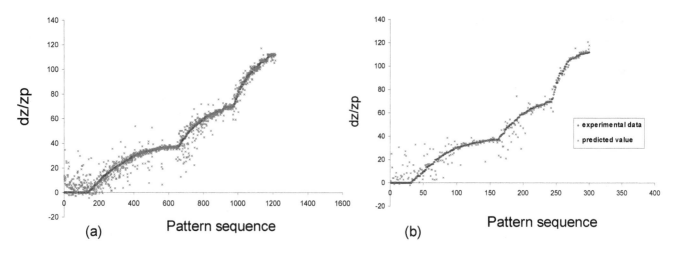

Figure 8. Relative length of jet's lower boundary and pattern sequence for topology 4-7-7-1. (a) Train data and (b) test data (the x axis denotes row number of arrange data from low high values of z/dp).

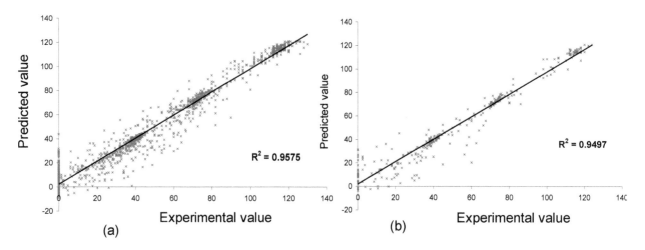

Figure 9. Predicted values of jet's upper boundary using optimum network versus experimental values and determination coefficient of optimum network (a) training step (b) test step.

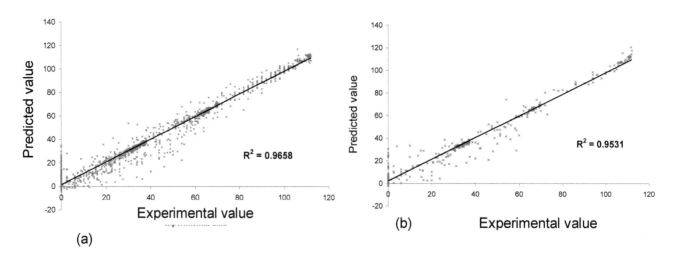

Figure 10. Predicted values of jets down boundary using optimum network versus experimental values and determination coefficient of optimum network (a) training step (b) test step.

parameters affect the jet outfalls in the stagnant ambient fluid; ANN is able to simulate jet outfalls characteristics very successfully.

ACKNOWLEDGEMENTS

The authors would like to acknowledge Shahid Chamran University of Ahwaz and the Centre of Excellence on Operation Management of Irrigation and Drainage Networks for financial support and facilitation of the experiments. The financial support of Khuzestan Province Water and Sewage Organization is appreciated.

REFERENCES

Adineh VR, Aghanajafi C, Dehghan GH, Jelvani S (2008). Optimization of the operational parameters in a fast axial flow CW CO2 laser using artificial neural networks and genetic algorithms. Opt. Laser Technol. 40:1000-1007.

Adrian WL, Stephan GM (2004). Double diffusive effect on desalination discharges. J. Hyd. Eng. 122:450-457.

Ahadiyan J, Musavi-Jahrom SH (2008). Investigation of variation of efflux momentum in shallow receiving water using FLOW-3D. Proceeding of International Symposium of Water Resource Management Tabriz, Iran. pp. 551-557.

Albertson ML, Dai YB, Jenson RA, Rouse H (1950). Diffusion of submerged jets. Trans. Am. Soc. Civil Eng. 115:639-664.

Ben M, Davies P, Malcangio D, Mossa M, Petrillo AF (2004). Turbulence of vertical round buoyant jets in a cross flow. In: Greco Carravetta, Della Morte (eds) River Flow 2004: Proc. An International workshop held at Napoli, Italy. London: AA Balkema, 2:1167-1174.

Cuthberston JS, Peter A, Davis PA (2008). Deposition from particle-laden round turbulent horizontal buoyant jets in stationary and coflowing receiving fluids. J. Hyd. Eng. 134:390-402.

Demuth H, Beale M, Hagan M (2007). Neural network toolbox 5 user's guide. The Mathworks Inc.

Fischer HB, List EJ, Koh RCY, Imberger J, Brooks NH (1979). Mixing in inland and coastal waters. Academic Press.

French RH (1986). Open channel hydraulics. McGraw-Hill Book Company. pp. 509-548.

Gallant SI (1993). Neural network learning and expert systems. Cambridge: MIT Press.

Girosi F, Jones M, Poggio T (1995). Regularization theory and neural network architectures. Neural Comp. 7(2):19-69.

Hagan MT, Menhaj MB (1994). Training feed forward networks with the Marquardt algorithm. IEEE Trans Neural Netw. 5:989-993.

Kasabov NK (1998). Foundations of neural networks fuzzy systems and knowledge engineering. Cambridge: MIT Press.

Kozma R, Sakuma M, Yokoyama Y, Kitamura M (1996). On the accuracy of mapping back propagation with forgetting. Neurocomp. 13:295-311.

Kunze E (1987). Limits on growing, finite-length fingers: A Richardson number constraint. J. Mar. Res. 45:533-556.

Lee JHW, Chu V H (2003). Turbulent Jets and plumes- a lagrangian approach. Kluwer Academic Publishers. Boston.

Maxworthy T (1983). The dynamics of double diffusive gravity currents. J. Fluid Mech. 128:259-282.

Pantokratoras A (2003). Vertical penetration of double diffusive water plumes discharged vertically downward. J. Hyd. Eng. 129:541-545.

Papanicolau PN, List EJ (1988). Investigation of round vertical turbulent buoyant jets. J. Fluid Mech. 195:341-391.

Pirmoradian N, Safshekan F, Sharifan AR (2009). Simulating hydrograph's peak time of occurrence using artificial neural networks in kasilian represent basin. ICWR 2009 International Conference, Shahrood, Iran.

Rajaratnam N (1976). Turbulent jets. Elsevier Scientific Publishing Company.

Turner JS (1998). Stratification and circulation produced by heating and evaporation on a shelf. J. Mar. Res. 56:855-904.

Turner JS (1967). Salt fingers a density interface. Deep-sea Res. Oceanogr. Abstr. 14:599-611.

14

Control response of electric demand by means of fuzzy logic using programmable logic controller (PLC)

J. L. Rojas-Rentería[1,3] , G. Macias-Bobadilla[1], R. Luna-Rubio[1,3],
C. A. Gonzalez-Gutierrez[1], A. Rojas-Molina[1] and J. L. González-Pérez[2]

[1]División de Estudios de Posgrado, Facultad de Ingeniería, Universidad Autónoma de Querétaro. Cerro de las Campanas S/N, C. P. 76010, Querétaro, Qro., México.
[2]Aplicaciones Computacionales y Biotecnología, Facultad de Ingeniería, Universidad Autónoma de Querétaro. Cerro de las Campanas S/N, C.P. 76010, Querétaro, Qro., México.
[3]Universidad Tecnológica de Corregidora, Carretera a Coroneo km 11.5, Querétaro, Qro. México.

This paper presents a controller of the electricity energy consumption for intelligent buildings. Special reference is made to a fuzzy control structure implemented in a programmable logic controller (PLC). Here the function of PLC is not only to connect and disconnect loads in the building, but to make use of vague terms from fuzzy reasoning. Using the class schedule, estimated consumption demand and the actual value, temperature and electric rates were used as a variables input to the controller for taking control action on the percentage of activation of ballasts for lighting lamps inside the building. A monitoring system was performed to forecast energy consumption in the building by means of artificial neural networks (ANN) as support for fuzzy control. The electricity consumption control has become an issue at the monthly bill that keeps record of that electricity consumption. The goal is to have a control that allows us a better management of the energy system and therefore savings on the final consumer, having a more uniform distribution of electricity consumption for building loads.

Key words: Fuzzy control, artificial neural networks, energy, programmable logic control.

INTRODUCTION

The control of electric power has become an issue at the monthly bill that keeps record of electricity consumption. It is essential these days to avoid penalties imposed by the various companies supplying energy, and obtaining significant energy savings and possible rebates, not only in industry but also in public and private buildings (Yan, 2006). The sum of the nominal values of all the loads of the building represents the maximum possible demand; peak load of the consumption may be the maximum instantaneous peak or average interval. The higher the energy demands at any given time for a period of 15 min, the higher the consumption charge. Due to the increasing demand for electricity in buildings, the complexity of systems and energy generation by companies increases according to their ability to supply energy. It is necessary to make an energy analysis for the construction of buildings through the professional application of technology by engineers and architects that design energy efficient buildings. After finishing the design and construction of the building, energy consumption is decided mainly by its control, maintenance and number of occupants; to achieve functional and satisfactory environments in intelligent buildings, the overall reduction in energy consumption through control systems is required (Doukas et al., 2007). In recent years there has been a concern for meeting the energy supply, covering the rapid pace of urban and industrial growth that the country has at present (Godoy and Cruz, 2011).

Currently, this demand shows a boom, since electricity is used in all sectors. Therefore, the electricity consumption in addition to being the best indicator of workload which is undergoing the entire electrical system is also a clear reflection of the economic activity and welfare of a country (Nguene and Finger, 2007). As the values of the electricity energy consumption are constantly changing, this variation depends on many factors difficult to measure; the most important are the pace of economic activity, population growth, the level of development, climatic and geographical conditions, the structure, luminosity and rate levels depending on the day of the week; besides technological changes as well as the efficiency of electricity production processes and appliances. That is, in just one day the electricity energy consumption can change by time in a year depending on the season (Vandad et al., 2009). It also depends on the day's consumption of the week before. On a hot day, energy consumption in buildings has increased significantly due to the use of energy for cooling (Basaran et al., 2011).

The problem above can be addressed through intelligent control systems, such as fuzzy control of electricity consumption. Where the inability to present the traditional algorithms to solve the uncertainties inherent in many problems related to the real world (character recognition, mathematical modeling of multivariable systems, etc...), it initiated a new trend in Computer Science Artificial Intelligence. Compared with conventional approaches to control, intelligent control uses information from the experts. It is also preferable, especially when the low cost and easy operation are involved (Mirnaser, 2010).

In recent years, several literature describes numerous techniques applied to fuzzy control following through the speculation and showing that "fuzzy sets" was the foundation of any logic, regardless of the number of truth levels. The implementation in control systems demonstrated the viability of fuzzy logic and facilitates decisions habitability and reparability of buildings. The mathematical foundation of fuzzy logic control was provided by Wang who showed that fuzzy systems are universal approximators (Ilyas and Yunis, 2006). Fuzzy logic is often an effective approach to these uncertainties. Fuzzy logic control is being increasingly applied to solve the power system problems in areas where system complexity, development time, cost and economics are the major issues about the buildings; in this situation fuzzy logic shows advantages over conventional control techniques either in terms of robustness and ease in implementing the control rules, where it describes development and optimization of the control system along with simulations of its performance (Chenthur et al., 2005). A training scheme for a fuzzy controller is derived for it minimizes the output error between reference

models. The trainings are conducted off-line for a class of set points conforming to the normal operating condition (Ahmed et al., 2001). Fuzzy set theory applications have received increasing attention in various areas of power systems such as operation, planning, and control. An approach based on the measure of potential losses, as well as a measure of potential gains, through the measure of an economic performance indicator through the use of fuzzy numbers and the concept of linguistic variable has been able to model the uncertainty and the economic risk that a company could face in an electricity market to satisfy the buildings in the public and private sectors opened to competition (Nguene and Finger, 2007). Modern production units and methods require increased flexibility, in highly nonlinear behavior of partly unknown systems. It is in this area that fuzzy modeling and control methods can play an important role, because an available qualitative operator and design knowledge can easily be implemented (He et al., 2003).

The aim of this study is to implement an intelligent control system for electric consumption in classrooms of the Faculty of Engineering of the Autonomous University of Queretaro, to avoid penalties imposed by the electricity supplier, as an alternative for saving money in efficiency, changing patterns of energy consumption and controlling its operation by means of automatic control.

MATERIALS AND METHODS

Fuzzy logic

Models based on fuzzy logic, are a set of modeling tools of representation or that belong to the field known as "soft computing". The fuzzy logic is a technique for incorporating human knowledge in efficient algorithms structured (Kazemian, 2004).

Many of the human intellectual processes are based on inductive reasoning; best exemplified are the arguments that linguistically respond to logical structures of the type: IF ... THEN..." We can thus argue that human knowledge is structured in rules like "IF ... THEN ..." and that this combination of rules leads to actions and decisions. One such rule is a function of multiple variables related with the association the "If" and called antecedents or causes, the variables associated with the "THEN", called consequence or effect.

Also, a characteristic of human knowledge is to characterize the situations, components, properties, etc., in a vague or diffuse term. Thus, for the human mind, for example, a skyscraper is not a building of over 100 m, but is a "high" building. Although this latest idea is an inherent uncertainty: What is the boundary between a very tall building and one that is not? This uncertainty can be bounded in mathematical terms through what is called membership function, which is the mathematical expression of degree (between 0 and 1) that values of an element belonging to a particular set by a specific fuzzy term (in this case "very high").

A fuzzy set is represented by a label, such as Z, taking values within the universe of discourse X, or limits within which it is defined, and characterized by a membership function μ_z takes values between 0 and 1 (Treesatayapun, 2008). The mathematical expression for a fuzzy set is reflected in Equation (1).

$$A = \{(x, \mu_z(x) \mid \in X)\}$$

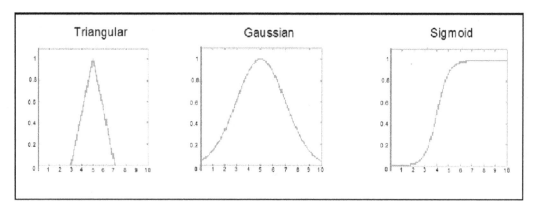

Figure 1. Membership functions.

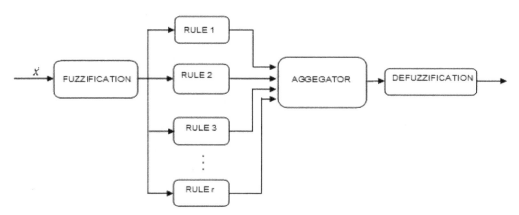

Figure 2. Fuzzy inference system structure.

$$\mu_z \colon X \to [0,1] \tag{1}$$

The membership function is a function that associates to each element (the fuzzy set) a value within the interval [0, 1] and within the universe of discourse. The most common membership functions are triangular, trapezoidal, Gaussian, sigmoid and bell. Figure 1 shows three membership functions, for as many fuzzy sets defined for a universe of discourse in the interval [0, 20].

Figure 2 shows the general structure of a fuzzy inference system. The input vector is represented by $\vec{X}$ and corresponds to the set of numerical values of the input variables of the system. The first task of the system is to convert these variables into numeric variables that you can manipulate the fuzzy inference system. This work is performed by the block "fuzzification" that calculates the membership levels of input values to the different fuzzy sets which has divided the universe of input variables to the system.

The basis of fuzzy reasoning is the rule like "IF ... THEN ...". The set of rules (rule base) is the linguistic knowledge that "has" the fuzzy inference system that allows you to solve the problem. Each rule corresponds to an expression as reflected in Equation (2). Where x_1 and x_2 represent two of the input variables and y represents the output variable.

$$IF\ x_1\ is\ A\ and\ x_2\ is\ B\ THEN\ y\ is\ C \tag{2}$$

In the Equation (2) A, B and C are fuzzy sets defined in the universe of discourse x_1, x_2 and y, and represented by the corresponding linguistic label. A fuzzy proposition "x_1 is A and x_2 is B" is called antecedent or premise and fuzzy proposition "y is C" is called the consequent or conclusion. A rule that expresses a relationship between **A, B** and **C** is called logical implication. The aggregator block manipulates the results of different rules to produce a result, still in vague terms, which the block "defuzzification" is responsible for converting a numeric variable.

Several types of fuzzy inference systems differ fundamentally in the consequent of the rules: the aggregation method and the corresponding "defuzzification" later. Such systems may include those of Mandini, Takagi-Sugeno y Tsukamoto (Pan et al., 2011). Of these, used in the research reflected in this document was fuzzy inference system of Takagi-Sugeno.

Artificial neural network

The study of artificial neural networks (ANN) is another one in expert systems. During the last ten years there has been a substantial increase in the interest on artificial neural networks. The ANNs are good for tasks involving incomplete data sets, fuzzy or incomplete information and for highly complex and ill-defined problems, where humans usually decide on an intuitional basis. They can learn from examples and are able to deal with nonlinear problems. Furthermore, they exhibit robustness and fault tolerance. Learning of a network shortly can be determined as the adjustment of the weights and the variables of the activation and transfer functions in order to perform a desired function (Kalogirou, 2000).

Neural network is composed of interconnected neurons as processing elements having similar characteristics as inputs, synaptic strength, activation output and bias. The interconnections between neurons carry the weight of the network (Singh et al., 2007). The advantage of ANN from other methods is its accomplishment in modeling the complex problems having many variables easily (Gonzalez and Zamarreno, 2005). A back propagation network is the most popular network because of the capability to find non-linear solutions to undefined complex problems. The errors of the output of a back propagation network are propagated back by means of the same connections used in feed forward mechanism by the derivation of the feed forward transfer function.

In the structure of hidden nodes, the nonlinear transfer function is modeled to process the information received by the input nodes. The network can be written as:

$$Y_t = \alpha_0 + \sum_{j=1}^{n} \alpha_j \ f\left(\sum_{i=j}^{m} \beta_{ij} Y_t + \beta_{0j}\right) + \varepsilon_t \tag{3}$$

Where m is the number of input nodes, n is the number of hidden nodes, f is a sigmoidal transfer function, as the logistic function:

$$f(x) = \frac{1}{1 + exp^{(-x)}} \tag{4}$$

The weight vector can be adapted for minimizing the energy function over the gradient descent direction. β_{ij} is the threshold value of the node activation or bias; α_0 y β_{0j} are the weights of the main arches of partial terms, which always have values equal to 1 (Gareta et al., 2006).

To prevent saturated connections, it is convenient to normalize input data and output for the same manner. If the neurons are saturated, there is a small change in the value of the item that can cause an error in the output value. To this end, data must be normalized before being presented to the neural network. The normalization compresses the range of the training data between 0 and 1:

$$X_n = \frac{(x - x_{min})*range}{x_{max} - x_{min}} + \textbf{starting value} \tag{5}$$

Where X_n is the value of the normalized data and x_{min} y x_{max} are the minimum and maximum of the entire data set.

Forecasting electricity consumption

We made a proposal from the estimation of electricity consumption in buildings, by an artificial neural network model with the Levenberg-Marquardt algorithm, in order to carry out the electricity consumption control in buildings, and have a comparison of the peak consumption of electrical energy demand. A number of runs of the software were done to generate 975 data for training and validation of the network. Also a number of different network sizes and learning parameters were tried aiming at finding the one that could result in the best overall performance. The network is a feed

forward back propagation neural network with four neurons in the input layer, four in the hidden layer and one in the output (Figure 3). The activation function used in the input layer is purely linear while for the other layers logarithmic sigmoid function was used. With this network architecture the best average of the absolute differences between measured and estimated values was selected, and expressed as a percentage of the measured values since its result as a percentage does not depend on aspects such as the magnitude of the input data. The objective of an ANN is to find an optimal configuration of weights, so that it can learn a set of patterns. Then the training becomes a nonlinear programming problem. The description of the algorithm was: a) determining the input and output variables; b) requires a subset of data covering the entire space of the same; c) the data set is divided into two parts: one part is used as a training set to determine the parameters of the neural classifier and the other part (called test set or set of generalization) is used to estimate the generalization error. Given various input vectors similar to existing patterns in the training set, the network will recognize the similarities between these patterns. The training set is divided into a validation subset to fit the model: d) a conventional model is developed to train the network with the data set; e) the relationship between inputs and outputs of the neural network is estimated. These steps are repeated to find the appropriate number of hidden nodes, using different training parameters for the network. 80% of the data was used to train the network, another 10% for the validation set and the remaining 10% to estimate the generalization. The initial weights were randomly initialized and a number of networks were simulated, each for a maximum of 1000 epochs, out of which the network with the best performance was selected. In back-propagation networks, the number of hidden neurons determines how well a problem can be learned.

RESULTS

The implementation of fuzzy control of electricity consumption took place in the building of Graduate Engineering School at the Universidad Autonoma of Queretaro (UAQ). The structure has five classrooms with an area of 40 m^2 and a conference room with an area of 56 m^2; one room is equipped with a brand air conditioner 18000 BTU Split York. Each classroom has independent lighting together with four fluorescent lamps 2×75 W. The design of the classroom included two windows 4 m long × 2 m high on the north side and another window of the same dimensions for the south side. The structure is a single level of 3 m in height (Figure 4).

It requires a monitoring system to acquire data on the behavior of demand through the power readings on the monthly billing of the building, measured per classrooms graduate in the engineering school at the Universidad Autonoma of Queretaro with a building management system (BMS) developed by us in the Engineering School and embedded on a web server. This BMS is based on a microcontroller module that allows checking out to monitoring building energy demand in real time via internet. The temperature data were obtained from February 25th to July 14th, 2011 with HOBO Pro V2 sensors that enable a rapid response information and data storage (Rojas et al., 2013).

Once the electricity power consumption of the building

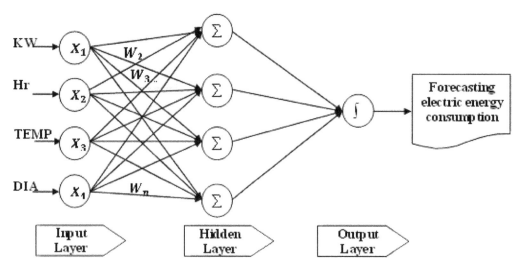

Figure 3. Artificial neural network architecture.

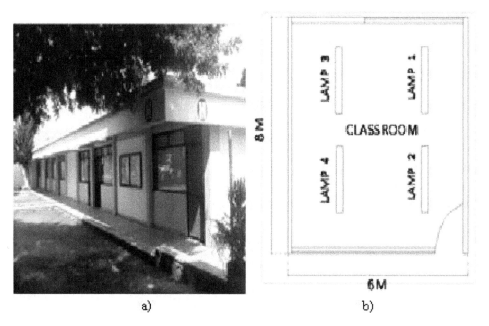

Figure 4. a) Engineering School building b) Classroom lamps.

was estimated, the proposal to control the electricity consumption in the buildings was the implementation of a fuzzy control on the structure of a programmable logic controller (PLC). A PC is used as a control center for the operation of the PLC programming protocol through a serial RS-232 interface for communication of user instructions. The programmable logic controller receives the commands through an input module from the control center. The generic control algorithms and instructions are written according to the protocol of the PLC logic in a ladder diagram (Function Block Diagram, or Structured Text) using an instruction Add-On (AOI) allowing a

transfer to the implication in the form of expert knowledge of linguistic IF-THEN rules to improve the functionality of control and decision-making in the PLC. Hierarchical structure enables the designer to decompose a complex fuzzy system into smaller and simpler parts, which reduces the internal complexity of a fuzzy model and results in fewer fuzzy rules and easier insight into the system operation. This simulation mode allows you to watch the influence of individual component values. 2D and 3D graphs with many options allow insight into the complex nonlinear mappings realized by the fuzzy algorithm. The function of the PLC algorithm not only is to

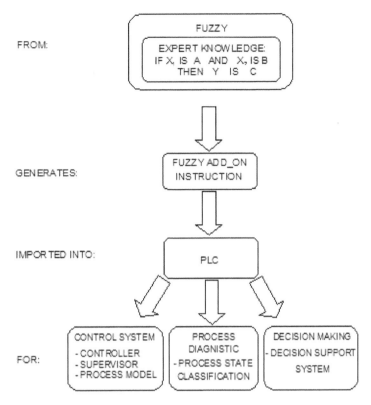

Figure 5. Fuzzy control application.

energize and de-energize the loads at the consumer side, but to use vague terms from fuzzy reasoning. Using estimated consumption demand, class schedules, temperature and electric rates as control variables in direct functions of rules, the number of rules then increases rapidly with the number of inputs and fuzzy terms for inputs dimensionality can, however, are reduced by hierarchical structuring of the rule base of the controller, which is supported by fuzzy logic (Figure 5). Based on these, we take the control action on the percentage of activation of ballasts for lighting lamps inside the classrooms.

For the present work along a period of five months the energy demand due to lighting in Engineering School classrooms was monitored. A fuzzy control of electric power consumption in the buildings was implemented and tested on the structure of a programmable logic controller (PLC). The input variables for the fuzzy controller are the error defined as the difference between the desired value of the estimated consumption demand and the actual value, besides schedules, temperature and electric rates, as control variables for the percentage of activation of the lighting ballasts inside of classrooms (Figure 6). The behavior of the system is influenced by the percentage of the overlapping of the fuzzy sets, that is, the limits of the defined functions. Every time that a new error, (and its derivative, of) is computed, the software produces a vector with new elements,

each one representing the membership degree of the input variables to the fuzzy sets.

According to the scheduling of classes and the temperature in summer time, the control is determined in Table 1, where the ballasts of lamps are operated in such a way that can provide the percentage of light intensity necessary to maintain the lighting conditions in classrooms (Figure 7).

An intelligent fuzzy logic controller to adjust the percentage of lamps intensity in intelligent buildings has been described in this paper combining the PLC structure with fuzzy logic theory and using the software RSLogix 5000 V16. The system has been experimentally demonstrated and its performance was verified. The configuring of a diffuse system of feed forward compensation gain and control of the electricity energy consumption in lighting a classroom is shown in Figure 8.

Figure 9 shows step function responses of the system have been derived. The experimental results show minimization of the response time of the system when fuzzy control is used to adjust the parameters of controller.

Each combination of error of the intensity lamps fuzzy set and a percentage of intensity change fuzzy set requires a control action. Ninety control rules are developed and presented in Figure 10. Each pair of error and of change inputs activates several rules.

The percentage of activation of the ballasts lamps in

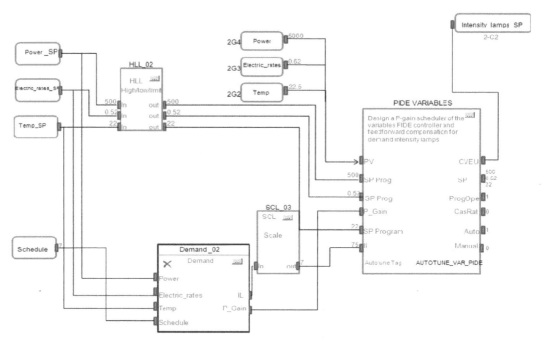

Figure 6. Add-On instructions.

Table 1. Intensity in lamps classroom.

Class schedule	Lamps intensity (%)	
	1 y 3 lamps	2 y 3 lamps
7 - 9	50	75
9 - 11	25	50
11 - 17	25	25
17 - 19	25	50
19 - 20	50	75
20 – 22	75	100

INTENSITY_LAMPS

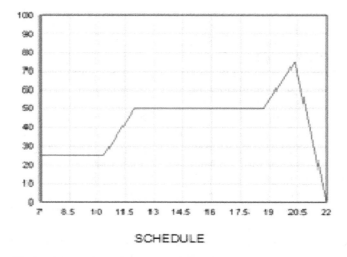

SCHEDULE

Figure 7. Lamp intensity percentage.

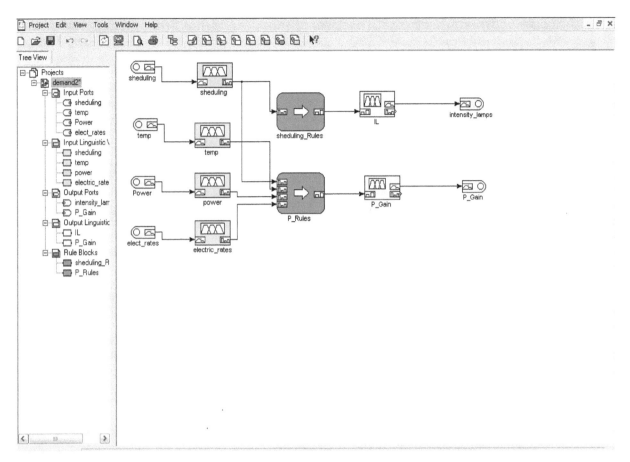

Figure 8. Add-On instructions for components.

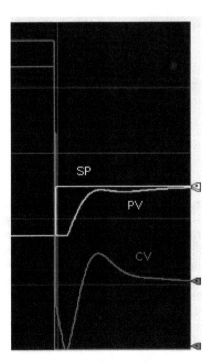

Figure 9. System under fuzzy logic control response.

classrooms intelligent building control was determined to ensure lighting considering the ranges of 200 to 500 lux, showing the estimation of combinations between data sets, based on the fit of the model to establish an optimal relationship between the variables in Figure 11 with a response surface generated by the controller.

Conclusions

A fuzzy control system for electric energy consumption in a control logic program was tested. A fuzzy logic controller is very responsive, practical and simple and meets all requirements with the advantage of a knowledge based approach with unknown system structure to produce reasonable control action in the sense of fast response of control; thus this methodology is considered effective. It was shown that the flexible structure of the fuzzy logic control leaves the designer to decide about the input–output universe of discourse and linguistic variables in terms of their shape, number and meaning, the construction of the rule base and the meaning of their operators and the defuzzification method.

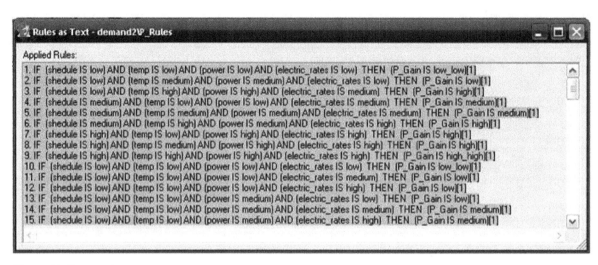

Figure 10. Fuzzy rules.

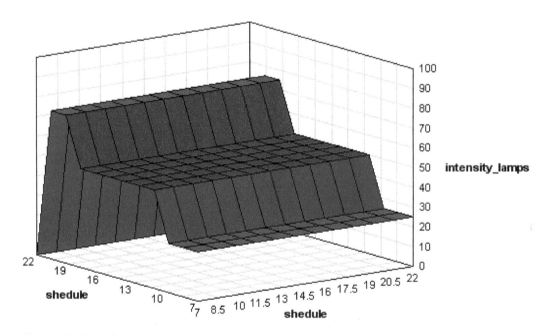

Figure 11. Controller response surface generated.

The field of general control, specifically in the intelligent control, is much focused that the control is executed in real time, where response time of this systems is critical. To reduce the time optimized algorithms can be used or implemented on programmable devices with many configuration options, combining hardware-software implementations and therefore the advantages of both.

In relation to additional works on the proposed scheme, it can be directed towards stability analysis of such controllers in the intelligent control applications. The fuzzy controller shows better performance than a simple PID controller, especially in load disturbance suppression.

The fuzzy logic controller can effectively incorporate linguistic IF-THEN expert rules. The fuzzy system has the network structure and the training procedure of a neural network. A fuzzy logic control initially creates a rule base from existing load data. Once trained, these data can be used to forecast future loads. In Trobec et al. (2006), the inside illuminance and luminous efficacy of the available solar radiation were analyzed with an automatic illuminance control based on fuzzy logic but for the positioning of the roller blind to take full advantage of daylight for inside illumination.

The proposed fuzzy control for electricity consumption system is a flexible tool that can be easily implemented and adapted to future applications. The system offers an improved solution due to its reliability, flexibility and efficiency. It allows consumers to control electric power consumption based on their priorities. This design of control at the customer side may be integrated with a digital energy meter to form a complete energy management system on saving energy up to 30 % in the billing. The fuzzy logic provides a better solution for all these cases, and the fuzzy based load forecasting is much closer to the actual load.

The control system meets the objective of this study to allow better management of the energy system with a more uniform distribution of electricity consumption for building loads just as significant savings in your monthly bill on electricity consumption.

REFERENCES

Ahmed MS, Bhatti UL, Al-Sunni FM, El-Shafei M (2001). Design of a fuzzy servo-controller. Fuzzy Sets Syst. 124:231-247.

Basaran UF, Omer GN, Kurban M (2011). A novel modeling approach for hourly forecasting of long-term electric energy demand. Energy Convers. Manage. 52:199-211.

Chenthur PS, Duraiswamy K, Christober A, Kanagaral N (2005). Fuzzy approach for short term load forecasting. Electr. Power Syst. Res. 76:541-548.

Doukas H, Patlitzianas KD, Iatropoulos DK, Psarras J (2007). Intelligent building energy management system using rule sets. Build. Environ. 42:3562-3569.

Gareta R, Romero LM, Gil L (2006). Forecasting of electricity prices with neural networks. Energy Convers. Manage. 47:1770-1778.

Godoy A, Cruz M (2011). Optimal scheduling and self-generation for load management in the Mexican power sector. Electr. Power Syst. Res. 81:1357-1362.

Gonzalez PA, Zamarreno JM (2005). Prediction of hourly energy consumption in buildings based on a feedback artificial neural network. Energy Build. 37:595-601.

He YB, Lim GH, Chua PS (2003). Comparison and application of three integral-improved methods on conventional fuzzy control strategy. Eng. Appl. Artif. Intell. 16:723-726.

Ilyas E, Yunis T (2006). Fuzzy logic control to be conventional method. Energy Convers. Manage. 47:377-394.

Kalogirou SA (2000). Applications of artificial-networks for energy systems. Appl. Energy 67:17-35.

Kazemian HB (2004). Comparative study of a learning fuzzy PID controller and a self-tuning controller. ISA Trans. 40:245-253.

Mirnaser M (2010). Fuzzy-logic and Neural network Fuzzy forecasting of Iran GDP growth. Afr. J. Bus. Manage. 4(6):925-929.

Nguene GN, Finger M (2007). A fuzzy-based approach for strategic choices in electric energy supply. The case of a Swiss power provider on the eve of electricity market opening. Eng. Appl. Artif. Intell. 20:37-48.

Pan I, Das S, Gupta A (2011). Tuning of an optimal fuzzy PID controller with stochastic algorithms for networked control systems with random time delay 2011. ISA Trans. 50:28-36.

Rojas R, Luna R, Gonzalez P, Gonzalez G, Rojas M, Macias B (2013). Estimated electric power consumption by means of artificial neural networks and autoregressive models with exogenous input methods. Afr. J. Phys. Sci. 8(14): 585-592.

Singh TN, Sinha S, Singh VK (2007). Prediction of thermal conductivity of rock through physico-mechanical properties. Build. Environ. 42:146-155.

Treesatayapun C (2008). Fuzzy-rule emulated networks, based on reinforcement learning for nonlinear discrete-time controllers. ISA Trans. 47:362-373.

Trobec ML, Zupancic B, Peternelj J, Krainer A (2006). Daylight illuminance control with fuzzy logic. Sol. Energy 80:307-321.

Vandad H, Furong L, Robinson R (2009). Demand response in the UK's domestic sector. Electr. Power Syst. Res. 79:1722-1726.

Yan M (2006). Demand side management in Nepal. Energy Pol. 3:2677-2698.

15

Modeling and simulation of watershed erosion: Case study of Latian dam watershed

Mirzai M., Sajadi A. and Nazari A.

Water- Energy Research Center-Sharif, Iran.

The Latian Dam is one of the important drinking water resources of Tehran, and it also has a role in preventing the flood. It is very important to keep the quality of water and preventing the dam from filling. Considering the special aspects of RUSLE model, it was used for estimating the amount of erosion in the watershed of dam including the sub-basins: Jajrood River, Kond River and Afjeh River, and then compared with the actual values measured. The results of modeling show that the degree of erosion is high because of steep slopes, lack of plant coverage. The results of modeling the amount of erosion in The Jajrood basin have been estimated about 1,524 ton/year, in Kond basin about 228.5 ton/ year, and in the Afjeh basin about 103.1 ton/year. By using the results of the water samples analyses, the amount of phosphorus entering the reservoir by the rivers were calculated. This research shows that, by using the proper coverage in the basin, the amount of sediment and phosphorus entering the reservoir, decreases considerably.

Key words: Latian Dam, phosphorus, reservoir.

INTRODUCTION

Soil erosion can cause ecological changes in the region. With regard to the role of planning and study of human and natural changes in erosion, assessment and adaptation model applied to each region, it is important. Latian Dam watershed is one of the areas where soil erosion is serious; the study of soil erosion in the area, as one of the water sources of Tehran is very important, particular area, population expansion, land use changed faces (Water and Energy Center of Sharif University, 2003a). Human sewage entering the river increased risk of erosion and sedimentation, pollution and nutrients in the reservoir. Including research done in this area;

Quantitative modeling of soil erosion using AHP (Analytic hierarchy process) in the watershed Latian (Maleki et al., 2011), evaluate the accuracy and efficiency of computer models II SEDIMOT in estimating runoff and sediment (Sadeghi, 1994), and the application and model evaluation M.P.S.I.A.C. Using satellite imagery, geographic information systems (GIS) in the sub-basin Lavarak (Tahmasebipoor, 1995) and comparison of models RUSLE and SWAT to estimate Erosions in the sub-basin Amameh (Poorabdollah, 2007). In this study, RUSLE model helping GIS system for modeling soil erosion in the watershed Latian was used. And modeling results are

Table 1. The data used in the model.

S/N	Model inputs	Applied data
1	Slope steepness and slope length	GIS map 1:50,000 Scale
2	Rainfall erosivity	Rainfall intensity got from Tehran's Regional Water Organization for 2 years
3	Meteorology	Temperature and rainfall Values at the different sub-basins
4	Soil erodibility	The soil map (1:50,000), separate reports including: the percentage of silt, sand, organic materials, soil structure and soil.
5	Land-use	1:50,000 maps containing the layers of orchards, pastures and farmlands with the related reports from Iranian National Geography Organization

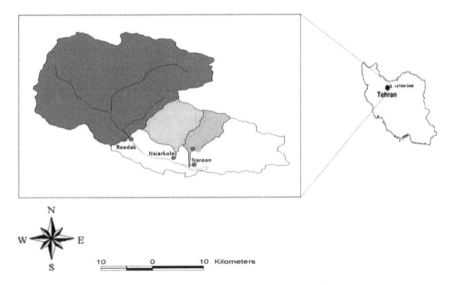

Figure 1. The location of stations and their upstream sub-basins.

compared with the actual values measured. The application of the RUSLE model has some advantages: (i) the data required are not very complex or unavailable in a developing country; (ii) this model is compatible properly with GIS software (Blonn, 2001), (iii) the use of this model is simplified by the presence of a graphical environment. Using this model with GIS information in raster format, the potential erosion can be found in any cell (Cox and Madramootoo, 1998). Also in regards to land use, based on management decisions, simulated erosion and its impact on the amount of sediment and phosphorus transport into the reservoir is shown. Study and modeling of the sub-basin Jajrood, and sub-basins kond and Afjeh is performed.

METHODS AND MATERIALS

The base equation of RUSLE model is as follows (Yazidhi, 2003):

$$A = LS \times R \times K \times C \times P$$

Where: A = the average annual soil loss (ton/ha/year); LS = the combination of the slope steepness and slope length (the factor without dimension); R = the rainfall erosivity factor; K = the factor of soil erodibility; C = the coefficient of plant coverage, and P = the coefficient of support practice.

The definition and application of every one of the above mentioned coefficients have been presented (Wischmeier and Smith, 1978; Desmet and Govers, 1996; Wischmeier et al., 1971).

The collected information about the watershed of Latian Dam is shown in Table 1. These stations together with their upstream sub-basins are shown in the Figure 1 and characterized in Table 2.

Input data

Figure 2 shows map of the river and its subdivisions, watershed boundaries and sub basins. Figure 3 shows the digital elevation map of the watershed (DEM) and the average slope values for each region. Figure 4 shows the type of vegetation in the watershed. Coefficients related to the vegetation which should be used in RUSLE model are shown in Table 3 and the values have been obtained from studies conducted in the region (Tehran's Agricultural Organization, 2002a).

Table 2. The specifications of measuring stations in the watershed of Latian dam.

Basin area (km²)	Sub-Basin	Elevation (m)	Latitude	Longitude	River	Station
403	Garmabdar, Meygoon, Ahar, Emameh and Roodak	1700	35-53	51-32	Jajrood	Roodak
58	Kond	1670	35-49	51-38	Kond	Najarkola
31	Afjeh	1790	35-50	51-40	Afjeh	Naroon

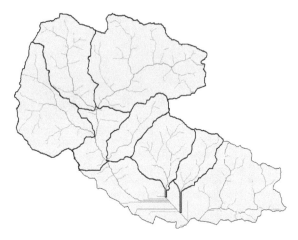

Figure 2. Distinguishing the boundaries of sub-basins with the help of arc view.

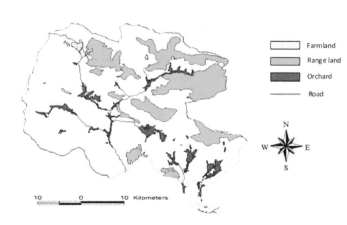

Figure 4. The map of plant.

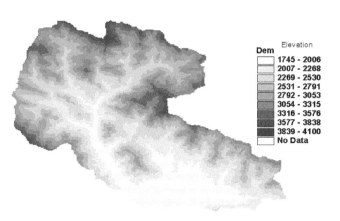

Figure 3. The DEM of the Latian Dam watershed.

The necessary inputs for the RUSLE model are: Average monthly temperature, the average amount of rainfall in month, the erosivity factor (R) and were obtained by studying the measured data in the stations (Tehran's Agricultural Organization, 2002b).

Soil types in this area include: Loamy, sandy loam, and clay loam. Types of Watershed soils are: 1 – Mountains; 2-hills; 3- flats and upper terraces; 4- Plains. Watershed land units, as part of the soil types are mentioned and Have the same physical characteristics, as of 1.1, 1.2, 1.3, 1.4, 2.1, 2.2, 3.1, 4.1 as shown in Figure 5 (Water and Energy center of Sharif University, 2003b).

The existing hydrological groups are shown in Table 4.

RESULTS AND DISCUSSION

The amounts of erosion, obtained from the model for any type of soil and any type of Land cover were presented for every sub-basin in Table 5. So, the whole amount of erosion per year in the basins of Roodak, Afjeh and Kond can be calculated by adding up the results of erosion in their sub-basins.

Due to the global equation erosion between any two regions with similar characteristics, whatever the place, the slope is greater or less vegetation or soil permeability is less, The amount of erosion in the area further. The result shows due to high slope and low vegetation in most areas, soil erosion is high.

Comparison with actual amounts and determining the model precision

A part of the eroded soil is transferred to downstream area by the flowing water in the form of sediment. This proportion is defined in the following way:

$$\text{Sediment delivery ratio (SDR)} = \frac{\text{The amount of sediment delivered to a point}}{\text{The amount of eroded soil at upstream of the point}}$$

To determine SDR and estimation of suspended load, the formulas proposed in this regard has been used (Foster, 2003).

Table 3. RUSLE input parameters for plant coverage.

Kind of plants	Canopy cover (%)	Falling height (m)	Residue	Canopy shape	Rock cover
Range land	50	0.2	Range litter	Rectangle	30
Farmland	30	0.3	The roots and branch residue	Rectangle	30
Orchard	35	2.1	Bushes and branches and leaves	Rectangle	30
barren land	-	-	-	-	30

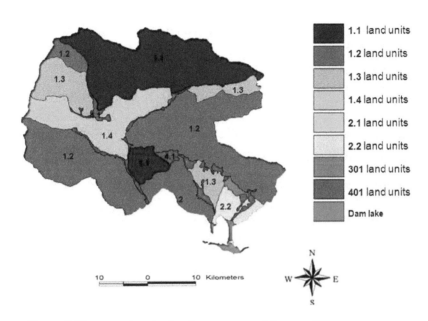

Figure 5. The map of evaluating the sources and the capability

Table 4. Hydrological groups of soil in the Latian Dam watershed.

Hydrological group	Minimum permeability (cm/h)	Runoff generation potential
A	7.5 - 11.5	Low
B	3.5 - 7.5	Low to moderate
C	1.5 - 3.5	Relatively high
D	< 1.5	High

The summary of the results (Including sediment calculated values and measured values and Model precision) are shown in Table 6.

Estimating the phosphorus load entering the water due to erosion

Total phosphate in the water consists of dissolved phosphorus and particulate phosphorus. The phosphorus existing in the sediments from soil erosion is particulate phosphorus. The amount of phosphorus in the unit of suspended sediment load is calculated from dividing particulate phosphorus load by suspended sediment load. This amount can be used for estimating the particulate phosphorus load entering the water after using the management procedures for preventing the erosion (the change of land-use) and investigating the change of the amount of phosphorus using these procedures. For calculating the phosphorus load, the results of the tests done by Sharif University of Technology were used. Figure 6 shows the variation of phosphorus-discharge at the mentioned stations.

The amounts of particulate phosphorus are shown in Table 7 based on the results of existing data.

Table 5. The results of erosion modeling in the sub-basins.

Sub-basin	The type of soil	Permeability (cm/h)	Land cover	Slope (degree)	Area (km^2)	Erosion (ton/ km^2/year)	Erosion (ton/year)
Garmabdar	SL (1.1)	1.5	P	23.7	25.8	3362	86833
			F-L	23.6	0.173	425.8	73.67
			B-L	26.7	52.8	4482	236844
	L (1.3)	5.5	P	22.2	10.0	3138	31376
			O	16.4	1.16	2465	2860
			B-L	19.8	3.49	3138	10950
	L (1.2)	2.5	P	23.7	23.6	3810	89953
			B-L	26.2	19.4	4931	95701
	SL (4.1)	5.5	O	18.1	0.76	2241	1703
			B-L	17.7	1.52	2241	3407
	SL (1.4)	2.5	O	15.8	0.871	2465	2147
			B-L	22.6	15.4	3586	55093
			P	27.9	2.75	3810	10481
Meygoon	SL (1.1)	1.5	F-L	18.3	1.94	336.2	650.8
			P	20.3	8.50	2913	24773
			B-L	25.7	21.5	4482	96531
	L (1.2)	2.5	F-L	20.7	0.331	358.6	118.7
			P	14.2	0.217	1860	403.7
			B-L	21.9	8.19	3586	29350
	L (1.3)	5.5	B-L	24.8	18.4	3362	61822
			O	18.5	0.600	2465	1479
	SL (4.1)	5.5	B-L	18.4	1.96	2465	4832
			O	11.5	1.23	1345	1655
	SL (1.4)	2.5	O	18.5	0.917	2914	2672
			F-L	24.6	0.283	403.4	114.2
			B-L	25.0	12.6	3810	48173
Ahar	L (1.3)	4	B-L	27.8	10.2	3810	38679
	SL (1.4)	5.5	B-L	25.2	24.7	3362	83169
			F-L	20.7	0.041	448.2	18.38
	SL (4.1)	5.5	B-L	19.1	1.57	2465	3878
			O	13.2	0.520	1569	815.8
	L (1.2)	2.5	O	14.8	1.76	2241	3940
			F-L	10.4	0.162	269	43.57
			B-L	23.9	55.2	3810	21085
Roodak	SL (1.4)	2.5	O	11.1	0.612	1591	973.8
			B-L	22.0	4.78	3586	17155
	SL (4.1)	5.5	O	10.4	0.290	1233	357.5
			B-L	22.4	1.79	3138	5626
	L (1.2)	2.5	P	22.5	1.19	3362	4000
			O	14.9	0.085	2465	210
			B-L	22.8	4.88	3810	18574
	SL (1.1)	1.5	B-L	27.2	7.58	4931	37378
	L (1.2)	2.5	O	5.7	0.212	672.3	142.5
			B-L	19.3	15.4	3138	48260
Emameh	L (1.2)	2.5	P	29.9	5.81	4483	26042
			O	26.8	0.472	4706	2221

Table 5. Contd.

Station	Soil		Land use				
			B-L	24.0	12.3	4706	57969
	SL (4.1)	5.5	O	8.9	2.18	1009	2197
			B-L	13.1	0.711	1726	12267
	SL (1.1)	2.5	O	16.1	0.073	2465	180.0
			B-L	22.2	8.35	3586	29952
	L (1.2)	2.5	P	26.6	2.82	4034	11380
			B-L	22.2	4.38	4482	19641
Afjeh	L (1.2)	2.5	O	22.0	0.307	3586	1101
			P	29.3	3.08	4258	13128
			B-L	25.3	15.0	4931	73894
	SL (3.1)	5.5	O	12.7	0.27	1569	423.6
			B-L	18.2	1.37	2465	3375
	SL (4.1)	5.5	O	10.2	1.68	1188	1990
			B-L	8.7	1.39	1031	1427
	CL (2.2)	2.5	B-L	12.5	4.53	1031	4672
			O	11.3	0.984	874.1	860.1
	CL (2.2)	2.5	B-L	14.7	1.68	1233	2075
			O	10.6	0.09	806.8	72.61
	SL (3.1)	5.5	O	2.30	0.34	150.2	51.50
			B-L	2.00	0.336	145.7	48.95
Kond	L (1.2)	2.5	P	31.3	6.46	4931	31827
			O	19.5	0.094	3362	316.00
			B-L	29.4	14.4	6051	87166
	SL (4.1)	5.5	O	11.0	1.24	1390	1716
			B-L	13.5	4.01	1860.	7465
	SL (3.1)	5.5	B-L	22.1	1.38	3138	4330
	L (1.3)	5.5	O	12.6	2.21	2062	4563
			B-L	13.5	8.5	2241	19050
	CL (2.2)	2.5	B-L	15.1	3.09	1345	4155
	L (1.2)	2.5	O	12.0	0.536	1927	1033
			P	22.8	1.93	3586	6921
			B-L	21.5	13.4	4482	59929

SL=Sandy loam, L= Loamy, CL= Clay loam; F= Farm land, Barren land, Pasture=P, Orchard=O.

Table 6. The results of calculated sediment load by the model and measurement.

Station	Soil loss (ton/year)	SDR (%)	Estimated total sediments (ton/year)	Calculated suspended load (ton/year)	Actual suspended load (ton/year)	Model precision (%)
Roodak	1524	16	243.8	187.6	216.0	86.8
Najarkola	228.5	24.7	56.49	43.38	50.09	86
Naroon	103.1	28	288.9	22.22	40.64	55*

*In Afjeh because the lack of actual suspended load data, this number (40637) in the above table is not a good indicator for this parameter. Therefore the obtained precision is not a suitable value for model in Afjeh basin.

The change of land-uses and estimating the erosion variation

Now, with the change of the land-uses in the basin according to the Figure 7, erosion modeling was performed. The results of running the model again are presented in Table 8. The compared results are presented in Table 9.

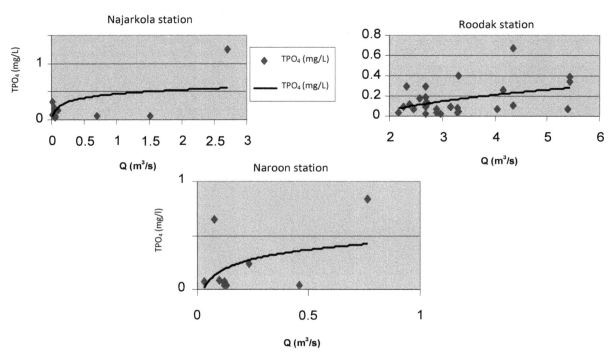

Figure 6. Variation of total phosphate (TPO$_4$) and river discharge (Q) at the Najarkola, Roodak and Naroon stations.

Table 7. The amounts of particulate phosphorus due to erosion in the stations.

Basin	The particulate phosphorus resulted from erosion (ton/year)	The amount of phosphorus in the suspended sediment load (g/ton)
Roodak	12.10	56.21
Kond	1.587	31.7
Afjeh	0.295	7.3*

* In Afjeh because the lack of actual suspended load data, this number in the above table is not a good indicator for this parameter.

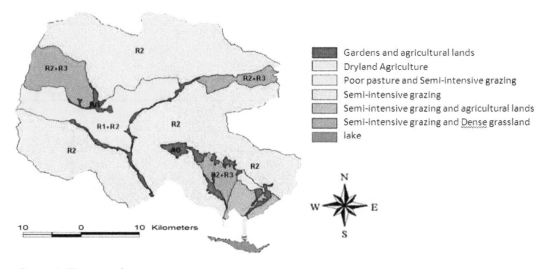

Figure 7. The map of present land use.

Table 8. The result of erosion modeling in the basin with new land.

Basin	Area	The recommended land-use	Slope (degree)	Area (km^2)	Erosion (ton/km^2 /year)	Erosion (ton/year)
Garmabdar	1.1	R2	25.98	78.90	1569	123700
	1.3	R2+R3	22.39	14.60	538	7864
	4.1	AO	15.58	2.28	1569	3773
	1.4	R1+R2	24.32	19.00	2465	46840
	1.2	R2	25.58	42.90	1726	73980
Meygoon	1.1	R2	25.42	31.90	1524	48554
	1.2	R2	21.10	8.73	1345	11739
	1.3	R2+R3	24.93	19.00	650	12348
	1.4	R1+R2	22.65	13.80	2174	30043
	4.1	AO	17.43	3.19	1905	6077
Ahar	1.2	R2	24.15	57.11	1905	108793
	1.3	R2+R3	28.08	10.15	1053	10691
	1.4	R1+R2	25.22	24.77	2689	66616
	4.1	AO	21.28	2.09	2465	5457
Roodak	1.1	R2	29.10	7.55	1927	14556
	1.2up	R2	23.03	6.15	1905	11721
	1.2down	R2	21.18	15.60	1726	26921
	1.4	R1+R2	22.50	5.41	2465	13344
	4.1	AO	20.26	2.08	2465	5428
Emameh	1.1	R2	23.73	8.46	1793	15161
	1.2up	R2	26.90	18.61	2241	41708
	1.2down	R2	24.97	7.15	2107	15054
	4.1	AO	12.25	2.89	1277	3688
Kond	1.2up	R2	29.78	20.96	2465	51672
	1.2down	R2	21.33	15.86	1748	27725
	4.1	AO	12.88	5.25	1412	7413
	1.3	R2+R3	13.25	10.71	426	4562
	3.1	DF	21.93	1.37	538	739
	2.2	R2+F	15.10	3.06	359	1098
Afjeh	1.2	R2	25.91	18.37	1121	20582
	4.1	AO	9.43	3.06	874	2674
	2.2up	R2+F	12.02	5.53	269	1488
	2.2down	R2+F	14.55	1.75	336	588
	3.1up	DF	16.72	1.65	381	627
	3.1down	DF	2.49	0.679	29.1	19.8

Table 9. The comparison of the results of erosion modeling in the present condition with the suggested land-use conditions.

Basin	The erosion with new land-use (ton/year)	The erosion with the former land-use (ton/year)	The calculated suspended load with new land-use (ton/year)	The percentage of erosion reduction	The particulate phosphorus entering after the new land-use (ton/year)
Roodak	703.5	1524	86.58	54	4.87
Kond	93.21	228.5	17.71	59	0.56
Afjeh	25.98	103.1	5.595	75	0.041

Conclusion

By comparing the results of sediment load calculated by the model with the actual values, the precision of the model in estimating the erosion and the sediment yield for the upstream basins of Roodak, Kond and Afjeh was respectively of 86.8, 86 and 55%, although depend on the percentage assumed valid for SDR. These results show the suitable precision of the model for Roodak and Kond basins (if in the basin of Afjeh, more measuring data for suspended load could be gathered, the more precise outputs of the model can be obtained in this basin).

The results show that the use of vegetation to areas without coverage and use of appropriate vegetation density appropriate land, the amount of erosion and the phosphorus load are reduced considerably. As a result, by using the suggested methods of land-uses for the basins discussed so far, the degree of erosion reduction in the upper basins of Roodak is about 54%, for Kond basin is about 59% and in the basin of Afjeh is about 75%.

Conflict of Interests

The author(s) have not declared any conflict of interests.

REFERENCES

Yazidhi B (2003). A comparative study of soil erosion modeling in Lom Kao-Phetchabun, Thailand. International institute for geo-information science and earth observation enschede, the Netherland.

Cox C, Madramootoo C (1998). Application of geographic information systems in watershed management planning in ST. Lucia. Ministry of Agriculture, Forestry, Fisheries and the Environment.

Desmet PJJ, Govers G (1996). A GIS procedure for automatically calculating the USLE LS factor on topographically complex landscape units. J. Soil Water Conserv. 51(5):427-433.

Foster GR (2003). "User's Reference Guide, RUSLE2, Oxford, Mississippi.

Maleki M, Ahmadee H, Jafaree M, Ghoddousee J, Azarniuvand H, Mosayyebee M (2011). Quantitative modeling of water erosion using Analytic hierarchy process (Latian dam watershed). Fourth National Conference sediment Department of Watershed Management Engineering College of Natural Resources Tarbiat Modarres University.

Blonn P (2001). A GIS-based model of diffuse pollution in the oak creek and menomonee river watersheds. project sponsored by the USEPA Grant No. R82-5759 to Marquette University from the USEPA/NSF/USDA STAR Watershed Program.

Poorabdollah M (2007). Comparison of models RUSLE and SWAT to estimate Erosions in the sub-basin Amameh Thesis Sharif University.

Sadeghi H (1994). Evaluate the accuracy and efficiency of computer models in estimating runoff and sediment II SEDIMOT. Thesis Tarbiat Modarres University.

Tahmasebipoor N (1995). Evaluate the erosion model M.P.S.I.A.C. Thesis Tarbiat Modarres University.

Tehran's agricultural organization (2002a). Meteorology and climatology of Latian Dam watershed.

Tehran's agricultural organization (2002b). Land cover studies of Latian Dam watershed.

Water and Energy center of Sharif University (2003a). Environmental studies of Latian Dam watershed. 2003.

Water and Energy center of Sharif University (2003b). Soil studies of Latian Dam watershed. 2003.

Wischmeier WH, Johnson CB, Cross BW (1971). A soil erodibility nomograph for farmland and construction sites. J. soil water conservat. 26(5):189-193.

Wischmeier WH, Smith DD (1978). Predicting Rainfall erosion losses-A guide to conservation planning. The USDA agricultural handbook No.537.

16

Estimated electric power consumption by means of artificial neural networks and autoregressive models with exogenous input methods

J. L. Rojas-Rentería[1,3] , R. Luna-Rubio[1,3], J. L. González-Pérez[2], C. A. González-Gutiérrez[1], A. Rojas-Molina[1] and G. Macías-Bobadilla[1]

[1]División de Estudios de Posgrado, Facultad de Ingeniería, México.
[2]Aplicaciones Computacionales y Biotecnología, Facultad de Ingeniería, México.
Universidad Autónoma de Querétaro. Cerro de las Campanas S/N, C.P. 76010, Querétaro, Qro., México.
[3]Universidad Tecnológica de Corregidora. Carretera a Coroneo km 11.5, Querétaro, Qro., México.

The growth electric energy demand in the industrial and commercial sectors and in public and private buildings represents a problem to estimate electrical consumption in these sectors in order to avoid fines imposed by the respective companies supplying electricity. This study presents artificial neural networks (ANN) and autoregressive models with exogenous input (ARX) models to calculate and to predict the electrical consumption for public sector using heuristic procedures. This system allows estimating the electric power consumption of the next few months ahead, and therefore, a better management of electric energy. The model validation is performed by comparing the results with a nonlinear regression model, ANN and autoregressive models with exogenous input models and the real data with analysis of variance (ANOVA). The ANN models results are estimate confidence intervals of 95%. The variables used as inputs to the neural model estimated are temperature, relative humidity, power consumption and time (day and hour). The algorithm used to estimate is Levenberg-Marquardt.

Key words: Analysis of variance (ANOVA), artificial neural networks (ANN), autoregressive models with exogenous input (ARX), energy management, estimating power consumption.

INTRODUCTION

Estimated electric power consumption in public sector requires advanced intelligent tools such as artificial neural networks (ANN) and autoregressive models with exogenous input (ARX). Electric energy is used in the buildings' comfort as cooling, heating and lighting, electrical and electronic equipment. In this sense, buildings are responsible for approximately 40% of the annual energy consumption worldwide with respect to these sectors (Omer, 2008). The main problem to estimate the electric power consumption is the complex dynamic behavior exhibited by the load series.

As the electric power consumption in these sectors grows, the complexity of the generation systems and energy consumption in the electricity companies increases according to their ability to supply power. These companies performs a measurement of all the variables (voltage, current, frequency and magnetic flux variations in the electrical network) from a central control room, plotting in real-time the average values of the programmed energy production and performing adjustments according to the demand of the day (Yik and Lee, 2005). Currently, it is necessary to make an energy analysis for the buildings construction of different economic sectors through the professional application of technology by engineers and architects that design energy-efficient buildings. After finishing the design and construction of the building, electrical consumption is decided mainly by its control, maintenance and number of occupants; in order to achieve functional and satisfactory environments in intelligent buildings, the overall reduction in electrical consumption through control systems is required (Mrabti et al., 2011; Young-Sub and Kang-Soo, 2007). This improves the energy efficiency of electrical and control devices as well as the estimated algorithms of electric power consumption.

The electric power consumption on a given day depends not only on the previous day's demand, but also of day electrical consumption of the previous week. Furthermore, they are several aspects that significantly influence the patterns of electrical consumption, particularly related to climate variables. By example on a hot day, the power consumption in buildings increases significantly due to the energy used for cooling (Basaran et al., 2010). To estimate the electric consumption in the short-term it is necessary to consider operations in electrical systems. Storage, generation and distribution of power are the most significant variables in buildings optimization (Nguyen-Vu et al., 2008).

This problem can be solved through models estimation of electric power consumption. These models have caused a great interest on study from the time when power grids were installed as a system of power transmission and distribution. Estimated models are useful for different applications and for mass proliferation of the use of electricity in the industrial, commercial and domestic sector. Within these environments, there are many applications for estimated models, such as cost reduction, planning, maintenance, human resource generation, design and research.

In recent years, literature describes numerous works of techniques applied to the estimate of electric power. Recently, the estimate of electric power has used ANN. To predict buildings energy needs benefiting from orientation, insulation thickness and transparency ratio by using ANN. Engineers have developed models of neural networks for lighting in office buildings, using the temperature and days of the week to estimate the demand for heat and electricity consumption (Wong and Wang, 2009). These networks are connected by a great number of links carrying out a nonlinear operation through different software. The use of neural networks applied to the internal temperature of buildings, reports an air conditioning control used to predict the electric energy demand (Ruano et al., 2005). Engineers have proposed self-organized maps as neural network models to predict short-term electric energy consumption, resulting in a demand curve for the following hours as

well as the use of predictive models of power load with neural networks combined with error correction (RBFNN), based on the energy demand consumption for air conditioning in buildings (Doukas et al., 2007). The ARX is dynamic mathematical models derived from the system identification theory that predict the behavior of air temperature inside buildings (Shina et al., 2001).

The objective of this study was to develop a model to estimate the electric power consumption for public sector based on a multilayer perceptron neural network that allows estimating the electricity consumption the next few months to get a better management of electric power with the classification by supervised learning models. The variables used as inputs to the model estimate are temperature and relative humidity, as well as power consumption and time. A validation model performance was made by comparing results with ARX and measured data, by analysis of variance (ANOVA).

MATERIALS AND METHODS

Neural networks models

Nowadays, neural networks are excellent tools to perform various tasks: pattern recognition (objects in images and drawings), speech recognition, explosive detection, and identification of human faces (in airports to identify the people that move in and out of it), perform data compression, videogames, artificial learning and estimated electric power consumption. Often they are also used to solve a problem when there are no existing algorithms to solve certain processes (such as image recognition); this is because the algorithms are accurate, while neural networks have more flexibility (Ayata et al., 2007). Besides, neural network models can be applied to engineering problems with nonlinear nature, where a key feature is the response rate for solutions.

An ANN model was developed for office buildings with daylighting for subtropical climates. There were four nodes at the output layer with the estimated daily electricity use for cooling, heating, electric lighting and total building as the output building energy (Wong et al., 2010). A short-term load estimation using ANN was applied to the Nigeria Electric Power System to the load estimate 1 h in advance. The inputs used for this ANN are the previous hour load, previous day load, previous week load, day of the week, and hour of the day (Adepoju et al., 2007).

A neural network consists of input neurons, hidden neurons and output neurons. Each of these is grouped into layers. The data are spread throughout the network starting from the input neurons to the output neurons (Mohammad et al., 2011). The neurons are connected by a large number of weighted links; neuron nodes that are adjusted so as to obtain certain specific results over which signals or information can pass. Basically, a neuron receives inputs over its incoming connections, combines the inputs, performs generally a nonlinear operation, and then outputs the final results. Generally, what matters is only the final weight of the output neurons. When the output signals are transmitted to the input neurons, all signals are processed again by changing the neural weights. The discussion about whether this process converges to specific states for each neuron through the iterations is complex. That is, those neural networks are minimized or maximized to find optimal values. Hidden nodes with nonlinear transfer functions are used to process the information received by the input nodes. The network can be written as:

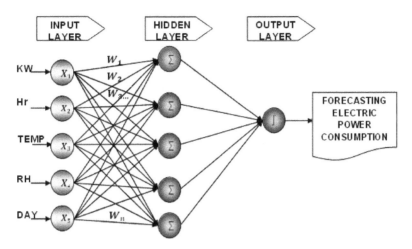

Figure 1. The schematic of ANN.

$$y_t = \alpha_0 + \sum_{j=1}^{n} \alpha_j f(\sum_{i=1}^{m} \beta_{ij} y_t + \beta_{0j}) + \varepsilon_t \qquad (1)$$

The connection that link neurons of an ANN have an associated weight, which is what makes the network, acquires knowledge. Considering y_t as the output value of the neuron i at a given instant, this signal is transmitted from neuron i to j but this signal is modified by the value of the connection weight between neurons in question. The nomenclature for the synaptic weight between neuron j and neuron i is β_{ji}. The first subscript (j) indicates the neuron or unit where you are going to connect. The second subscript (i) indicates the neuron or unit where the connection comes from. The entry of the function is the sum of all input signals by the weight associated with the connection of the signal input. Where the number of input nodes is m, the number of hidden nodes is n, a sigmoidal transfer function is f, as the logistic function:

$$f(x) = \frac{1}{1 + exp^{(-x)}}$$

$$(2)$$

Equation 2 represents a vector of weights from hidden nodes to output nodes that introduce nonlinearity into the model. In Equation 1, α_0 and β_0 are the weights of the main arches of partial terms, which always have values equal to 1 (Gareta et al., 2006). Among the units or neurons that form a neural network there is a set of connections that bind them. Each unit transmits signals to those connected to its output. Associated with each unit, there is an activation function that transforms the net input to the unit which comes as a result of being connected to other units that supply information in the output value. Maybe a linear or nonlinear function, chosen depending on the specifications of the problem has to be solved neuron.

Normalization of data necessary to avoid conditions of the neurons is saturated. If the neurons are saturated, there is a small change in the value of the item that can cause an error in the output value (Wong et al., 2010). To this end, data must be normalized before being presented to the neural network. The range considered as input any value between minus infinity and plus infinity and generates an output between 0 and 1. The starting value of the number of nodes in the hidden layer is equal to the average of the number of inputs and outputs.

Normalization is carried out through the following expression:

$$X_n = \frac{(x - x_{min})*range}{x_{max} - x_{min}} + \text{starting value} \qquad (3)$$

Where X_n is the value of the normalized data, and x_{min} and x_{max} are the minimum and maximum of data set, with an initial value of the weights of the neural network according to the model.

Several iterations are required to train a small network, even for a simple problem. To reduce the number of iterations and speed up the learning time of ANN, several topics of recent research have been developed; some improvements of the algorithm of retropropagation are the gradient descent and the algorithm of Levenberg-Marquardt (Ngoo et al., 2011).

The ranges of applications of ANNs are steadily increasing. Its use in applications related to the administration and management of energy begins in the early 90's, and provides a thorough description of the applications of ANNs in renewable energy systems (Wong et al., 2010).

The ANN applied in this study, is a layered network with 5 input nodes and one hidden layer with a variable number of hidden nodes, such as temperature (Temp), relative humidity (RH), time (Hr and Day) and energy consumption (kW) as variables that influence energy consumption, directly on multiple factors such as power consumption heating systems, air conditioners, and refrigerators (Kim et al., 2011) with an output layer with one node. A schematic diagram of the basic architecture is shown in Figure 1. Each layer was interconnected together by the connection strengths called weights. In such networks, all neural signals propagate forward through the network layers. There are no connections back and neither side usually either recurrent self, useful in recognition or pattern classification.

Autoregressive models with exogenous input model

The parameters for a linear ARX model were determined from values sampled at an interval of time T of the input and output. This determination is performed by a multivariable linear regression that determined the parameters a_1, a_{na} and b_1 minimizing the squared values difference between actual and calculated by the following autoregressive model:

$$y_n = -a_1 y(t-1) - \cdots - a_{na} y(t-n_a) + b_1 u(t-1) \tag{4}$$
$$+ \cdots + b_{nb} u(t-n_b) + e(t) + c_1 e(t-1)$$
$$+ \cdots + c_{nc} e(t-n_c)$$

This is also called equation error structure, where y = output signal, n = input signal, t = discrete time, a_n, b_n, c_n = model parameters, e = error, y n_a, n_b, n_c = number of poles. The output at the sampling instant t is obtained from past values of the output and input (in $t-1$, $t-n_a$ etc). The selection of the values of the best model is obtained through the estimation process (Harunori et al., 2001; Preminger et al., 2007). The ARX structure has a system which can be defined by means of the number of the poles, the number of zeros, and the time delay.

The values are obtained by the estimation procedure by entering the coefficients as parameters for determining the vector θ to be estimated:

$$y(t, \theta) = G(z, \theta) u(t) + H(z, \theta) e(t) \tag{5}$$

To avoid the white noise as a direct error in the equations, the parameters of ARX structural adjustment will be:

$$\theta = [a_1 \ a_2 \dots a_{na} \ b_1 \ b_2 \dots b_{na}]^T \tag{6}$$

Often the ARX model Equation 4 is represented as:

$$V(z) y(t) = W(z) u(t-n_k) + e(t) \tag{7}$$

Where the matrices $V(z)$ and $W(z)$ are given by:

$$V(z) : 1 + a_1 z^{-1} + \cdots + a_{n_a} z^{-n_a} \tag{8}$$

$$W(z) : 1 + b_1 z^{-1} + \cdots + a_{n_b} z^{-n_b} \tag{9}$$

The number of entries is represented by the number of n_u and n_y outputs, $V(z)$ and $W(z)$ are n_y by n_y and n_u and n_u matrices, respectively, which elements are the polynomials in the shift operator z^{-1} (with m any natural number). The inputs $a_{ij}(z)$ and $b_{ij}(z)$ of the matrices $V(z)$ and $W(z)$ can be expressed as:

$$a_{ij}(z) = \delta_{ij} + a_{1_{ij}} z^{-1} + \cdots + a_{n_{ij}} z^{-n_{aij}} \tag{10}$$

and

$$b_{ij}(z) = b_{ij} z^{-nk_{ij}} + \cdots + b_{n_{kij}} z^{-n_{kij} - n_{kij} + 1} \tag{11}$$

and z^{-1} is the backward shift operator

$$z^{-1} u(t) = u(t-1) \tag{12}$$

Measures of accuracy

The accuracy of prediction is the most important and decisive performance measurement applied to ANN and ARX models. A measure of accuracy is often defined in terms of prediction error,

which is the difference between the measured and the estimated value. There are a number of measures of accuracy in the literature of prediction, with different advantages and limitations. Among the most frequently used are: the mean square error (MSE), the root mean square error (RMSE), and the mean absolute percentage error (MAPE).

$$MSE = \frac{\sum (e_t)^2}{N} \tag{13}$$

$$RMSE = \sqrt{MSE} \tag{14}$$

$$MAPE = \frac{1}{N} \sum \left| \frac{e_t}{y_t} \right| (100) \tag{15}$$

Where e_t is the individual prediction error; y_t is the present value, and N is the number of terms of the error. Electric power consumption in public sector depends largely on the variables of temperature and relative humidity to maintain an atmosphere of comfort and functionality (lighting, ventilation, heating and cooling) (Zhiwei et al., 2007).

The time and energy consumption in kWh are considered as inputs to the ANN. Time is necessary because some tasks must be carried out at different schedules, and hence the energy consumption (kWh) will change.

Description of public sector building

The procedure to design the estimate model of electric power consumption based on an ANN algorithm was carried out in the graduate engineering building at the Universidad Autonoma of Queretaro. The structure has five classrooms each with an area of $42 \ m^2$ and a conference room with an area of $58 \ m^2$. One classroom is equipped with York 18000 BTU Split air conditioning unit. The structure of the building is a single level with 3 m high.

The energy consumption data used to train the model come from measuring in the main substation in the Engineering school at the Universidad Autonoma of Queretaro, with a quality power monitoring system. The temperature data and relative humidity were measured in classrooms with HOBO Pro V2 sensors that allow a rapid response to information and data storage. The HOBOware software was used to transport field data for temperature and relative humidity analysis. This data were obtained, as well as the time and day of measurements. These data were divided into two groups: the first one used a series of 780 h to train the neural network and the second group worked with 195 h to test the neural network model.

ANN algorithm description

The objective of an ANN is to find an optimal configuration of weights, so that it can learn a set of patterns. The proposal for the prediction of electric power consumption in the buildings was an ANN model with the Levenberg-Marquardt algorithm. With this network architecture the highest average of the absolute differences between measured and estimated values was selected, expressed as a percentage of the measured values since its result as a percentage does not depend on variables such as the magnitude of the input data (Rempel et al., 2008). The ANN construction may include hidden layers (not directly connected to inputs or outputs), where neurons in each layer have the same structure of a single neuron, but the inputs are the outputs of the neurons of the preceding layer. The learning rule or data training algorithm is a procedure for modifying the weights of a network and

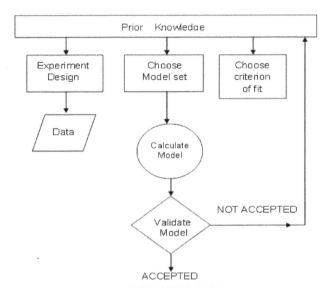

Figure 2. ARX and system identification.

its purpose is to train the network to perform some task. These training data are composed of multiple pairs of input training patterns and output. The best model was compared with data from the ARX and regression models using the MAPE to comparing the best results from the tests of equality of two or more means with the ANOVA techniques to be validated. Then the training becomes a nonlinear programming problem. The description of the algorithm was: a) determining the input and output variables; b) a data set describing the relationship between input-output model is grouped; c) the data set is divided into 2 parts: one part is used as a training set to determine the parameters of the neural classifier and the other part (called test set or set of generalization) is used to estimate the generalization error. The training set is divided into a validation subset to fit the model: d) a conventional model is developed to train the network with the data set; e) the relationship between inputs and outputs of the neural network is estimated. These steps are repeated to find the appropriate number of hidden nodes, using different training parameters for the network. 80% of the data were used to train the network, another 10% for the validation set and the remaining 10% to estimate the generalization.

ARX algorithm description

The measured data were used to obtain the coefficients in the ARX model based on analysis of input variables: temperature (TEMP), relative humidity (RH), time (Hr) and day, and as an output variable: the energy consumption (kW). Once data are registered, they are divided into 2 subgroups: the first data set was used to determine the model coefficients; the remaining group was used in the ARX model validation (Abhijit et al., 2011). Once the coefficients were calculated, it performs a comparison of the best prediction with the measured data of electricity consumption in real time in the Engineering building. a) The input and output data are recorded during an experiment of identification, which identifies the signals to measure, as well as its time and its restrictions, b) A set of candidate models is obtained considering its specifications in order to select the most suitable. The formal properties of models are combined with an intuition of engineering and priori knowledge (Figure 2). Then a model with some unknown physical parameters is constructed from basic physical laws and other well-established relationships. A set model built for data fitting, is called "black box", c) It was determined the best model in the set, guided by the data. This is the method of identification. The quality assessment is often based on a self-improvement of the models by the reproducibility of the input variables maintaining its structure. The quality assessment is often based on how the models seek to improve when they try to reproduce the basic approach of the structure of the model.

RESULTS AND DISCUSSION

Several models of ANN and ARX were generated and tested according to their performance and structured with 975 data which were obtained from electrical energy consumption monitoring, as well as of the temperature and relative humidity variables. The error of the MAPE was used to examine the quality of prediction models in order to determine the best ANN performance and ARX. Error MAPE values were calculated for each of the models and Tables 1 and 2 show the best models, their reliability, and better performance for ANN and ARX models, respectively. The 5-5-1 ANN model is the one that had the best results with a 0.0216 MAPE, 0.9908 R^2 and 0.0927 SEP compared with the results of the remaining models in Table 1. The best ARX model was 3-2-1 with a 0.0439 MAPE, 0.9856 R^2 and 0.1341 SEP, shown in Table 2.

Table 3 shows the prediction results obtained from the ANN, ARX and linear regression models and compares them to the real data. The table shows the MAPE of each model and indicates the most appropriate prediction and most likely to be a successful prediction.

Figure 3 compares the ANN, ARX and regression models in terms of MAPE, SEP and R^2. The prediction model with ANN has a lower error compared with the results of the remaining models.

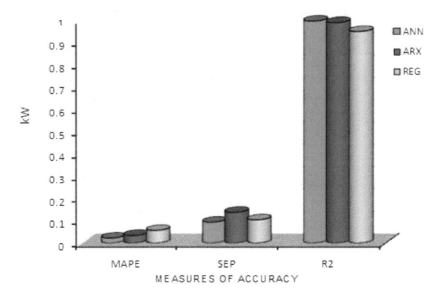

Figure 3. Comparison error or neural network, ARX and regression models.

The real data and ANN, regression, and ARX results were selected and compared using analysis of variance to estimate the variability of the components for the various methods of analysis, in order to compare the systematic errors with the obtained by performing random tests with different mean values to determine if any of them differed significantly from the rest (Table 4).

Propositions were made on the values determined in the models to make a decision in order to accept or reject a test by a data analysis tool called hypothesis testing.

Ho: $\mu = \mu 0 = \mu 1$ H1: $\mu \neq \mu 0$

Duncan's multiple range test (DMRT)

Before the DMRT was performed, the standard deviation for each treatment was calculated as:

$$S\bar{x} = \sqrt{\frac{MS(error)}{nj}} \qquad (16)$$

Where MS (error) is the MSE, and nj is the number of blocks for the four treatments (real data, ANN, ARX and regression), calculated by the state values of Rp as follows:

$$Rp = r\alpha(p, f)S\bar{x} \qquad (17)$$

$Rp(p, \alpha)$ was obtained from the table in the Duncan test. After classification of the average, treatment was compared as follows:

$S\bar{x}$ = 186.7

$r_{0.05}(3.96) = 2.79$

$r_{0.05}(96.288) = 1.86$

$R_2 = r_{0.05}(3.288)\ S\bar{x} = 2.79 \times 186.7 = 520.95$

$R_2 = r_{0.05}(96.288)\ S\bar{x} = 1.86 \times 186.7 = 347.45$

Comparing treatments 1 y 3 = 8721.45 – 8252.30 = 469.15

443.3 > 347.45 $\longrightarrow \mu_2 \neq \mu_3$

Comparing treatments 1 y 4 = 8721.45 - 9749.33 = 1027.88

3015.6 > 520.95 $\longrightarrow \mu_2 \neq \mu_3$

Comparing treatments 1 y 2 = 8721.45 – 8648.14 = 73.31

64.95 < 347.45 $\longrightarrow \mu_1 = \mu_2$

From the above we can see that the average of the first treatment (real data) and the second treatment (selected ANN) is equal to $\alpha = 0.05$. These results show that the average of the estimated power consumption of the selected ANN and real data are approximately equal at 95% confidence level, significantly higher than the results of treatment with regression and ARX. When the four estimate models (with $\alpha = 0.05$) were compared the null hypothesis of the test was accepted with 95% confidence, considering that the interval contains the measured value of the population; this indicates that the

Table 1. Comparison of estimated error for different neural network models.

Model	R^2	MAPE	SEP
5-2-1	0.9632	0.0412	0.1224
5-3-1	0.9308	0.0560	0.1713
5-4-1	0.9744	0.0327	0.1125
5-5-1	0.9908	0.0216	0.0927
5-6-1	0.9741	0.0455	0.1244

Table 2. Comparison of estimated error for different ARX models.

Model	R^2	MAPE	SEP
3,2,1	0.9856	0.0439	0.1341
4,1,0	0.9722	0.0445	0.1158
4,1,2	0.9374	0.0564	0.0811
4,1,3	0.9312	0.0595	0.0856
4,4,2	0.9415	0.0519	0.0844

Table 3. Comparison of measurements and estimated values in neural networks, nonlinear regression and ARX models.

Hour	Measurement	ANN	ARX	Regression
148	9700.2	9674.43	9998.21	9680.39
148.5	9800.4	9716.29	9691.43	9677.73
149	9780.5	9677.00	9683.47	9722.24
149.5	9710.6	9678.31	9678.36	9682.95
150	9679.8	9660.31	9676.50	9684.26
150.5	9609.9	9653.89	9678.42	9666.27
151	9589.8	9619.36	9684.21	9659.84
151.5	9470.3	9587.80	9693.86	9625.31
...	...	...	...	...
MAPE error		0.0216	0.0439	0.0993

Table 4. ANOVA data comparison between the nonlinear regression, ARX and neural network models.

Summary			
Group	**Count**	**Sum (kW/h)**	**Average (kM/h)**
Meassured	97	845980.911	8721.45
Neural networks	97	838869.77	8648.14
Regression	97	800473.17	8252.30
ARX	97	944812.869	9740.34

Source	**Sum square degree**		**Mean square F**	**Critical value for F**
Between groups	117065635	3	39021878.33 25.02	2.63
Blocks	598749526	96	6236974.23	
Total	715815162			

estimate of electric power consumption for selected values of the model of ANN and real data were significantly more accurate than the values obtained by nonlinear regression and ARX models.

Conclusions

A method for predicting the electric power consumption in a multilayer perceptron neural network was tested. The construction of the model 5-5-1 in the algorithm in ANN was able to produce the best results in predicting electric power consumption in the building, with an estimated error of 0.0216 with the real data. The ANOVA statistical method for estimation of variation was used, comparing the results of the model of ANN with measured data and the results of nonlinear regression and ARX model was obtained at 95% reliability in neural network models. This model is closer to the measured data to predict the electric power consumption in public sector buildings. This ANOVA was used to compare whether the values of a set of numerical data are significantly different than the values of one or more other data sets to achieve a statistical F ratio and error treatment. DMRT was used to identify which model is closer to the real data.

Moreover, it was shown that the selected ANN has better estimated values for total electricity power consumption. Additionally, the utility of neural networks was effective in the prediction process of electricity in terms of MAPE. Finally, neural networks, in most cases measures exhibited the lowest prediction error. It concludes the advantages of neural networks to be easier to implement models and allow obtaining low prediction errors. The approach described in this paper could be used to design an intelligent control strategy for electrical consumption in buildings.

REFERENCES

Abhijit S, Sachin C, Ravindra D (2011). Closed-loop identification using direct approach and high order ARX/GOBF-ARX models. J. Process Control. 21:1056-1071.

Adepoju GA, Ogunjuyigbe SO, Alawode KO, Tech B (2007). Application of Neural Network to Load Forecasting in Nigeran Electrical Power System. Pacific J. Sci. Tech. 8:68-72.

Ayata T, Yıldız O, Arcaklıoğlu E (2007). Application of ANN to explore the potential use of natural ventilation in buildings in Turkey. Appl. Therm. Eng. 27:12-20.

Basaran UF, Omer NG, Kurban M (2010). A novel modeling approach for hourly forecasting of long-term electric energy demand. Energy Convers. Manage. 52:199-211.

Doukas H, Patlitzianas KD, Iatropoulos K, Psarras J (2007). Intelligent building energy management system using rule sets. Build. Environ. 42:3562-3569.

Gareta R, Romero LM, Gil L (2006). Forecasting of electricity prices with neural networks. Energy Convers. Manage. 47:1770-1778.

Harunori Y, Sanjay K, Yasunori M (2001). Online fault detection and diagnosis in VAV air handling unit by RARX modeling. Energy Build. 33:391-401.

Kim H, Stumpf A, Kim W (2011). Analysis of an energy efficient building design through data mining approach. Autom. Constr. 20:37-43.

Mohammad G, Sahar S, Mohammad AV (2011). Artificial neural networks applied to DGA for fault diagnosis in oil-filled power transformers. Afr. J. Electr. Electron. Eng. Res. 3:1-10.

Mrabti T, El Ouariachi M, Malek R, Kassmi KA, Tidhaf B, Bagui F, Olivié F, Kassmi K (2011). Design, realization and optimization of a photovoltaic system equipped with analog maximum power point tracking (MPPT) command and detection circuit of the dysfunction and convergence the system (CDCS). Afr. J. Phys. Sci. 35:7865-7888.

Ngoo LM, Muriithi CM, Nyakoe GN, Njoroge SN (2011). A neuro fuzzy model of an induction motor for voltage stability analysis using continuation load flow. J. Electr. Electron. Eng. Res. 3:62-70.

Nguyen-Vu T, Wang L, Wong PK (2008). Modelling and short-term forecasting of daily peak power demand in Victoria using two-dimensional wavelet based SDP models. Electric. Power Energy Syst. 30:511-518.

Omer AM (2008). Energy, environment and sustainable development. Renew. Sustain. Energy Rev. 12:2265-2300.

Preminger A, Franck R (2007). Forecasting exchange rates: a robust regression approach. Int. J. Forecasting 23:71-84.

Rempel E, Harter F, Velho H, Chian A (2008). Neural networks in auroral data assimilation. J. Atmos. Sol. Terr. Phys. 70:1243-1250.

Ruano AE, Crispim EM, Conceicao EM, Lucio MM (2005). Prediction of building's temperature using neural networks models. Energy Build. 38:682-695.

Shina S, Kumar S, Matsumoto T, Kojima T (2001). Application of system identification modelling to solar hybrid systems for predicting radiation, temperature and load. Renew. Energy 22:281-286.

Wong HL, Wang SW (2009). Intelligent building research: Review. Autom. Constr. 14:143-159.

Wong SL, Wan KW, Lam NT (2010). Artificial neural networks for energy analysis of office buildings with day lighting. Appl. Energy 87:551-557.

Yik FW, Lee WL (2005). Rebate as an economic instrument for promoting building energy efficiency in Hong Kong. Build. Environ. 40:1207-1216.

Young-Sub K, Kang-Soo K (2007). Simplified energy prediction method accounting for part-load performance of chiller. Build. Environ. 42:507-515.

Zhiwei L, Weiwei L, Zhijian H, Yao Y (2007). An innovate air-conditioning load forecasting model based don RBF neural network and combined residual error correction. Int. J. Refrig. pp. 528-538.

17

Kinematics of the human hand applied to the design of prosthesis

Luis Antonio Aguilar-Pérez[1], Christopher René Torres-San Miguel[1], Guillermo Urriolagoitia-Sosa[1], Luis Martínez-Sáez[2], José Alfredo Leal-Naranjo[1], Beatriz Romero-Ángeles[3] and Guillermo Urriolagoitia-Calderón[1]

[1]Instituto Politécnico Nacional, Escuela Superior de Ingeniería Mecánica y Eléctrica; Unidad Profesional Zacatenco, Av. Instituto Politécnico Nacional s/n, Col. Lindavista, Delegación. Gustavo A. Madero, Distrito Federal, C.P. 07738, México.
[2]Instituto Universitario de Investigación del Automóvil, Industriales, Universidad Politécnica de Madrid. Carretera de Valencia, km.7. Madrid, España. CP. 28031, México.
[3]Instituto Politécnico Nacional, Escuela Superior de Ingeniería Mecánica y Eléctrica, Unidad Profesional Azacapotzalco, Av. De las Granjas No. 682, Col. Santa Catarina. Del. Azcapotzalco, Distrito Federal C.P. 02250 México.

This work shows the application of a mechanism of four bars synthetized function used in the development of a prosthetic device with an underacted movement, for its application in people with a mutilation level close to the distal dislocation of the wrist. A methodology is exposed for this, from which the procedure for obtaining the trajectory of the four bars mechanism through the function synthesis, which was formulated upon two mathematic models expressed in terms of anthropometric values and ranges of movement for the index and thumb, respectively. As a result of the synthesis of these mechanisms a hand prosthesis prototype was obtained, which counts with seven degrees of liberty separately from each other, which allows to develop punctual and cylindrical holdings, with the purpose of applying this prototype to the subsequent study of grip patterns and interpretation of myoelectric signals that allow to determine an easier to interpret mechanism of control that permits to generate dynamic grips instead of static average grips.

Key words: Computer Aided Design (CAD), Biomechanics, synthesis of mechanisms.

INTRODUCTION

The purpose of generating a grip movement with the hand is to achieve the thumb, along with any of the other fingers, wraps the object of interest within the workload of the entire hand. A precise simulation of this behavior represents such a high degree of complexity due to all implicit variables during the custom scan features of the human being (Belter and Dollar, 2011). Therefore, it is important to mention that the design process of prototypes must satisfy the best possible way, the personal characteristics of each patient which are defined under three general points of view: the description of anthropometric and morphological characteristics of the hand (Zollo et al., 2007; Naik and Kumar, 2010), the work device capabilities (Kutz, 2003), and the control exerted by the person itself.

The opposition movement is the most important, being described by Kapandji and Lacomba (2006) as a set of three consecutive moves: first the preemption of the full osteoarticular column, followed by its flexion to suit the action to perform, and ending with the complete opposition of the thumb on the hand. In Santos (Barrientos et al., 2007) analysis of the five axes of motion that make up the complete thumb osteoarticular column was proposed, finding that the major joints were the carpal metacarpal joint (CMC) and the metacarpophalangeal (MCP), which is why the authors conclude that the study of these two joints is impossible to perform separately, so Kapandji and Lacomba (2006) established that the movements of the thumb may be explained with only three motion axes, joining the CMC and MCP joints in a single joint, and neglecting the offset of the multangular-metacarpal joint (TMC). In Light (Cimadevilla and Herrera, 2006) it was mentioned that the main importance of flexing moves is due to the fact that through these, it is possible to "wrap" the object with the fingers, while the abduction-adduction allows, in a certain way, to "guide" the finger so that it can stably hold the object.

Furthermore, Barrientos et al. (2007) mentioned that a singular configuration is acquired due to the alignment of two or more phalanges able to reach the same point, but using different angular positions, so that in the work reported by Cimadevilla and Herrera (2006) and Hernández and Montoya (2007), it was shown that there was a slight dependence between the movement of the last joints from the fingers II and III, but this became larger between fingers IV and V. Anatomically fingers II to V have the same type of metacarpophalangeal joint (MCP), which is a condylar type, allowing to generate flexion and extension as well as abduction and adduction movement, but since the range of motion of the latter is too small, between 10° and 15°, compared with the first type of movement is a range of about -20° to 110°, generally this type of movement is omitted in the prosthetic design.

Due to the wide range of objects that people manipulate daily, usually the types of grips are divided into two, depending on the action seeking to perform, either manipulate (dynamic grip) or hold (static grip) any element by a previously established position for an undefined time. According to the results shown by Vergara et al. (2012) it was found that the main types of static grip used in daily life were the cylindrical type (determined for force grips) and precise (determined for precision grips), while eating was the activity with a longer allotted time as well as the tasks associated with this, giving it an average of 1.604 h a day, followed by leisure tasks (1.086 h/day) and grooming (0.76 h/day).

On the other hand, the index and middle fingers of a human hand exert a maximum average force of 50 to 60 N, while the ring and little finger exert a maximum force of 25 to 35 N average as reported in Gregory (2002). A study by Alcalde et al. (2006) in Spain, shows that the thumb can exert a maximum average force of 91 to 101.6 N, concluding that when the force is exerted by a finger individually, the range of applied force is greater than the one that would be determine if this were other fingers participating during grip (Table 4) (Li et al., 1998).

The literature reports that the statically interaction with objects takes two forms; first if the item is held for a long time and its size is medium or even small, then a precision grip is required (Feix et al., 2009) performed between the index finger and thumb (although it also interacts with the medium finger), on the other hand, if it's necessary to hold a heavy object for a short time or if its size is medium or even large, a grip with force will be done by the whole hand, being named this as grip power grip (Cipriani et al., 2006).

There is a third type of movement that is performed from the junction between the two above, but due to the redundancy of positions that should be adopted to perform this grip, the study of this would be repetitive in terms of the positions a hand adopts during gripping. Because of this wide variability of objects, it is difficult to determine a specific design under which the special characteristics of each task is defined, combined with, due to amputation suffered by the patient, the control exercised by the person on the prosthesis, commonly is used to take positions of the remaining member, which will be performed by the device so that these can be translated into a static position defined as grip (Feix et al., 2009). Thus, this paper proposes the development of a methodology for sizing four-bar mechanisms, which are adaptable to custom prosthetic hands design at the level range of motion and specific anthropometric dimensions of the persons hand.

MATERIALS AND METHODS

The methodology presented in this paper consists of the kinematic analysis of the open chain representing the fingers, performed from the procedure described by Denavit and Hartembergy following the convention of signs and symbols given by Craig (2006); Lewis et al., (2004) and Shigley and Uicker (2001) from where the equations that describe the position of the fingertip are obtained, which can be adapted to a mathematical function that is used as a movement pattern for the synthesis of the mechanism function and are solved by Shigley and Uicker (2001) and Montúfar et al. (2009), method, obtaining as a result the dimensions of two types of mechanisms, one for the thumb and one for the index finger, to be finally adapted to the dimensions of a physical prototype, which will be generated by the CAD/CAE/CAM methodology described by Costa-de-Morais (2003) and Candal (2005) which is adapted to this case study.

Miralles and Puig (2000) and Portilla et al. (2010) proposed various ranges of values used to define the kinematics of the hand, Table 1 summarizes several sources regarding to the anthropometric measurements of the index finger, which are referenced in the following schematic figure from the index finger.

Table 1. Measures of the forefinger offered by different authors.

Joint	Kind of movements	Forefinger			
		Miralles and Puig (2000)	Velázquez Sánchez (2008)	Portilla et al. (2010b)	Aguilar (2013)
MCP	Extension	22°	…	…	30°
	Flexion	86°	98°	83°	84°
	Length	45 mm	43 mm	43 mm	45 mm
IPP	Extension	7°	…	…	15°
	Flexion	102°	115°	105°	104°
	Length	22 mm	26 mm	26 mm	22 mm
IPD	Extension	8°	…	…	3°
	Flexion	72°	78°	78°	78°
	Length	27 mm	23 mm	16 mm	25 mm

Table 2. Measures of the thumb offered by different authors.

Joint	Kind of movement	Thumb		
		Chang and Matsuoka (2006)	Deshpande et al. (2013)	Aguilar (2013)
TM	F-E	53°	40° - 40°.	35°, 40°.
	A-A	42°	40° - 40°.	40°, 10°.
	Length	52.9 mm	43.1 mm	46 mm
	F-E	70°	60° - 60°.	70°, 40°.
MCP	A-A	30°	15° -15°.	50° - 40°.
	Length	40.3 mm	36.5 mm	34.5 mm
	F-E	95°-100°	20° - 80°	60° - 40°
	A-A	---	---	---
IP	Length	30.7 mm	20 mm	30 mm

Due to the previously described anatomical and morphological similarity between the finger II (index) and fingers III to V, the study and application of the methodology proposed herein will be omitted. Likewise, in Table 2, the anthropometric values and ranges of motion of the thumb reported by several authors are summarized, these were measured from the reference shown in Figure 2, being the result of simplified joint raised previously. Using the values reported in the last column of Tables 1 and 2 -beside from the use of the methodology described by Barrientos et al. (2007) from

Figures 1 and 2, Equations (1) to (5) are obtained, which describe the position of the fingertips from the direct kinematics of the open string that represent them.

$$posx_{ff} = l_1 \cos(q_1) + l_2 \cos(q_1 + q_2) + l_3 \cos(q_1 + q_2 + q_3) \tag{1}$$

$$posy_{ff} = l_1 \sin(q_1) + l_2 \sin(q_1 + q_2) + l_3 \sin(q_1 + q_2 + q_3) \tag{2}$$

$$posx_{th} = l_1 c_{q_1} + l_2\left(c_{(q_1+q_2)}c_{q_1} - s_{(q_1+q_2)}c_{\alpha_1}s_{q_1}\right) - l_3 a\left(c_{(\alpha_1+\alpha_2)}s_{(q_1+q_2)}c_{q_1} - s_{(\alpha_1+\alpha_2)}s_{\alpha_1}c_{q_1} + c_{(\alpha_1+\alpha_2)}c_{(q_1+q_2)}c_{\alpha_1}s_{q_1}\right)$$
$$+ l_3 b\left(c_{(q_1+q_2)}c_{q_1} - s_{(q_1+q_2)}c_{\alpha_1}s_{q_1}\right) \tag{3}$$

$$posy_{th} = l_1 s_{q_1} + l_2\left(c_{(q_1+q_2)}s_{q_1} + s_{(q_1+q_2)}c_{\alpha_1}c_{q_1}\right) - l_3 a\left(c_{(\alpha_1+\alpha_2)}s_{(q_1+q_2)}s_{q_1} + s_{(\alpha_1+\alpha_2)}s_{\alpha_1}c_{q_1} - c_{(\alpha_1+\alpha_2)}c_{(q_1+q_2)}c_{\alpha_1}c_{q_1}\right)$$
$$+ l_3 b\left(c_{(q_1+q_2)}s_{q_1} + s_{(q_1+q_2)}c_{\alpha_1}c_{q_1}\right) \tag{4}$$

$$posz_{th} = l_2 s_{(q_1+q_2)}s_{\alpha_1} + l_3 a\left(s_{(\alpha_1+\alpha_2)}c_{\alpha_1} + c_{(\alpha_1+\alpha_2)}c_{(q_1+q_2)}s_{\alpha_1}\right) + l_3 b\left(s_{(q_1+q_2)}s_{\alpha_1}\right) \tag{5}$$

Where;

$$a = s_{(q_1+q_2+q_3)}$$

$$b = c_{(q_1+q_2+q_3)}$$

From the above equations, the ideal workspace for both fingers shown in Figure 3a and b for the index to the thumb was plotted, so they were the visual references for the evaluation of the operating range and determining the movement pattern proposed in this research. it was mentioned before that the morphology of the

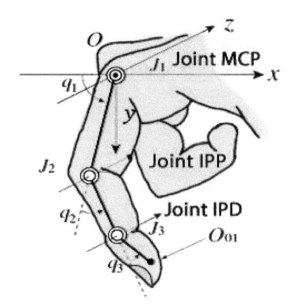

Figure 1. Links that represent the forefinger.

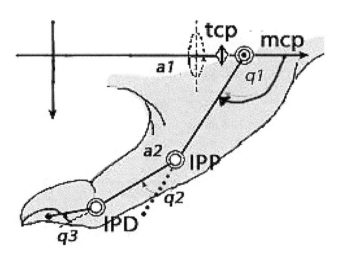

Figure 2. Links that represents the thumb.

forefinger it is dependent between phalanx, that is why the value of input like function of the previous phalanx was determine and was expressed in Equation (6), limited by the range of movements shows in Table 1 at the last column.

$$f\left(\theta_{1_{ff}}\right) = \sin\theta_i$$

(6)

Thus, for the thumb an anthropometric relationship between this parameter and its mathematical relationship was established with respect to a parametric function modeled on the approximation of the workspace volume reported by Li and Tang (2007) and Zhang et al. (2005).

$$f(u,v,k) = \begin{bmatrix} x(u,v,k) \\ y(u,v,k) \\ z(u,v,k) \end{bmatrix} = \begin{bmatrix} r*\cos(u) \\ r*\sin(u) \\ v \end{bmatrix}$$

(7)

Whose equation is shown below was established.

$$r = f(X) = \left(\frac{posy2 - posy1}{posx2 - posx1}\right)(X - posx2) + posy2$$

$$v = TM_{length} + MCP_{length} + IP_{lenght}$$

To do the synthesis of mechanism it was necessary to establish some precision points which are result of the evaluation of Equations (6) and (7), which are in the range of values of Tables 1 and 2. That evaluation was made by using the Chevichev equation, which is shown in Equation (8).

$$x_j = \frac{1}{2}(x_0 + x_{n+1}) - \frac{1}{2}(x_{n+1} - x_0)*\cos\left(\frac{\pi(2j-1)}{2n}\right)j = 1,2,\dots n$$

(8)

For the use of Equation (8), for each set of mechanisms 21 precision points were determined, plus the synthesis of the mechanism from the thumb was performed only in the XY plane, since in this plane is possible to describe the motion of flexion - extension of the thumb. The result of this evaluation was substituted in the Freudenstein equations shown by Equations (14) and (15), so that, in attempting to satisfy these values, it was necessary to solve a system of equations with 21 unknowns quantities, for which we used the Newton-Raphson method shown in Equation (16), besides being considered the procedure described by Shigley and Uicker (2001) and Montúfar et al., (2009).

$$K_2\cos\theta_4 - K_3\cos\theta_2 + K_1 = \cos(\theta_2 - \theta_4)$$

(14)

$$K_2\cos\theta_3 - K_5\cos\theta_2 + K_4 = \cos(\theta_2 - \theta_3)$$

(15)

$$X_{k+1} = X_k - \frac{f(X_k)}{J(X_k)}$$

(16)

Where:

$$K_1 = \frac{a_1^2 + a_4^2 + a_2^2 - a_3^2}{2*a_2*a_4}$$

$$K_2 = \frac{a_1}{a_2}$$

$$K_3 = \frac{a_1}{a_4}$$

$$K_4 = \frac{a_1^2 + a_2^2 + a_3^2 - a_4^2}{2*a_2a_3}$$

$$K_5 = \frac{a_1}{a_3}$$

$$J = \begin{bmatrix} j_{1,1} & \cdots & j_{m,n} \\ \vdots & & \vdots \\ j_{m,1} & \cdots & j_{m,n} \end{bmatrix}$$

(17)

$$j_{1,1} = \frac{\delta F_1}{\delta X_1}; \ j_{1,2} = \frac{\delta F_1}{\delta X_2}; \ \cdots \ ; j_{1,n} = \frac{\delta F_1}{\delta X_n}$$

$$j_{m,1} = \frac{\delta F_m}{\delta X_1}; \ j_{m,2} = \frac{\delta F_m}{\delta X_2}; \ \cdots \ ; j_{m,n} = \frac{\delta F_m}{\delta X_n}$$

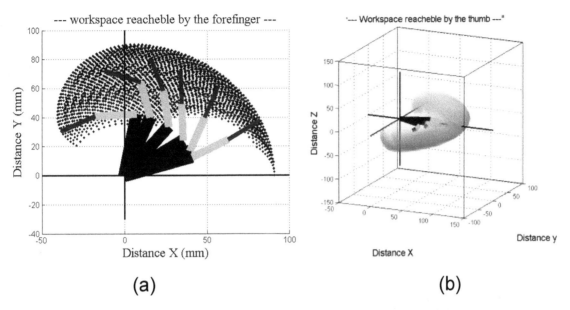

Figure 3. Plot of the ideal workspace for the fingers (a) Forefinger, (b) Thumb.

Table 3. Results of the synthesis of mechanism.

Bar	Forefinger (mm)	Thumb (mm)
R1	10	10
R2	47.5	39
R3	6	11
R4	46	52

RESULTS

Once the synthesis of the mechanisms, in Table 3 the results obtained for the measures used in this work are shown. Finally, using as reference Figure 4a and b, the physical sizing of the links using a Computer Aided Design (CAD) program (Figure 8), whereas during the design process that the measures of the model do not exceed the anthropometric dimensions of the hand. In Figure 5 the prototype made from the methodology outlined here exposed for sizing mechanisms 4 prosthetic hand bars is shown. From the design of the mechanisms, a case study is proposed to evaluate the performance of the entire device, considering as a hypothesis the results shown in Vergara et al. (2012) where it is mentioned that the activity to which he devotes much time the process is feeding. When analyzing Figure 6, the free body diagram is observed during the holding of a water glass with a cylindrical grip power.

To evaluate the performance of the proposed mechanism in this paper, the free-body diagrams shown in Figure 7 were done, while the entire procedure for the calculation of reaction forces is shown in Aguilar (2013), and the obtained values are summarized in Table 4.

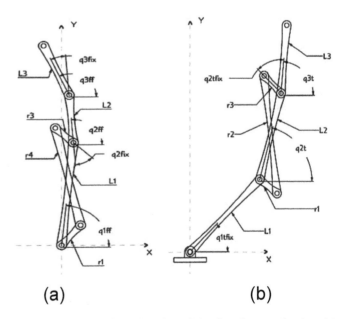

Figure 4. Scheme of the location of the four bar mechanism (a) Forefinger, (b) Thumb.

After determining the loads acting on the complete mechanism due to the case study, we proceed to perform the simulation program for the loads within the finite element calculation, in order to verify the deformation suffered by the pieces, for this the results of static analysis mechanisms were imported, then an automatic meshing part (Figure 8) is created, and finally the stress range at which the material undergoes during the case study is obtained as a result.

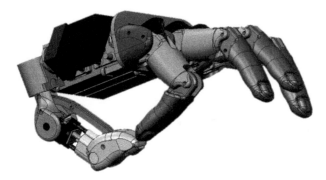

Figure 5. The model of prosthesis of human hand, doing a punctual grip (Aguilar, 2011).

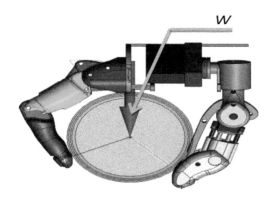

Figure 6. Prototype of the personalized hand prosthesis from the measuring of the anthropometric values.

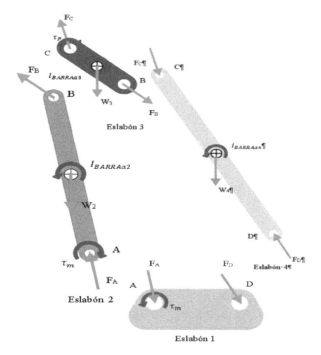

Figure 7. Free body diagrams applied to 4-bar mechanism for the thumb.

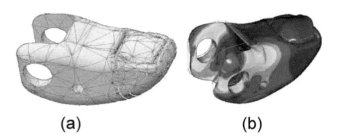

Figura 8. Piece that represent the distal phalanx a) automatic Mesh obtained b) stress field.

Table 4. Force applied by the link at the end.

Extremo del eslabón	Fuerza aplicada
A	2.61
B	-1.66
C	44.3
D	43.95

Table 5. Average force exerted by the fingers in certain grips.

Type of grip	Exerted force (N)
Precisiongrip	24-95 N
Lateral grip	37-106 N
Cylindrical grip	
1 finger	30-109 N
2 fingers	7-38 N
3 fingers	23-73 N

DISCUSSIONS

The human hand has 21° of freedom, people generally only have conscious control of about 16. This coupled with the uniqueness of the fingers due to the alignment of the axes of its movement, allows to perform the simplification proposed in this paper given the number of phalanges moving from finger II to V, but such simplification is only valid for prosthesis designs in which generate static grips from sub-actuated mechanisms is planned. The mechanisms calculated in this work are solely responsible for generating flexion movement, leading to define these different locations within the phalanges of the fingers. This is shown in Figure 3a, showing the configuration of the mechanism for the fingers II to V, where the mechanism is located on the first link considered in the kinematic chain of the finger, whereas for the thumb mechanism (Figure 3b) its location is in the second link in the kinematic chain.

This is because it was proposed to split into two coordinated movements the range of flexion and abduction, as proposed in the description of the opposition movement described by Kapandji and Lacomba (2006), so that the position of the first link only affect the orientation of the second link. For this reason, the position of this link at 45° was fixed, a value according to Cailliet (2006), is designated as the angle at which that section is relaxed thumb, when not performing any flexion.

Furthermore, the research conducted in this paper used the equations of Denavit and Hartemberg so that a mechanism could be synthesize from these equations, but it should be noted that the equation proposed only describes ideal workspace for each finger, which is adapted to a movement pattern that remains within the this workspace, and as presented by Zheng et al. (2011) is possible to improve this equation to define a tangent path to the surface, which would sustain the most common objects of daily use for all activities submitted by Vergara et al. (2012).

Finally, as mentioned in the work of Leal-Naranjo et al. (2013), the four-bar mechanism proposed in this paper is a reduction type of a kinematic chain, which means that the acting force is missing, this can be improved from the use of a kinematic inversion that would modify the position where the force is applied, without having to modify the mechanism already calculated.

Conclusions

Considering the objective of generating flexion and extension moves for the fingers II to V, and allowing to exist a controlled abduction-adduction movement for the thumb, performed automatically by a servomotor. To achieve this throughout this paper, various kinematic relationships were exposed to simplify 14° of the existing freedom degrees of the hand, from which, a methodology for designing kinematic strings of motion was proposed, expressed in terms of the specific anthropometric parameters of the human hand, which is translated in the custom level design prosthetic hand mechanism. Furthermore, the approach undertaken, in mathematical terms, expressed the function to describe the position of the mechanism, which will be used in future studies to develop a control law based on the study of the movement patterns generated by different types of gripping and its relationship with the corresponding myoelectric signal.

Conflict of Interests

The author(s) have not declared any conflict of interests.

ACKNOWLEDGEMENTS

The authors fully appreciate the support granted for this research work by Instituto Politécnico Nacional and the collaboration of the biomechanics group of the Universidad Politécnica de Madrid for all the support given on the makeover of this work.

REFERENCES

Alcalde LV,. Álvarez ZJM, Bascuas; HJ, García F, Ana A, Germán A, Rubio YCE (2006), La carga física de trabajo en extremidades superiores, los límites del sistema mano-brazo, Mapfre Seguridad, 1(101):30-39.

Aguilar-Pérez LA (2013). Dise-o de una protesis de dedo pulgar, Instituto Politécnico Nacional.PMCid:PMC3585368

Belter JT, Dollar YAM (2011). Performance characteristics of anthropomorphic prosthetic hands, Rehabilitation Robotics (ICORR), 2011 IEEE Int. Confer. on pp. 1-7.

Barrientos AL, Pe-ín F, Balaguer C, Aracil, YR (2007). Fundamentos de robótica, 2a:93-131.

Cailliet R (2006). Anatomía funcional, biomecánica, 1:152-191.

Candal MV (2005). Integración CAD/CAE/CAM-PR en la optimización del dise-o de productos plásticos: caso de estudio, Ciencia e Ingeniería, 26(3):121-130.

Cimadevilla LH, Herrera YPJG (2006). Dise-o de un sistema articulado emulando el movimiento de una mano, Centro Nacional de Investigación y Desarrollo Tecnológico, P. 125.

Craig J (2006). Robótica. Publisher. Pearson Prentice Hall J3:62-100.

Chang LY, Matsuoka YY (2006). A Kinematic Thumb Model for the ACT Hand, Proceedings of the 2006 IEEE International Conference on Robotics and Automation.

Deshpande AD, Xu Z, Vande WMJ, Brown;J. Ko BH, Chang LY, Wilkinson DD, Bidic SM, Matsuoka YY (2013). Mechanisms of the Anatomically Correct Testbed (ACT) Hand.

Feix T, Pawlik R, Schmiedmayer HB; Romero J, Kragic YD (2009). A comprehensive grasp taxonomy, Robotics, Science and Systems Conference: Workshop on Understanding the Human Hand for Advancing Robotic Manipulation Cipriani CF. Zaconne G. Stellin;L. Beccai; G. Capiello; M. C. Carroza y P. Dario, Cloosed-loop controller for a Bio-inspered multi-fingered underactuated Prosthesis, IEEE International conference on robotics and automation, 2006.

Hernández SC, Montoya YMCF (2007). Dise-o de un sistema emulando el movimiento articulado de una mano, brazo y antebrazo, Centro Nacional de Investigación y Desarrollo Tecnológico, P. 105.

Kutz M (2003). Standard Handbook of Biomedical Engineering. Design, 6:821-882.

Kapandji AI. Lacomba YMT (2006), Fisiología articular: Esquemas comentados de mecánica articular. Hombro, codo, pronosupinacion, mu-eca, mano. 1(6):198-333.

Leal-Naranjo JA, Torres San Miguel CR, Carbajal-Romero MF, Sáez YLM (2013) Structural numerical analysis of a three fingers prosthetic hand prototype, int. J. Phys. Sci. 8(13):526-536.

Lewis. FL, Dawson DM, Abdallah YCT (2004). Robot Manipulator Control: Theory and Practice.

Li, ZM, Latash ML Zatsiorsky YVM (1998). Force sharing among fingers as a model of the redundancy problem, Exper. Brain Res. 119(3):276-286.http://dx.doi.org/10.1007/s002210050343, PMid:9551828

Li Z-M, Tang YJ (2007). Coordination of thumb joints during opposition. J. Biomechan. 40(3):502-510. http://dx.doi.org/10.1016/j.jbiomech.2006.02.019PMid:16643926

Montúfar CPC, Flores JA, García RI, Tapía YHR (2009). Cinemática de mecanismos y máquinas, mmmm,---.Costa-de-Morais, F. R. J., CAD/CAE/CAM/CIM, (2003), Instituto superior de ingeniería de Porto, P. 123.

Miralles MRC, Puig YCM (2000), Biomecánica clínica del aparato locomotor, Barcelona; Espa-a, 1:133-169.

Naik GR, Kumar YDK (2010). Identification of hand and finger movements using multi run ICA of surface electromyogram. J. Med. Syst. 36(2):841-851. http://dx.doi.org/10.1007/s10916-010-9548-2, PMid:20703649

Shigley JE, Uicker YJJJ (2001). Teoría de máquinas y mecanismos, 300-325:343-380, 448-480.

Portilla FÉA, Aviles SOF, Pi-a OR, Ni-o SPA, Moya SE, Molina YVMA (2010). Análisis cinemático y dise-o de un mecanismo de cuatro barras para falange proximal de dedo antropomórfico, Ciencia e Ingeniería Neogranadina, 20-1:45-49.

Portilla FE, Pi-a OR, Avilés SO, Ni-o SP, Molina YVM (2010). Dise-odel mecanismo actuador de un dedo robot antropomórfico, Revista Facultad de Ingeniería Universidad de Antioquia. 58:153-162.

Vergara M, Serrano CJ, Rodriguez PJ, Pérez YGA (2012). Resultados de un trabajo de campo sobre agarres utilizados en tareas cotidianas, XIX Congreso Nacional de ingeniería Mecánica. Gregory, R. W., Biomechanics and control of torque production during prehension, The Pennsylvania State University, P. 210.

Velázquez Sánchez AT (2008) Caracterización cinemática e implementación de una mano robótica multiarticulada, Instituto Politécnico Nacional, P. 326.

Zollo LS, Roccella E, Guglielmelli M, Carrozza C, Dario PY (2007), Biomechatronic design and control of an anthropomorphic artificial hand for prosthetic and robotic applications, IEEE/ASME Transactions on Mechatronics, 12(4):418-429. http://dx.doi.org/10.1109/TMECH.2007.901936

Zhang X, Braido P, Lee S-W, Hefner R, Redden YM (2005). A normative database of thumb circumduction *in vivo*: center of rotation and range of motion, Human Factors: The Journal of the Human Factors and Ergonomics Society. 47(3):550-561. http://dx.doi.org/10.1177/154193120504901216, http://dx.doi.org/10.1177/154193120504902224, http://dx.doi.org/10.1518/001872005774860069

Zheng JZ, De La Rosa S, Dollar YAM (2011). An investigation of grasp type and frequency in daily household and machine shop tasks, Robotics and Automation (ICRA), 2011 IEEE International Conference on, pp. 4169-4175.

18

Optimal transformer allocation in electrical distribution using genetic algorithm

Oluwole Charles Akinyokun, Gabriel Babatunde Iwasokun and Akinwale Michael Ojo

Department of Computer Science, Federal University of Technology, Akure, Ondo State, Nigeria.

The optimization of transformers allocation is a major challenge to the operators of electrical energy distribution in several developing countries. In this research, a Generic Algorithm model for the optimization of transformer allocation in electrical distribution networks is developed. The algorithm employed the principles of selection, crossover and mutation to allocate transformers of different capacities to various substations in order to achieve their optimum performance. The objective function was subjected to cost and power capacity of each transformer as well as the growth rate and power consumption of the region. The initial population of chromosomes was generated at random with each consisting of potential solution to the problem. The chromosomes were decrypted and used to estimate the objective function. The GA operations were carried out on the chromosomes to know the ones that are best fit for consideration in the next generation. Results of a case study of transformer allocation in Osogbo District of Power Holding Company of Nigeria exhibited best-fit strategies for massive exchange (redistribution) of transformers in the district.

Key words: Genetic algorithm, transformer allocation, power distribution network, optimization and power generator.

INTRODUCTION

Electricity is one of the major driving forces behind modern machines and it is the backbone of a progressive economy. A nation with erratic supply of electricity will definitely be a nation with unstable economic growth. In modern times, the supply of electricity is manned by major electricity companies and passes through the stages of generation, transmission, distribution and consumption. Most electricity is generated using coal, oil, natural gas, nuclear energy, or hydropower. Some production is done with alternative fuels like geothermal energy, wind power, biomass, solar energy or fuel cells (Milbrandt and Mann, 2009). Majority of the electricity is

produced at power plants with the use of steam turbines where mechanical energy is changed into electrical energy by using various energy sources such as coal, natural gas and oil. These fuels heat water in a boiler to produce steam. The steam under tremendous pressure is used to turn a series of blades mounted on a shaft turbine. The force of the steam rotates a shaft that is connected to a generator. The spinning turbine shafts turn electromagnets that are surrounded by heavy coils of copper wire inside generators. This creates a magnetic field which causes the electrons in the copper wire to move from atom to atom creating electricity (Culverco, 2005).

Utility companies anticipate demand for electricity and transmit it at very high voltage along system of power lines to consumers through transformers where the high voltage is "step up" or "step down". The power lines can be high as 765,000 volts which travel many hundreds of miles in a transmission grid (BOPL, 2012). Electric power distribution reliability is a measurement of how well the system provides customer adequate and secured supply of power to meet daily requirements. The concept of adequacy is generally considered to be the existence of sufficient facilities within the system to satisfy customers' demand. Several methods in which Generic Algorithm (GA) formed the bedrock have been proposed for sufficient and constant transmission of electricity to consumers through suitable and appropriate allocation of transformers. GA is a programming technique that mimics biological evolution as a problem-solving strategy. They are based on a biological metaphor, which view learning as a competition among a population of evolving candidate problem solutions (Luger, 2002; Adam, 2004). This paper presents a suitable case study, a GA-based optimization procedure for transformers allocation as one of the key elements in electrical distribution networks.

Related works

The theoretical foundations for GA were presented in (Holland, 1975; Kumara et al., 2009; Melanie, 1999) as a global search technique for solving optimization problems which is basically focused on the theory of natural selection, the process that drives biological evolution. Genetic algorithms consist of a population of binary string and searching many peaks in parallel (Bhasker et al., 2013; Li, 2009). The authors in (Mahela and Ola, 2013) studied the possibility of reducing the value of real power losses for global system transmission lines by choosing the best location to install shunt capacitors. GA is used to calculate the optimal allocation and sizing considering the value of real power losses with injection of reactive power as an indicator of the ability of reducing losses at load buses. In Carpinelli et al. (2010) optimal sizing and allocation of dispersed generation, distributed storage systems and capacitor banks are presented. The optimization focused on minimizing the sum of the costs sustained by the distributor for the power losses, network upgrading, reactive power service and the storage and capacitor installation over the planning period. A hybrid procedure based on a GA and a sequential quadratic programming-based algorithm was implemented on an 18-busbar MV balanced 3-phase network and the results confirmed its feasibility.

A heuristic backtracking search algorithm is proposed in Chia-Hung et al. (2007) for adjusting the phasing arrangement of primary feeders and laterals for phase balancing of distribution systems. The phase unbalance index of distribution feeders is calculated based on the phasing current magnitude of each line segment and

branch which has been solved by a 3-phaseload flow program. Bogdan et al. (2013) proposed a method for achieving optimization through the reconfiguration of distribution systems taking into account various criteria in a flexible and robust approach.

A method for finding the optimal values of the fixed and switched capacitors in the distribution networks based on the Real Coded GA (RCGA) is presented in (Rahmat-Allah and Mohammad, 2007). The modeling of the loads at different levels is simulated with low and medium voltage capacitors. With various parameters in the optimization problem, RCGA is used to find the real optimal network with the best rate for the capacitors. A determination method of optimal allocation and transfer of Step Voltage Regulators (SVRs) in distribution feeders with Renewable Energy Sources (RES) is presented in (Takahashi et al., 2012). The proposed method determines the optimal allocation and transfer of SVRs based on the forecasted amount of Photovoltaic (PV) system. In the proposed method, voltage margin is maximized under a constraint that all the node voltages are controlled within the proper range for a certain period of years.

Sreejaya and Iyer (2012) presents a GA based reactive power optimization for voltage profile improvement and real power loss minimization in AC-DC system. The reactive power control devices such as generators, tap positions of on-load tap changer of transformers, shunt capacitors, converter transformer tap positions and firing angles (Al-Abdulwahab, 2007; Ellithy et al., 2008) were used to correct voltage limits violations while simultaneously reducing the system power losses. Shahram (2006) proposed a system for evaluating the optimum allocation of any power system elements such as power plant, substation and capacitors. The system operates on GA and uses heuristic rules for its operations. The system finds substation allocation in optimum point with regard to its place and size. The mathematical model of the problem uses minimum investment costs and power loss to obtain the goal. Tiago et al. (2011) made a comparison between GA and particle swarm optimization (PSO) as tools for providing solution to switch allocation problem. The two algorithms used fuzzy expert system (FES) for making engineering judgment in the solution of the switch allocation problem. The models and techniques proposed were validated and applied in a large scale substation with the results showing the performance level of the two algorithms. The authors in Lijun et al. (2008) present optimal choice and allocation of devices in multi-machine power systems using GA. Focus was on achieving the power system economic generation allocation and dispatch in deregulated electricity market.

PROPOSED GA MODEL FOR OPTIMAL TRANSFORMER ALLOCATION

The first phase of the algorithm is concerned with the survey of some baseline data of transformer in each substation. The baseline data include power rating of transformer, estimated power consumption in the service area that is being serviced by the transformer, age of the transformer, classification of consumer (residential/commercial/industrial) and estimated percentage load growth of the area.

The second phase is concerned with developing a model of genetic algorithm procedure with a view of placing transformers in a substation for maximum capacity utilization. The model is characterized by a database of substation. The system employs a mono-objective optimization technique which is aimed at maximizing the capacity utilization of a transformer relative to its position in the electrical distribution network. The technique has a mechanism for guiding against over-utilization which can lead to quick ageing or breakdown of the transformer. Moreover, it involves the re-allocation of the existing transformers in the distribution network and resizing of an existing network by providing the capability of adding new nodes.

The third phase is concerned with the repositioning of transformers for better performance such that, the transformers that have less power to supply their substation are replaced. The design is presented under the transformer allocation in electrical distribution networks and data entry, genetic algorithm processing and result presentation design.

A typical substation comprises a distribution transformer, an incoming high voltage line, switches, circuit breakers, and other equipment needed to deliver electric power to the customer at the required voltages (U.S. Department of Labor, 2009). The factors that affect and determine the performance of transformers in an electrical distribution network include weather (storms, snow, temperature and humidity), contamination and humidity, excessive ambient temperature, excessive load and ageing. The design of transformer allocation in electrical distribution networks is driven by power flow analysis, load growth analysis and ageing factor.

Genetic representation of transformers in distribution network

The basis of genetics in nature is a chromosome. In the search space, each solution to the problem at hand, need to be encoded so that it can be thought of as a chromosome. Originally, genetic algorithm was designed with the idea of using binary string as a means of encoding (Mitchell, 1999). However, in a problem such as this, encoding binary string is not a natural way for representing the problem instead, what is designed is an encoding based upon the ordinary value where the position of each value represents where the transformer should be transferred to. In transformer allocation, the transformers are represented by 3-digits, while the position of the 3-digit gene in the chromosome represents the substation where the transformer is to be taken to. Each chromosome in the population is associated with a fitness value that is calculated using the fitness function. The fitness value indicates the satisfactory level of the solution being offered by the chromosome (Mitchel, 1999). This information is used to select the chromosomes that will contribute to the formation of the next generation of solution.

Crossover basically means that first part of the chromosome is exchanged with a part of the second chromosome, while the other parts of the chromosomes are equally exchanged. In a nutshell, crossover involved the genes of two chromosomes to be exchanged in an orderly manner. The individual chromosomes randomly organized pair wise, have their space location consumed in such a way that each former pair of individuals give rise to a new pair. The prompt to be used for Crossover is chosen randomly, different result is achieved by positioning the crossover point randomly.

Some individuals in the chromosome are randomly modified, that is, one (1) will change to 0 and 0 will change to one (1). Mutation is required after crossover because it prevents the solution from converging towards local optimal. Mutation involves selecting a gene represented by 3-digits in the chromosome and randomly altering one of the 3 digits.

Design of optimal allocation of transformers

Genetic algorithms are mainly used for optimization techniques (either to minimize or maximize). The model here is to maximize the capacity utilization of each transformer in the distribution system subject to the various parameters attached to each substation. The framework for the design in the system is provided in Figure 1 and has data entry, optimization procedure and result presentation.

The data to be entered into the system will basically serve as input to the genetic algorithm processing procedure. The kind of data required are not the type that is processed in peace-meal, but is bounded for processing as a whole. The required data for the system are divided into the following:

a. Genetic algorithm control parameters: The value of the control parameters influences the performance of the genetic algorithm processing module (Ellithy, 2007). It is used to alter the behavioral pattern of how the algorithm operates. For example, generations required by the optimization depends on the value of the control parameters. The control parameters that will be entered into the system include population size, crossover type, mutation probability, number of years for the model and number of iterations.

b. Substation records: Depending on the number of substations to be considered in the optimization system, the following parameters are used to test the objective function for optimizing the transformer in each substation:

i. Power rating of the transformer,
ii. Estimated power consumption of the area,
iii. Age (years) of the transformer,
iv. Consumer classification (Residential or Industrial),
v. Growth rate of the area.

The data are obtained and sent to the genetic algorithm procedure for processing and storage into a database for future retrieval and reprocessing. The database is as follows:

a. District {district name, state of origin, substation, population size, mutation probability, crossover type, number years of model, number of iteration},
b. Substation {substation id, transformer id, transformer power rating, transformer type, age of transformer, power consumption in the area, consumer classification},
c. Optimized transformer {substation id, initial substation id, transformer id, transformer power rating, transformer type, power consumption in the area, consumer classification}.

The data entry system represents an interface between the genetic algorithm processing and the stored substation records. At the data entry system, users request is transformed into a structured query language (SQL). The system dynamically fetches all the substation records regarding the district and is sent to the genetic algorithm processing unit.

Objective function: Based on the factors that affect the performance of a transformer in a distribution network, the mono-objective task of this genetic algorithm is based on the maximization of capacity utilization of individual transformers in the distribution networks considering the following parameters relating to a substation:

a. Power rating of the transformer,
b. Power consumption of the area (load demand),

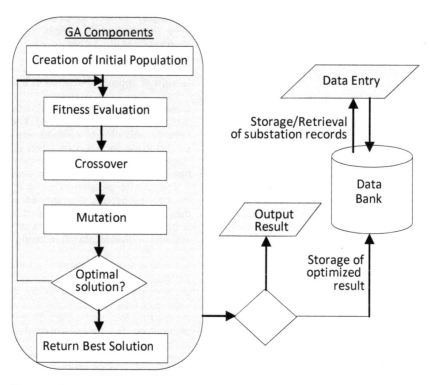

Figure 1. The design architecture.

c. Appreciation of power demand of the area for the specified period of time (load growth),
d. Ageing factor of the transformer,
e. Marginal fluctuation in power demand in the area.

The objective function, Z for the optimal transformer allocation in electrical distribution networks is given as:

$$Max\ Z = (T[i] - A[i]) - (P[i] + L[i] + M)$$

Subject to the decision variables: $T[i]$ = power rating of the transformer, $A[i]$ represents ageing factor of the transformer, $P[i]$ = the power consumption at the substation, $L[i]$ = the annual load growth of the area, and M = electricity marginal variation in demand.

Optimization procedure

Genetic algorithms use a "chromosomal" representation which requires the solution to be coded as a finite length of string (Ellithy, 2007). The procedure for optimizing the allocation of transformers in electrical distribution networks is based on the following processes:

a. String representation: In genetic algorithm, a chromosome represents a potential solution in a way to the domain problem. In the context of transformer allocation, a chromosome is a string of bits (comprising of 0's and 1's) which when decoded, represent a complete arrangement of the transformers in the distribution network. In the context of genetic algorithm for optimizing the allocation of transformers in electrical distribution networks, a gene

is a group of 3 digits, which when decoded, represent the substation number (position) in which the transformer is to be placed in the distribution system. The substations in the distribution network are numbered from 1, 2, 3, ..., N, where N is the number of substations.

Hence, a chromosome comprises of bits that are three times the number of substations in the distribution network. Each 3 group of digits which is a gene is decoded to represent the substation position of the transformer in the distribution network. For example, supposing T1, T2, T3, ...T_N are transformers in substations S1, S2, S3, ..., S_N respectively, a chromosome defined as: 020 017 005.....128 will give the arrangement as in Table 1.

This means that Transformer T1 is allocated to substation 20, Transformer T2 is allocation to substation 17, transformer T3 is allocated to substation 5 and transformer T_N is allocated to substation 128.

b. Initial population generation: The population refers to the number of chromosomes which will undergo evolutionary procedure to eventually produce a single chromosome that will be picked as the optimal value. The illustration above represents just one chromosome. For instance, if the population size selected for the algorithm is 700, then this number of chromosomes will be generated at random. Initially, they may hold no promise, but after they have undergone the evolutionary procedure of genetic algorithm, they will eventually produce a single chromosome that 'best-fit' the arrangement of transformers in the distribution network.

c. Fitness evaluation: The gene (location) for each transformer is tested in their environment (substation) using the various parameters relating to that substation such as:

i. Power rating of the transformer,
ii. Power consumption of the area (load demand),
iii. Power load growth of the area for the specified period of time,
iv. Ageing factor of the transformer,

Table 1. Chromosome arrangement of the transformers.

T1	T2	T3	....	T$_N$
020	017	005	....	128

v. Marginal fluctuation in power demand in the area.

The estimated value of the fitness of all the transformers in their virtual substation are added together to form the objective function value. This fitness evaluation is carried out on all the chromosomes to see which of them will have the highest objective function value. The chromosomes with low fitness values are replaced with newly generated ones, while the ones with high fitness value will undergo selection, crossover and mutation (evolutionary procedures) and move to the next generation (iteration) with the hope of producing better fitness.

d. Selection and reproduction: A set of old chromosomes are selected to reproduce a set of new chromosomes according to the probability which is proportional to their fitness. They are carried out to preserve better solution candidates. Less fit candidates are discarded and new ones are generated to replace them.

e. Crossover: This is performed on two chromosomes at periods that are selected from the population. Each of the two strings is splinted into two and the head of the first is joined to the tail of the second, while the head of the second is joined to the tail of the first. The conceptual diagram of the process of a Crossover of Parents 1 and 2 chromosomes is shown in Figure 2.

f. Mutation: This involves selecting a chromosome and changing one of its bits from 0 to 1 or vice versa as shown in Figure 3.

The optimization procedure requires an objective function and the encoding techniques for the parameters of each transformer in each of the substations, which are used to estimate its fitness. After the substation records and control parameters have been entered, the methodology employed is as follows:

a. The solution begins with the random generation of initial population of chromosomes,
b. For each chromosome, evaluate the objective function and the fitness value. The objective function is determined according to the summation of the capacity utilization of all the transformers in the network,
c. If chromosome population converge or the specified number of iterations has been carried out (optimum solution likely reached), then the chromosome with the highest fitness value is obtained as the optimal solution,
d. Select the new population using the principle of selection and reproduction described above (evolutionary principle),
e. Apply crossover and mutation on the new population and go to Step b.

The block diagram of the procedures described above is shown in Figure 4. At the end of the optimization procedure, the chromosome with the highest fitness value is taken as the optimal solution.

IMPLEMENTATION OF THE PROPOSED ALGORITHM

Prior to implementation, several choices were made concerning the parameters that serve as tools in controlling the GA procedure. Care was taken to ensuring that the set of choices is fit enough to produce optimal

Figure 2. A visual diagram for crossover.

Figure 3. A visual diagram for mutation.

results. Before optimization, the position of transformers in electrical distribution system is processed, the required information, which comprise of the control parameters for the processing and substation in the District were determined. The input forms for creating the control parameters and the substation databases are shown in Figures 5 and 6, respectively. Parameters such as population size, the number of substations/transformers in the system, crossover type (Single Point) in this case, mutation probability, number of years and iterations were appropriately selected.

Processing via GA begins with the reading of district and substations record from the database as shown in Figure 7. Read data are then converted into a set of strings where a substation is represented by a 3-digit string which the GA procedure can work upon. Therefore, the number of strings that form a chromosome will be three times the number of substation. The procedure is iterative and at the end of each iteration, genetic operators act on the chromosomes that allocate each transformer in the system (crossover and mutation). At the end, the fitness of each chromosome is evaluated using the objective function. The one that has the highest fitness is temporarily stored for future comparison. Those with the least fitness are discarded and new chromosomes are generated to continue the processes until the number of required iteration is reached. At the end of the whole process, the best-fit chromosomes

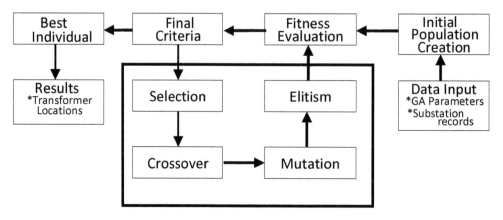

Figure 4. Optimization procedural block diagram for optimal transformer allocation in electrical distribution networks.

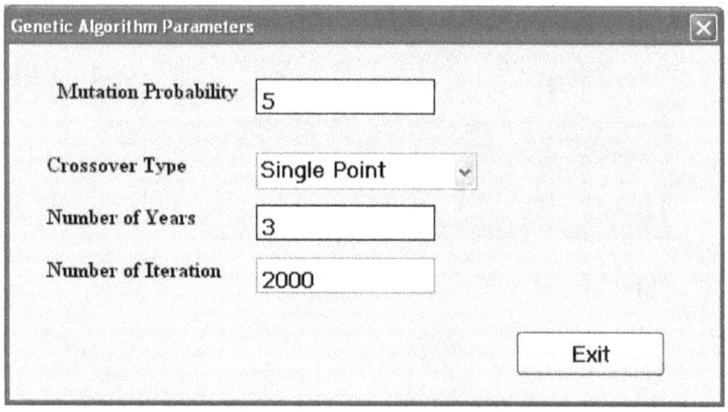

Figure 5. Input form for GA control parameters.

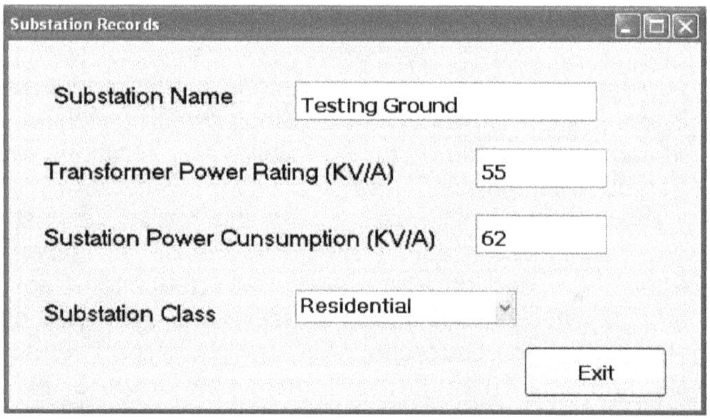

Figure 6. Entering form for substations data.

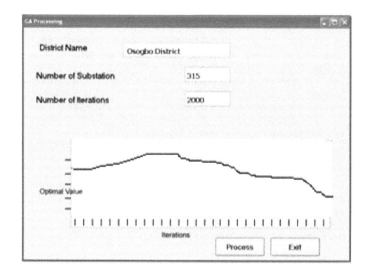

Figure 7. Processing via GA.

stored for each of the iterations are compared and the one that evaluates to best fitness is chosen for the allocation of transformers into the appropriate substations. For optimal performance, all underused or overused transformers are relocated to appropriate and rightful substations.

A case study of Osogbo electricity distribution district (OEDD) of Power Holding Company of Nigeria (PHCN) was carried out. The schematic diagram of the district is shown in Appendix 1. OEDD is one of the oldest districts of the electricity company in Nigeria and several other districts had been carved out from it. Presently, the district has a customer population of about 571,056 spreading across its 135 substations in five geographical units or undertakings that include Osogbo, Okefia, Ayetoro, Ikirun and Ila. Electricity is distributed to the end users in the district from a 33 KVA power source (Ojo, 2012). The matrix of the current and optimized transformer allocations in the district is presented in Table 2. Optimization of transformer allocations via GA indicates a fair but un-optimized allocation of transformers in the network with significant numbers of sub-utilized (SU) as well as over-utilized (OU) transformers.

Table 2. Current and optimized transformer allocation in Osogbo District, Nigeria.

Sub Id	Name of substation	Current transformer allocation		Optimized transformer allocation	
		Capacity Distr. T/F (KVA)	Loading (KVA)	Capacity Distr. T/F (KVA)	From Sub Id
1	Nulge	500	280	500	113
2	Osogbo Local Govt.	300	399	200	35
3	Idi Baba	300	105	200	38
4	Oke Ijetu	300	330	200	77
5	Federal Housing	300	120	200	80
6	Owode Village	200	198	100	47
7	Egbeda	200	136	200	9
8	Cooker III	200	110	300	3
9	Cooker II	200	100	200	10
10	Cooker I	200	106	200	11
11	Oredunmi	200	106	100	134
12	Gaa Fullani	200	156	200	8
13	Industrial Park	1000	820	1000	13
14	LAUTECH (Asubiaro)	500	440	300	62
15	OSBC	500	475	500	53
16	Uniosun	500	280	300	61
17	UNESCO	500	365	300	4
18	Nursing School Hostel	300	204	300	64
19	Crown Hotel	200	240	300	5
20	Fountain University	200	196	200	78
21	Asubiaro State Hospital	200	144	100	87
22	Mini Water Works	200	132	300	122
23	Auxilliary (Odi Olowo)	100	92	100	133
24	MTN Idi Baba	50	37.5	50	24
25	MTN (Ife Oluwa)	50	38.5	50	25
26	Ebenezer	500	385	500	115
27	Station Rd.	500	365	500	49
28	Terminus	500	440	300	58
29	Old garage	500	380	500	17
30	Igbonna	500	535	500	27
31	Fagbewesa	300	243	300	65
32	Adenle	300	219	315	129
33	Orisunbare Market	500	530	500	72
34	LAUTECH Teaching Hosp	500	610	500	29
35	TIB/Spring Bank	200	174	300	125
36	UBA	300	195	300	124
37	Wema Bank	300	291	200	82
38	Fist Bank PLC	200	176	200	131
39	OSICOL Water	200	148	200	22
40	Computer	200	200	200	81
41	STB/UBA	100	61	100	41
42	Union Bank	100	72	100	68
43	District Office	100	73	100	45
44	O'Net Otakiti	100	94	100	100
45	SKYE Bank Fagbewesa	100	65	100	94
46	Ademola Rasaq	100	89	300	130
47	Intercontinenter Bank	100	99	100	42
48	MTN Opp.Post Office	50	56.5	50	135

Table 2. Contd.

49	Coca-Cola	500	335	500	69
50	Baruwa	500	540	500	26
51	Eleyele Estate	500	385	500	51
52	Ogo-Oluwa	500	570	500	116
53	Omigade	500	320	500	117
54	Odetoyinbo	500	645	500	55
55	Sazo	500	395	500	120
56	Ibuamo Abija Area	500	190	300	123
57	Olosan II Ogo-Oluwa Area	500	295	300	2
58	Folakunle	300	354	300	66
59	Heritage	300	150	500	56
60	Olosan	300	225	300	127
61	Zarah	300	321	300	36
62	Ataoja Est.	300	318	200	20
63	Oladipo	300	423	200	6
64	Ibukunoluwa	300	177	200	40
65	Palm Crest Hotel	300	177	300	18
66	Olasamson	300	186	200	83
67	Kamar Dairo	200	80	200	7
68	Raji Kolade	100	64	100	100
69	Gov's Office I	500	380	500	114
70	Gov's Office II	500	270	500	118
71	Abere I	500	485	500	74
72	CBN I Opposite NECO	500	375	500	111
73	CBN II Abere	500	440	300	63
74	Amorite	500	410	300	32
75	House of Assembly I	300	237	500	14
74	House of Assembly II	300	144	500	121
75	Fed. High Court	300	225	300	128
76	Custom	300	291	300	60
77	Olaniyi Aina Petrol	200	176	200	86
78	First Bank	200	120	300	126
79	Access Bank	200	142	200	79
80	Health Trust Fund	200	176	200	21
81	INEC	200	134	300	74
82	NTA Osogbo	200	184	200	39
83	Fidelity Bank	200	210	300	59
84	Tantalizer	200	154	200	84
85	Federal Pay Office	200	166	200	12
86	Bank PHB	200	138	300	129
87	Oceanic Bank	100	120	100	134
88	Zenith Bank	100	80	100	43
89	Ayinke Tower	100	86	100	132
90	GTB	100	79	100	102
91	Diamond Bank	100	75	100	91
92	FCMB	100	89	100	90
93	MTEL Ogo-Oluwa	100	94	100	99
94	Fed. Inland Revenue	100	69	200	67
95	FRSC	100	85	100	88
96	Living Spring Hotel	100	97	100	103
97	MTN Oke Pupa	100	95	100	101
98	AIG Office	100	93	100	108

Table 2. Contd.

99	Celtel, Owode Abere	100	79	200	133
100	Celtel, Gbongan /Ibadan Rd	100	68	100	89
101	Abere Streetlighting	100	83	100	104
102	Afri Bank	100	74	100	46
103	Street Lighting	100	82	100	92
104	Heritage Hotel	100	86	100	23
105	Streetlighting	100	96	100	98
106	Union Bank Gb/Ib Road	100	94	100	44
107	Streetlighting	100	95	100	93
108	Sterling Bank	100	84	100	106
109	SSS Office	50	48	50	109
110	Zain Opp. Access Bank	50	53.5	50	110
111	Jaleyemi	500	415	500	28
112	Matanmi	500	605	500	73
113	Exchange	500	300	500	15
114	Oja-Oba	500	400	500	71
115	Kajola	500	330	500	33
116	Oke Abesu	500	385	500	30
117	Oke Baale	500	385	500	50
118	Custain	500	405	500	52
119	Fadilulahi	500	230	500	112
120	ST Charles	500	395	500	34
121	Fadilulahi II	500	215	500	54
122	Osogbo Local Govt	300	120	300	75
123	Jimoh Buraimoh	300	396	500	119
124	BetterLife	300	183	300	75
125	Asubiaro I	300	123	200	19
126	Asubiaro II	300	138	300	131
127	Onireke	300	192	300	31
128	Ifelodun	300	222	500	70
129	Isale Aro	300	159	500	1
130	Ikolaba	300	69	500	57
131	Iso Ewe	300	240	500	16
132	Ita-Olokan	300	288	300	76
132	Bishop's Court(Oke Ayepe)	300	285	200	85
133	Etisalat	300	285	300	132
133	Iso Ata(Back of Palace)	200	84	100	97
129	IDC II	315	179.55	300	133
130	IDC I	300	165	300	132
131	Palace	200	128	100	107
132	Street Lighting Jaleyemi	100	73	300	130
133	Sttreet Lighting, Ita-Olokan	100	60	300	37
134	Tajudeen Oladipupo	100	108	100	105
134	MTN Oke Ayepe	100	72	100	96
135	Yetty Guest House	50	44	50	48

Visual inspection of the figures presented in Table 2 revealed that practical implementation of the algorithm will require several exchanges of transformers to where they best fit in the distribution network. For instance, transformers at substations with identifier 113, 35, 38, 77 and 80 could have been located at Nulge, Osogbo Local government, Ido Baba, Oke Ijetu and Federal Housing, respectively. It is also shown that some transformers are to be disposed for new ones, for smooth and reliable distribution of electricity. Future research focuses on improving the algorithm to attain fully optimized transformer allocations in an electricity distribution network. This is expected to be achieved via the inclusion of some other relevant decision variables like customers' social class (private, commercial government) and environmental factors (temperature, humidity) in the objective function.

Conclusions

GA optimization technique has been proposed for resolving inadequacies inherent with the conventional or manual allocation of transformers in electrical distribution networks. The optimization procedure adequately allocated transformers to where they are best fit for energy transmission over reasonable lifespan in an electrical distribution. The system has an advantage over the manual system because it can be executed repeatedly and very helpful in the determination of how existing electricity distribution network could accommodate expansion.

REFERENCES

Adam M (2004). GAs and Evolutionary Computation. Talk Origins Archives.

Al-Abdulwahab A (2007). "Radial Electrical Distribution Systems Automation Using GA", J. King Abdulaziz University Eng. Sci. 18(2).

Bhasker K, Vijay M, Albert W, Debmalya B (2013). Mathematical Modeling of Optimizing Power Stream Measurement Using GA, Am. J. Eng. Res. (AJER), 2(10):71-79.

Bogdan T, Mircea C, Andreas S, Sudria-Andreu A, Roberto VR (2013). Pareto Optimal Reconfiguration of Power Distribution Systems Using a GA Based on NSGA-II, Int. J. Energies 6:1439-1455; doi:10.3390/en6031439

BOPL (2012) Broadband Over Power Lines. A White Paper (www.state.nj.us/rpd/BLPw Hitepaper.pdf), Accessed 23/07/2013.

Carpinelli G, Mottola F, Proto D, Russo A (2010). Optimal Allocation of Dispersed Generators, Capacitors and Distributed Energy Storage Systems in Distribution Networks, Modern Electric Power Systems 2010, Wroclaw, Poland.

Chia-Hung L, Meei-Song K, Hui-Jen C, Chin-Ying H (2007). Phase Balancing of Distribution Systems Using a Heuristic Search Approach (www.jicee.org/inc/download.asp? PR_Idx=148), Accessed 12/10/2013.

Culverco (2005). Electricity Generation and Distribution; Science and Safety of Electricity http://www.culverco.com/sse/power.

Ellithy K (2007). Optimal shunt capacitors allocation in distribution networks using GA. Int. J. Innov. Energy Syst. Power 3(1).

Ellithy K, Al-Hinai AS, Moosa AH (2008). "Optimal Shunt Capacitors Allocation In Distribution Networks Using Genetic Algorithm- Practical Case Study". Int. J. Innovations Energy Syst. Power, IJIESP. 3(1).

Holland J (1975). GA (http://www.cc.gatech.edu/~turk/bio_sim/articles/genetic_algorithm.pdf), Accessed 27/02/20143

Kumara S, David G, Graham K (2009). GAs (.http://citeseerx.ist.psu.edu/viewdoc/download?doi=10.1.1.61.6575&rep=rep1&type=pdf), Accessed 27/02/2014

Lijun C, István E, Georgios S, Yicheng L (2008). Optimal choice and allocation of facts devices in deregulated electricity market using GAs (https://www.uni-due.de/ean/downloads/papers/irep-erlich-08.04.pdf), Accessed 05/11/2013.

Luger GF (2002). Introduction to GA, working principle: Electrical Power Distribution Engineering; North Maharashtra University, Jalgaon.

Mahela OMP, Ola SR (2013). Optimal capacitor placement for loss reduction in electric transmission system using GA, Int. J. Electr. Electron. Eng. Res. (IJEEER) 3(2):59-68.

Milbrandt A, Mann M (2009). Hydrogen resource assessment hydrogen potential from coal, natural as, nuclear, and hydro power, technical report of united states national renewable energy Laboratory-NREL/TP-560-42773 (http://www.nrel.gov/docs/fy09osti/42773.pdf).

Mitchell M (1999). An Introduction to GAs, Bradford Book The MIT Press, Cambridge, Massachusetts. London, England.

Ojo AM (2012). Development of genetic algorithm for optimal transformer allocation in electrical distribution networks, M. Tech. Thesis, Department of Computer Science, Federal University of Technology, Akure, Nigeria.

Rahmat-Allah H, Mohammad A (2007). Optimal capacitor placement in actual configuration and operational conditions of distribution systems using RCGA. J. Electr. Eng. 58(4):189-199.

Shahram J (2006). Software development for optimum allocation of power system elements based on GA, Proceedings of the 6th WSEAS International Conference on Power Systems, Lisbon, Portugal, September 22-24, 2006.

Sreejaya P, Iyer RS (2012). Reactive Power Control by GA in AC-DC Systems, Lecture Notes in Information Technology, International Conf. Future Electr. Power Energy Syst. Vol. 9.

Takahashi S, Yasuhiro H, Masaki T, Eiji K (2012). Method of optimal allocation of svr in distribution feeders with renewable energy sources. J. Int. Counc. Electr. Eng. 2(2):159-165.

Tiago A, Anselmo R, Maria da Guia da S (2011). Switches Allocation in Distribution Network Using Particle Swarm Optimization Based on Fuzzy Expert System, Proceedings of 7th Power Systems Computation Conference Stockholm Sweden.

U.S. Department of Labor (2009). Occupational Safety and Health Administration: Electricity Generation, Transmission and Distribution. www.osha.gov.

Li Y (2009). Using Niche GA to Find Fuzzy Rules, Proceedings of the 2009 International Symposium on Web Information Systems and Applications (WISA'09), Nanchang, P. R. China, pp. 64-67.

Appendix 1. Conceptual diagram of Osogbo, Nigeria District 11KVA.

19

Application of soft computing techniques for multi source deregulated power system

S. Baghya Shree[1] and N. Kamaraj[2]

[1]Department of Electrical and Electronics Engineering, Anna University, Dindigul Campus, India.
[2]Department of Electrical and Electronics Engineering Thiagarajar College of Engineering, Madurai, India.

In this paper, an interconnected power system is proposed for Automatic Generation Control (AGC) in restructured power environment. The customized AGC scheme is projected in deregulated environment for multi-source combination of hydro, reheat thermal and gas generating units in entire area. Proportional integral derivative controller is offered for AGC scheme and the gains are optimised through soft computing techniques such as Hybrid Chaotic Particle Swarm Optimization (HCPSO) algorithm, Real Coded Genetic Algorithm (RCGA) and also with Artificial Neural Network (ANN). The PSO chosen here carves out the AGC problem through the addition of adaptive inertia weight factor and adaptive constriction factors. The intense trend in deregulated system leads to the aggressiveness in frequency and tie line power deviations. It is observed that the chaos mapping of PSO enhance the rate of convergence using logistics map sequence. The proposed algorithms are tested on three area power system for different electricity contracted scenarios under various operating conditions with Generation Rate Constraint (GRC). Analysis reveals that proposed HCPSO improves significantly the dynamical performances of system such as settling time and overshoot. The comparative results show the robust performance of HCPSO against parametric uncertainties for a wide range of load demands and disturbances.

Key words: Automatic generation control (AGC), hybrid chaotic particle swarm optimisation (HCPSO), proportional integral derivative (PID), restructured power system.

INTRODUCTION

In restructured situation, Automatic generation control (AGC) is one of the essential subsidiary services to be maintained for diminishing frequency deviations (Abraham et al., 2011; Tan, 2011; Shayeghi, 2008). The requirement for improving the efficiency of power production and delivery with intense participation of independent power producers stimulates restructuring of the power sector. The demand being fluctuating and increasing one, it is necessary to maintain the same constraint with the combination of various sources of generation and hence an attempt on research is made on the three area power system with various combinations of hydro, thermal and gas generation. Many researchers have been made their contribution in analyzing the restructured system (Ibrabeem and Kothari, 2005; Bevrani et al., 2005; Shayeghi and Shayanfar, 2005;

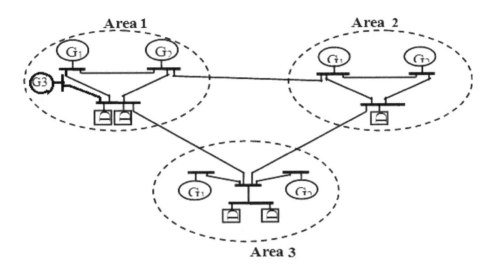

Figure 1. Three area restructured power system.

Menniti et al., 2004; Bevrani et al., 2004). Various control strategies have been opted for the better performance of the open market system (Demiroren and Zeynelgil, 2007; Shayeghi et al., 2006). The restructured three area power system is shown in Figure 1. Now-a-days the electric power industry has been transformed from Vertically Integrated Utilities (VIU) providing power at regulated rates to an industry that will incorporate competitive companies selling unbundled power at lower rates (Shayeghi et al., 2009). In the new power system structure, Load Frequency Control (LFC) acquires a fundamental role to enable power exchanges and to provide better conditions for electricity trading (Sedghisigarchi et al., 2002; Bevrani, 2002; Donde et al., 2001). Since to maintain the area control error to be zero so as to assure the generation and demand to be same, LFC are required for the power system (Christie and Bose, 1996; Lim et al., 1996). To keep the dynamic response of the power system to be stable, a controller like HCPSO (Cheshta and Verma, 2011) is required so as to perform the LFC of system shown in Figure 1. Under open market system (deregulation) the power system structure changed in such a way that would allow the evolving of more specialized industries for Generation (GENCOs), Transmission (TRANSCOs) and Distribution (DISCOs) (Tan, 2010). The concept of Independent System Operator (ISO) is an unbiased coordinator who has to balance the consumer and power generators reliably and economically (Bhatt et al., 2010; Rakhshani and Sadeh, 2010; Tan, 2009).

The AGC task is done through the error signal produced during generation and net interchange between the areas, that error is known as Area Control Error (ACE) (Liu et al., 2003).

$$ACE = \sum_j (\Delta P_{tie,i,j} + b_i \Delta f_i) \tag{1}$$

Where b_i be the frequency bias coefficient of the ith area, Δf be the frequency error of the ith area, $\Delta P_{tie,i,j}$ be the tie line power flow error between ith area and jth area.

The DISCO Participation Matrix (DPM) is proposed here to carry out the electricity contracts, the conventional control uses the integral of ACE as the control signal (Abraham et al., 2011; Tan, 2010, 2011; Shayeghi, 2008) and it has been found that the ACE which is used as a control signal results in reduction in frequency and tie line power error to zero in steady state (Tan, 2011). From the literature it is pointed out that very few of them concentrates on AGC problem in restructured environment. Since Proportional Integral Derivative (PID) holds the better results and hence, RCGA and HCPSO (Shayeghi et al., 2006), Artificial Neural Network (ANN) algorithm are introduced to independently determine optimal gain parameters of three area multi source AGC problem. In all PSO algorithms, inertial, cognitive and communal behaviour governs the movement of a particle. In HCPSO, an extra feature is introduced to ensure that the particle would have a predefined probability to maintain the diversity of the particles. The HCPSO algorithm converges to the best optimization results consistently and moderately rapid for all the test cases. The proposed work compares the performances for scenarios with ANN algorithm and RCGA-PID, while comparing the algorithms, the optimizing performance of HCPSO algorithm has been established to be the best for all the test cases with the controllers.

SYSTEM ANALYZED

The three area multi source generating system is considered here, in which each area has different combinations of GENCOs and DISCOs. Area 1 comprises of two DISCOs and three GENCOs with thermal reheat turbine, mechanical hydraulic turbine and gas turbine, Area 2 includes one DISCO and two GENCOs with hydro and thermal turbines and Area 3 consists of two GENCOs with thermal and Gas turbines combination with two DISCOs as shown in Figure 3. In this restructured environment, any GENCO in one area may supply DISCOs in the same area as well as DISCOs in other areas. In other words, for restructured system having several GENCOs and DISCOs, any DISCO may contract with any GENCO in another control area independently. This is termed as bilateral transaction.

The transactions have to be carried out through an Independent System Operator (ISO). The main purpose of ISO is to control many ancillary services, one of which is AGC. In open access scenario, any DISCO has the freedom to purchase MW power at competitive price from different GENCOs, which may or may not have contract with the same area as the DISCO (Shayeghi et al., 2009). The contracts of GENCOs and DISCOs described by 'DISCO participation matrix' (DPM). In DPM, the number of rows is equal to the number of GENCOs and the number of columns is equal to the number of DISCOs in the system. Any entry of this matrix is a fraction of total load power contracted by a DISCO towards a GENCO. The sum of total entries in a column corresponds to one DISCO be equal to one. The DPM for the nth area power system is as follows:

$$DPM = \begin{bmatrix} cpf_{11} & cpf_{12} \cdots & cpf_{1n} \\ cpf_{21} & cpf_{22} \cdots & cpf_{2n} \\ \vdots & \vdots & \vdots \\ cpf_{n1} & cpf_{n2} \cdots & cpf_{nn} \end{bmatrix} \quad (2)$$

$$\sum_{j=1}^{n} cpf_{ij} = 1$$

$$AGPM = \begin{bmatrix} AGPM_{11} & .. & AGPM_{1N} \\ : & : & : \\ AGPM_{N1} & .. & AGPM_{NN} \end{bmatrix} \quad (3)$$

Where, $AGPM_{ij} = \begin{bmatrix} gpf_{(si+1)(zj+1)} & .. & gpf_{(si+1)(zj+mj)} \\ : & : & : \\ gpf_{(si+ni)(zj+1)} & .. & gpf_{(si+ni)(zj+mj)} \end{bmatrix}$

For i,j=1,2,....N, and $s_i = \sum_{k=1}^{i-1} n_i;$ $z_j = \sum_{k=1}^{j-1} m_j$;$s_1 = z_1 = 0$

In the above, ni and mj are the number of GENCOs and DISCOs in area i and gpf$_{ij}$ refer to 'generation participation factor' and shows the participation factor GENCOi in total load following the requirement of DISCOj based on the possible contract. The Equation (3) shows the Augmented Generation Participation Matrix (AGPM), which depicts the effective participation of DISCO with various GENCOs in all the areas with Generation Rate Constraint (GRC).

The sum of all entries in each column of AGPM is unity. To demonstrate the effectiveness of the modeling strategy and proposed control design, a three control area power system is considered as a test system with GRC. As there are many GENCOs in each area, the ACE signal has to be distributed among them due to their ACE participation factor in the AGC task. The scheduled contracted power exchange is given by (Shayeghi et al., 2009):

$\Delta P_{tieij}^{scheduled}$ = (Demand of DISCOs in area j from GENCOs in area i) - (Demand of DISCOs in area i from GENCOs in area j)

$$d_i = \Delta P_{loc,i} + \Delta P_{di} \quad (4)$$

Where, $\Delta P_{loc,i} = \sum_{j=1}^{mi} \Delta P_{Lj-i}$, $\Delta P_{d,i} = \sum_{j=1}^{mj} \Delta P_{ULj-i}$,

$$\eta_i = \sum_{\substack{j=1 \\ j \neq i}}^{N} T_{ij} \Delta f_j, \quad (5)$$

$$\xi_i = \Delta P_{tie,ik,sch} \sum_{\substack{k=1 \\ k \neq i}}^{mj} \Delta P_{tie,ik,sch}, \quad (6)$$

$$\Delta P_{tie,ik,sch} = \sum_{j=1}^{ni} \sum_{t=1}^{mk} apf_{(si+j)(zk+t)} \Delta R_{Lt-k} - \sum_{t=1}^{nk} \sum_{j=1}^{mi} apf_{(sk+t)(zi+j)} \Delta P_{Lj-l} \quad (7)$$

$$\Delta P_{tie,i,error} = \Delta P_{tie,i-actual} - \xi_i \quad (8)$$

$$\rho_i = [\rho_{1i} \cdots \rho_{ki} \cdots \rho_{nii}]^T \quad (9)$$

$$\rho_{ki} = \sum_{j=1}^{N} \left[\sum_{t=1}^{mj} gpf_{(si+k)(zj+t)} \Delta R_{Lt-j} \right]^T ; \Delta P_{m,k-i} = P_{ki} + apf_{ki} \sum_{j=1}^{mj} \Delta P_{ULj-i} \quad (10)$$

Where k=1,2.....n$_i$

In a power system having steam plants, power generation can change only at a specified maximum rate. The structure for ith area in the presence of GRC is shown in Figure 2. A typical value of the GRC for thermal unit is 3%/min, that is, GRC for the thermal system be $\Delta PGt(t) \leq 0.0005 p.u.MW / s$ .Two limiters, bounded by±0.0005 are employed within the AGC of the thermal and gas system to prevent the excessive control action. Likewise, for hydro plant GRC of 270%/min. for raising generation and 360%/min. for lowering generation has been deemed.

HCPSO-PID controller strategy

The Proportional-Integral-Derivative (PID) controller is intended for this multi area multi source generation system. Since this controller provides zero steady state deviation with good dynamic response of frequency and tie-line power in a multi area power system. The control vector is given by:

$$U_i = -[K_{pi} + ACE_i + K_{Ii} \int ACE_i \, dt + K_{di} \frac{dACE_i}{dt}] \quad (11)$$

Where K$_{pi}$, K$_{di}$, K$_{Ii}$ are the proportional, derivative and integral gains of PID controller.

In PID controller, the tie line power deviation and frequency deviation are weighted together as a linear combination to a single variable called ACE, which is given as control signal to governor set point in each area. Here, ITAE is used as a performance criterion. To achieve a preeminent performance and to improve the dynamics of LFC in a deregulated power system, Hybrid Chaotic Particle Swarm Optimization Algorithm is used to optimize the gains of PID controller. The evaluation of proposed controller has been made by simulating the same structure using RCGA optimization (Demiroren and Zeynelgil, 2007) and ANN has been trained through Back Propagation Algorithm (Demiroren, 2001) for ACE and Differentiation of ACE.

Hybrid chaotic particle swarm optimisation

In conventional approach, it involves more number of iterations to

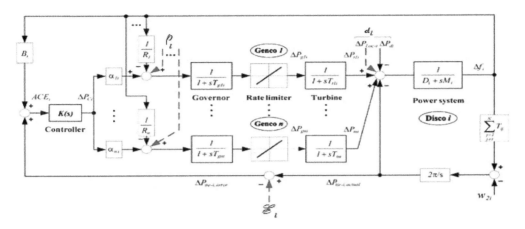

Figure 2. Control structure with GRC for ith area.

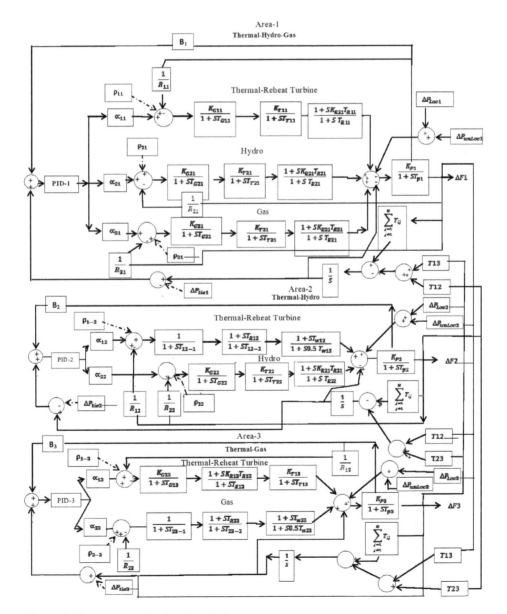

Figure 3. Three area restructured control area.

Table 1. Fitness value (ITAE) comparison.

Scenario	Fitness function		
	HCPSO-PID	RCGA-PID	ANN
1	4.5236	4.5099	4.8932
2	8.3976	9.0656	9.8035
3	8.111	9.4837	10.1235

optimize the objective function and hence it is a time consumable one (Cheshta and Verma, 2011; Shayeghi and Shayanfar, 2006; Barjeev and Srivastava, 2003; Rerkpreedapong and Feliache, 2002). To conquer this intricacy, Hybrid Chaotic Particle Swarm Optimization is proposed to optimise the gains of PID Controller. In general PSO depends on its parameter and after certain iterations, the parameter sets are approximately identical (Cheshta and Verma, 2011). To enhance the performance of particle swarm optimization algorithm the application of adaptive inertia weight factor and adaptive constriction factors is proposed. The extreme trend in deregulated power system leads to the aggressiveness in frequency and tie line power deviations. It is observed that the chaos mapping upgrade the rate of convergence using logistics map sequence and Chaotic based optimisation offers diversity in population. A chaotic sequence for inertia weight and constriction factor for optimization is as follows:

Adaptive inertia weight factor (AIWF)

The rate of inertia weight is set for the entire particles be similar for all iteration (Cheshta et al., 2011). Therefore difference among particles is omitted. This adaptive method declares that the better particle should have a tendency to utilize its neighbour particles. This strategy provides the huge selection pressure. The AIWF is obtained as (Cheshta et al., 2011):

$$w_i^k = w_{min} + f_{pbest}^k \mid f_i^k \cdot f_{pbest}^k \mid / f_i^k \mid f_i^k \cdot f_{gbest}^k \mid \qquad (12)$$

Where w_i^k be inertia weight of ith population at k^{th} iteration, w_{min} be minimum inertia weight, f_{pbest}^k be fitness function of pbest solution at k^{th} iteration, f_i^k be fitness function of ith population at k^{th} iteration and f_{gbest}^k be fitness function of gbest solution at k^{th} iteration.

Adaptive constriction factors

Constriction factor are extremely depend on fitness function of current iteration (that is) pbest and gbest solution and c1 and c2 controls the utmost step size. This factor can be determined as:

$$c1_i^k = \sqrt{f_i^k / f_{pbest}^k} \qquad (13)$$

$$c2_i^k = \sqrt{f_i^k / f_{gbest}^k} \qquad (14)$$

The velocity up gradation of particle modified as:

$$v_i^{k+1} = w_i^k v_i^k + c1_i^k z1_i^k \left(pbest_i^k - x_i^k\right) + c2_i^k z2_i^k \left(gbest_i^k - x_i^k\right) \qquad (15)$$

Where, v_i^k be the velocity of the ith population at k^{th} iteration, z_i^k be Chaotic sequence based on logistic map for i^{th} population at k^{th} iteration, x_i^k be position of particle of ith at k^{th} iteration.

The position of each particle is updated using the velocity vector that is:

$$x_i^{k+1} = x_i^k + v_i^{k+1} \qquad (16)$$

Fitness-objective function

The focal intention of this effort is to reduce the frequency deviation and tie line power flow deviations and these parameters are weighted together as ACE. The fitness function is taken along with an optional penalty factor to take care of transient responses; the fitness function is given by:

$$\text{ITAE} = \int_0^{tsim} t \mid e(t) \mid dt \qquad (17)$$

Where $e(t)$ be error considered.

The fitness function to be minimized is given by:

$$j = \int_0^{tsim} \left(\beta_1 \mid \Delta f_1 \mid + \beta_2 \mid \Delta f_2 \mid + \mid \Delta p_{tie12}^{error} \mid\right) dt + FD \qquad (18)$$

Where, $FD = \alpha_1 OS + \alpha_2 ST$; Where Overshoot (OS) and settling time (ST) for 2% band of frequency deviation in all three areas are considered for evaluation of the Frequency Discrimination (FD), by adjusting the values of α_1 and α_2 the frequency discrimination can be obtained. The fitness value for all the three scenarios are listed Table 1.

Pseudo code

Step 1: Choose the population size and number of iteration.
Step 2: Generate randomly 'n' particles for gains and frequency biases with uniform probability over the optimized parameter search space [x_{min}, x_{max}], similarly generate initial velocities of all particles, v^i which is given by: $v^i = 0.4 \, rand(v_{max} - v_{min})$
Step 3: Run AGC model and calculate the fitness function for each particle (Equation18) at k^{th} iteration.
Step 4: Calculate gbest value and pbest value.
Step 5: Calculate fitness function at gbest and pbest solution.
Step 6: Calculate AIWF (Equation 12), constriction factor (Equations 13-14) and z1, z2 (Equation 10).
Step 7: Update velocity of each particle (Equation 15).
Step 8: Based on updated velocities, each particle changes its position according to Equation (16).
  If particle infringes the position limit in any dimension, set its position at the proper limit.
Step 9: If the last change of the best solution is greater than a pre

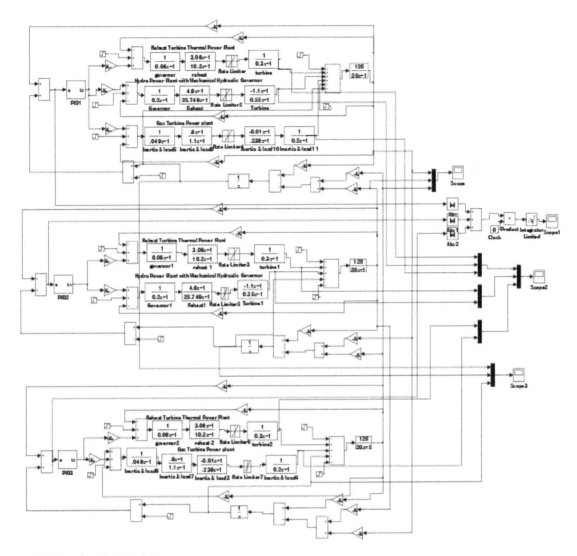

Figure 4. Simulink model.

specified number or the number of iteration reaches the maximum iteration, stop the process, otherwise go to Step 3.

RESULTS AND DISCUSSION

The three area control structure with GRC considering multi source generation has been simulated for restructured structure as shown in Figure 4. To demonstrate the robustness of proposed control strategy against parametric suspicions and contract variations, simulations are carried out for three scenarios of possible contracts under various operating conditions and large load demands. The plant parameters for three area deregulated power system is presented in Table 2. Performance of the proposed controller is compared with RCGA-PID (Demiroren and Zeynelgil, 2007) and ANN (Demiroren, 2001) controller. The parameters of the controllers are given in appendix (Table 3).

Scenario1 poolco based transactions

In this scenario, GENCOs participate only in the load following control of their areas. It is assumed that a large step load 0.1 pu is demanded by each DISCOs in areas 1, 2 and 3 with GRC. The poolco based contracts between DISCOs and available GENCOs is simulated based on the following AGPM. The variations in tie line power flows and frequency is shown in Figures 5 and 6 and the values are depicted in Tables 4 and 5.

Scenario 2 combination of poolco and bilateral based transactions

In this case, DISCOs have the freedom to contract with any of the GENCOs within or with other areas. All the GENCOS are participating in the AGC task as per the following AGPM. The discrepancies based on this

Table 2. Power system plant and control parameters.

Area 1			Area 2		Area 3	
Thermal-Hydro-GAs			Hydro-Thermal		Thermal-Hydro	
GENCO-1	GENCO-2	GENCO-3	GENCO-1	GENCO-2	GENCO-1	GENCO-2
Thermal	Hydro	Gas	Thermal	Hydro	Thermal	Gas
Tg=0.06s	Tg=0.2s	Tg=0.049s	T1=0.06s	Tg=0.2s	Tg=0.06s	T1=0.049s
Tt=0.3s	Tt=0.55s	Tt=0.2s	T3=10.2s	Tt=28.149s	Tt=10.2s	T3=1.1s
R=0.3333Hz/p.u.MW	Kr =0.3113	Kr =0.5	T2=0.3s	R=.29633Hz/p.u.MW	Kr =0.33	T2=0.2s
Tr=10.2s	Tr=10.6 s	Tr=1.1s	Tw =1s	Kg=1	Tr=10s	Tw =1.5s
	R=0.32Hz/p.u.MW	R=.33Hz/p.u.MW	R=0.32Hz/p.u.MW	Kt=1	R=0.2899Hz/p.u.MW	R=0.3077Hz/p.u.MW
Kg=1	Kg=1	Kg=1	Kg=1		Kg=1	Kg=1
Kt=1	Kt=1	Kt=1	Kt=1		Kt=1	Kt=1
Kp=20 Hz/ p.u. MW Tp=120s B=0.532p.u. MW/Hz Prated=2000 MW (Nominal Load) P°= 1000 MW f=60Hz			Kp=20 Hz/ p.u. MW Tp=120s B=0.495p.u. MW/Hz Prated=2000 MW (NominalLoad) Po= 1000 MW f=60Hz		Kp=20 Hz/ p.u. MW Tp=120s B=0.542 p.u.MW/Hz Prated=2000 MW (Nominal Load) Po= 1000 MW f=60Hz	
T12=T13=T23= 0.543 p.u/Hz						

Table 3. Controller parameter.

Parameter	RCGA	HCPSO	ANN
Number of population	20	20	Number of hidden layers 10
Number of Generation	200	200	1000
	Probability crossover -0.8	W_{max}-0.6	Sampling interval-0.05s
	Mutation function taken as Gaussian	W_{min}0.1	Number of delayed inputs-2
	Fitness scaling function is Rank	$C_1=C_2=1.5$	Number of delayed output-1

transaction are shown in Figures 7 and 8 prevailing to frequency and tie line power deviations.

Scenario 3 contract violation

In this scenario, the DISCOs may violate the contracts by demanding more power than that specified in the contract. This excessive power is reflected as a located load of that area (un contracted demand).The AGPM of this case follows the scenario 2 and the un contracted loads for DISCO 1 in area1 is 0.018 p.u, DISCO 2 in area1 is 0.0230 p.u, DISCO1 in area is 0.3800 p.u, DISCO 1 in area 3 is 0.0125 p.u, DISCO 2 in area3 0.0125 p.u. The purpose of this scenario is to test the effectiveness of the proposed controller against the uncertainties and sudden large load disturbances in the presence of GRC (Figures 9 and 10).

The Table 6 demonstrates the comparison of GENCO power deviation for the three scenarios with theoretical and the simulated values by Equation (10). The deviation in tie line power flows for these possible contracts are presented in appendix. The results thus obtained

through simulation depicts that the proposed HCPSO-PID controller holds good performance as compared to RCGA-PID and ANN controller for all possible contracts and for wide range of load disturbances.

Conclusions

Multi source generation is universal for any real time grid in function. It is incredibly hard to synchronize the various areas in a deregulated environment by means of frequency and tie line power flows. However, the conventional PID controller can be able to coordinate but with large overshoots and settling time. Hence soft computing techniques proposed for this AGC problem. The HCPSO-PID controller is proposed here for multi source generation system for a deregulated environment. This controller accomplishes consistency over tracking frequency and tie line power deviations for a wide range of load disturbances and system uncertainties. To prove its robustness the performance has been compared with RCGA-PID and ANN controller. The simulated result shows that the proposed controller is

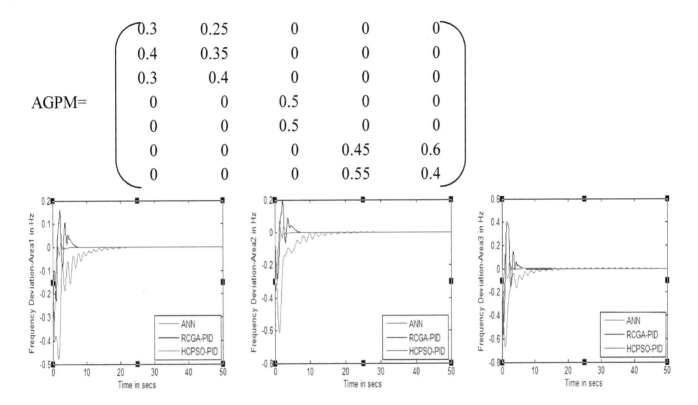

Figure 5. Frequency deviation for scenario 1.

$$
AGPM=
\begin{pmatrix}
0.2 & 0.15 & 0.1 & 0 & 0.2 \\
0.25 & 0.2 & 0 & 0.1 & 0.15 \\
0.1 & 0 & 0.3 & 0.25 & 0.15 \\
0.3 & 0.15 & 0.3 & 0.25 & 0.2 \\
0 & 0.2 & 0 & 0.15 & 0.2 \\
0.15 & 0.2 & 0.15 & 0.15 & 0 \\
0 & 0.1 & 0.15 & 0.1 & 0.1
\end{pmatrix}
$$

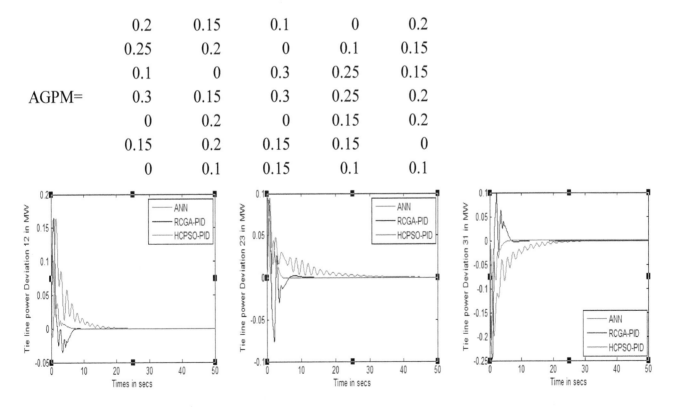

Figure 6. Tie line power deviation for scenario 1.

Table 4. Tie line power deviations.

Controller	Area	Peak overshoots (MW)			Peak Undershoot(MW)			Settling time(secs)			Computational time (secs)
		Scenario 1	Scenario 2	Scenario 3	Scenario 1	Scenario 2	Scenario 3	Scenario 1	Scenario 2	Scenario 3	
HCPSO-PID	1	0.120428	0.118588	0.141012	-0.00813	-0.05842	-0.10009	7	6	4	
	2	0.094645	0.139323	0.19326	-0.00436	-0.00656	-0.02693	8	6	5	0.45
	2	0.000912	0.03702	0.052313	-0.21249	-0.25369	-0.30557	4	8	6	
RCGA-PID	1	0.165357	0.126169	0.160866	-0.03485	-0.00822	-0.00821	14	20	18	
	2	0.093712	0.111066	0.11627	-0.07594	0	0	15	21	18	0.85
	3	0.098728	0	0	-0.24801	-0.23711	-0.27666	11	19	19	
ANN	1	0.164209	0.172452	0.208209	-0.01273	-0.01034	-0.01637	34	38	19	
	2	0.093889	0.093077	0.090079	-0.0001	0	0	36	41	20	0.23
	3	0.000762	0	0	-0.19951	-0.22226	-0.24809	36	28	25	

Table 5. Frequency deviations.

Controller	Area	Peak overshoots (Hz)			Peak Undershoot (Hz)			Settling time (secs)			Computational time (secs)
		Scenario 1	Scenario 2	Scenario 3	Scenario 1	Scenario 2	Scenario 3	Scenario 1	Scenario 2	Scenario 3	
HCPSO-PID	1	0.03352	0.083241	0.128561	-0.31716	-0.286	-0.34254	7	6	4	
	2	0.06948	0.148039	0.221594	-0.35658	-0.28115	-0.37978	8	6	5	0.45
	2	0.12463	0.168112	0.228224	-0.57114	-0.56928	-0.70162	4	8	6	
RCGA-PID	1	0.16183	0.193253	0.365623	-0.28816	-0.30916	-0.39173	14	20	18	
	2	0.19515	0.296932	0.480645	-0.30682	-0.23067	-0.36772	15	21	18	0.85
	3	0.40514	0.341415	0.572651	-0.56879	-0.56651	-0.71862	11	19	19	
ANN	1	0.16420	0.000799	0.017762	-0.01273	-0.47493	-0.63228	34	38	19	
	2	0.09388	0.00333	0.018313	-0.00023	-0.58227	-0.75234	36	41	20	0.23
	3	0.00091	0.002363	0.028305	-0.19951	-0.67788	-0.85948	36	28	25	

most excellent for real time application. In future, all techniques like ANFIS can be incorporated to get online coordination for the deregulated environment.

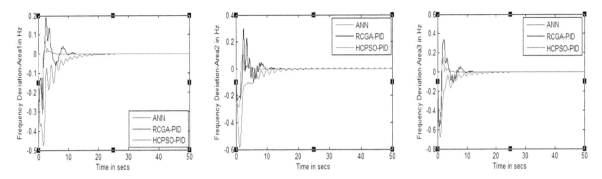

Figure 7. Frequency deviation for scenario 2.

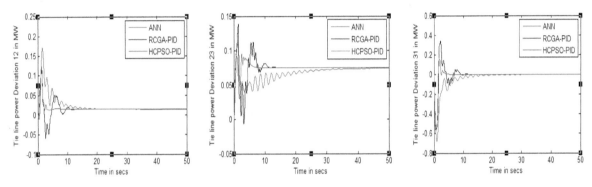

Figure 8. Tie line power deviation for scenario 2.

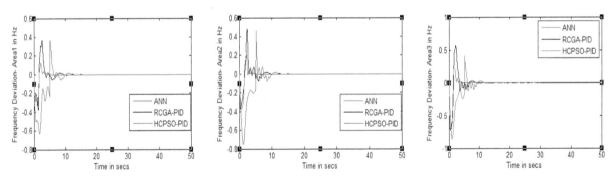

Figure 9. Frequency deviation for scenario 3.

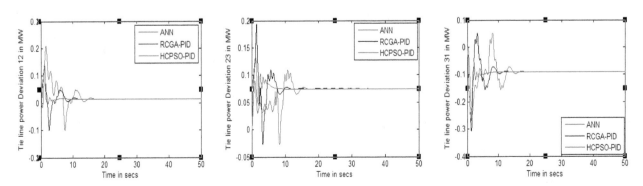

Figure 10. Tie line power deviation for scenario 3.

Table 6. Genco power deviations for 0.1 p.u. load disturbance.

Genco power deviation	Scenario	Theoretical value	Value obtained through Simulation			Error Value		
			RCGA	HCPSO	ANN	RCGA	HCPSO	ANN
Area 1								
GENCO 1 – Thermal	1	0.055	0.055006	0.055005	0.055006	-6×10^{-6}	-5×10^{-6}	-6×10^{-6}
	2	0.065	0.065005	0.065005	0.065005	-4.9×10^{-6}	-4.6×10^{-6}	-4.9×10^{-6}
	3	0.085	0.085025	0.085008	0.085025	-2.5×10^{-5}	-8×10^{-5}	-2.5×10^{-5}
GENCO 2 Hydro	1	0.075	0.074982	0.074983	0.074982	0.18×10^{-6}	0.17×10^{-6}	0.18×10^{-6}
	2	0.07	0.079996	0.079999	0.079996	-4.3×10^{-6}	-1×10^{-6}	-4.3×10^{-6}
	3	0.085	0.084994	0.084992	0.084994	6.1×10^{-6}	7.8×10^{-6}	6.1×10^{-6}
GENCO 3 Gas	1	0.07	0.070013	0.070014	0.070013	-1.3×10^{-5}	-1.4×10^{-5}	-1.3×10^{-5}
	2	0.08	0.079996	0.079999	0.079996	-4.3×10^{-6}	-1×10^{-6}	-4.3×10^{-6}
	3	0.095	0.095008	0.095001	0.095008	0.49×10^{-4}	-1.3×10^{-6}	0.49×10^{-4}
Area 2								
GENCO 1 Thermal	1	0.055	0.049999	0.049999	0.049999	0.1×10^{-6}	0.1×10^{-6}	0.1×10^{-6}
	2	0.12	0.119999	0.119998	0.119999	1.1×10^{-6}	2.3×10^{-6}	1.1×10^{-6}
	3	0.144	0.143862	0.143998	0.143862	0.138×10^{-6}	2.3×10^{-6}	0.13×10^{-6}
GENCO 2 Hydro	1	0.05	0.050001	0.049994	0.050001	-1×10^{-6}	0.6×10^{-6}	-1×10^{-6}
	2	0.055	0.054998	0.055	0.054998	1.7×10^{-6}	2.5×10^{-6}	1.7×10^{-6}
	3	0.071	0.071028	0.071006	0.071028	-2.8×10^{-5}	-6.2×10^{-6}	-2.8×10^{-5}
Area 3								
GENCO 1 Thermal	1	0.105	0.104981	0.105	0.104981	0.19×10^{-6}	-1×10^{-7}	0.19×10^{-6}
	2	0.065	0.064978	0.06497	0.064978	2.19×10^{-5}	0.3×10^{-5}	2.19×10^{-5}
	3	0.144	0.079403	0.079976	0.079403	0.597×10^{-6}	2.42×10^{-5}	0.59×10^{-6}
GENCO 2 Gas	1	0.095	0.095012	0.095002	0.095012	0.12×10^{-6}	0.2×10^{-6}	0.12×10^{-6}
	2	0.045	0.045028	0.045039	0.045028	-2.8×10^{-5}	-3.8×10^{-5}	-2.8×10^{-5}
	3	0.06	0.061845	0.06002	0.061845	-0.184×10^{-5}	-2×10^{-5}	-0.18×10^{-5}

Conflict of Interest

The authors have not declared any conflict of interest.

ACKNOWLEDGEMENT

The authors acknowledges the Regional Director, Dean, Head of the Department, Faculty Members of University College of Engineering Dindigul and Management, Principal and Faculty Members of Thiagarajar college of Engineering, Madurai who cooperated to work on this article.

REFERENCES

Abraham RJ, Das D, Patra A (2011). Load following in a bilateral market with local controllers. Int. J. Electr. Power Energy Syst. 33(10):1648–1657. http://dx.doi.org/10.1016/j.ijepes.2011.06.033

Barjeev T, Srivastava SC (2003). A fuzzy logic based load frequency controller in a competitive electricity environment. IEEE Power Engineering Society General Meeting. 2003.

Bevrani H (2002). A novel approach for power system load frequency controller design. IEEE/PES Transmission and Distribution Conference Exhibition. pp. 184–189. http://dx.doi.org/10.1109/TDC.2002.1178281

Bevrani H, Mitani Y, Tsuji K (2004). Robust decentralized AGC in a restructured power system. Energy Conver. Manage. 45:2297–2312. http://dx.doi.org/10.1016/j.enconman.2003.11.018

Bevrani H, Mitani Y, Tsuji K, Bevrani H (2005). Bilateral based robust load frequency control. Energy Conver. Manage. 46(7–8):1129–1146. http://dx.doi.org/10.1016/j.enconman.2004.06.024

Bhatt P, Roy R, Ghoshal S (2010). Optimized multi area AGC simulation in restructured power systems. Int. J. Electr. Power Energy Syst. 32(4):311–322. http://dx.doi.org/10.1016/j.ijepes.2009.09.002

Cheshta J, Verma HK (2011). Hybrid Choatic Particle Swarm Optimisation based gains for deregulated automatic generation control. Int. J. Electronics Commun. Comput. Eng. 2(2):1-9

Christie RD, Bose A (1996). Load frequency control issues in power system operations after deregulation. IEEE Trans. Power Syst. 11(3):1191–1200. http://dx.doi.org/10.1109/59.535590

Demiroren A (2001). Automatic generation control by using ANN technique. Electrical Power Components and systems (Electric Machines and Power systems). 29(10):883-896. http://dx.doi.org/10.1080/15325000152646505

Demiroren A, Zeynelgil HL (2007). GA application to optimization of AGC in three area power system after deregulation. Int. J. Electr. Power Energy Syst. 29:230–240. http://dx.doi.org/10.1016/j.ijepes.2006.07.005

Donde V, Pai A, Hiskens IA (2001). Simulation and optimization in an AGC system after deregulation. IEEE Trans. Power Syst. 16(3):481–

489. http://dx.doi.org/10.1109/59.932285

Ibrabeem PK, Kothari DP (2005). Recent philosophies of automatic generation control strategies in power systems. IEEE Trans. Power Syst. 20(1):346–357. http://dx.doi.org/10.1109/TPWRS.2004.840438

Lim KY, Wang Y, Zhou R (1996). Robust decentralized load-frequency control of multi-area power systems. IEEE Proceedings Part C. 143:377–386.

Liu F, Song YH, Ma J, Mei S, Lu Q (2003). Optimal load-frequency control in restructured power systems. IEEE Proceedings on Generation Transmission Distribution. 150(1):87–95.

Menniti D, Pinnarelli A, Scordino N (2004). Using a FACTS device controlled by a decentralized control law to damp the transient frequency deviation in a deregulated electric power system. Electr. Power Syst. Res. 72(3):289–298. http://dx.doi.org/10.1016/j.epsr.2004.04.013

Rakhshani E, Sadeh J (2010). Practical viewpoints on load frequency control problem in a deregulated power system. Energy Conver. Manage. 51(6):1148–1156. http://dx.doi.org/10.1016/j.enconman.2009.12.024

Rerkpreedapong D, Feliache A (2002). Decentralized load frequency control for load following services. IEEE Proceeedings on Power Engineering Society Winter Meeting. pp. 1252–1257.

Sedghisigarchi K, Feliache A, Davari A (2002). Decentralized load frequency control in a deregulated environment using disturbance accommodation control theory. Proceedings on 34th South eastern Symposium on System Theory. pp. 302–306.

Shayeghi H (2008). A robust decentralized power system load frequency control. J. Electr. Eng. 59(6):281–293.

Shayeghi H, Shayanfar HA (2005). Design of decentralized robust LFC in a competitive electricity environment. J. Electr. Eng. 56(9–10):225–236.

Shayeghi H, Shayanfar HA (2006). Decentralized robust AGC based on structured singular values. J. Electr. Eng. 57:305–317.

Shayeghi H, Shayanfar HA, Jalili A (2006). Multi-stage fuzzy PID power system automatic generation controller in deregulated environments. Energy Conver. Manage. 47:2829–2845. http://dx.doi.org/10.1016/j.enconman.2006.03.031

Shayeghi H, Shayanfar HA, Jalili A (2009). Load frequency control strategies: a state of-the-art survey for the researcher. Energy Conver. Manage. 50(2):344–353. http://dx.doi.org/10.1016/j.enconman.2008.09.014

Tan W (2009). Tuning of PID load frequency controller for power systems. Energy Conver. Manage. 50(6):1465–1472. http://dx.doi.org/10.1016/j.enconman.2009.02.024

Tan W (2010). Unified tuning of PID load frequency controller for power systems via IMC. IEEE Trans. Power Syst. 25(1):341–350. http://dx.doi.org/10.1109/TPWRS.2009.2036463

Tan W (2011). Decentralized load frequency controller analysis and tuning for multi-area power systems. Energy Conver. Manage. 52(5):2015–2023. http://dx.doi.org/10.1016/j.enconman.2010.12.011

Appendix

Nomenclature

i: Subscript referred to area,
F: Area frequency,
P$_{tie}$: Tie line power flow,
P$_T$: Turbine power,
P$_V$: Governor valve position,
P$_C$: Governor set point,
ACE: Area control error,
AGC: Automatic generation control,
GRC: Generator rate constraint,
DPM: DISCO participation matrix,
AGPM: Augmented generation participation matrix,
cpf: Contract participation factor,
gpf: Generation participation factor,
K$_P$: Subsystem equivalent gain constant,
T$_P$: Subsystem equivalent time constant,
T$_T$: Turbine time constant,
T$_G$: Governor time constant,
R: Droop characteristic,

B: Frequency bias,
FD: Frequency Deviation,
ITAE: Integral time multiplied absolute error,
Tij: Tie line synchronizing coefficient between areas i and j,
Pd: Area load disturbance,
P$_{Lji}$: Contracted demand of DISCO j in area I,
P$_{ULji}$: Un-contracted demand of DISCO j in area I,
P$_{M,ji}$: Power generation of GENCO j in area I,
P$_{Loc}$: Total local demand,
η: Area interface,
ξ: Scheduled power tie line power flow deviation.

20

An efficient technique for morphing zero-genus 3D objects

A. Elef, M. H. Mousa and H. Nassar

Department of Computer Science, Faculty of Computers and Informatics, Suez Canal University, Egypt.

In this paper, we present an algorithm to morph a zero-genus mesh model to a topologically equivalent one based on spherical parameterization, as it is the natural parameterization method for this kind of objects. Our algorithm starts by normalizing the two objects to the cube of unity, as a preprocessing step. Then, the two normalized models are parameterized onto a common spherical domain. We reposition the points of the objects on the sphere in accordance to the relative areas of their triangles. Repositioning on the sphere prevents point clustering and overlapping during the matching process. Experimental results are presented to demonstrate the efficiency of the algorithm.

Key words: 3D morphing, zero-genus mesh, spherical parameterization, nearest neighbor matching.

INTRODUCTION

Shape changing has gained attention due to the attraction of scenes people see on the screen. Indeed, morphing is derived from the biological term "metamorphosis", meaning the change in form and often habits of the individual during normal development after the embryonic stage. Therefore, it suits very well modeling computer animation techniques dealing with the design of algorithms changing one object into another over time (Sompagdee, 2009). In other terms, morphing is an interpolation technique used to create from two objects a series of intermediate objects that change continuously to make a smooth transition from the source object to the target object. Morphing has been done in two dimensions by varying the values of the pixels of one image to make a different image, or in three dimensions by doing the same. We are presenting here a new type of morphing, which is applied to the geometry of three dimensional models, creating intermediate 3D objects which can be translated, rotated, scaled, and zoomed into.

The history of morphing can be categorized into two categories: 2D and 3D morphing. 2D morphing seems to have reached its goals in finding the solutions for the transformations as well as feature handling, while 3D morphing is still far behind 2D success (Sompagdee, 2009).

Two-dimensional morphing

In general, 2D morphing techniques require a lot of manual processes. They can be classified into two categories: image-based and geometric-based.

Image-based morphing

Image-based approaches are used enormously in the entertainment industry. Algorithms here are generally composed of three major steps: control, warping and cross dissolving. For controlling the morphing process, these algorithms rely heavily on the experience and knowledge of animators to define correspondence points. Good results can be obtained by using images captured from similar angles and positions regarding the lack of the depth information for generating intermediate objects. Beier and Neely (1992) proposed the line segment feature based method. Where, animators have less work but the complexity of calculation is increased. Lee et al. (1995) used moving curves called snakes in order to capture features accurately and fasten the process of feature defining.

Geometric-based morphing

For geometric–based approaches, 2D polygons are given as input. Sederberg and Greenwood (1992) proposed a minimization method without user interaction. New vertices are added to the polygon that has less number of vertices. All possible paths are calculated but only the best path, the one that gives a minimum amount of work or less shrinkage, is selected. Gao and Sederberg (1998) improved the method to measure the amount of work as well as the way to find the least work path. Shapira and Rappoport (1995) embedded skeletons inside each polygon by decomposing the polygon into star-shaped pieces with a star origin inside each piece then they connected those star origins. For interpolation, skeletons are interpolated and star pieces are unfolded.

Three-dimensional morphing

Three- dimensional morphing algorithms transform a 3D model into another. The complexity of an algorithm depends on many factors, such as: the object representation, genus, and convexity. The simplest morphing can be done when the initial and final shapes are convex and similar in their geometry and topology. Usually, 3D methods have restrictions on object models and how models are represented. Concave objects are more difficult to morph than convex ones. Objects with a different genus, e.g. with holes or with a closed surface are very complicated to transform. Without user intervention, it is not possible to get the desirable results. The existing solutions are categorized by object representations as follow (Sompagdee, 2009):

(i) Polygonal-based representation: The objects are represented by their boundaries. This representation is commonly used and is easy to obtain.

(ii) Volumetric representation: The 3D models are described either by their geometric primitives or by volumes (volumetric data sets). A volumetric representation is ideal for modeling the behavior of objects with complex interior structures. In particular, this representation helps overcome the limitation on model types.

CONTRIBUTION

Our approach is focused on creating the series of intermediate objects, using spherical parameterization as a common domain of the source and target zero-genus objects. This parameterization domain is the natural domain to use, given when our object is a sphere, and as such- makes the mapping step easier.

To create this series of intermediate objects, we start by parameterizing the source and target objects on the sphere. We use progressive meshes (Hoppe, 1996; Zhou et al., 2004) in combination with a local smoothing strategy (Shen and Makedon, 2006) to find the final spherical parameterization. Then we create the point-to-point correspondence between the objects using the AABB tree search technique (CGAL, 2010). The spherical parameterization which we have used makes the mapping step easier since the objects are mapped to their natural parameterization domain.

Initial spherical parameterization

Parameterization of 3D mesh data is important in such applications as, texture mapping, remeshing and morphing. Closed manifold genus-0 meshes are topologically equivalent to a sphere; hence this is regarded as the natural parameterization domain for it. Parameterizing a triangle mesh onto a sphere means assigning a 3D position on the unit sphere to each of the mesh vertices, such that the spherical triangles induced by the mesh connectivity are not too distorted and do not overlap. Satisfying the non-overlapping requirement is the most difficult and critical component of this process. Moreover, it is usually an expensive optimization procedure for large meshes. Here, we describe the spherical parameterization algorithm we use, which is based on the algorithm proposed in (Praun and Hoppe, 2003; Zhou et al., 2004; Shen and Makedon, 2006). The later algorithm incorporates a local parameterization scheme into the progressive mesh representation (Hoppe, 1996). This reduces the complexity of global optimization for large meshes.

Given a triangle mesh M, the problem of spherical parameterization is to form a continuous invertible map ψ from the unit sphere to the mesh. That's, $\psi : S^2 \rightarrow M$. The map is specified by assigning for each mesh vertex v a parameterization $\psi^{-1}(v) \in S^2$. Therefore, each mesh

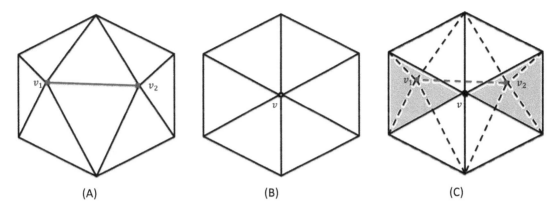

Figure 1. An edge collapse operation. (A) (Left) the edge v to be collapsed. (B) (Middle) The mesh after the edge contraction. (C) (Right) Parameterizing the deleted vertices using the created triangles.

edge is mapped to a great circle arc, and each mesh triangle is mapped to a spherical triangle bounded by these arcs. The spherical parameterization algorithm consists of two major steps:

(i) A progressive mesh representation, $\mathcal{M} = \{M^0, M^1, \cdots, M^k = M\}$, with embedded local parameterization information is generated from the original mesh M. This is performed by iterating the successive edge collapse operations until the current simplified mesh becomes a convex polyhedron M^0. The obtained polyhedron is considered as the base mesh of $\mathcal{M}$. For each edge collapse, the two decimated vertices are parameterized over the resulting simplified mesh. The local parameterization information is recorded in $\mathcal{M}$.

(ii) Suppose that the centroid of the base mesh M^0 is the center of the unit sphere. The projection of the vertices of M^0 onto the considered sphere produces an initial spherical mesh. Starting from this initial spherical mesh, the sequence of vertex split operations, the inverse of the edge collapse, in $\mathcal{M}$ is performed progressively. For each vertex split operation, the two split vertices are positioned on the unit sphere using the recorded connectivity and embedded parameterization information.

The key point of the progressive mesh hierarchical structure is the choice of the order of the edges to be collapsed. Here, we use the selection strategy proposed by Garland and Heckbert (1997) to determine the edge collapse order and to position the newly created vertices. In the classical progressive mesh representation (Hoppe, 1996; Zhou et al., 2004), the geometrical and topological information of each removed vertex are recorded in a vertex splitting operation during the decimation process. Thus the vertex can be completely recovered during progressive refinement process. However, this information is not suitable to reposition the recovered vertex on the unit sphere when the same vertex split sequence is performed on the corresponding spherical mesh. In what follows, we present how to reposition the

recovered vertex according to the relative position with respect to its first order neighborhood in the original mesh. As shown in Figure 1 (left and middle), edge $e = v_1 v_2$ is collapsed and a new vertex v is created. Let $star(v)$ be first order neighborhood of the vertex v. Using the MAPS algorithm (Lee et al., 1998), $star(v)$ is flattened into a planar region Ω. The vertices v_1 and v_2 are embedded into Ω and find the triangles T_1 and T_2 containing v_1 and v_2 respectively. The barycentric coordinates $(\alpha_i, \beta_i, \gamma_i)$, $i = 1,2$ of the embedding of v_1 and v_2 inside T_1 and T_2 respectively. Therefore, v_1 and v_2 can be locally parameterized with respect to the containing triangles T_1 and T_2 using the barycentric coordinates $(\alpha_i, \beta_i, \gamma_i)$. The local parameterization information of the two decimated vertices, together with all collapse information of the edge, is recorded in a vertex split operation for later reconstruction on the sphere. The final form of the progressive hierarchy of the given mesh is $\mathcal{M} = \{M^0, sp^1, sp^2, \cdots, sp^k\}$, where M^0 is the convex base mesh and the sp^i are the ordered split operations. That is, $M^i = M^0, sp^1, \cdots, sp^i$.

Starting from this base spherical mesh which is generated by projecting the convex base mesh M^0 onto the unit sphere, the vertex split operations in $\{sp^1, sp^2, \cdots, sp^k\}$ are performed progressively to simultaneously recover the original mesh and construct the spherical parameterization. Let M^i be the recovered mesh after performing the i ths vertex split operation, M^i_s be its corresponding spherical mesh. The $(i + 1)$ ths vertex split operation is then performed as follows. With the containing triangles T_1, T_2 and barycentric coordinates $(\alpha_i, \beta_i, \gamma_i)$ of the two new vertices v'_1 and v'_2 retrieved from sp^{i+1}; two new vertices v'_1 and v'_2 are inserted into M^{i+1}_s with the same connectivity as in M^{i+1} and positioned on the unit sphere by:

$$v'_1 = Normalize\,(\alpha_1 p_1^1 + \beta_1 p_1^2 + \gamma_1 p_1^3)$$
$$v'_2 = Normalize\,(\alpha_2 p_2^1 + \beta_2 p_2^2 + \gamma_2 p_2^3)$$

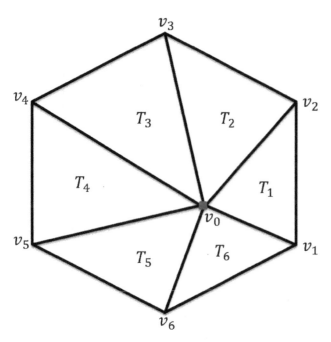

Figure 2. The local neighborhood *star* projected on the 2D plane.

Where (p_1^1, p_1^2, p_1^3) and (p_2^1, p_2^2, p_2^3) are the triangles in M_s^i corresponding to T_1 and T_2 respectively.

Local spherical improvement

The local spherical improvement uses iterations over the vertices of the initial parameterization on the unit sphere (Shen and Makedon, 2006). At each vertex, it tries to reposition in the local neighborhood *star* to gradually improve the mapping quality. The triangles composing the local neighborhood *star* is piece-wise linear. Therefore it can be projected on the 2D plane while preserving the relative area of each spherical triangle. Given that the vertex to reposition, Figure 2 shows an example of the projection of *star* on a 2D plane. Supposing that $v_i = (x_i,$ the signed area of the triangle can be computed by:

$$A_1 = \frac{1}{2}\left((x_2 - x_1)(y_0 - y_1) - (x_0 - x_1)(y_2 - y_1)\right)$$

Thus, replacing A_1 with A_{ideal} and treating x_0 and y_0 as the only unknowns in the previous equation, we can formulate a system of linear equations using all the triangles in the spherical $star(v_0)$ and solve it in the least squares sense to locate a new center vertex position. This new center position minimizes the square sum of the relative area differences between $star(v_0)$ on the object and $star(v_0)$ on the sphere S^2. Note that only the center position is concerned here. This indicates that the border

of spherical $star(v_0)$ is fixed, and consequently that. the total area of the spherical $star(v_0)$ cannot be changed. Therefore, each triangle in the spherical $star(v_0)$ aims to achieve not its correct absolute area but the correct area relative to the other triangles in $star(v_0)$. For example, Let $T_1, T_2, \cdots, T_6$ be the set of projected triangles depicted in Figure 2 and $T_1', T_2', \cdots, T_6'$ be the corresponding triangles on the object. If we use $A(\cdot)$ to denote the area of a triangle, the relative area of T_i' can be given by:

$$T_i = \frac{A(T_i')}{\sum_{j=1}^{6} A(T_j')}$$

In order to preserve this relative area, on the 2D project should have an ideal area of,

$$A_i = \frac{A(T_i')}{\sum_{k=1}^{6} A(T_k')} A_{Total}$$

Where A_T, is the total area of the 2D projection of the parameter submesh. To calculate the new location (x) for the parameter submesh center on its 2D projection, the following system of linear equations is formulated:

$$
\begin{aligned}
(x_2 - x_1)(y - y_1) - (x - x_1)(y_2 - y_1) &= 2A_1 \\
(x_3 - x_2)(y - y_2) - (x - x_2)(y_3 - y_2) &= 2A_2 \\
(x_4 - x_3)(y - y_3) - (x - x_3)(y_4 - y_3) &= 2A_3 \\
(x_5 - x_4)(y - y_4) - (x - x_4)(y_5 - y_4) &= 2A_4 \\
(x_6 - x_5)(y - y_5) - (x - x_5)(y_6 - y_5) &= 2A_5 \\
(x_1 - x_6)(y - y_6) - (x - x_6)(y_1 - y_6) &= 2A_6
\end{aligned}
$$

The new center location $(x$ is obtained by solving this linear system in a least squares sense.

MESH MAPPING

Now that we have the source and the target 3D objects parameterized on the sphere, the objective here is to find the point-to-point correspondence between the two parameterized objects. According to the number of points in the two objects, we have two kinds of mesh mapping:

(i) M to M mapping: The two input objects have the same number of points. We use the nearest neighbor algorithm (Manolis et al., 1997) to find the point to point correspondence. To avoid the case that multiple points are matched to a single point, we associate with each point an attribute, valued by true or false, to indicate whether that point is selected before or not.

(ii) M to N mapping: The source and the target objects have not the same number of points. Without loss of generality, assume that the source object has more points than the target object. To overcome this inequality problem we subdivide the target object using the subdivision algorithm (Kobbelt, 2000) such that the two

Figure 3. (A) Left two images. The input triangular mesh of the Stanford Bunny (39 k points, 70 k triangles) and, its spherical parameterization, (B) Right two images. The target triangular mesh of the Gargoyle (100 k points and 200 k triangles) and its spherical parameterization.

objects have an equal number of points. We fall again in the first kind-- M to M mapping. It can be seen that M to N mapping is more costly than M to M mapping, simply since we apply M to M mapping in addition to the subdivision step.

M to N mapping has the disadvantage of being time consuming. We use an enhanced implementation of nearest neighbor searching called AABB tree (CGAL, 2010). The AABB tree features a static data structure and algorithms to perform efficient intersection and distance queries against sets of finite 3D geometric objects. Using this static data structure, we build a tree with the vertices of the target object. We then use the tree to find for each point of the source object the corresponding nearest neighbor from the tree.

RESULTS

The methods described in the preceding sections have been implemented in C++ and using CGAL the Computational Geometry Algorithms Library (CGAL, 2010). The experiments are carried out on a PC with a 2.8 GHZ dual-core processor and 2GB of memory. The input objects are in the form of triangular meshes. Before constructing the spherical parameterization of our objects, we apply the following two preprocessing steps:

(1) Normalize the input models to a cube of unityto get a smooth and a robust transition between the input and output objects. This normalization of each object is performed separately. For each object, the centroid of the object is translated to the origin of the coordinates. Then, calculate the distance, of the farthest point with respect to the origin. Finally, divide the coordinates of each point, $p = (p_x, p_y, p_z)$, by d to get the normalized point

Figure 4. The AABB tree for the set of the spherical triangles of the gargoyle.

$$p_{Norm} = \left(\frac{p_x}{d}, \frac{p_y}{d}, \frac{p_z}{d}\right).$$

(2) If the objects are not sufficiently sampled, apply surface subdivision to enhance the mapping between the input and output objects.

Figure 3 shows the spherical parameterization of two triangular meshes the input object is the Stanford bunny and the target object is the Gargoyle. In our experiment, the parameterization time is 79 s for the Gargoyle (100 k points and 200 k triangles). Once the spherical parameterization is constructed for the input and target objects, we construct the AABB tree for the set of spherical triangles of the target object (the gargoyle, in our case) for the mapping step, as shown in Figure 4.

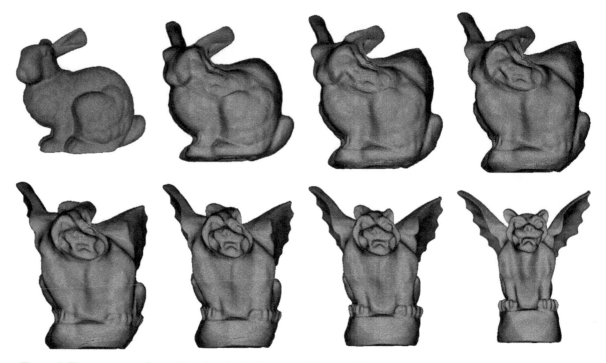

Figure 5. The sequence of morphing the stanford bunny to the gargoyle.

Each point in the spherical parameterization of the Bunny is matched with the closest spherical point in the AABB tree.

Once the matching step is performed, a linear interpolation is performed between the set of points of the Bunny and the corresponding points in the Gargoyle. This interpolation creates the set of frames to be visualized as the final morphing animation. Figure 5 shows the series of the frames that creates the morphing of Bunny-Gargoyle.

CONCLUSIONS

In this paper, we propose a novel technique for 3D mesh morphing capable to interpolate between arbitrary zero-genus objects. The technique can be presented as an animation by creating a series of intermediate objects using the spherical parameterization as a common domain of the source and target objects. We converted both objects into the same spherical domain with suitable modifications to reposition of the points on the sphere. This repositioning prevents the morphing from creating overlapping or clustering of points on the sphere during the mapping step. Then we carry out mesh mapping to realize the morphing process and this happened by using the point-to-point correspondence between the objects of the AABB tree search algorithm. The spherical parameterization which is used to make the mapping step easy since the objects are mapped to their natural parameterization domain.

Conflict of Interest

The author(s) have not declared any conflict of interest.

REFERENCES

Beier T, Neely S (1992). Feature-Based Image Metamorphosis. Proceedings of SIGGRAPH 92:35-42.

CGAL (2010). Computational Geometry Algorithms Library, http://www.cgal.org.

Garland M, Heckbert PS (1997). Surface simplification using quadric error metrics. Proceedings of the 24th annual conference on Computer graphics and interactive techniques, ACM Press/Addison-Wesley Publishing Co. 209-216.

Gao P, Sederberg TW (1998). "A Work Minimization Approach to Image Morphing," Visual Computer, pp. 390-400.

Hoppe H (1996). Progressive meshes. Proceedings of the 23rd annual conference on Computer graphics and interactive techniques, ACM. pp. 99-108.

Kobbelt L (2000). sqrt(3)-subdivision. Computer Graphics (Proc. SIGGRAPH '00). 34:103-112.

Lee AWF, Sweldens W, Schroder P, Cowsar L, Dobkin D (1998). MAPS: multiresolution adaptive parameterization of surfaces. Proceedings of the 25th annual conference on Computer graphics and interactive techniques, ACM: pp. 95-104.

Lee S, Chwa K, Shin SY, Wolberg G (1995). "Image Metamorphosis Using Snakes and Free-form Deformations. Proceedings of SIGGRAPH 95.

Manolis K, Hoomanvassef MDB, Krzysztof G (1997). "3D MOrphing." MIT project (6.837) http://web.mit.edu/manoli/morph/www/morph.html.

Praun E, Hoppe H (2003). "Spherical parametrization and remeshing." ACM. Trans. Graph. 22(3):340-349.

Sederberg TW, GreenWood E (1992). A Physically Based Approach to 2D Shape Blending. Proceedings of SIGGRAPH 92. In Computer Graphics Proceedings, Annual Conferences Series.

Shapira M, Rappoport AA (1995). "Shape Blending Using Star-Skeleton Representation." IEEE Computer Graphics and Applications. pp. 44-50.

Shen L, Makedon F (2006). "Spherical mapping for processing of 3D closed surfaces." Image Vision Computing. 24(7):743-761.

Sompagdee P (2009). Survey of Morphing. C. S. Department, Thammasat University. pp.1-8.

Zhou K, Bao H, Shi J (2004). "3D surface filtering using spherical harmonics." Computer-Aided Design. 36(4):363-375.

21

Computational calculation of the electronic and magnetic properties of 1x1-MN/GaN (M = V, Cr and Mn) multilayers

Miguel J. E. R.[1], **Gladys C. J.**[2] **and César O. L.**[2]

[1]GEFEM Group, Distrital University Francisco José de Caldas, Bogotá, Colombia.
[2]Grupo Avanzado de Materiales y Sistemas Complejos GAMASCO, Departamento de Física, Universidad de Córdoba, Montería Colombia.

We employed density functional theory (DFT) in order to study the electronic and magnetic properties of 1x1-MN/GaN (M = V, Cr, and Mn) multilayers, in the wurtzite-type hexagonal structure. The calculations were carried out using a method based on full-potential linearized augmented plane waves (FP-LAPW), employed exactly as implemented in Wien2k code. For the description of the electron-electron interaction, generalized gradient approximation (GGA) was used. We found that the VN/GaN multilayers exhibited a half-metallic ferromagnetic behavior and all 1x1-MN/GaN (M = V, Cr and Mn) multilayers have magnetic properties with a magnetic moment of 2, 3 and 4 μ_β per cell, respectively. Additionally, we found that the magnetic moment/cell multilayers increase linearly with an increase in the atomic number Z of the transition metal. Analysis of the density of states reveals that ferromagnetic behavior of the multilayers can be explained by the strong hybridization between states (V, Cr and Mn)-d and N-pcrossing of the Fermi level. The magnetism in the multilayers essentially comes from the d orbitals of the atoms of V, Cr and Mn.

Key words: DFT, 1x1-MN/GaN (M = V, Cr, and Mn) multilayers, structural and electronic properties.

INTRODUCTION

Gallium nitride, GaN, a semiconductor that crystallizes as wurtzite (Koide et al., 2005), is a material of great interest because of its wide potential application in technology, in light-emitting devices in the blue and near-ultraviolet ranges, diodes based on Schottky contact, and laser diodes (Nakamura, 1997; Morkoc et al., 1994). Its efficiency in blue, green, and yellow light-emitting emitting diodes, laser injection, and ultraviolet detectors is truly extraordinary (Steckl and Birkahn, 1998). The high value of the dielectric constant, high thermal conductivity, and favorable transport properties make it a good candidate for new applications in devices that must operate at high temperatures and in high-power electronic devices (Nakamura et al., 1994). In recent years, there has been great interest in the GaN compound, its alloys, and when doped with transition metal, due to their potential applications in diluted magnetic semiconductors (Dietl et al., 2000), as spin injectors, in magnetic memories, and in other spintronics applications (Zhang and Kuech, 1998; Dietl, 2002). At the same time, recent advances in techniques of the growth of materials and the ability to control the growth of semiconductor materials have opened the door to the manufacture of high-quality multilayers in different geometries and for different kinds of semiconductors. Rawat et al. (2009) demonstrated that it is possible to grow a multilayer of transition metal nitrides and GaN, despite the difference in the crystalline structures of NaCl, titanium nitride TiN, and GaN wurtzite. They grew a TiN/GaN multilayer using the reactive pulsed laser deposition technique (PLD), while Birch et al. (2006) grew a ScN/CrN multilayer epitaxially, using the magnetron sputerring technique. This fact shows that it is worthwhile to carry out theoretical studies of 1x1-MN/GaN (M = V, Cr, and Mn) multilayers that will provide information on the structural, electronic, and magnetic properties of these multilayers and enable the design of new devices that will contribute to the development of current semiconductor technology.

COMPUTATIONAL METHODS

The calculations were carried out within the framework of density functional theory (DFT), and full potential augmented plane wave (FP-LAPW) was used as implemented in the Wien2k software package (Schwarz et al., 2010). The exchange and correlation effects of the electrons were dealt with using the generalized gradient approximation (GGA) of Perdew, Burke, and Ernzerhof (PBE) (Perdew et al., 1997). In the LAPW method, the cell is divided into two types of regions, namely spheres centered at the atomic nuclear sites and an interstitial region between non-overlapping areas. Within the atomic spheres, wave functions are replaced by atomic functions, whereas in the interstitial region, the functions are expanded in the form of plane waves. The charge density and potential expand to form spherical harmonics up to l_{max} = 10 inside the atomic spheres, and the wave function in the interstitial region expands in the form of plane waves with a cutoff parameter $R_{MT}K_{max}$ = 8, where R_{MT} is the smallest radius of the atomic level within the unit cell and K_{max} is the magnitude of the largest k vector of the reciprocal lattice. To ensure convergence in the integration of the first Brillouin zone, 1600 points were used, which corresponds to 140 k-points at the irreducible part of the first Brillouin. The integrals over the Brillouin zone were solved using the special approximation of k points provided by Monkhorst and Pack (1976). Self-consistency was achieved by requiring that the convergence of the total energy be less than 10^{-4} Ry. To achieve expansion of the potential in the interstitial region, G_{max} was considered to be = 12. The corresponding muffin-tin radii were 1.6 bohr for N, 1.95 bohr for Ga, and 1.85 for V, Cr and Mn. Calculations were performed taking into consideration the spin polarization caused by the presence of V, Cr and Mn in the superlattice.

To calculate the lattice constant, the minimum volume, the bulk modulus, and the cohesive energy of the two structures studied, calculations were fit to the Murnaghan equation of state (Murnaghan, 1944), Equation (1)

$$E(V) = E_0 + \frac{B_0 V}{B_0'} \left[\frac{(V_0/v)^{B'}}{B_0' - 1} + 1 \right] - \frac{B_0 V_0}{B_0' - 1} \tag{1}$$

Where B_0 is the bulk modulus, its first derivative is B'_0, V_0 is the equilibrium volume of the cell, and E_0 represents the cohesive energy.

In other to study the relative stability of 1x1-MN/GaN (M = V, Cr, and Mn) multilayers in a 50-50 concentration, namely, x = 50% GaN molecules and x = 50% MN (M = V, Cr, and Mn) molecules, the energy of formation was calculated. For the ternary compound, the formation energy is defined as the difference between the total energy of the ternary phase $M_{1-x}Ga_xN$ and the total energy of the binary compounds in their ground state (more stable phase: fme) MN and GaN wurtzite, namely, E_{MN}^{fme} and $E_{GaN}^{wurtzita}$, respectively. Therefore, the formation energy is given by Equation (2)(Zhang and Veprek, 2007; Sheng et al., 2008).

$$\Delta E_f = E_{M_{1-x}Ga_xN}^{fme} - (1-x) E_{MN}^{fme} - x E_{GaN}^{wurtzita} \tag{2}$$

The 1x1-MN/GaN multilayer were modeled according to special quasirandom structures approach (Zunger et al., 1990) and the disorder aspects were ignored. The 1x1-MN/GaN multilayer an hexagonal unit cell with alternating [0001] layers of MN (V, Cr and Mn) and GaN in conventional wurtzite structure was employed, as show in Figure 1. Where a and c are the lattice constants, u denotes the dimensionless parameter of the internal structure and the positions of the atoms are: for Ga or M (0,0,0), (1/3,2/3,1/2) and N (0,0,u), (1/3,2/3,u+1/2).

RESULTS AND DISCUSSION

Structural properties

The multilayers were modeled in the wurtzite structure belonging to space group 156 (P3m1), interspersing a monolayer of GaN and one of MN (M = V, Cr and Mn) along the z axis. Figure 2 shows the energy as a function of the volume of 1x1- MN/GaN (M = V, Cr and Mn) multilayers. The calculated total energy was fit to Murnaghan's equation of state. It can be noted that each of the curves has a minimum energy value, and thus the crystallization phase of the multilayers is stable or metastable.

The lattice constant, the c/a value, the bulk modulus (B_0), the minimum volume (V_0), the minimum energy (E_0), the magnetic moment (μ_β) per cell, and the energy of formation of 1x1-MN/GaN (M = V, Cr and Mn) multilayers are shown in Table 1. Table 2 shows the values of the structural parameters of the binary compounds VN, CrN, MnN and GaN, calculated and reported by other authors. The calculated lattice constant for each of the binary compounds accords well with values reported theoretically and experimentally, since it differs by less than one percent. The values of the bulk modules of the multilayers are higher, which confirms that they are quite rigid, making them good candidates for possible applications in devices operated at high temperature and high power, as well as hard coatings. On the other hand, despite the difference in the crystalline structure between VN NaCl, zinc blend of CrN, MnN, and GaN wurtzite, joining of the layers of the 1x1-MN/GaN (M = V, Cr and Mn) compounds with GaN to form a multilayer does

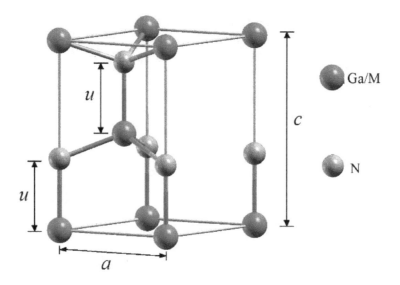

Figure 1. Unit cell 1x1-MN/GaN (M = V, Cr and Mn) multilayers.

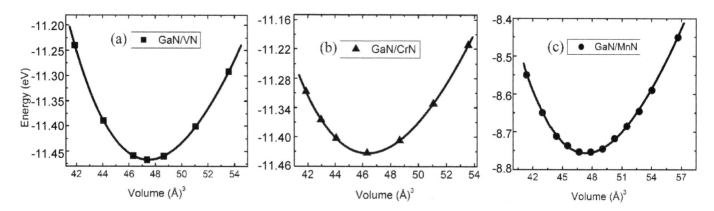

Figure 2. Total energy as a function of volume for 1x1-(a) VN/GaN, (b) CrN/GaN, (c) MnN/GaN multilayers.

Table 1. Structural and magnetic parameters and the energy of formation ΔE_f of 1x1-MN/GaN (M = V, Cr and Mn) multilayers.

Multilayer	a_0 (Å)	c/a	V_0 (Å^3)	B_0 (GPa)	E_0 (eV)	μ (μ_β)	ΔE_f (eV)
VN/GaN	3.227 3.267[a]	1.631	47.41	176.07	- 11.47	~2.0	+ 0.621
CrN/GaN	3.210	1.628	47.19	191.50	- 11.48	~3.0	+ 0.461
MnN/GaN	3.190	1.626	46.31	181.00	- 8.570	~4.0	+ 0.403

not change the GaN wurtzite structure, as seen in Table 1 in the value of the lattice constant and the c/a value of the multilayers, which are very close to the value of the lattice constant and the c/a value of GaN in Table 2.

In order to verify the relative stability of the multilayer, we calculated the energy of formation of each multilayer. For this purpose, we calculated the total energy E_0 (Table 2) of the binary compounds VN, CrN, MnN and GaN in their ground states. Table 1 shows the values of formation energy ΔE_f calculated using Equation 2.

The energy of VN, CrN, MnN and GaN binary compounds in their ground state is negative, whereas, according to the results of Table 2, the value of the energy of formation of each multilayer is positive.

Table 2. Structural parameters of binary compounds VN, CrN, MnN and GaN in ground state.

Binary	a_0 (Å)	c/a	B_0 (GPa)	E_0 (eV)
VN	4.129		306.01	- 15.25
	4.127[b]	-	305.3[c]	
	4.139[c]			
CrN	4.148		211.15	- 14.95
	4.146[b]	-	204.15	
	4.135[c]			
MnN	4.271	-	291.5	- 9.524
	4.256[d]			
GaN	3.222	1.629	184.50	- 8.933
	3.221[f]	1.631[f]	170.56[f]	
	3.190[g]		188.00[g]	

A (González et al., 2009) Theoretical, b (Liangcai et al., 2013) Theoretical, c (International center for diffraction data, 2007) Experimental, d (Suzuki et al., 2000) Experimental, e (Lukashev and Lambrecht, 2004) Theoretical, f (Shultz and Thiemann, 1977) Theoretical, g (Arbouche et al., 2009) Experimental.

Therefore, 1x1-MN/GaN (M = V, Cr and Mn) multilayers are metastable. This means that the multilayer cannot grow under equilibrium conditions, so in order to grow them, it is necessary to supply power to the system, as Rawat et al. (2009) did in order to grow a 1x1-TiN/GaN multilayer using the reactive pulsed laser deposition technique (PLD). These results for the energy of formation are important, because through knowing these values, growing conditions can be improved, and therefore 1x1- MN/GaN (M = V, Cr and Mn) multilayers of excellent quality can be grown.

Table 1 shows that energy of formation of the 1x1-MN/GaN (M = V, Cr and Mn) multilayer. The smallest value of the energy of formation corresponds to the 1x1-MnN/GaN multilayer; therefore, it is the most energetically stable.

Electronic properties

Figure 3(a), (b) and (c) shows the calculated band structures of 1x1-MN/GaN (M = V, Cr and Mn) multilayers in their ferromagnetic state phase. Figure 4b and 4c shows that the 1x1-CrN/GaN and 1x1-MnN/GaN multilayers are not half-metallic behavior due valence and conduction bands cross the Fermi level, however 1x1-VN/GaN multilayer is half-metallic and ferromagnetic, since in the valence band near the Fermi level the majority spin (spin-up) is metallic, and the minority spin (spin-down) is semiconducting. The 1x1-VN/GaN multilayer exhibit 100% polarization of the conduction carriers in the ground state, which is required in spin injection. This suggests that it can be used efficiently for injection of spin polarized charge carriers.

Figure 4(a), (b) and (c) show the total density of states (TDOS) and partial density of states (PDOS) of the orbitals that more contribute near the Fermi level of 1x1-MN/GaN (M = V, Cr, and Mn) multilayers in the ground state. The calculations were performed with spin polarization up and down.

Figures 4a confirm the half-metallic and ferromagnetic nature of 1x1-VN/GaN multilayer, since the up-spin density is metallic, whereas the down-spin density is of semiconductor character, namely, the spin-up channel is completely occupied and the spin-down channel is completely empty. Whereas that 1x1-CrN/GaN and 1x1-MnN/GaN have metallic behavior of the two spin channels.

The 1x1-MN/GaN(M = V, Cr, and Mn) multilayers, have magnetic behavior with magnetic moments of 2, 3 and 4 μ_β respectively, is mainly determined by the orbitals (M = V, Cr, and Mn)-d, and to a lesser extent by the N-p orbitals that cross the Fermi level. However, as seen in Figure 4, the contribution of the N-p (up-spin) orbital near the Fermi level increases with the increase in the atomic number Z of the transition metal in the multilayer, the contribution of orbital N-p being lower in the VN/GaN and higher in the CrN/GaN multilayer. Additionally, according to the theory by Jhi et al. (1999), the hybridization of the metallic states (M = V, Cr, and Mn)-d and nonmetallic electrons N- p that cross the Fermi level results in a strong covalent bond, which is responsible for the high degree of stiffness of the multilayer.

Figure 5 shows the variation of the magnetic moment as a function of the atomic number of the transition metal present in the1x1-MN/GaN (M = V, Cr, and Mn) multilayer, with Z = 23, 24 and 25 respectively. It can be observed that the magnetic moment increases linearly with an increase in the atomic number.

This increase in the magnetic moment value can

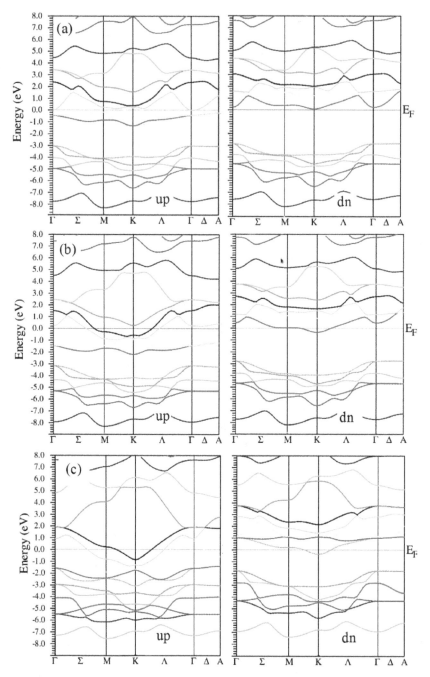

Figure 3. Band structure (a) 1x1-VN/GaN, (b) 1x1-CrN/GaN and (c) 1x1-MnN/GaN.

understood as follows: the magnetic moments of 2, 3 and 4 μ_β are due V^{3+}, Cr^{3+} and Mn^{3+} configuration, respectively; with electronic configurations V^{3+} =:[Ar]$3d^2$, Cr^{3+} =:[Ar]$3d^3$ and Mn^{3+} =:[Ar]$3d^4$; because, when the V, Cr and Mn atoms are in the multilayer each atom gives three electrons. Then, the V atom remain two valence electrons, Cr atoms three and Mn atom four valence electrons (configurations d^2, d^3 and d^4, respectively). This valence electrons couple ferromagnetically, as result the two electrons produce a total magnetic moment of 2

μ_β/atom-V, the three electrons produce a total magnetic moment of 3 μ_β/atom-Cr and the four electrons produce a total magnetic moment of 4 μ_β/atom-Mn.

Conclusions

We reported first principles calculations to determine the structural, electronic, and magnetic properties of a 1x1-MN/GaN (M = V, Cr, and Mn) multilayer. The calculated

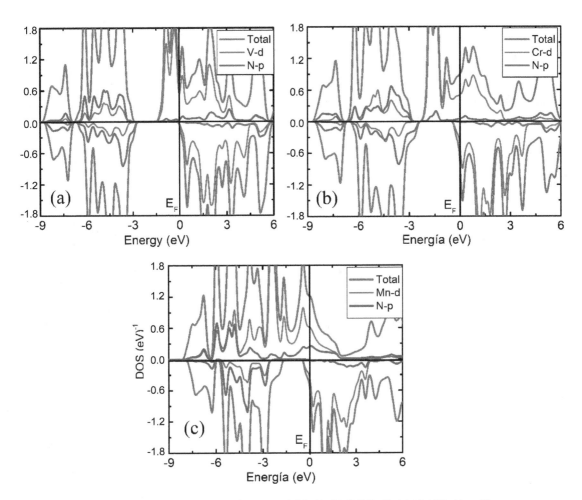

Figure 4. Total and partial density of states of 1x1 (a) VN/GaN, (b) CrN/GaN, (c) MnN/GaN multilayers.

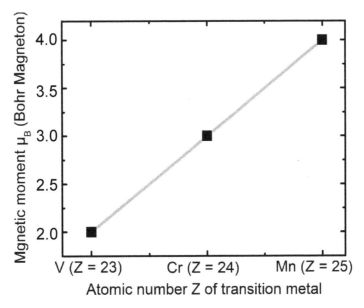

Figure 5. Magnetic moment as a function of the atomic number of the transition metal present in the1x1-MN/GaN (M = V, Cr, and Mn) multilayer. The line is a visual guide.

values of the bulk modules were quite high; therefore, the multilayers are quite rigid, which makes them attractive for potential applications at high temperatures and for hard coatings. Also, we found that the magnetic moment increases linearly with an increase in the atomic number of the transition metal present in the multilayer. On the basis of the density of states, we found that the multilayer exhibits a half metallic behavior, due to the orbital M-d(M = V, Cr, andMn) andN-p that cross the Fermi level in each corresponding multilayer. Finally, we found that 1x1-MN/GaN (M = V, Cr, and Mn) multilayers exhibit magnetic properties with magnetic moments 2, 3 and 4 μ_β, respectively. These properties show that multilayers are good candidates for possible applications in diluted magnetic semiconductors, spin injectors, and other spintronics applications.

Conflict of Interest

The authors have not declared any conflict of interest

ACKNOWLEDGEMENT

The authors thank the Research Center of the University of Cordoba CUIC for its financial support.

REFERENCES

Arbouche O, Belgoumène B, Soudini B, Driz M (2009). First principles study of the relative stability and the electronic properties of GaN. Computational Materials Sci. 47(2):432–438. http://dx.doi.org/10.1016/j.commatsci.2009.09.007

Birch J, Joelsson T, Eriksson F, Ghafoor N, Hultman L (2006). Single crystal CrN/ScN superlattice soft X-ray mirrors: Epitaxial growth, structure, and properties. Thin Solid Films 514(1-2):10–19. http://dx.doi.org/10.1016/j.tsf.2006.02.011

Dietl T (2002). Ferromagnetic semiconductors. Semicond. Sci. Technol. 17(4):377-392. http://dx.doi.org/10.1088/0268-1242/17/4/310

Dietl T, Ohno H, Matsukura F, Cibert J, Ferrand D (2000). Zener Model Description of ferromagnetism in Zinc-BelndeMagnwticSemicondutors. Science 287(5455):1019-1022. http://dx.doi.org/10.1126/science.287.5455.1019

González HR, López PW, Fajardo F, Rodríguez M, Jairo A (2009). Pressure effects on the electronic and magnetic properties of Ga$_x$V$_{1-x}$N compounds: Ab-initio study. Materials Science and Engineering B. 163(3):190–193. http://dx.doi.org/10.1016/j.mseb.2009.05.029

International center for diffraction data (2007). Powder diffraction files 00-045-0978 (ScN), 00-035-0779 (YN), 03-065-0565 (TiN), 00-035-0753 (ZrN), 00-033-0592 (HfN), 00-035-0768 (VN), 03-065-5011 (NbN), 03-065-9404 (TaN), 00-065-2899 (CrN), International center for diffraction data, PDF-2/release 2007 (2007).

Jhi SH, Ihm J, Louie SG, Cohen ML (1999). Electronic mechanism of hardness enhancement in transition-metal carbonitrides. Nature. 399:132–134. http://dx.doi.org/10.1038/20148

Koide N, HikosakaT, Honda Y, Yamaguch M (2005). Incorporation of carbon on a (1 1̄ 01) facert of GaN by MOVPE. J. Crystal Growth. 284(3-4):341–346. http://dx.doi.org/doi:10.1016/j.jcrysgro.2005.07.021

Liangcai Z, David H, Paul HM (2013). Ab initio study of the alloying effect of transition metals on structure, stability and ductility of CrN. J. Phys. D: Appl. Phys. 46(36):365301. http://dx.doi.org/10.1088/0022-3727/46/36/365301

Lukashev P, Lambrecht WRL (2004). First-principles study of the preference for zinc-blende or rocksalt structures in FeN and CoN. Phys. Rev. B. 70:245205. http://dx.doi.org/10.1103/PhysRevB.70.245205

Monkhorst HJ, Pack JD (1976). Physical Review B. Special points for Brillouin-zone integrations. 13(12):5188-5192. http://dx.doi.org/10.1103/PhysRevB.13.5188

Morkoc H, Strite S, Gao GB, Lin ME, Sverdlov B, Burns M (1994). Large-band-gap SiC, III-V nitride, and II-VI ZnSe-based semiconductor device technologies. J. Appl. Phys. 76(3):1363-1368. http://dx.doi.org/10.1063/1.358463

Murnaghan FD (1944). The Compressibility of media under pressure. Proceedings of the National Academy Science U.S.A. 30(9):244-247. http://www.ncbi.nlm.nih.gov/pmc/articles/PMC1078704/

Nakamura S (1997). III-IV Nitride based light-emitting devices. Solid State Communications. 102(2-3):237-243. http://dx.doi.org/doi:10.1016/S0038-1098(96)00722-3

Nakamura S, Mukai T, Senoh M (1994). Candela-class high-brightness InGaN/AlGaN double-heterostructure blue-light-emitting diodes. Appl. Phys. Lett. 64(13):1687-1692. http://dx.doi.org/10.1063/1.111832.

Perdew J, Burke K, Ernzerhof M (1997). Generalized Gradient Approximation Made Simple: Physical Review Letter. 77(18):3865-3868. http://dx.doi.org/10.1103/PhysRevLett.77.3865.

Rawat V, Zakharov DN, Stach EA, Sands TD (2009). Pseudomorphic stabilization of rocksalt GaN in TiN/GaN multilayers and superlattices. Phys. Rev. B. 80:24114. http://dx.doi.org/10.1103/PhysRevB.80.024114

Schwarz K, Blaha P, Trickey SB (2010). Electronic structure of solids with WIEN2k. Molecular Physics: Int. J. Interface between Chem. Phys. 108(21-23):3147–3166. http://dx.doi.org/10.1080/00268976.2010.506451

Sheng SH, Zhang RF, Veprek S (2008). Phase stabilities and thermal decomposition in the Zr$_{1-x}$Al$_x$N system studied by ab initio calculation and thermodynamic modeling. ActaMaterialia. 56(5):968–976. http://dx.doi.org/10.1016/j.actamat.2007.10.050

Shultz H, Thiemann KH (1977). Crystal structure refinement of Al Nans GaN. Solid State Commun. 23(11):815-819. http://dx.doi.org/10.1016/0038-1098(77)90959-0

Steckl AJ, Birkahn R (1998). Visible emission from Er-doped GaN grown by solid source molecular beam epitaxy. Appl. Phys. Lett. 73(12):1700-1702. http://dx.doi.org/10.1063/1.122250

Suzuki K, Kaneko T, Yoshida H, Obi Y, Fujimori H, Morita H (2000). Crystal structure and magnetic properties of the compound MnN. J. Alloys Compounds 306(1-2):66–71. http://dx.doi.org/10.1016/S0925-8388(00)00794-5

Zhang R, Kuech TF (1998). Photoluminescence of carbon in situ doped GaN grown by halide vapor phase epitaxy. Appl. Phys. Lett. 72(13):1611-1613. http://dx.doi.org/10.1063/1.121144

Zhang RF, Veprek S (2007). Phase stabilities and spinodal decomposition in the Cr$_{1-x}$Al$_x$N system studied by ab initio LDA and thermodynamic modeling: Comparison with the Ti$_{1-x}$Al$_x$N and TiN/Si$_3$N$_4$ systems.Acta Materialia. 55(14):4615-4619. http://dx.doi.org/10.1016/j.actamat.2007.04.029

Zunger A, Wei SH, Ferreira L, Bernard JE (1990). Special quasirandom structures. Phys. Review Lett. 65:353. http://dx.doi.org/10.1103/PhysRevLett.65.353

Permissions

List of Contributors

Yu Wuyang
Institute of Management Decision and Innovation, Hangzhou Dianzi University, 310018, Zhejiang, P. R. China

Adnan Salih
College of Science for Women, Baghdad University, Iraq

Khawla J. Tahir
College of Science, Karbala University, Iraq

Fred Otieno
Durban University of Technology, P. O. Box 1334, Durban, 4000, South Africa

Josiah Adeyemo
Durban University of Technology, P. O. Box 1334, Durban, 4000, South Africa

Noradin Ghadimi
Department of Electrical Engineering, Ardabil Branch, Islamic Azad University, Ardabil, Iran

Behrooz Sobhani
Department of Electrical Engineering, Ardabil Branch, Islamic Azad University, Ardabil, Iran

Khaled Ouni
The High Institute of Applied Sciences and Technology of Kairouan, Kairouan, Avenue Beit ElHekma, 3100 Kairouan, Tunisia

Hedi Dhouibi
The High Institute of Applied Sciences and Technology of Kairouan, Kairouan, Avenue Beit ElHekma, 3100 Kairouan, Tunisia

Lotfi Nabli
The National Engineering School of Monastir, Avenue Ibn ElJazzar, 5019 Monastir, Tunisia

Hassani Messaoud
The National Engineering School of Monastir, Avenue Ibn ElJazzar, 5019 Monastir, Tunisia

Quanjin Liu
College of Science, Nanjing University of Aeronautics and Astronautics, Nanjing 210016, China
School of Physics and Electronic Engineering, Anqing Normal College, Anqing 246011, China

Zhimin Zhao
College of Science, Nanjing University of Aeronautics and Astronautics, Nanjing 210016, China

Ying-xin Li
Institute of Machine Vision and Machine Intelligence, Beijing Jingwei Textile Machinery New Technology Co., Ltd., Beijing 100176, China

Xiaolei Yu
Jiangsu Institute of Standardization, Nanjing 210029, China

Saddam Akber Abbasi
Department of Statistics, the University of Auckland, Auckland, New Zealand

Muhammad Riaz
Mathematics and Statistics Department, King Fahd University of Petroleum and Minerals, Dhahran, Saudi Arabia

Kun Li
Tianjin University, Tianjin 300072, China

Chao Song
Tianjin University, Tianjin 300072, China

Jingyu Yang
Tianjin University, Tianjin 300072, China

Jianmin Jiang
Tianjin University, Tianjin 300072, China

Lili Pan and Mei Xie
University of Electronic Science and Technology of China, 2006 Xiyuan Avenue, Gaoxin West Zone, 611731, Chengdu, China

Waseem Shahzad
National University of Computer and Emerging Sciences Department of Computer Science, Sector H-11/4, Islamabad, Pakistan

Salman Asad
National University of Computer and Emerging Sciences Department of Computer Science, Sector H-11/4, Islamabad, Pakistan

Muhammad Asif Khan
National University of Computer and Emerging Sciences Department of Computer Science, Sector H-11/4, Islamabad, Pakistan

Y. Elmahroug
Unité de Recherche de Physique Nucléaire et des Hautes
Energies, Faculté des Sciences de Tunis, 2092 Tunis,
Tunisie

B. Tellili
Unité de Recherche de Physique Nucléaire et des Hautes
Energies, Faculté des Sciences de Tunis, 2092 Tunis,
Tunisie
Université de Tunis El Manar, Institut Supérieur des
Technologies Médicales de Tunis, 1006 Tunis, Tunisie

S. Chedly
Université de Carthage, École Polytechnique de Tunisie,
B.P. 743 - 2078 La Marsa, Tunisie

Chihi Adel
Laboratoire Photovoltaïque, Centre des Recherches et des
Technologies de l'Energie Technopole BorjCedria B.P No.
95 2050 - Hammam Lif - Tunisie

Boujmil Mohamed Fethi
Laboratoire Photovoltaïque, Centre des Recherches et des
Technologies de l'Energie Technopole BorjCedria B.P No.
95 2050 - Hammam Lif - Tunisie

Bessais Brahim
Laboratoire Photovoltaïque, Centre des Recherches et des
Technologies de l'Energie Technopole BorjCedria B.P No.
95 2050 - Hammam Lif - Tunisie

Seyed Habib Musavi-Jahromi
Faculty of Water Sciences Engineering, Shahid Chamran
University (SCU), Ahwaz, Iran

Javad Ahadiyan
Faculty of Water Sciences Engineering, Shahid Chamran
University (SCU), Ahwaz, Iran

J. L. Rojas-Rentería
División de Estudios de Posgrado, Facultad de Ingeniería,
Universidad Autónoma de Querétaro. Cerro de las
Campanas S/N, C. P. 76010, Querétaro, Qro., México
Universidad Tecnológica de Corregidora, Carretera a
Coroneo km 11.5, Querétaro, Qro. México

G. Macias-Bobadilla
División de Estudios de Posgrado, Facultad de Ingeniería,
Universidad Autónoma de Querétaro. Cerro de las
Campanas S/N, C. P. 76010, Querétaro, Qro., México

R. Luna-Rubio
División de Estudios de Posgrado, Facultad de Ingeniería,
Universidad Autónoma de Querétaro. Cerro de las
Campanas S/N, C. P. 76010, Querétaro, Qro., México
Universidad Tecnológica de Corregidora, Carretera a
Coroneo km 11.5, Querétaro, Qro. México

C. A. Gonzalez-Gutierrez
División de Estudios de Posgrado, Facultad de Ingeniería,
Universidad Autónoma de Querétaro. Cerro de las
Campanas S/N, C. P. 76010, Querétaro, Qro., México

A. Rojas-Molina
División de Estudios de Posgrado, Facultad de Ingeniería,
Universidad Autónoma de Querétaro. Cerro de las
Campanas S/N, C. P. 76010, Querétaro, Qro., México

J. L. González-Pérez
Aplicaciones Computacionales y Biotecnología, Facultad
de Ingeniería, Universidad Autónoma de Querétaro.
Cerro de las Campanas S/N, C.P. 76010, Querétaro, Qro.,
México

M. Mirzai
Water- Energy Research Center-Sharif, Iran

A.Sajadi
Water- Energy Research Center-Sharif, Iran

A. Nazari
Water- Energy Research Center-Sharif, Iran

J. L. Rojas-Rentería
División de Estudios de Posgrado, Facultad de Ingeniería,
México
Universidad Tecnológica de Corregidora. Carretera a
Coroneo km 11.5, Querétaro, Qro., México

R. Luna-Rubio
División de Estudios de Posgrado, Facultad de Ingeniería,
México
Universidad Tecnológica de Corregidora. Carretera a
Coroneo km 11.5, Querétaro, Qro., México

J. L. González-Pérez
Aplicaciones Computacionales y Biotecnología, Facultad
de Ingeniería, México

C. A.González-Gutiérrez
División de Estudios de Posgrado, Facultad de Ingeniería,
México

A. Rojas-Molina
División de Estudios de Posgrado, Facultad de Ingeniería,
México

G. Macías-Bobadilla
División de Estudios de Posgrado, Facultad de Ingeniería,
México

Luis Antonio Aguilar-Pérez
Instituto Politécnico Nacional, Escuela Superior de Ingeniería Mecánica y Eléctrica; Unidad Profesional Zacatenco, Av. Instituto Politécnico Nacional s/n, Col. Lindavista, Delegación. Gustavo A. Madero, Distrito Federal, C.P. 07738, México

Christopher René Torres-San Miguel
Instituto Politécnico Nacional, Escuela Superior de Ingeniería Mecánica y Eléctrica; Unidad Profesional Zacatenco, Av. Instituto Politécnico Nacional s/n, Col. Lindavista, Delegación. Gustavo A. Madero, Distrito Federal, C.P. 07738, México

Guillermo Urriolagoitia Sosa
Instituto Politécnico Nacional, Escuela Superior de Ingeniería Mecánica y Eléctrica; Unidad Profesional Zacatenco, Av. Instituto Politécnico Nacional s/n, Col. Lindavista, Delegación. Gustavo A. Madero, Distrito Federal, C.P. 07738, México

Luis Martínez-Sáez
Instituto Universitario de Investigación del Automóvil, Industriales, Universidad Politécnica de Madrid. Carretera de Valencia, km.7. Madrid, España. CP. 28031, México

José Alfredo Leal-Naranjo
Instituto Politécnico Nacional, Escuela Superior de Ingeniería Mecánica y Eléctrica; Unidad Profesional Zacatenco, Av. Instituto Politécnico Nacional s/n, Col. Lindavista, Delegación. Gustavo A. Madero, Distrito Federal, C.P. 07738, México

Beatriz Romero-Ángeles
Instituto Politécnico Nacional, Escuela Superior de Ingeniería Mecánica y Eléctrica, Unidad Profesional Azacapotzalco, Av. De las Granjas No. 682, Col. Santa Catarina. Del. Azcapotzalco, Distrito Federal C.P. 02250 México

Guillermo Urriolagoitia-Calderón
Instituto Politécnico Nacional, Escuela Superior de Ingeniería Mecánica y Eléctrica; Unidad Profesional Zacatenco, Av. Instituto Politécnico Nacional s/n, Col. Lindavista, Delegación. Gustavo A. Madero, Distrito Federal, C.P. 07738, México

Oluwole Charles Akinyokun
Department of Computer Science, Federal University of Technology, Akure, Ondo State, Nigeria

Gabriel Babatunde Iwasokun
Department of Computer Science, Federal University of Technology, Akure, Ondo State,Nigeria.

Akinwale Michael Ojo
Department of Computer Science, Federal University of Technology, Akure, Ondo State, Nigeria

S. Baghya Shree
Department of Electrical and Electronics Engineering, Anna University, Dindigul Campus, India

N. Kamaraj
Department of Electrical and Electronics Engineering Thiagarajar College of Engineering, Madurai, India

A. Elef
Department of Computer Science, Faculty of Computers and Informatics, Suez Canal University, Egypt

M. H. Mousa
Department of Computer Science, Faculty of Computers and Informatics, Suez Canal University, Egypt

H. Nassar
Department of Computer Science, Faculty of Computers and Informatics, Suez Canal University, Egypt

J. E. R.Miguel
GEFEM Group, Distrital University Francisco José de Caldas, Bogotá, Colombia

C. J. Gladys
Grupo Avanzado de Materiales y Sistemas Complejos GAMASCO, Departamento de Física, Universidad de Córdoba, Montería Colombia

O. L. César
Grupo Avanzado de Materiales y Sistemas Complejos GAMASCO, Departamento de Física, Universidad de Córdoba, Montería Colombia

Printed in the USA
CPSIA information can be obtained
at www.ICGtesting.com
JSHW051443221024
72173JS00006B/1563